The Architecture
of Medical Imaging

Designing Healthcare Facilities
for Advanced Radiological Diagnostic
and Therapeutic Techniques

Bill Rostenberg, FAIA, FACHA

Chapters 6 and 7 written by

Steven C. Horii, M.D., FACR, FSCAR

WILEY

John Wiley & Sons, Inc.

For my wife, Debbie, who encouraged me to research, write, and publish.
Each time I have written a book, she taught me the importance
of balancing that work with the other aspects of our lives.

Copyright © 2006 by John Wiley & Sons, Inc. All rights reserved

Published by John Wiley & Sons, Inc., Hoboken, New Jersey

Published simultaneously in Canada

For general information about our other products and services, please contact our Customer Care Department within the United States at (800) 762-2974, outside the United States at (317) 572-3993 or fax (317) 572-4002.

Wiley also publishes its books in a variety of electronic formats. Some content that appears in print may not be available in electronic books. For more information about Wiley products, visit our web site at www.wiley.com.

Library of Congress Cataloging-in-Publication Data

Rostenberg, Bill.
The architecture of medical imaging : designing healthcare facilities for advanced radiological diagnostic and therapeutic techniques / Bill Rostenberg.
   p. ; cm.
   Includes bibliographical references and index.
   ISBN 13: 978-0-471-71661-7 (cloth : alk paper)
   ISBN 10: 0-471-71661-8 (cloth : alk paper)
   1. Health facilities–Design and construction. 2. Health facilities–Planning. 3. Diagnostic imaging–Equipment and supplies. I. Title.
   [DNLM: 1. Diagnostic Imaging–methods. 2. Facility Design and Construction.
WX 140 R839a 2006]
RA967.R67 2006
725'.51–dc22
                                        2006009318

Printed in the United States of America

10 9 8 7 6 5 4 3 2 1

Contents

About the Authors

Bill Rostenberg, FAIA, FACHA

Bill Rostenberg, FAIA, FACHA, is a principal and director of research of Anshen + Allen, an international architectural firm specializing in innovative health care, academic, and higher education facility design. He is based in Anshen + Allen's San Francisco office.

Bill is an editorial board member of *Advance for Imaging and Oncology Administrators* and frequently writes topical articles and editorial opinions for both architectural and medical journals, including *Healthcare Design, Diagnostic Imaging, Health Imaging and IT, Radiology Today, OR Manager, Modern Healthcare, AIArchitect, Health Facilities Management, Building Research and Information,* and *Hospital Management International.*

He has written numerous books and articles about the design and planning of healthcare facilities, including *The Architecture of Imaging, Design Planning for Freestanding Ambulatory Care Facilities,* "Medical Technology and Facility Design in a Managed Care Environment," "Facility Design for Medical Imaging Workstations," "Surgology Is Coming," "Design Considerations in a Filmless Enterprise," "Ergonomics Straightens Its Posture at SCAR 2004," "Desperately Seeking Solutions (to Reading Room Design)," "Convergent Thinking: Blurring the Boundaries Between Surgery and Interventional Imaging," "The Architecture of Reform," "Imaging Revolution: Meeting the Department's Changing Design Requirements," "Reading Rooms Should Be Designed to Accommodate Future Changes," "Success by Design: Maximizing Your Digital Environment," "21st Century Imaging for Hospitals and Health Care Systems of the Future," "Building a Competitive Image with Innovative Facility Design," and "Alternative Healthcare Facilities: Design Reflects Quality Image."

Bill has been an instructor at Harvard University Graduate School of Design–Office of Executive Education, the Radiological Society of North

America (RSNA), the Society for Computer Applications in Radiology (SCAR), the Association of Healthcare Radiology Administrators (AHRA), PACS 2004 and 2005, the American College of Healthcare Executives (ACHE), the American Institute of Architects (AIA), the American Hospital Association (AHA), the American Society for Healthcare Engineering (ASHE), the Center for Health Design, the Healthcare Symposium, the International Academy for Design and Health, the Association of periOperative Registered Nurses (AORN), ORManager, Clemson University Graduate Program in Architecture + Health, Cornell University Department of Environmental Design, UCLA Lake Arrowhead Retreat, and numerous other medical and architectural professional organizations and institutions.

Bill is an advisory board member for a National Institutes of Health (NIH) research grant pioneering applications of intraoperative MRI (I-MRI). He has served on the board of directors and has been the national program chair of the American Institute of Architects/Academy of Architecture for Health, chair of the National AIA/AAH Technology Committee, vice chair of the National AIA/AAH Strategic and Facility Master Planning Committee, and chair of the Health Facilities Committee of the American Institute of Architects' San Francisco chapter and the advisory board for the Center for Health Design. He was elevated to Fellowship in the American Institute of Architects in 2001 for his notable contributions in advancing the practice standards of architecture.

Mr. Rostenberg is a founding fellow of the American College of Healthcare Architects (ACHA) and has been awarded presidential citations, both nationally and locally, from the AIA/Academy of Architecture for Health for extraordinary service to the profession. Bill is also a recipient of the AIA/AHA National Fellowship in Health Facility Design. He received his master of architecture and bachelor of architecture degrees from the University of Arizona and holds a bachelor of science degree in architecture from Washington University. He maintains professional registration in California and Arizona.

Bill resides in the San Francisco Bay area with his wife, Debbie, and son, Nathan.

Steven C. Horii, MD, FACR, FSCAR

Dr. Horii, the author of chapters 6 and 7, did his undergraduate work at the Johns Hopkins University, earning a BA in natural sciences and graduating with departmental honors in chemistry. He went on to New York University School of Medicine and earned his MD in 1976. He stayed at NYU as a resident in radiology and later as a fellow in abdominal radiology. Dr. Horii passed his diagnostic radiology board examination in 1980 and joined the faculty at NYU. Dr. Horii remained at NYU until 1988, when he left to become clinical director of the Image Management and Communications Section in the Radiology Department at Georgetown University. He subsequently joined the faculty in the Department of Radiology at the University of Pennsylvania Medical Center in 1992 as associate director of the Medical Informatics Group and professor of radiology. Dr. Horii was elected to Fellowship of the American College of Radiology in 1998 and of the Society for Computer Applications in Radiology (SCAR) in 2000.

Dr. Horii's clinical specialty is diagnostic ultrasound, and his research interests are in picture archiving and communications systems (PACS), particularly the evaluation and human factors aspects of such systems and the design of reading rooms appropriate for workstations. He has presented papers at most of the major conferences on PACS in the United States and abroad. His interest in the design of health care facilities for digital imaging results from growing up as the son of an architect. He still recalls that his first Radiological Society of North America meeting in Chicago was as memorable for visiting the famous buildings there as it was for the new science and technology being shown at the meeting.

Dr. Horii resides with his wife in the Philadelphia suburbs. When he has time, he enjoys his hobbies of restoring vintage electronic and optical equipment and working on his collection of space program hardware.

Foreword

Imaging has increasingly become one of the most important branches of modern medicine. It is indispensable for diagnosis, selection of appropriate treatment, identification of complications, and treatment follow–up. It is also increasingly used in guiding interventions.

In the last decade there has been a shift in how and where patients are treated, with great emphasis on outpatient medicine and surgery. Today only patients afflicted with severe, complex, and critical conditions require admission to the hospital for complicated treatments and major surgery. Imaging is essential for most procedures and makes hospital stays shorter and outcomes more favorable. Generally all other conditions are handled in outpatient facilities.

Medical and surgical practice, today as before, depends on the proper design of facilities that provide infection control, fire safety, and basic sanitary and comfort requirements, while payers demand designs that make rapid throughput possible and keep costs and risks down. A high level of skill is essential to achieve these difficult and often contradictory demands on modern architectural design.

Much of the content of the previous edition of this remarkable book has become outdated by the revolution of technology in medical imaging. The introduction of new modalities has brought tectonic changes into how medicine is practiced today, and they affect every aspect of architectural design of medical imaging facilities. In writing this book the authors have realized that in order to write meaningfully about design, one must rely on many experts. They have been successful in enlisting the advice and guidance of key leaders and even pioneers of new technologies, advanced communication systems, and health care delivery methods. These technologies and up–to–date information and communication systems are essential not only for the function of a modern medical imaging department but also for the conduct of care in the whole institution. Modern imaging is ubiquitous in a functional hospital, as well as in an outpatient facility, and is practiced today by many specialties. The authors are to be congratulated for objectively covering all these aspects and seeking the views of other acknowledged leaders in the multiple areas of medical practice involved with imaging.

While the arrangement of chapters is similar to the previous edition, the content is brand-new, up-to-date, and practical. Reading it is essential for anyone designing a contemporary facility involved with medical imaging.

Alexander R. Margulis, MD, DSc (HC)
Professor emeritus of radiology, University of California, San Francisco, and clinical professor of radiology, Weill Medical College of Cornell University, New York.

New York City

Preface

In 60 seconds, a healthy heart beats some 60 to 80 times. In 60 seconds, electron beam tomography records over a thousand views of cardiac activity in rapid succession. A thousand pictures in just a minute! A dozen images of every heartbeat! We acquire more information in a few seconds than we can examine in a day.

Not only does medical imaging acquire information rapidly, but its technology changes almost as fast. In contrast, architecture is a slower and more deliberate process. Accommodation of rapid changes in equipment and technology can lead to costly changes in facility construction when flexibility is not incorporated into design. Because the building sciences probably will never evolve at the pace of the medical sciences, proactive planning coupled with an understanding of imaging's ever-evolving role in medicine can reduce both the likelihood of costly design and construction mistakes and the magnitude of those that do occur.

The breadth of knowledge needed to develop even a simple imaging facility can easily overwhelm the inexperienced or misinformed. Furthermore, a misunderstanding of technology often compromises design opportunities that should not be sacrificed.

Armed with their own priorities and reasons for developing an imaging facility, architects and healthcare professionals sometimes approach problem solving differently. Often they are unaware that each may be speaking a different language. One of the goals of *The Architecture of Medical Imaging* is to provide designers and healthcare providers with a common language so that they can establish a team approach to creating quality through collaboration.

This book simplifies the design and planning process for both nonmedical and medical professionals. It provides a detailed, step-by-step explanation of design and planning activities to enable radiologists and healthcare administrators to work closely with architects. In addition, it equips architectural designers with a broad understanding of medical imaging as a basis for framing the proper questions that must be asked of facility users.

The Architecture of Medical Imaging is divided into six parts. Part 1 serves two functions: it explains the importance of quality design, and then it correlates various design approaches with both general changes in the health care industry and specific changes in medical imaging. This part provides an overview for both design professionals and medical practitioners.

Part 2 describes how to organize and manage an architectural project from the owner's perspective. Intended as a primer for health care professionals, it also will interest architects because it offers a comprehensive list of owner expectations. In addition, the chapter on equipment planning highlights some of the common areas of confusion that typically surround the equipment planning process, and thus should benefit both architects and health care professionals.

Part 3 explains the vast range of imaging techniques in use today, as well as newer modalities that are still in research and development. It also describes the evolutionary transition from film-based to digital image and information management, which has dramatically altered the rules of medical imaging facility design. Together, parts 1 through 3 establish a common language for architects and medical practitioners, so that collaboration can grow and communication can be strengthened.

Part 4 builds on the preceding chapters and explains important planning and design concepts for medical imaging facilities. It forms the heart of the book and offers both conceptual and detailed suggestions for state-of-the-art medical imaging facility design, ranging from departmental planning guidelines to suggestions for detailed room layout and special utility needs.

Part 5 offers a vision of the future, describing medical imaging trends and their impact on facility design–such as the deployment of medical imaging services beyond the radiology department and beyond hospital boundaries–and suggests how tomorrow's imaging projects may differ from those of today.

The useful appendices in part 6 examine specific imaging facility projects and include excerpts from relevant regulatory guidelines.

The architecture of medical imaging is both changing and constant. New equipment and procedures challenge the brightest and most focused professionals to envision future trends. Yet with each new development, it becomes more apparent that imaging is here to stay as a superstar of contemporary healthcare delivery.

Acknowledgments

Periodically, when I want to learn about a topic unknown to me, I end up writing a book about it. In the 1980s it was freestanding ambulatory care facilities; in the 1990s it was medical imaging facilities. Now, some ten years after writing my previous book on the design of imaging facilities, I find that so much has changed—and there are so many new things to know—that it is time to learn all over again. *The Architecture of Medical Imaging* significantly updates its predecessor, *The Architecture of Imaging* (no longer in print), because medical imaging today is radically different than it was just a decade earlier.

On each writing excursion, I have learned a remarkable amount from stellar leaders in both the medical and architectural fields. This has certainly been the case in writing *The Architecture of Medical Imaging*, and I am grateful to all who have assisted me with this challenging endeavor. My heartfelt thanks go out to many individuals without whom this book would not have been possible. In particular, I am grateful to Steven C. Horii, MD, FACR, FSCAR, the author of chapters 6 and 7 of this book. Dr. Horii also reviewed, commented on, and contributed to many other sections herein, as well as those within my previous book. Dr. Horii is clinical director of the Medical Informatics Group and professor of radiology at the Hospital of the University of Pennsylvania, and is well known for his pioneering work in developing the DICOM (digital imaging and communications in medicine) standards, which enable medical imaging devices from various equipment vendors to be able to communicate with each other. Thus, DICOM has made digital image and information management and communications in radiology possible. A recent cover story in the magazine *Imaging Economics* suggested that DICOM warrants a Nobel prize, and if such a prize were given, its logical recipient would be Dr. Steven C. Horii.[1]

Dr. Alexander Margulis, MD, is professor emeritus of radiology at the University of California, San Francisco, and clinical professor of radiology at Weill Medical College of Cornell University, New York. Dr. Margulis has guided and mentored me–as he has done for so many others throughout his illustrious career–in my quest for knowledge about all things radiologic. He has been both a trusted advisor and a friend throughout the writing of both imaging facility design books.

I am grateful to Richard Satava, MD, professor of surgery at the University of Washington, who has pioneered visionary concepts of merging advanced communications systems with advanced medicine; James Atkinson, MD, professor and chief, Divisions of General and Pediatric Surgery, University of California, Los Angeles, who provided executive leadership in the challenges of building his institution's academic medical center of the future; Osman Ratib, MD, PhD, FAHA, professor and chief of nuclear medicine, Department of Radiology, University Hospital of Geneva (previously professor and vice chair of information systems, Department of Radiological Services, University of California, Los Angeles), who has pioneered novel concepts of twenty-first-century radiology reading room design; Theodore L. Phillips, MD, FACR, Wun-Kon Fu Distinguished Professor, Department of Radiation Oncology, University of California, San Francisco, who is recognized internationally for his work in cancer treatment, and whom I had the distinct pleasure of working closely with in the design of the UCSF/Mount Zion Comprehensive Cancer Center (figure 8-7); Paul Barach, MD, MPH, Associate Professor, Department of Anesthesiology, Medicine and Epidemiology, Associate Dean, University of Miami Medical School, an advocate of improving safety and minimizing medical errors; Eliot Siegel, MD, vice chairman and professor of diagnostic radiology, University of Maryland School of Medicine, and chief of radiology, Maryland Department of Veterans Affairs, who has perhaps more experience with filmless radiology than anyone else due to his leadership since the inception of the Department of Veterans Affairs' first filmless hospital, which was conceived in the late 1980s (before PACS technology became commercially available). Dr. Siegel has also been instrumental in developing prototype reading room environments and collecting the "evidence" used in many radiology-related evidence-based design decisions.

I am grateful for the assistance and advice from several individuals at Brigham and Women's Hospital, including Dr. Ferenc Jolesz, MD, the B. Leonard Holman Professor of Radiology and vice chairman for research and director, Division of MRI and Image Guided Therapy Program, Department of Radiology, who is well known for developing the first intraoperative MRI over a decade ago and subsequent versions of this fascinating technology; John Carrino, MD, MPH, assistant professor of radiology, clinical director, Magnetic Resonance Therapy, co-director, Spine Interventional Service; Angela Roddy Kanan, RN, charge nurse, Magnetic Resonance Therapy; Daniel Karcher, MS, MRI senior engineer; and Marsha O'Neil, senior project manager and financial analyst, Image Guided Therapy Program.

Many other renowned medical leaders contributed their insights to this book. I am thankful to Peter Fitzgerald, MD, associate professor of medicine and engineering, and director, Cardiovascular Core Analysis Lab, Stanford University Medical Center; Edward Panacek, MD, MPH, professor and clinical trials office director, emergency medicine and clinical toxicology, University of California, Davis; Warren Sandberg, MD, director of anesthesia, Operating Room of the Future Project, Department of Anesthesia and Critical Care, Massachusetts General Hospital; and Chester Szerlag, executive administrator, radiation and cellular oncology, University of Chicago. Each of these well-known and respected luminaries has shared insights with me, reviewed and commented on portions of this book, and taught me many valuable lessons.

Similarly, many architects and design professionals have contributed their time and knowledge by assisting me with *The Architecture of Medical Imaging*. My colleagues at Anshen + Allen have supported this research endeavor and encouraged me to help guide our firm in upholding our place as an international leader in evidence-based design and innovative sustainable health care architecture. In particular, my thanks go to Roger Swanson, Felicia Borkovi, Derek Parker, the late Alex Bonutti, Ann Killeen, Annie Coull, Jenifer Altenhoff, Todd Tierney, Zigmund Rubel, Tony Rinella, Bob Dooley, Lynn Befu, Marty Waldron, William Lee, Scott Benjamin, Rodrigo Diaz Montero, Joshua Richardson, Rachel Ginsberg, Tatiana Guimaraes, Monika Kejriwal, Richard Sarao, Brooks Hunt, Jeff Thompson, Jenifer Pechacek, Ryan McBrayer, and Allyson Kovas. Special thanks go to Steve Riffe for his tireless efforts helping me coordinate the myriad components of this book, for being a second pair of eyes and ears as an internal editor, for diplomatically reminding the contributors of graphics to send their materials in before the final deadline, and for miraculously enabling me to leverage my time efficiently in my primary responsibilities at Anshen + Allen, thus allowing me to write effectively in all my "spare" time.

A host of other design and allied professionals assisted in the development of *The Architecture of Medical Imaging*. Special thanks go to Elizabeth Brott, senior project manager, National Facilities Services, Kaiser Permanente; Scott Jenkins, president, EDI Design Services, Inc.; Siemens Medical Solutions USA, Inc.; Philips Medical Systems, GE Healthcare; Jay Clark, western regional sales manager, Medical Products, ETS-Lindgren; Morris Stein, president, Stein-Cox Group; Ray Brovold, president, Brovold Associates, Radiology Planning Consultants; Michael Roughan, director of healthcare planning and programming, Payette Associates, Inc.; Marty McIntyre, vice president and account executive, EQ International; Kathryn M. Pelczarski, program manager, ECRI; Walter Vernon, principal, Mazzetti & Associates; and Kenneth Caldwell.

Finally, I would like to extend my appreciation to the staff at John Wiley and Sons for helping me prepare my manuscript for publication and for their professionalism in developing it into a final publication. In particular, I am grateful to John Czarnecki, acquisitions editor, architecture and design.

Note

1. G. Wiley, "The Prophet Motive: How PACS Was Developed and Sold," available at http://www.imagingeconomics.com//library/200505-01.asp.

The Architecture of Medical Imaging is written in memory of Alexander C. Bonutti, AIA, mentor, colleague, and friend. Alex inspired me to write the three books I authored and advised me with each. Alex departed far too soon, but he left his indelible mark during the all too brief time he was with us.

How to Use This Book

A book devoted to a tightly focused topic and intended for a limited audience can be difficult to write. Conceptualizing that same book for a diverse audience is even more challenging because both its content and its style are likely to be more appropriate, in some instances, for one audience than for another. Add to this a topic that is both broad and constantly changing, and the task of writing becomes a very difficult one indeed.

As mentioned in the preface, *The Architecture of Medical Imaging* is written for all the professionals involved in the design of medical imaging environments. My intent is to provide a much-needed resource that will be of value to everyone involved in the process of designing imaging facilities: architects, radiologists and other healthcare providers, administrators, and interior designers, regardless of whether they are seasoned specialists or newly practicing professionals.

For those readers whose interests include history, philosophy, management, medical science, design, systems analysis, regulation, and the future of imaging facilities, welcome to all that resides between the front and back covers of this book. For those who are focused on a narrower range of issues rather than the entire spectrum, consider the following road map.

Begin with part 1, the overview, if you want to learn more about the context in which medical imaging has evolved. If you are familiar with project schedules and budgets but wish to learn more about magnetic resonance imaging (MRI), computed tomographic angiography (CTA), and positron emission tomography (PET), you might skim through part 2, "Development of an Imaging Facility," and then proceed to part 3, "Imaging Techniques."

If, however, you are more familiar with methods of image acquisition and picture archiving and communications systems than with departmental gross square footage, schematic design, design development, and contract documents, you might concentrate on part 2 and only skim through part 3.

Some readers will head straight for part 4, "Design and Planning." It provides both a broad and a detailed array of design and planning information. However, many of these data will be even more meaningful when read in conjunction with the preceding chapters. Certainly everyone will be interested in part 5, "Trends Influencing Tomorrow's Imaging Facilities," and the appendices that follow.

However, before you begin to read the book, please consider a word of caution. It is hoped that the information contained herein will be useful to all readers. However, because the subject matter is continuously changing, many of the topics and details may not apply to some facilities; they may have been accurate at the time of publication but may have since been superseded, or they may be based on individual opinions rather than universally accepted rules. Because medical imaging and its architecture are both complex and always changing, readers are encouraged to seek specific direction from design and planning professionals, health care delivery experts, and equipment manufacturers regarding particular projects. Therefore, the information contained in this book should not be considered to be more than general background information.

PART ONE

OVERVIEW

CHAPTER 1

Design Considerations for Imaging Facilities

The architecture of a medical imaging facility reflects an image of its medical providers, the neighborhood surrounding the facility, and the community of patients and families who come to the facility for medical care (figure 1–1). Good design increases a medical provider's visibility and also provides a productive and supportive environment that will help attract and retain healthcare employees.

Like medicine, architecture embraces both science and art. Subject to the laws of gravity and the effects of weather, the facility must endure over time. Healthcare architecture must go beyond just serving the needs of patients, staff, and the public; it must promote interaction among people, between people and technology, and between people and their communities.

Unfortunately, the need for supportive human interaction within a medical imaging facility sometimes is difficult to satisfy as planners and designers wrestle with the myriad technical requirements that challenge them daily. Consequently, medical imaging facilities too often are viewed simply as places for advanced technology. Such a view fails to consider the human aspect of the imaging environment and therefore does not address design requirements in their entirety. It is vital that design professionals do not focus on technology requirements so closely that they forget the needs of the people who will use that technology. Coordinating the technical demands of medical equipment often usurps precious design time that the designer originally allocated for less technical tasks. When this happens, the design team can become reactive instead of visionary, creating architecture that merely solves immediate or short-term problems. The overreaching design goal for medical imaging facilities is producing solutions that create opportunities for human interaction and support the healing process.

Figure 1-1 Architecture reflects the quality of care provided within. © Richard Barnes. Architect: Anshen + Allen.

As imaging technology becomes more complex, so does the challenge of integrating form and function. One way to prevent functional requirements from overpowering design is for the architectural team to thoroughly understand both the processes and the equipment used for medical imaging, and for the medical team to understand how the design process will be orchestrated. Using this approach, design professionals learn what questions to ask and when to ask them, and healthcare professionals are better prepared to provide input into the design of their facility. Armed with this knowledge, the architectural and medical members of the project team can set the stage for quality healthcare architecture that meets the needs of both patients and staff. This chapter focuses on identifying those needs.

Special Needs of Medical Imaging Facilities

How does the design of a medical imaging facility differ from those of other building types? It must accommodate the special needs of imaging patients and their families, the needs of imaging personnel (including radiologists, technologists, other healthcare providers, administrators, clerical personnel, and housekeeping staff), and the needs of equipment in terms of its function, installation, maintenance, modification, and replacement.

The Needs of Patients

Patients and their families have many needs that can be addressed through effective medical imaging facility design. Some of these include the efficient flow of information, stress reduction, comfort, dignity, and privacy. If these requirements are seamlessly accommodated while patients are being treated at the imaging facility, patients will have a head start toward their ultimate goal of coping with their medical condition and attaining wellness.

Most patients come to an imaging facility to solve a medical mystery. Ultrasound, magnetic resonance, computed tomography, or any number of other imaging modalities make it possible to visualize what otherwise would be invisible. Information provided by these imaging modalities is relied upon by the medical staff to determine a patient's course of treatment. Facility design must take into account the imaging equipment and its proper installation. Failing to do this not only risks damage to the equipment itself but has dire consequences for the reliability, accuracy, and timeliness of the results upon which patients and caregivers depend.

Solving a medical mystery can be stressful. The diverse array of machinery that enables radiologists and other physicians to diagnose and treat otherwise unknown conditions often appears foreign and even frightening to many patients. The odd postures patients must assume, the duration for which they must hold still, and the overall sense that their health and well-being may be determined in part by an electronically rendered illustration of their inner anatomy and physiology can be intimidating. However, usually it is not the instrumentation itself that patients are most frightened of but rather what it will reveal about them.

> There are severe anxiety-related reactions associated with magnetic resonance imaging (MRI). Patients who experience such reactions may disrupt the examination or move so much that the image is degraded. This experience may also influence patients' perceptions of the quality of care they receive.[1]

Designers should account for the high degree of stress patients often have upon arrival at an imaging facility. The architecture should provide inherently clear wayfinding, minimize the need for patients to make unnecessary navigational decisions, afford privacy and dignity throughout the course of an imaging exam, and provide reassuring positive distractions to enable patients to momentarily take their minds off their immediate medical concerns. Facility design that adds difficulties–circuitous circulation, unnecessarily long routes of travel, or impersonal settings for interaction with caregivers–only heightens patients' levels of anxiety.

Figure 1-2 Waiting areas should be large enough to for families to be together, yet intimate to reduce anxiety. © Erich Ansel Koyama. Architect: Anshen + Allen.

Patients often feel alienated in imaging facilities. Therefore, general waiting areas should be comfortable and personal, large enough to allow family members to be together yet intimate enough to reduce patient anxiety (figure 1-2). Additional gowned waiting areas should be located adjacent to procedure rooms, to minimize the need for patients who have already changed into gowns to travel through the corridors. Patients undergoing a nuclear medicine procedure may need to ingest or be injected with radioactive substances before their scans, and those waiting for ultrasound scans may need to drink large quantities of water. Therefore, toilet rooms should be appropriately located near waiting areas and procedure rooms.

A well-designed imaging facility supports a patient's right to respectful treatment. When asked to remove their clothing, patients may feel that their sense of dignity has been diminished. However, when the surroundings afford privacy and are appropriately illuminated, patients tend to feel more self-assured and secure. Beyond the basic privacy mandates of HIPAA (Health Insurance Portability and Accountability Act), patients appreciate additional privacy amenities, such as doors and partitions that enhance visual privacy, and offices and public spaces that are treated with sound-absorbing materials to prevent their conversations with caregivers from being overheard. Patient privacy also is enhanced when acoustic separation of patient and staff areas restricts the sounds of business within work areas.

Procedure room design should integrate function with ambience. For example, high ceiling heights, dictated by equipment clearances, provide ample opportunities to vary the ceiling plane—which patients lying in a supine position may see more than they will see wall surfaces. Similarly, many procedure rooms benefit from external windows and views to land-scaped courtyards. Procedures that involve viewing a monitor within the procedure room, however, require control of the daylight admitted through exterior windows.

The Needs of Staff and Faculty

If based solely on the needs of equipment, the enclosures for medical imaging services would be dark and monolithic. Too often, the weight of equipment and requirements for radiation, radio-frequency, or magnetic shielding result in windowless subterranean environments. However, faculty and staff work long hours and perform difficult tasks. Their work environment affects how they respond to each other and how they serve patients. Facility layout should include both an "off-stage" zone where staff can speak freely to each other without concern of being overheard and an "on-stage" zone where they can comfortably interact with patients and family members without disturbing other staff. For example, break rooms and private offices are best placed with views to the outdoors and ample natural daylight. Staff areas such as reading rooms and control rooms–while best designed without exterior windows–deserve the same attention to detail and their unique lighting requirements that public lobbies and waiting areas do (figure 1-3). Supportive staff work environments have been shown to improve staff satisfaction and thus help improve the quality of care administered by staff. Consequently, a well-designed work environment can improve both patient and staff satisfaction.

Figure 1-3 Staff areas deserve the same attention to detail as do patient areas. © Michael Dersin Photography. Architect: Anshen + Allen.

Flows of people, data, supplies, and equipment must be carefully planned in order to enable imaging facility staff members to perform their functions effectively. Each form of traffic moves with different characteristics and at different rates. Facility design greatly impacts the variety of traffic patterns and work flows within the environment. Enhancements to the design can have positive effects on staff productivity. Other factors that allow staff members to perform their work effectively are adequate task lighting, the correct size and configuration of treatment rooms, close proximity of treatment rooms to their associated support spaces, and adequate space for housekeeping and maintenance activities.

The Needs of Equipment

As imaging equipment becomes more computer-based, the need for "clean" uniform power and efficient air-conditioning systems is magnified. Therefore, infrastructure systems designed by engineers must be sized for excess capacities and carefully coordinated with architectural and other engineering design requirements.

Medical technology is changing at an increasingly rapid rate, and the need for flexibility in every aspect of design becomes more crucial. Therefore, alternatives for future growth and modification should be part of the initial design, not an afterthought. For example, power and cooling system requirements tend to double or triple, rather than increase by a small margin, when new technology is introduced.

Although some imaging equipment itself is shrinking in size, the capabilities of any single piece of equipment are expanding. As a result, multiple ancillary instruments may be used in the exam room. Therefore, needs for both examination space and support space (such as patient preparation areas and equipment storage rooms) are likely to increase even as individual equipment components become more compact.

Note
1. R. McKenzie, C. Sims, R. G. Owens, and A. K. Dixon, "Patients' perceptions of magnetic resonance imaging," *Clinical Radiology* 50, 3 (1995): 137–43.

CHAPTER 2

Forces of Change in Medical Imaging Facility Design

I n recent years we have witnessed significant advances in medical imaging service delivery. For example, the proliferation of enterprise-wide electronic picture archiving and communications systems (PACS) and image and information archiving and communications systems (IMACS) have radically altered the core drivers of traditional (film-based) imaging facility design. Add to this the development of functional and molecular imaging, the convergence of interventional imaging and minimally invasive surgery, the transformation of traditional radiology from an ancillary service to an integral collaborative component of every aspect of healthcare delivery, and ongoing turf battles among myriad medical specialists for access to knowledge in the form of medical informatics, and it is easy to see that the rules guiding the design and planning of future medical imaging facilities need to be reinvented.

Awareness and understanding of the drivers that affect both healthcare delivery in general and medical imaging in particular are important for anyone involved in the design of medical imaging facilities. Ironically, the wave of change is sometimes so rapid that new design drivers are likely to emerge within the course of designing and constructing a single project.

This chapter reviews concurrent developments in both healthcare and medical imaging throughout the past century and discusses factors that influence the design of medical imaging facilities. The chapter concludes with a set of challenges that architects and healthcare staff must address when planning a successful imaging facility.

Historical Developments in Healthcare and Radiology

Key developments in healthcare that have taken place in the United States since the late nineteenth century can be divided into three primary segments: (1) the growth of American medical schools and hospitals and concurrent events in radiology (circa 1880 to 1920), (2) the outpatient explosion (circa 1970s to the present), and (3) the integration of advanced information management (circa 1990 to the present).

The Growth of American Medical Schools and Hospitals and Concurrent Events in Radiology

Prior to 1880, fewer than 200 acute care hospitals and only three professional medical schools existed in the United States. By the first decade of the twentieth century, that number had grown to more than 5,000 acute care hospitals and 1,000 medical schools. This thirty-year period of explosive growth has been characterized by some as the first healthcare revolution in the United States.

This healthcare revolution coincided with Roentgen's discovery of X-rays in 1895, Salvioni's description of the fluoroscopic "cryptoscope" in 1896, and Edison's development of the fluoroscope during the same year (figure 2-1). In the years immediately following these discoveries, not only was it difficult simply to obtain the electrical power needed to take X-rays, but the application of X-rays to patient care was often overlooked; instead, this new tool was viewed more as a curiosity than as a diagnostic device.[1] As Dr. Ronald Eisenberg points out in his book *Radiology: An Illustrated History,*

> The first x-ray department at the [Boston] Children's Hospital was limited in its function by reason of the fact that the hospital was not equipped with electric current, and was obliged to obtain its power from the Opera House nearby. A wire was run from the Opera House to the Hospital, but when there was no music there was no current. No opera, no x-rays![2]

In the years following the first healthcare revolution, radiology slowly evolved from a novelty into an interpretive function that assisted other medical components of the hospital (figures 2-2 and 2-3), such as the emergency department and surgery. During this period, X-ray services (for those institutions that had X-ray equipment) often depended on the hospital's general budget for funding and usually were given little financial support. The lack of funding was evident in the architecture of early medical facilities. Frequently, spaces used for radiography were small, dark, and situated below grade.

> [T]he meager space and equipment which were available in 1899 is illustrated by . . . experience at the Philadelphia General Hospital . . . [T]he importance of the subject can be best gauged by the fact that a special ground floor room was built of concrete 12 by 15 feet–180 square feet of floor space; three feet were separated for a photographic developing room, leaving a total space of 12 by 12 feet for the equipment and furnishings.[3]

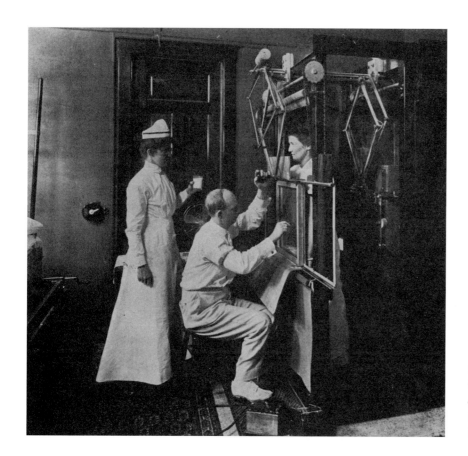

Figure 2-1 Thomas Edison developed the first fluoroscope one year after Roentgen's discovery of x-rays. From: Edward Stevens, *The American Hospital of the Twentieth Century*, 1918.

However, architect Edward F. Stevens–one of the first to write about turn–of–the–century healthcare architecture in the United States–described some early arrangements of X-ray facilities, and in 1918 wrote about the growing interest in the use of "Roentgen–rays."

> The Roentgen-ray [X-ray], in its diverse uses, has become invaluable. While it is true that the best results can be obtained by only the expert roentgenologists, nevertheless even the limited use of the x-ray in the small hospital is most helpful.[4]

Stevens' vision at the turn of the twentieth century foresaw many of the design challenges that still face architects today. He described functional and safety considerations inherent in medical imaging facility design of his day and even advocated that X-ray rooms not be placed in basement locations.

> We know . . . that the recurrent use of this powerful medium has caused serious burns and the destruction of live tissue so that the operators should have every possible protection. Lead screens afford this protection against both direct and reflected rays. It is more common now to provide control rooms heavily lined with lead at least one-eighth inch thick; and where vision is required, lead glass is used for the operator. . . . A few precautions may be mentioned in

GROUND FLOOR

Figure 2-2 The first x-ray departments were closely associated with the "Accident Room" (or emergency room). From: Edward Stevens, *The American Hospital of the Twentieth Century*, 1918.

providing for this department: avoid cellar, particularly if it is damp; moisture causes trouble with the transformer and high tension wiring. . . . [T]he room should be sufficiently high studded to allow overhead high tension system. . . . [T]he x–ray transformer requires a special electric current supply. Do not rely on the word of a local electrician or power company. . . . This department should be planned for at the beginning, not left to chance.[5]

Design considerations often were secondary because early imaging departments were not seen as being financially self–supporting, and pioneering radiologists did not always share the stature of their fellow physicians. The desire to control the use of an institution's X–ray equipment was perhaps a precursor of today's medical turf battles. It was not until later that medical imaging advanced as a distinct branch of medicine, responsible initially for diagnosis and later for treatment of disease and injury. Eventually, imaging became a fundamental service essential to all aspects of the practice of medicine. As diagnostic and therapeutic radiology developed, imaging departments were reorganized as profit centers capable of generating considerable revenue. Dr. Eisenberg describes the economic challenges that radiologists faced at the turn of the twentieth century:

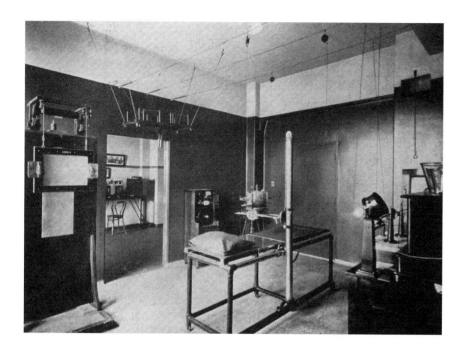

Figure 2-3 While the basic principles of radiography have remained constant, the rooms in which these procedures are performed have changed dramatically. From: Edward Stevens, *The American Hospital of the Twentieth Century*, 1918.

At the Peter Bent Brigham Hospital, a letter written as early as 1911 saw no need for the services of a roentgenologist, specifying: "in regard to a roentgenologist we have put down no salary figure. This Department will probably involve the employment of one or more technical assistants not graduates in medicine." One reason for the generally low opinion of radiologists among other medical specialists was the fact that in the early days radiologists were not willing to delegate the operation of their machines. Thus they were perceived as something lower than physicians, more like technicians.[6]

The Outpatient Explosion

Beginning in the late 1970s and continuing to the present, a second healthcare revolution has occurred. Economic concerns, technologic developments, and consumer education have led to questioning the need for lengthy hospitalization. Insurance companies and regulators have begun examining alternatives to inpatient treatment. Additionally, federal cost-containment policies and diminishing reimbursement structures have begun to diminish the profit-generating potential of many imaging departments.

In 1985, the prospective payment system first limited reimbursement for treatment provided to hospitalized patients by using a standardized listing of diagnosis-related payments, known as diagnosis-related groups (DRGs). DRGs limited the amount of reimbursement a hospital could expect, and as a result, much of the healthcare industry shifted its focus to outpatient treatment.

Consequently, patients who were hospitalized tended to be more acutely ill than was the case before the shift. Patients with less acute illnesses soon chose their place of diagnosis and treatment from among a number of outpatient settings. It was during this period that outpatient imaging centers first grew rapidly in number, and nonhospital healthcare facilities such as surgery centers, urgent care centers, and freestanding imaging centers flourished. The migration of imaging services to ambulatory care facilities–both freestanding and hospital-based–continues today. The transition to outpatient care has also been fueled by financial pressures favoring minimally invasive and noninvasive forms of treatment over traditional treatments requiring lengthy hospitalization.

By the late 1980s, imaging had developed a dual role. On one hand, it was integral to centralized medical treatment within acute care hospitals; on the other hand, it provided an important link in the referral network served by diverse, decentralized, and often independent outpatient settings. These settings included hospitals, clinics, and physicians' offices. In addition, imaging data were beginning to be remotely transmitted among these and other settings, such as physicians' homes and distant reading centers.

The Era of Electronic Information Management

Beginning in the early 1990s, escalating healthcare costs dominated the nation's economic concerns and even became a national political issue. Proposed reform initiatives and trends toward managed care placed focus upon providing universal healthcare coverage and promoting incentives for cost reduction and eliminating waste. The advent of enterprise-wide electronic information management systems–and the resulting improved methods of medical information management–became a key component in the effort to contain operating costs, while at the same time requiring enormous initial capital expenditures and infrastructure upgrades.

The impact of these initiatives on medical imaging was evident in three areas. First, utilization of expensive imaging modalities such as magnetic resonance imaging (MRI) and computed tomography (CT) fell under intense scrutiny as insurance companies and other payers began requiring preauthorization for the use of imaging procedures. Second, the preventive aspects of imaging (for example, early screening for suspected disease) increased in importance as managed care shifted from an emphasis on disease treatment to an emphasis on health maintenance. Third, the perceived value of hospital information systems (HIS), radiology information systems (RIS), picture archiving and communications systems (PACS), and image management and communications systems (IMACS) began to grow.

The concepts behind advanced medical information management began to take shape at a time when the workforce was becoming increasingly computer-literate. Computer networks, e-mail, and wireless communication networks were beginning to herald what would soon become known as the information revolution. This increased reliance on electronic information management, coupled with computer-literate personnel, created the opportunity to restructure both the operational and architectural aspects of healthcare in general, and medical imaging in particular.

Electronic information management had begun to affect healthcare and medical imaging services by enabling electronic linkages, and thus operational integration, both among departments within hospitals and among facilities across the country. Financial, medical, and personal data–which previously had been stored on paper–now became electronically based and could be transmitted via comprehensive communication networks.

It seemed as if overnight the fundamental rules of traditional imaging facility design (such as minimizing technologists' footsteps for transporting an exposed film cassette between X-ray room and darkroom) had been erased by ubiquitous and instantaneous electronic transmission of digital data. The impact of advanced image and information management systems on facility design was revolutionary and has been constantly evolving ever since.

Parallel Changes in Healthcare and Medical Imaging

If a time line showing the milestones in medical imaging during the past century is compared to one showing key events in healthcare, a parallel pattern emerges. First, the discovery of X-rays coincided with the development of medical schools in the United States. Next, many of the new powerful and sophisticated imaging techniques, such as CT and MRI, were introduced during or just before the explosion in outpatient services. Finally, the first large-scale installations of picture archiving and communications systems, image management and communications systems, radiology information systems, teleradiology, computed radiography, and other forms of digital medical image management coincided with the emergence of the information revolution. (A more detailed chronology of medical imaging milestones is shown in table 2-1.)

The Role of Imaging Today

Recently, much attention has focused on imaging's role in preventive medicine. New techniques of viewing metabolic activity, combined with noninvasive procedures that provide exquisite detail of internal anatomy, now identify the potential for disease before it occurs. In this sense, medical imaging has evolved from a reporting function, interpreting data about patients' past and present conditions, into a predicting and treating function, warning of and actually preventing physical deterioration beyond the early stages of involvement.

Additionally, healthcare cost containment policies and trends toward noninvasive medical treatment have enabled certain imaging techniques to replace surgery as the procedure of choice for diagnosing many, if not most,

continues on page 18

TABLE 2-1 A CHRONOLOGY OF MEDICAL IMAGING MILESTONES

Imaging Technique	First Described	First Described By	Source
X-rays discovered	1895	Roentgen	
Fluoroscopy	1896	Salvioni, Edison	
Cineradiography	1896	Bleyer	
First chest X-ray	1896	F. H. Williams	a
Portable X-ray	1901	Williams	
First scattered radiation grid developed	1913	Bucky	b
Cardiac catheterization	1929	Forssmann	c
Transverse axial tomography	1937, 1938	Watson, Kieffer	d
Automatic film processor	1942		e
Principles of magnetic resonance	1946	Purcell, Bloch	
Magnetic resonance spectroscopy	1946		
Diagnostic ultrasound: first described	1947–1948	Dussik	f
Fluoroscopic image intensifier	1948	Coltman	g
Scintillation scanner	1949	Cassen	h
Multidirectional tomography	1951		i
Nobel prize for description of MRI principles	1952	Purcell, Bloch	
Positron scanner	1953	Brownell, Sweet	j
Principles of PET introduced	mid-1950s		k
SPECT (single-photon emission computed tomography)	1963	Kuhl, Edwards	l
Percutaneous transluminal angioplasty	1964	Dotter, Judkins	m
Mass-produced dedicated mammography unit	1965	CGR Company	n
Radionuclide multiplane tomographic scanner	1965	Anger	o
Diagnostic ultrasound: first clinical use	1966		p
Computed tomographic head scan	1972	Hounsfield	q
Computed tomographic body scan	1973		r
Magnetic resonance imaging: first image of a heterogeneous object	1973	Lauterbur	s
Magnetic resonance imaging: first image of a live animal	1976		t
Magnetic resonance imaging: first human image	1977	Damadian	u
First commercial PET scanner introduced	late 1970s		v
Digital fluoroscopy/digital subtraction angiography	1979	Mistretta	w
Hounsfield and Coumads awarded Nobel prize for invention of CT	1979		x
Commercial superconducting MR imager	1980		y
Magnetic resonance imaging: first routine clinical use	1981		
Picture archiving and communications systems	1982	Boyd	z

Imaging Technique	First Described	First Described By	Source
Electron beam tomography	1982		
Photo-stimulable phosphors, computed radiography	1984	Fuji	aa
Biomagnetics/superconductive quantum interference device	1988		bb
First spiral CT scanner in routine operation	1989		cc
Magnetic resonance angiography	1990		
Functional MR imaging introduced	early 1990s		
Optical coherence imaging	1991	J. G. Fujimoto	dd
Computed tomographic angiography	1992		ee
First intraoperative MRI installed	1994	Jolesz (et al.)	ff
PET/CT introduced	1996	Townsend and Nutt	gg
Multidetector CT technology introduced	1998		hh
MRI safety guidelines white paper published	2002, 2004	American College of Radiology	
Nobel prize for first MRI device	2003	Lauterbur and Mansfield	

Sources

a. Siemens AG. Medical Solutions. *Computed Tomography: Its History and Technology*. 2003. Document number A91100-M2100-A844-1-7600.

b. Siemens AG.

c. Bushong, S.C. *Radiologic Science for Technologists: Physics, Biology, and Protection.* 5th ed. (St. Louis: Mosby Year Book, 1993).

d. Eisenberg, R. L. *Radiology: An Illustrated History* (St. Louis: Mosby Year Book, 1992).

e. Bushong, 1993.

f. Eisenberg.

g. Bushong, 1993.

h. Eisenberg.

i. Bushong, 1993.

j. Eisenberg.

k. ECRI, *Healthcare Product Comparison System,* May 2004.

l. Bushong, 1993.

m. Eisenberg.

n. Eisenberg.

o. Eisenberg.

p. Bushong, 1993.

q. Eisenberg.

r. Eisenberg.

s. Eisenberg.

t. Eisenberg.

u. Eisenberg.

v. ECRI.

w. Bushong, S. C. *Radiologic Science for Technologists,* 3rd ed. (St. Louis: Mosby Year Book, 1984).

x. Siemens, AG.

y. Bushong, 1984.

z. Bushong, 1984.

aa. Bushong, 1984.

bb. Bushong, 1984.

cc. Siemens AG.

dd. Research Laboratory of Electronics at MIT. *Timeline: 1980–1999.* Available online: http://www.rle.mit.edu/about/about_history_timeline8099.html, accessed November 2005.

ee. Siemens AG.

ff. ECRI.

gg. University of Pittsburgh Medical Center, *"University of Pittsburgh research shows combined PET/CT finds cancerous lesions standard CT misses."* Available online: http://www.scienceblog.com/community/older/2002/B/20026559.html, accessed November 2005.

hh. ECRI.

continued from page 15

injuries and illnesses. Similarly, multidetector computed tomography (MDCT), computed tomography angiography (CTA), magnetic resonance angiography (MRA), and certain nuclear medicine techniques are beginning to replace diagnostic interventions (such as radiographic angiography and diagnostic cardiac catheterization) as procedures of choice, resulting in a decline in diagnostic angiography volumes but growth in therapeutic interventional angiography.

> Rapidly advancing multislice CT technology has paved the way for its inroads into the cardiovascular suite, especially the introduction of the 16–slice machine in 2002 [and 64–slice CT in 2004]. . . . The 16–slice CT . . . offered image resolution and speed that made it conducive to capturing the small anatomy of a beating heart, from the arteries carrying life–giving blood to small lesions that could impede that flow. . . .
>
> CT has many advantages over diagnostic cardiac catheterization in patient turnaround. One CT machine can easily push through one patient every 15 minutes. . . . . Meanwhile, catheterization labs at best can turn around about one patient per hour. . . .
>
> Ultimately, taking the diagnostic procedures out of the catheterization lab to make more time for therapeutic procedures will bring in more revenue for the hospital. . . . .
>
> CT angiography costs about $600 per procedure and about the same for MRI images, but costs can run to as much as $3,000 for a diagnostic catheterization. . . . CT angiography will eventually substitute for coronary angiography, boosting the volume of invasive therapeutic procedures as the number of diagnostic catheterizations decline.[7]

The boundary between surgery and radiology has been further obscured by new interventional applications, allowing specific imaging rooms to function as suites for minimally invasive surgery. Such interventional suites pose new design challenges due to their increased requirements for air handling capacity, infection control precautions, and pre- and postprocedural patient holding areas than did their predecessors. Many interventional imaging suites are now located within the surgery department rather than within the radiology department. Interventional radiology is less traumatic than open surgery and thus requires less recovery time. For example, various minimally invasive cardiac procedures performed in the catheterization lab have replaced the need for open–heart surgery, which is more invasive and requires longer recuperation times for patients. Additional advantages of co–locating interventional imaging suites with surgical procedure rooms include the efficiency of a comprehensive controlled supply delivery system for both services, and a unified pre- and postprocedural holding and observation area.[8]

Imaging and image guidance has also become a significant component of surgical practice:

> The proliferation of image–guided surgery (IGS) systems has been driven by advances in the technology of image manipulation, development of innovative minimally–invasive surgical (MIS) procedures a well as the establishment of IT [information technology] networks capable of linking areas of image acquisition, such as radiology or orthopedics, to the operating suite. While neurosurgeons were the first clinicians to recognize the benefits of implementation of this sophisticated equipment, other specialists have come to rely upon the exquisite anatomic and increasingly physiologic roadmaps these systems provide.[9]

The extended role of medical imaging in diagnosis and treatment encourages researchers and equipment vendors to expand the limits of imaging technology. The cost of this research is significant, but the results have a considerable positive impact on patient outcome. Depending upon its application, medical imaging can be either one of the more cost–effective or one of the more costly healthcare services provided today.

Imaging's Complexity and Competitiveness Among Specialties

Medical imaging is a highly complex blend of diagnostic and therapeutic subspecialties and has broad implications for the delivery of healthcare services. Questions regarding a given modality's appropriateness, its cost in relation to its results, and the most qualified type of specialist to administer it are continually being debated. In addition, imaging referral patterns are shifting. In the past, referrals came primarily from surgical and medical specialists. In the future, more will come from primary care generalists and payer gatekeepers.

Many factors must be considered in determining which modality is best for a given condition. For example, are fast magnetic resonance imaging techniques able to reveal the same metabolic activity as single–photon emission computed tomography (SPECT) and positron emission tomography (PET)? Does MRI provide a better image of the spine than CT? Which modality is less expensive per procedure? Which is more cost–effective in terms of overall patient treatment? Who controls the imaging equipment? Who owns the information it renders?

Opinions vary regarding which specialist is best qualified to perform a particular procedure and who is best qualified to interpret the images. For example:

> Most cardiologists have agreements with their hospital that they will do all the (cardiology) interpretation. On the other hand, hospitals also have agreements with radiology groups that they will do all the study interpretations for MRI and CT. That's where the war

begins. . . . They both say they own it, and the only person that ends up in the middle is the hospital.[10]

Similarly,

- Is interventional angiography (which was pioneered by radiologists) the realm of vascular surgeons or interventional radiologists?
- With such interventional procedures, where does radiology end and surgery begin?
- Is a radiologist more qualified to interpret fetal ultrasound than an obstetrician?[11]

Competition among medical specialists–and even between specific imaging modalities–often leads to internal turf battles among allied healthcare providers. The politics of medicine complicate the planning process for imaging facilities but rarely can be avoided entirely. Territorialism is as fundamental to medical planning as the forces of gravity are to structural engineering. Therefore, a successful planning team must be trained in diplomacy, as well as in facility planning.

The Forces of Change

Some of the conditions that began to change healthcare architecture during the initial growth of outpatient services in the 1980s still exist today. Patient–oriented design, economic concerns, and technological developments now shape the nature of healthcare delivery to a greater extent than ever before. These factors directly influence health insurance premiums, federal approval of new drugs and equipment, and even television advertisements. Indirectly, but significantly, they give form to a new healthcare architecture.

Medical imaging and the design of medical imaging facilities appear to be facing similar challenges. Depending on the point of view, the key forces shaping healthcare and healthcare architecture today can be seen as either being restrictive or creating new opportunities. In either case, they must be factored into the decision–making process for design and planning.

Patient-Oriented and Evidence-Based Design

One significant development influencing the architecture of medical imaging facilities is the change in attitude toward reducing medical errors and accommodating the needs and desires of patients. Many healthcare providers recognize that the physical environment of the healthcare facility influences safety, patient compliance, consumer choice, and customer satisfaction.

The Picker Institute, a nonprofit leader in assessing patients' perceptions within healthcare settings, and the Center for Health Design (CHD), a nonprofit membership organization dedicated to promoting life-enhancing healthcare environments, have developed a "Patient-Centered Environmental Checklist" to help designers and facility administrators and clinicians assess their facilities "through the eyes of patients and their families." The checklist identifies eight attributes of the physical environment that have a substantial impact on patients' perceptions and those of their families:

- Promotes connections to staff
- Is considerate of well-being
- Is convenient and accessible
- Is confidential and private
- Shows caring for family
- Is considerate of impairments
- Facilitates connection to the outside world
- Is safe and secure[12]

Within the limitations of lean construction budgets, it is still possible to provide a safe environment with natural lighting, clear wayfinding systems, and pleasant furnishings. A soothing environment can improve compliance and hasten the recovery process.

A facility's measurable results can be related to health, economic, or organizational outcomes. There is a process, known as evidence-based design that can assist the design team to compete in categories that will contribute to improved outcomes in each of these areas. The Center for Health Design (www.healthdesign.org), for example, is a not-for-profit organization whose mission is to transform healthcare settings into healing environments that improve outcomes through the creative use of evidence-based design.[13]

Better buildings translate to bottom-line cost savings, as documented by Berry, Parker, Coile, Hamilton, O'Neill, and Sadler in their article supporting evidence-based design: "Evidence-based design considers three categories of benefits: stress reduction, safety, and ecological health. . . . [B]eneficial financial results can be found in all three categories."[14]

Patient-Oriented Design and Medical Imaging

One healthcare delivery concept, called patient-focused care, suggests that a drastic restructuring of the traditional healthcare delivery model (and thus the delivery of medical imaging services) can improve the patient's experience in the hospital, which in turn can generate operational savings. Although patient-focused care is not a new concept, it is being applied in a new way that modifies the traditional arrangement of hospital departments, with broad implications for the form and function of healthcare facilities in general and imaging services specifically.

About the time that some of the first digital image and information management and communications systems were being developed, some proponents of patient-focused care noted the inefficiencies in the traditional healthcare models, which required an inordinate amount of inpatient movement to and from centralized imaging departments with fixed equipment and specialized staff. Unnecessary patient transport not only was costly in terms of time and staffing resources but also contributed to both staff and patient injuries, as well as increased medical errors due to discontinuous patient care.

In contrast, evolving patient-focused concepts were beginning to utilize PACS systems to streamline the process and decentralize some radiology departments. Now staff and equipment could come to the patient, instead of the patient being transported throughout the hospital. As a result, the number of distinct patient encounters could be reduced, the number of staff full-time equivalents (FTEs) cut, the incidence of medical errors lowered, and opportunities for staff cross-training enhanced.

In one study, radiologists at the Baltimore Veterans Affairs Medical Center (led by Dr. Eliot Siegel) compared the process of ordering, conducting, and evaluating a traditional paper-based diagnostic exam with one done in a filmless, paperless operation. The traditional process consisted of fifty-nine individual steps, while the automated process required only nine steps:

1. Physician places order through the hospital information system (HIS)
2. Transportation aide takes patient to radiology department
3. Technologist selects patient from computerized modality work list
4. Technologist obtains image
5. Image checked for quality on computer system
6. Transportation aide returns patient to nursing unit
7. Radiologist verifies image and reports findings
8. Radiologist verifies study and dictates report using voice-recognition technology
9. Report available on HIS[15]

One key implication of the patient-focused model was that basic imaging services could be decentralized throughout various inpatient and outpatient care areas across the healthcare enterprise. Unfortunately, few robust image and information networks existed in the early days of this concept, and it was difficult to translate the theoretical advantages of the first patient-focused operations into tangible benefits. However, as information technology matured, significant benefits of decentralized imaging have now been realized. This is most evident with outpatient imaging providing convenient access to image acquisition for patients, and both inpatient and outpatient image distribution systems providing radiologists, referring physicians, and allied healthcare professionals with convenient access to images and information.

Patient-Oriented Design and Architectural Design

Patients' perceptions of the architecture of a medical imaging facility influence how they feel about the care provided within, so attention must be paid to facility design. Consumers of healthcare services demand buildings that are convenient and unintimidating, and designers–as with any other building type–should promote these qualities in medical imaging facilities. Imaging facilities–replete with technical complexity–provide both the need and the opportunity for crafting a humane environment. Today, there is greater awareness of a supportive environment's beneficial effect on patients and staff. Most designers recognize that properly designed, well-lit spaces both hasten patient recovery and increase staff productivity.

Patients respond to environments that are designed to meet their specific needs. They also respond to architectural design that "brands" or conveys a facility's personality and inspires good first and lasting impressions. Like people, buildings have unique personalities: some attract; others repel. All reflect the quality of care provided within the facility. The strength of a facility's image depends on the clarity of the design concept and the skill with which it is articulated.

Economics and Medical Imaging

Form follows financing! Economic variables have a profound influence on medical imaging facilities, affecting such diverse factors as operations, maintenance, staffing patterns, equipment acquisition, and the ability to adapt to new technology. Because facility construction represents a relatively small part of total healthcare expenditures, the most significant savings typically come from the effective utilization of healthcare personnel.

As the rules for medical reimbursement change, so do the referral patterns that affect imaging services. Because imaging services are so dependent on referrals from other physicians, and because reimbursement rates for imaging services are usually characterized by small margins, many radiologists–in association with other healthcare providers–have opened their own imaging centers in an effort to establish more efficient operations as compared to hospital-based imaging departments. However, questions of self-referral and excessive referral to imaging services have led to legislation that places strict limitations on such joint ventures and limits the profit-making potential of both hospital-based and freestanding imaging centers.

Proper facility layout is essential to ensuring efficient operations. As the workload capacity of imaging equipment increases, a facility's ability to improve employee productivity must also be supported. With regard to equipment, many facilities have responded to cost containment by seeking vendors that have developed "economy" equipment lines, emphasizing dependable technology without the bells and whistles found in some of their more expensive models. Much of the latest generation of equipment tries to minimize space and facility requirements. However, manufacturers' minimum dimensions are not necessarily conducive to optimal use of the space.

Increased Usage and Capabilities of Medical Imaging

Another way to increase operational efficiency and cut costs is to increase patient throughput, thereby enabling more patients to be examined with less equipment. Fast image acquisition and rapid postprocessing techniques now enable greater patient throughput and thus increase productivity. Continual improvements in imaging technology ensure that image acquisition is no longer the source of workflow bottlenecks, placing more responsibility on efficient facility planning and systems integration.

The rampant development of new imaging techniques raises philosophical, political, and economic questions about whether unrestricted medical treatment is a right or a privilege. Is it appropriate? Is it even a good idea? While some might suggest that technology is to blame for rising healthcare costs, an opposing view–held by both laypersons and medical practitioners–suggests that the high cost of healthcare is testimony to the overall success of modern medicine.

A study underwritten by the Blue Cross and Blue Shield Association concluded, not surprisingly, that greater availability of diagnostic imaging equipment itself is responsible for its increased utilization, contributing to rising healthcare costs.

> If you have more capacity to look for disease, the more you are going to find and the more you are going to find, the more you are going to do something about it even without evidence that doing something is particularly effective. . . .
>
> Despite the findings . . . many technologies save money and to a lesser extent, some save money and improve quality. . . .
>
> Using only the cost to insurance beneficiaries as a measurement, the study failed to recognize that technologies might lower cost in other areas such as lost workdays, [Blair Childs, president of a trade group representing medical device manufacturers,] said. "It talks about the increase in healthcare spending, but it doesn't talk about what we're getting for that. It only looks from the vantage point of spending and is not looking from the vantage point that patients are getting access to care they wouldn't otherwise have gotten."[16]

Medical professionals can now detect many diseases and illnesses early on because they can acquire precise data that enable them to discover these conditions. Our aging population is another indicator of medicine's success. People now live long enough to become affected by more chronic illnesses than was the case previously. Many believe it is not technology but rather society's expectations of longevity and quality of life that raise the cost of healthcare.

The Cost of Construction and the Value of Quality Facility Design

Compared to the price of commercial or retail construction, the cost of building an imaging facility includes many additional premiums. Floor-to-floor heights tend to be great because of the heating, ventilating, and air-conditioning (HVAC) requirements as well as the vertical clearance of the equipment itself (figure 2–4). This means more materials and therefore higher cost. The weight of equipment also leads to increased cost due to the need for greater structural capacities and special mounting assemblies. In addition, power requirements are extensive, and special lighting and air-conditioning often are required.

Another consideration unique to medical imaging facility design–protection against radiation, electromagnetic (EM), and radio-frequency (RF) emissions–adds expense. Most facilities designed to treat patients are subject to more restrictive and thus more costly construction codes and regulations than are other facility types. While regulatory design requirements vary widely from state to state, it is becoming increasingly common across the nation to house imaging equipment–especially those modalities with high outpatient utilization–within ambulatory care facilities designed to less stringent business (B) occupancy code requirements as compared to hospital (I) occupancy code requirements.

Given the higher cost inherent in building imaging facilities, how much more will good or even great design cost? Quality design in itself is not necessarily expensive; in fact, it should provide savings through effective use of space as well as interest and inspiration through innovation. Creative planning enables staffing and operational economies and allows for changes over time without disrupting present operations.

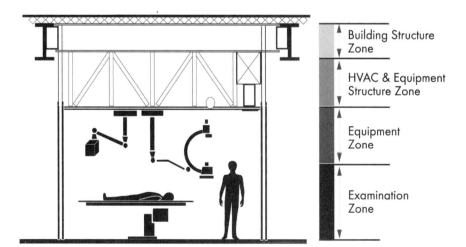

Figure 2-4 Imaging facilities require greater floor-to-floor heights than do other types of healthcare facilities.

The human element of imaging facility design–while sometimes over-looked–is crucial. The perceptions of staff, who spend much of their time within the space, and the emotions of patients, who are often terrified of the very events that necessitate their presence in the facility, pose significant design opportunities. Sensitivity to the dimensions of space and the creative use of materials and finishes can yield an exceptional environment without exceeding the realities and constraints of conservative budgets.

The Challenge

Resources are shrinking. Requirements are expanding. Designing and building a medical imaging facility was never easy, but now it is even more difficult. Addressing economic, technological, and patient mandates is not enough; today, the architecture of medical imaging facilities must satisfy these needs with a solution that is both innovative and affordable. The challenge is greater and the risks are higher than they were in the past.

In spite of, or perhaps because of, a more difficult challenge, today's imaging centers and hospital departments are more dynamic and patient-oriented than ever before. Successful imaging architecture blends dynamic space and form with logical planning and construction. If the design team does not understand imaging functions or equipment, it is all too likely that design efforts will either ignore or become overpowered by technical and functional constraints. On the other hand, if the nature of imaging is understood, design opportunities will be recognized and form and function will enhance each other.

Successful imaging facilities are those that address the following challenges:

1. *Improve the medical experience.* Simply stated, this means designing for people, their emotions, and how individuals function. Improving the medical experience will benefit patients, staff, referring physicians, owners, and visitors.
2. *Anticipate change and integrate flexibility with design.* Build into every design the ability to change, both internally and externally. Although the nature of future changes may be unknown, the fact that change will occur is a given. It is both possible and necessary to provide flexibility today to accommodate tomorrow's changing needs.
3. *Maintain quality with less expense.* Incorporate cost-effective imaging systems, plan spaces for efficient staff functioning, and specify appropriate building components.
4. *Avoid duplication.* As the potential for decentralized imaging services continues to grow, avoid unnecessary duplication of equipment, staff, and facilities and ensure that information transfer between remote sites is effective. Many medical im-

aging functions are becoming decentralized and distributed throughout the healthcare enterprise. Plan now for future advances in image and information management systems as a means to link remote sites.

Notes

1. R. L. Eisenberg, *Radiology: An Illustrated History* (St. Louis: Mosby Year Book, 1992), 51–52, 67–69.
2. Eisenberg, 68–69.
3. Eisenberg, 67.
4. E. F. Stevens, *The American Hospital of the Twentieth Century* (New York: Architectural Record Publishing Company, 1918), 142–143.
5. Stevens, 143–145.
6. Eisenberg, 69.
7. C. Becker. "Grudge Match." Modern Healthcare, December 1, 2003. http://www.modernhealthcare.com/storyPreview.cms?articleId=31111&archive=Y
8. B. Rostenberg, "The architecture of reform," *Modern Healthcare*, December 1, 2003, 20.
9. C. H. Harris, "IT in the OR: Image-guided surgery soups up need for networks," *Health Imaging & IT*, December 2003, 28–31.
10. Brett Hickman, cited in Becker.
11. D. E. Egerter, "Tool of the future: Ultrasound stethoscope," *Diagnostic Imaging*, July 1991, A64.
12. Picker Institute and Center for Health Design (Boston, MA), "Health care design patient-centered environmental checklist: Assessing the built environment from the patient and family perspective," 1999.
13. R. Cama, "Measurable results: Going for the gold!" *Healthcare Design*, November 2004, 6.
14. L. Berry, D. Parker, R. Coile, D. K. Hamilton, J. D. O'Neill, and B. Sadler, "The business case for better buildings," *Frontiers of Health Services Management* 21, 1 (2004): 3–24.
15. L. A. Runy, "Radiology: How technical breakthroughs are advancing the field," *Hospitals and Health Networks* 77, 11 (2003): 49–55 (special supplement sponsored by the American Hospital Association).
16. C. Becker, "If you have it, you use it," *Modern Healthcare*, November 10, 2003, 9.

PART TWO

DEVELOPMENT OF
AN IMAGING FACILITY

CHAPTER 3

Organization of a Medical Imaging Project

Of all building types, healthcare facilities are perhaps the most complex. Among the various types of healthcare facilities, medical imaging facilities may well be the most challenging to design. To successfully meet that challenge, the design team must be well organized and aware of the forces, both internal and external, that influence project development.

Medical imaging facilities encompass such a vast range of facility types and spaces that it is not possible to describe all the conceivable requirements for every imaging project. For example, the organizational needs of an internal remodel that replaces a single radiography room will differ from those of a new hospital replacement containing comprehensive, state-of-the-art diagnostic and treatment systems. Similarly, the needs of a major renovation project will differ from those of a small, newly constructed imaging center.

This chapter describes some of the activities that must take place prior to designing and planning an imaging facility and explains how the facility owner or administrator can best prepare for the decisions that will need to be made. It also discusses how to build a foundation for a well-organized design and management process. While much of this chapter focuses on the development of freestanding facilities, the strategies described can also be applied to designing hospital-based imaging departments.

Strategic Planning and Master Planning

The initial steps that set a project in motion are often the most important. The temptation to "make a building" before researching the context in which medical imaging services and the facility itself will operate should be resisted. Much of the groundwork preceding architectural design focuses not directly on a building itself but rather on the external forces that either enable or preclude the owner and the design team from creating a successful project and managing a successful process. Strategic planning and master planning address these external factors, as well as other important variables in the process.

Strategic planning, an essential prerequisite to site and facility development, is an external and internal analysis of the factors that determine an organization's future. In the context of a provider of medical imaging services, it is the process by which an organization evaluates its surroundings and sets goals to achieve its objectives for providing imaging services. This, in turn, leads to the creation of a responsive site and facility master plan that will guide the continued growth and development of real estate and facilities, as necessary, to achieve these goals.

A technology plan for medical imaging facilities defines strategies for implementing new medical technologies and should be a part of the strategic plan. The technology plan describes a rational basis for technology assessment and acquisition and thus provides an alternative to decision making that is driven solely by interdepartmental politics.

Although development of a single medical imaging project may not require a comprehensive strategic or master plan, reference to existing business and strategic plans and site/facility master plans serves as valuable guidance to any development project. If a strategic plan is not in place, one probably should be initiated whether or not immediate facility development is anticipated. Without a common strategy, it is doubtful that project team members are working toward a common goal, and without defined tactics, it is doubtful that they are working together at all.

A master plan provides a framework for growth by (1) mapping the conditions of existing property and structures, (2) identifying opportunities and obstacles to future development, and (3) charting the application of resources to effect sequential development consistent with the strategic plan's intentions. Like strategic plans, site and facility master plans specify various periods of time within which primary goals are targeted.

The components of strategic planning and master planning set the stage for purposeful design. Each step in this predesign process has particular objectives. The steps include:

1. Establish goals and evaluation criteria
2. Perform market analyses and feasibility studies
3. Perform site and facility evaluation studies
4. Develop a working budget
5. Develop a project schedule
6. Develop functional and space programs
7. Align scope, budget, and schedule
8. Develop site and facility concept plans

A brief discussion of these key predesign activities follows.

Step 1: Establish Goals and Evaluation Criteria

Quality design requires that the goals of a project be well defined and clearly stated. Clearly stated goals will in turn help align the expectations of each member of the project team. Examples of project goals for a medical imaging facility include:

Strategic
- To provide the most advanced imaging services in the region
- To become the imaging facility of choice for patients, referring physicians, and affiliated provider organizations

Economic
- To provide a physical environment that will maximize staffing efficiency
- To improve physical accessibility and allow for patient convenience by eliminating operational bottlenecks, thus reducing waiting time
- To avoid unnecessary duplication of equipment

Political
- To make imaging services accessible to patients residing in outlying areas of the region
- To minimize turf battles among medical specialists

Medical
- To reduce medical errors and improve the accuracy of diagnostic interpretations
- To offer noninvasive alternatives to traditional invasive procedures

Temporal
- To allow for incremental growth and modification over time without disrupting existing services

Physical
- To integrate building systems that will accommodate continuous change
- To separate inpatient and outpatient zones and circulation routes
- To create a physical image that reflects state-of-the-art medical technology without compromising personal interaction between patients and healthcare providers
- To reduce stress for both patients and staff

Project goals should be stated in terms of measurable evaluation criteria prior to commencing facility design. This will help project team members recognize if they are drifting away from the goals and objectives with which they began. Evaluation criteria to consider include:

Strategic
- Is the solution consistent with the core goals of the strategic plan?
- Does the solution give the organization a strategic advantage?

Economic
- Is the solution economically feasible and fiscally responsive?
- Does it make good business sense?
- Is it consistent with the demands of the marketplace?

Political
- Does the solution serve the community well?
- How does it affect, and how is it affected by, competitors?

Medical
- Does the solution enable the provision of high-quality healthcare?
- Are the medical needs of the community being met?
- Is the solution consistent with the institution's goals for focusing on certain medical programs?

Temporal
- Can the solution be implemented in such a manner as to maximize its impact?
- Does it provide for phased implementation?
- Does it provide flexibility for adapting to an unknown future?

Physical
- Is the solution durable?
- Does it enhance the organization's image?
- Does it reduce the stress levels of those who use it?

Step 2: Perform Market Analyses and Feasibility Studies

A market analysis should be considered an integral component of strategic planning. However, it is unlikely that a strategic plan is so current or so specifically targeted to imaging services that it can serve as an accurate guide to the feasibility of a new or newly expanded service. Implementation of new services represents such a significant expenditure of resources that analyzing of the current and anticipated market conditions is essential.

A market analysis should identify the anticipated demand for services and calculate the potential return on investment (ROI). It also should consider the likely introduction of similar services by nearby institutions. In this way, it offers a conceptual framework for determining the viability of new services and programs.

The market analysis should be as realistic as possible. Therefore, the opportunities for a new or expanded market should not be exaggerated. Conversely, overly conservative estimates of demand for imaging services may lead to an undersized facility or less efficient use of staff and equipment. A balanced and realistic view of external conditions will result in the greatest ROI.

Upon completion of a general market analysis that supports the viability of new imaging services, a more detailed feasibility study should be conducted to further assess the viability of the specific imaging project that is anticipated. The feasibility study should include realistic estimates of facility size, construction costs, equipment costs, additional project costs, and anticipated operational costs.

Preliminary estimates for building size can be calculated using generic guidelines, but these figures should be refined later (based on more accurate data) if they are to be used for anything other than feasibility studies. Similarly, preliminary unit construction costs (dollars per gross square foot of construction) can be obtained from a cost estimator, an architect, or a building contractor, provided these individuals are familiar with current projects that are similar in both scope and location.

Construction costs vary considerably by region, building type, and bidding climate. Unit cost per square foot will be affected by the size and nature of the project. For example, the cost of building an imaging facility as part of a hospital will differ from that of an imaging suite located within a medical office building. Similarly, the cost of an MRI suite will be greater than that of a basic radiographic room. A construction escalation cost factor also must be considered.

The cost of equipment will vary considerably depending on its capabilities, the vendor, and, most important, the purchaser's ability to negotiate a good price. If existing equipment will be reused, the cost of its removal and reinstallation should be factored into the budget. For the purposes of the feasibility study, the cost of equipment for a recent comparable project should suffice, provided an appropriate cost escalation contingency is added and the equipment budget is refined as additional details become known. The cost of equipment can exceed construction costs, and equipment maintenance contracts—paid over the useful life of the equipment—can exceed the purchase price of equipment.

If the project involves a freestanding building on a new site, the feasibility study should consider the need for delivery of electric, gas, water, and sewer services to the building. The study also should consider an evaluation of the geotechnical aspects of the site to determine any unusual subsurface conditions that might affect construction and thus construction costs. Similarly, building within a seismic zone will involve unique construction cost premiums.

If installation of the imaging project is to occur within an existing structure, the feasibility study should consider infrastructure capacity upgrades that may be needed in order for the existing building systems to support the anticipated increase in equipment load and demand for utility services. A renovation project may not allow for planning that is as efficient as it would be in new construction because of physical constraints inherent in the existing structure. As a result, the renovated project may require more space, be less efficient for staff, compromise future flexibility, and have a configuration that is limited by a restrictive infrastructure. (See chapter 14, "Renovation Versus New Construction.") It should be kept in mind that the cost of renovation is not necessarily less expensive than the cost of new construction.

Step 3: Perform Site and Facility Evaluation Studies

If an existing site is inadequate for the proposed program or if no site is currently owned by those proposing the new facility, a new site may need to be selected. Whatever site is proposed (new or existing), it will need to be analyzed to determine how well it will accommodate the needs of the new facility.

Site selection and site analysis are integral components of the market analysis and feasibility studies. As such, site data must be integrated based upon the assumptions made in the preceding steps. The site selection and analysis will generate financial data, such as the purchase price of the pre-ferred site and the cost of improvements required after purchase. Site evaluation and selection criteria (as defined by Lifton and Hardy in "Site Selection for Health Care Facilities") include:

- Proximity to patients and other providers
- Major road access
- Accessibility by public transportation
- Direct site access
- Size and usable area
- Site configuration and orientation
- Zoning restrictions
- Legal and physical restrictions
- Environmental impact[1]

If an existing facility is to be renovated or added to, it should be evaluated to determine how well it can accommodate its new function. Facility evaluation criteria include:

- Present age and remaining useful life expectancy
- Compliance with current codes
- Structural capacity
- Capacity of, and ease of adding to, the existing electrical and mechanical systems
- Presence of toxic or hazardous materials
- Size, shape, and configuration (for example, does the location of structural columns allow an efficient configuration of imaging rooms and adjacent support spaces?)
- Interior and exterior appearance of the existing facility

Step 4: Develop a Working Budget

The process of developing a working budget is cyclical, not linear. As the project progresses and more detailed data about the project's scope and complexity become available, the budget should be reevaluated and confirmed. (See chapter 4, "Management of the Process," for a discussion of types of costs and cost considerations at each phase of a project.)

During these iterative cycles of budget refinement the magnitude of the budget should remain stable. If cost estimates conflict with the proposed budget, the scope of the project might need to be modified at the outset to conform to the limitations of available capital. If the budget is arbitrarily changed in the middle of design, the programming, planning, and design processes will need to be revisited. For these reasons, the initial preparation of a working budget should be as comprehensive as possible.

Although the owner is primarily responsible for establishing a project's preliminary capital budget, it is the architect and cost consultants who are responsible for verifying that the budget is appropriate for the scope and quality of intended work. If these individuals are in conflict, they must be brought into alignment before detailed programming or design activities begin. Medical equipment consultants often provide an estimate of both fixed and movable medical equipment costs.

It is important that both the owner and the architect consider the capital budget in tandem with the operating budget for the facility, as the operating budget will eventually exceed the facility's construction cost. Sustainability–the concept of minimizing a construction project's initial and long-term impact on the environment and natural resources–will affect both the construction budget and the operating budget. (Sustainability is discussed further in chapter 8, "Design Concepts.")

An owner's construction contingency should appear as a line item in the budget. This contingency, often 10 percent of the estimated construction cost for new construction and up to 20 percent for renovation, is provided to account for unknown conditions that might arise during construction. It is not intended to be used to increase the project's programming or design scope. If it is, it will have been spent before construction begins and will not be available when needed.

A design contingency should be included in addition to the owner's construction contingency. The purpose of the design contingency is to account for the absence (at this early stage) of detailed drawings that describe how design concepts will be implemented. Prior to beginning schematic design, the design contingency might be equal to 10 percent of the estimated construction cost for new construction and 15 percent for renovation. It can be reduced after most design decisions have been made. The design contingency–like the construction contingency–is not intended to be used to increase project scope; rather, its purpose is to accommodate design refinement as the project progresses.

Contingency figures should be neither too lean nor too fat. An inflated estimate of cost might seem to limit the exposure to risk by guaranteeing that the construction project will be achieved within the assumed budget. However, the true risk of this is unnecessarily limiting the amount of program area by being too conservative in developing the project budget. Should construction bids or cost estimates reveal that more program area is possible within the original budget, the additional program area–if added late in the process–will be designed at a premium price and with considerable compromise.

Step 5: Develop a Project Schedule

The schedule is a road map that highlights milestones critical to the project's development. The schedule should be neither so loose that it has little meaning nor so rigid that it cannot accommodate important developments that will arise during the course of design and construction. Like the budget, the project schedule will require occasional adjustment.

Budget and schedule are intimately related. As the magnitude of one increases, in most cases so does the magnitude of the other. Both owners and architects should be careful not to squeeze either the budget or the schedule so tightly that it will have a negative impact on the quality of the project.

For imaging projects that require careful coordination of many diverse disciplines (architects and planners, equipment installation specialists, radiologists, technologists, and administrators), the project schedule is as much a tool for communication as it is a calendar. It describes the work for which individual team members are responsible and the time by which the results of their work must be made available so that other team members can accomplish their tasks.

A number of key questions should be asked prior to establishing the initial project schedule. These include:

- What is driving the schedule? Is there a critical date by which the project must be occupied?
- Can the project be occupied in stages?
- How long will construction likely take? Are there unusual factors that might extend the construction duration? Can some phases of construction–such as site preparation–be started early? Can the project be fast-tracked?
- What needs to be done before construction can begin? How long will preconstruction activities (programming, design, etc.) last? What other activities might delay commencement of construction?
- Has financing been secured? When will funds be made available?

- What regulatory or financing reviews will be required? Who needs to review the project? What time frame is anticipated for this?
- Are key milestone dates on a critical path of the schedule?
- Will there be financial penalties if the project is delayed?[2]

According to *The Architect's Handbook of Professional Practice*, if financial and regulatory agency approvals are needed, they need to be incorporated into scheduling plans:

> Financial and regulatory approvals usually involve go/no-go decisions, so they almost always lie on the critical path. For complex projects requiring many interconnected approvals . . . the architect providing project scheduling services may need to map out a "decision schedule" as well as a design and construction [or project] schedule.[3]

Figure 3-1 provides an example of a decision schedule, and figure 3-2 provides a sample project schedule. The project schedule will be determined, in part, by the selected method of project delivery, such as design-bid-build, fast track, or design/build. The project duration will in turn influence the level of compensation the architect will seek, especially if extensive on-site contract administration services are needed. For example, a very short duration may require that the architect employ additional staff

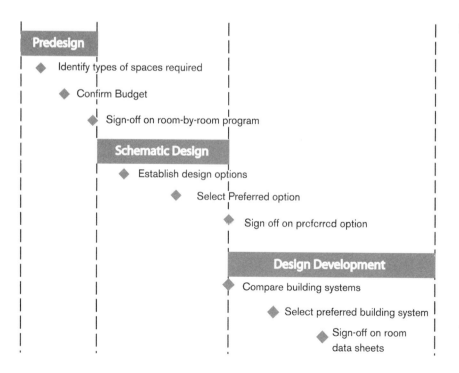

Figure 3-1 A decision schedule.

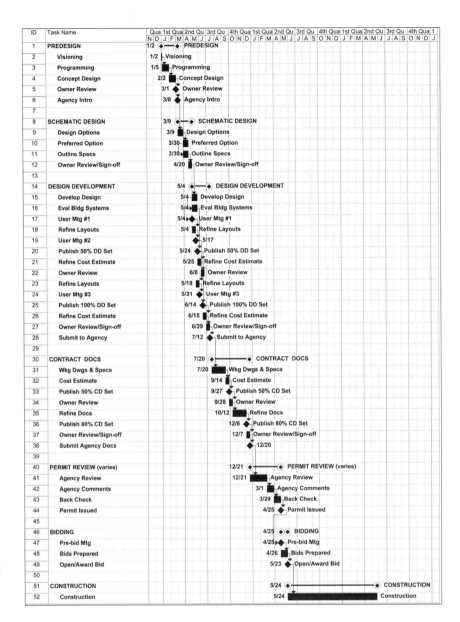

ID	Task Name			
		Qua	1st Qua	2nd Qu	3rd Qu	4th Qua	1st Qua	2nd Qu	3rd Qu	4th Qua	1st Qua	2nd Qu	3rd Qu	4th Qua	1
1	**PREDESIGN**	1/2 ◆—◆ PREDESIGN
2	Visioning	1/2 Visioning
3	Programming	1/5 Programming
4	Concept Design	2/2 Concept Design
5	Owner Review	3/1 ◆ Owner Review
6	Agency Intro	3/8 ◆ Agency Intro
7		
8	**SCHEMATIC DESIGN**	3/9 ◆—◆ SCHEMATIC DESIGN
9	Design Options	3/9 Design Options
10	Preferred Option	3/30 Preferred Option
11	Outline Specs	3/30 Outline Specs
12	Owner Review/Sign-off	4/20 Owner Review/Sign-off
13		
14	**DESIGN DEVELOPMENT**	5/4 ◆—◆ DESIGN DEVELOPMENT
15	Develop Design	5/4 Develop Design
16	Eval Bldg Systems	5/4 Eval Bldg Systems
17	User Mtg #1	5/4 ◆ User Mtg #1
18	Refine Layouts	5/4 Refine Layouts
19	User Mtg #2	◆ 5/17
20	Publish 50% DD Set	5/24 ◆ Publish 50% DD Set
21	Refine Cost Estimate	5/25 Refine Cost Estimate
22	Owner Review	6/8 Owner Review
23	Refine Layouts	5/18 Refine Layouts
24	User Mtg #3	5/31 ◆ User Mtg #3
25	Publish 100% DD Set	6/14 ◆ Publish 100% DD Set
26	Refine Cost Estimate	6/15 Refine Cost Estimate
27	Owner Review/Sign-off	6/29 Owner Review/Sign-off
28	Submit to Agency	7/12 ◆ Submit to Agency
29		
30	**CONTRACT DOCS**	7/20 ◆—◆ CONTRACT DOCS
31	Wkg Dwgs & Specs	7/20 Wkg Dwgs & Specs
32	Cost Estimate	9/14 Cost Estimate
33	Publish 50% CD Set	9/27 Publish 50% CD Set
34	Owner Review	9/28 Owner Review
35	Refine Docs	10/12 Refine Docs
36	Publish 80% CD Set	12/6 Publish 80% CD Set
37	Owner Review/Sign-off	12/7 Owner Review/Sign-off
38	Submit Agency Docs	12/20
39		
40	**PERMIT REVIEW (varies)**	12/21 ◆—◆ PERMIT REVIEW (varies)
41	Agency Review	12/21 Agency Review
42	Agency Comments	3/1 Agency Comments
43	Back Check	3/29 Back Check
44	Permit Issued	4/25 Permit Issued
45		
46	**BIDDING**	4/25 ◆◆ BIDDING
47	Pre-bid Mtg	4/25 Pre-bid Mtg
48	Bids Prepared	4/26 Bids Prepared
49	Open/Award Bid	5/23 ◆ Open/Award Bid
50		
51	**CONSTRUCTION**	5/24 ◆—◆ CONSTRUCTION
52	Construction	5/24 Construction

Figure 3-2 The project schedule is influenced by the project's scope as well as by the project's delivery method.

or pay overtime premiums. However, a prolonged schedule might require that the architect attend to the project for a longer duration than might otherwise be necessary. If the schedule (from the time of its inception) is either unusually long or unusually short, there should be good justification for this. If the architect feels that the schedule is inappropriate relative to the project scope, this should be brought to the owner's attention as soon as possible.

Step 6: Develop Functional and Space Programs

Functional and space programming provide a road map for facility planning and design. The functional program identifies past and present work–

load as well as operational characteristics and translates them into a model for future operations. For areas undergoing significant operational reengineering, however, past operational characteristics may have little relevance to future approaches.

Space programming translates the functional program into spatial data: size, quantity, quality, and space adjacencies. A detailed space program identifies each assigned space to be provided in the facility (public areas, patient areas, and staff areas) along with multipliers to account for wall thicknesses, unassigned circulation space, and rooms to house mechanical equipment. A room–by–room space program is a description of the individual spaces that constitute the entire imaging service. (See chapter 11, "Space Requirements.")

A well-written program is more than a list of rooms. Together, the functional and space programs serve as a virtual model of the imaging facility. As such, the program makes it possible to visualize the operation of the completed project. For example, adjacencies of one room to another present a logical progression of imaging service delivery. The space program for renovating an existing facility should consider the utilization of existing services and spaces and should address the implications of reusing existing construction. Such reuse, however, might introduce inherent inefficiencies into the space program.

Development of the functional and space programs should not be rushed. These are important tools and they provide an essential step between feasibility and design. The very process of programming will encourage the project team to reflect on important design and functional aspects that may not have been considered otherwise. It is easier and far less costly to make revisions to the building program than to effect the same changes while the building is under construction. Functional and space programs should consider and represent the flow of people, material, information, and equipment through the facility. The programs serve as a checklist and provide data useful in confirming preliminary budget estimates. The entire planning team should review and formally approve the space and functional programs before advancing to subsequent design phases.

Space and functional programming activities might include tours of other facilities that provide services and contain equipment comparable to those being planned. Such facility tours also are useful during schematic design.

Finally, the functional and space programs should reiterate the project goals and objectives set forth in the strategic plan. The project criteria should clearly describe scope, purpose, quality, schedule, and budget. (Figure 3–3 is an example of a functional and space program summary for a specific diagnostic imaging department.)

Figure 3-3 Example of a functional and space program summary.

Summary Example of a Functional and Space Program for Diagnostic Imaging

I. Existing Conditions
  A. Current and future programs
     1. Components of diagnostic imaging in this evaluation include inpatient imaging, MRI, and special procedures.
     2. All inpatient and outpatient angiographic, interventional fluoroscopic, and CT-guided biopsy procedures are performed in this area of service.
     3. All inpatient CTs and all inpatient and outpatient neuroradiology and head and neck CT scans are performed in this area of service.
  B. Current facilities
     1. The existing facility is approximately 15,000 DGSF.
     2. Digital image archive is located off-site.
     3. The existing facility includes: 1 MRI, 2 CTs, 3 general radiographic, 1 chest, 1 mammography/breast biopsy, 2 interventional fluoroscopy, and 3 angiographic special procedures.
  C. Facility deficiencies
     1. Traffic flow and circulation through the service are restricted, resulting in cross-traffic among staff, inpatients, and outpatients.
     2. Many of the inpatient holding areas are crowded, limit supervision, and have inadequate space for family and relatives to stay with patients.
     3. Most procedure rooms are undersized for current practices.
II. Planning Assumptions
  A. Operational policies and procedures
     1. MRI is to be located between the inpatient and outpatient areas. One MRI will be provided, initially, as part of the inpatient area. An adjacent area will be shelled for a future unit to be installed as part of the outpatient zone.
     2. All special procedures work for inpatients and outpatients will be located in the proposed facility. It is assumed that at least 60 percent of the special procedures work will be done on an outpatient basis. The staging and observation of post-procedure outpatients will occur in the adjacent day surgery area.
  B. Staffing and Scheduling
     1. Existing/projected staff by shift:

POSITION	DAY	EVENING	NIGHT
Faculty, administration, research	4	0	0
Residents/students	4	0	0
Technologists/nursing	12-14	0	0
Clerical	4	0	0
Other	6-7	0	0
Total	30-33	0	0

  C. Workload
     1. Historical data show inpatient procedures peaking in fiscal year 2005 at 35,225 examinations. The ratio of inpatient examinations to admissions has declined from 2.2 exams per admission in 2000 to 1.76 in 2005.
     2. Ultrasound and other procedures provided outside the main inpatient department accounted for 2,486 examinations in 2005. Workload within the inpatient service included 3,245 CT examinations, 1,463 angiographic procedures, 3,156 radiographic exams, 8,026 chest exams, 1,104 fluoroscopic examinations, and 489 MRI studies.
     3. Outpatient examinations provided in the department during 2005 included 2,204 MRI exams, 1,643 outpatient CT exams, and 734 angiographic procedures.

4. A one-month sample of patient records during September 2005 reported that 506 of the 3,408 examinations performed in the department were performed in the evening or on the weekend. This represents approximately 15 percent of the total workload for that period.

5. Special studies are currently under way to provide additional data regarding average procedure time and equipment utilization rates.

III. Planning Guidelines

  A. Desired relationships

    1. Access from the intensive care unit (ICU) and surgery is necessary for the provision of imaging to these patients.

  B. Design considerations

    1. Provide for future flexibility by providing some shelled space for future use and allowing for future external expansion.

    2. Consider universal room design for basic procedure rooms.

  C. Special and technical equipment

    1. MRI equipment, magnetic shielding, radio-frequency shielding

    2. CT units

    3. Special angiographic rooms

    4. Interventional fluoroscopy

    5. Standard radiographic and radiographic/fluoroscopic rooms

  D. Support systems considerations

    1. Movement of clean and soiled material between the service and central processing should be considered in the planning of the service.

  E. Building systems considerations

    1. Shielding for all radiographic, CT, and MRI equipment must be incorporated into the design of the building. The effect of imaging equipment on adjacent areas, and the effect of adjacent areas on imaging equipment, must be evaluated during design.

    2. MRI, CT, angiography, and interventional imaging rooms should be equipped with built-in suction, as well as compressed air.

IV. Room-By-Room Space Listing

AREA/ROOM	NSFA/UNIT	UNIT	TOTAL NSF	COMMENTS
MRI				
Scan room	520	2	1,040	
Control	130	2	260	
Computer room	200	1	200	
Laser imaging	100	1	100	
Patient valuables	60	1	60	
Archival storage	90	1	90	
Patient holding	80	6	480	
Patient toilets	60	4	240	
Interpretation/consult	0	0	0	See special procedures
Subtotal			2,470	
Special Procedures				
Angiography	520	4	2,082	
Control (angio)	120	4	480	Adjacent to angio
Storage/supply	180	3	540	
Patient holding/prep	100	6	600	
Postprocedure observation	0	0	0	In day surgery area

Figure 3-3 *continued* Example of a functional and space program summary.

AREA/ROOM	NSFA/UNIT	UNIT	TOTAL NSF	COMMENTS
Interpretation	240	1	240	
Clean/soiled utility	80	2	160	
Patient toilet	60	2	120	
Tray makeup	100	1	100	
Subtotal			4,320	
Radiographic/fluoroscopic				
Fluoroscopy	320	2	960	
Radiography	280	3	840	
Control	80	2	160	
Patient toilets	60	3	180	
Staff core	260	1	260	
Patient prep area	80	2	160	
Subtotal			2,560	
Patient Support				
Outpatient waiting	20	40	800	
Reception	80	2	160	
Public toilets	80	2	160	
Clean utility	100	1	100	
Patient gowning area	240	2	480	
Gowned waiting	20	30	600	
Patient toilets	60	2	120	
Soiled utility/trash	80	1	80	
Inpatient holding	80	4	320	
Dressing, standard	16	10	160	
Dressing, accessible	35	3	105	
Subtotal			3,085	
Staff Support				
Office, asst. chief	100	2	200	
Technologist work area	250	4	1,000	
Office, radiologists	120	4	480	
Secretarial/transcription	85	1	85	
Reading room	80	4	320	
Conference/education	240	1	240	
Lockers/lounge	180	2	260	
Staff toilets	60	4	240	
Storage	360	1	360	
Subtotal			2,285	
Total NSF			14,720	
Net to department grossing factor			1.6	
Total NSF $\times$ departmental gross square feet =			23,552	

[a]NSF stands for net square feet.

Step 7: Align Scope, Budget, and Schedule

Once the project scope, budget, and schedule are identified, these three variables should be compared to verify that they are in balance with one another. The verification process will likely require that one or all three be refined. The programming phase–rather than subsequent design phases–is the time to ensure alignment.

It usually is a good idea for each variable (scope, schedule, and budget) to be formally approved in writing. Later, a description of each can be incorporated into the agreement for design and planning services between the owner and the architect, where they will become terms of the contract. Formal written approval does not imply that no further changes will be made. However, it does suggest that if one variable changes, the other two are likely to change as well. Documenting the starting point at which all three were in balance makes it easier to monitor when and by what level of magnitude deviation occurs. It also helps identify whether budgetary deviations are due to changes in project scope.

Step 8: Prepare Site and Facility Master Plan and Concept Plans

Once scope, budget, and schedule are aligned, concept plans should be developed. The purpose of master planning and concept planning is to determine and test options available for initial and future growth on the site or within the confines of existing construction. Concepts should include options for:

- Site circulation, including that of patients, staff, and services
- Parking
- Circulation within the building(s), specifically the flow of people (staff, patients, and visitors), equipment, supplies, and waste
- Building massing and configuration
- Potential future site and building expansion options

A concept diagram is shown in figure 3–4. A variety of concept plans should be developed to examine alternative design solutions. Eventually the planning team should identify one preferred option to be developed in greater detail and, if warranted, develop one or two alternative versions of the preferred concept. Concept planning should conclude with a written evaluation of both the preliminary and preferred concepts, including the strengths and weaknesses of each and their associated implementation costs.

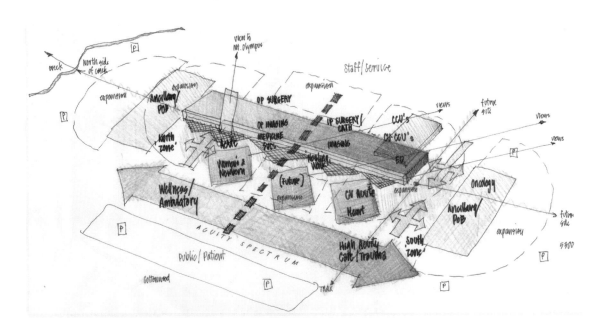

Figure 3-4 Example of a concept diagram.
Courtesy of Anshen + Allen, Architects.

Project Team Selection

As soon as the risks of moving forward with the project have been evaluated, the owner should assess the capabilities potentially available in-house for managing the design and construction processes. Does the organization include individuals who have experience with managing design and construction projects of this type? What is the cost of dedicating most of their time to the project and having others take over the remainder of their responsibilities? If sufficient experience does not exist internally, perhaps a project management or construction management consultant should be considered.

Except in the case of small projects developed by large healthcare institutions with in-house architects and engineers, a team of architectural and engineering consultants probably will be hired to design the project and assist in administering the contract documents during construction. If programming and master planning services are to be provided by the design architect, the architectural team should be selected soon after the preliminary budget and schedule have been established. The selected architect can help verify that the budget and schedule are in balance with project scope.

However, if programming and/or master planning services are to be provided by someone other than the design architect, two distinct selection processes may occur: one for programming and master planning consultants after establishment of a preliminary budget and schedule, and one for the architectural design consultant after programming and master planning are complete. Both consultant teams can help verify that schedule and budget are in balance with project scope.

Selecting the appropriate architectural team is an important and often difficult decision. An experienced team is needed to successfully complete the project. It is essential to select consultants who understand the special nature of imaging facilities in general, as well as the unique requirements of the specific project to be developed. The selection process should be composed of four sequential steps: (1) define the criteria that will be used to select qualified candidates, (2) prequalify firms that meet the stated criteria, (3) develop a short list consisting of four or five of the most qualified teams, and (4) interview the short-listed firms. During the architect selection process, interviewers should plan to participate actively during the interview and should be familiar with each candidate team's work and qualifications.

Selection factors to consider include individuals' direct experience on similar projects; team members' longevity with the firm and previous experience of each team member working with each other; references from other clients; and ultimately the owner's intuition.[4]

Notes

1. J. Lifton and O. B. Hardy, *Site Selection for Health Care Facilities* (Chicago: American Hospital Publishing, 1982).
2. D. Haviland, *The Architect's Handbook of Professional Practice*, Vol. 2: *The Project* (Washington, DC: American Institute of Architects, 1994), 380–81.
3. Haviland, 381.
4. J. A. Flaws, "Which architect should you pick?" *Health Facilities Management*, July 1992, 34–40.

CHAPTER 4

Management of the Process

This chapter examines the basic responsibilities of the owner, architect, and contractor within a medical imaging project, as well as describes the need to have a basic alignment of expectations for each of these parties, and the need for clear communications among all involved. It describes the design phases (from conceptual design through construction), as well as the process for aligning a project's budget with its scope.

Managing a medical imaging project may involve tasks that are more complex than those required for other healthcare design projects. The architect and the owner each should assign a manager with specific responsibilities to the project, and together these two managers will lead their respective teams. Specific project manager tasks include establishing goals, scheduling, budgeting, and directing in such a way that the design team can obtain consensus on critical issues. For example, radiologists will likely want to defer equipment selection until the latest date possible to ensure that the equipment is state-of-the-art (or at least the most current model available), but the manager of the design team must make sure that such decisions are made in a timely manner and that there is a mechanism in place to accommodate changes to those decisions when they become necessary.

Sometimes it is not apparent just how many steps in the design and planning process are contingent on detailed, site-specific equipment data. For example, the design of some procedure rooms must remain generic until the proposed equipment is specified. Although a generic or universal layout might be acceptable for simple, basic procedure rooms, delaying the specific layout of more specialized procedure rooms is likely to affect the entire project schedule, as items with long lead times will arrive late, requiring some of the construction trades to perform their work out of sequence.

In some states, the regulatory review required to obtain a building permit will not allow major equipment selections to be deferred.

In the case of magnetic resonance imaging, substituting one equipment model (or one magnetic field strength) for another could require replanning several rooms and modifying the structural, mechanical, and electrical systems, as well as shielding requirements. Postponing equipment selections will delay the preparation of contract documents, which in turn will delay construction.

The Project Team: Roles and Responsibilities

Successful architecture requires a team of skilled professionals who are willing and able to work together interactively. The team is made up of the owner, the architect, and the contractor, with the architect and contractor being responsible to the owner.

TABLE 4-1: TYPICAL PROJECT TEAM (DESIGN PHASES)

Owner	Architect/Engineers/Other Consultants	Contractor[a]
Project manager	Principal	Construction manager (optional)
Radiology administrator	Project manager	General contractor (optional)
Radiologist	Project architect	Cost estimators (optional)
Chief technologist	Designer	
Radiation physicist	Medical planner	
Facility operations and maintenance representative	Interior architect/interior designer	
Radiologic nurse	Programmer	
Equipment consultant[b]	Technical coordinator	
Equipment vendors[c]	Mechanical engineer	
	Electrical engineer	
	Structural engineer	
	Cost estimator	
	Equipment consultant[b]	

Notes

a- The contractor or construction manager's involvement during design phases is considered optional (but desirable). If a contractor or construction manager is involved at this time, it is usually to assist with recommendations regarding constructability, to provide a second cost estimate, or to help with complex issues of phasing or subdividing the project into separate bid packages.

b- An equipment consultant can be a consultant either to the owner or to the architect.

c- Equipment vendors are not actually consultants. Often, their services are tied to product sales. Nonetheless, their input can be helpful. Information from vendors is necessary in order for the architectural and engineering (A/E) team to perform design and planning services, but the A/E team has no contractual relationship with the vendors. Therefore, all vendor-furnished information should come to the A/E team via the owner.

For small projects, the team might be limited to an administrator, a radiologist, a technologist, a physicist, an architect, engineers, and equipment vendors. For large projects it might include most of the individuals listed in table 4–1. The first step in a successful collaboration is to define each team member's responsibilities.

The Owner's Responsibilities and Consultants

The owner's management responsibilities include stating the goals of the project and obtaining consensus from a diverse group of facility users. Radiologists, technologists, nurses, radiology administrators, hospital administrators, information technology managers, financial officers, and maintenance personnel all may have differing opinions on particular issues. In addition, the owner may seek the additional advice of consultants in the areas of finance, equipment procurement, radiation protection, and staffing. It is important to recognize that medical imaging extends beyond the radiology department and that decision makers from the emergency department, the ICU, and surgery should be involved in the design of imaging projects that will have an impact on their respective areas of responsibility.

Additional owner responsibilities include establishing a strategic plan, a project budget, and schedule parameters, as well as providing information about existing site and facility conditions. Specific owner responsibilities are defined in article 2 of AIA (American Institute of Architects) document B141: Standard Form of Agreement Between Owner and Architect.

Within any facility, a variety of groups will overlap in their use of various spaces, circulation routes, equipment, and functions. The owner should assist the architect in identifying all user groups potentially affected by planning and design decisions. User group input should be sought during the early phases of the process, such as programming, schematic design, and design development. The architect's ability to understand the nuances of medical imaging processes is critical at this phase.

The Architect's Responsibilities and Consultants

The architect provides design and management leadership for the project team, collects information from the various user groups, and coordinates the input of the many consultants needed to design a complex imaging facility. This planning is done by a multidisciplinary team led by the architectural project manager. Civil and structural engineers, landscape architects, mechanical and electrical engineers, medical equipment consultants, interior architects and designers, and cost consultants all play a role in facility design.

Planning, design, management, and technical expertise are provided by various members of the team. A principal-in-charge typically has overall responsibility for the project, while the project manager has day-to-day management responsibilities with the owner. Technical expertise usually is provided by the project architect and technical coordinator, who together coordinate the preparation of design and construction documents and establish standards for drawings and specifications. Project designers and planners give form to the building and work closely with the project architect to address the owner's design- and planning-related needs and goals. (The architect's responsibilities are defined in article 1 of AIA document B141: Standard Form of Agreement Between Owner and Architect.)

Alignment of Expectations

Medical technology continues to develop, growing increasingly more complex and demanding in terms of design requirements for new equipment and procedures. This makes it difficult to create comprehensive standards for imaging facilities that can be reused on different projects without being updated on a regular basis. It is thus necessary that the architectural team and the departmental users share their cumulative knowledge and experience during the initial design phases, in which physical and operation concepts for the project begin to take form.

The owner, architect, and contractor need to agree on the specific roles each party will play throughout the course of project development in order to establish a clear path for decision making. Project goals and parameters–such as types of service that will be accommodated, space allocations for each service, type of project delivery anticipated, and a description of the project budget–should be determined as early as possible.

Before work can begin, the owner and the architect must define the project scope so that both parties agree on the services each is responsible for providing. These should be spelled out for each phase of work and integrated into the project schedule. In addition, each party's services should be clearly defined in the owner–architect agreement. This agreement should spell out what basic services the architect is to provide and what additional services fall outside this scope. (See AIA document B141 for a description of both basic and additional services. Note that the AIA documents can be modified for each specific project.) For example, a renovation project should begin with a detailed assessment of existing building and site conditions. If no accurate existing-conditions drawings exist, an on-site survey should be performed. However, it should not be assumed that this survey is part of the architect's basic services unless it is specifically stated in the owner–architect agreement. Similarly, the kinds of information that must be provided by the owner and the owner's consultants also should be defined before the project begins.

The architect is responsible for meeting the stated budget, but this can occur only if budget and project scope are appropriately matched. At the end of each phase of work, three things must be in balance: cost, quality, and quantity. Two can be fixed, but one must remain flexible. If these factors are aligned during the initial (programming) phase, they should not drift apart in successive design phases. However, if an imbalance develops, the next phase of work should not begin until the discrepancy is corrected. If a serious deviation among cost, quality, and quantity arises, either the budget will need to be increased or the project scope must be decreased. If the latter alternative occurs well into design, potential construction cost savings are likely to be negated by the increased cost of completing the project.

Communication

Clear communication is essential to the successful management of the design and construction processes. Sometimes the information presented by the architect is not conveyed in a manner that is clearly understood by either staff members or administrators. An architect looking at an X-ray of a fractured wrist probably can recognize the individual fingers and bones of the hand but is unlikely to comprehend the severity of the fracture or its treatment implications. This is understandable because most architects are not trained in reading X-rays. Similarly, most radiologists, technologists, and administrators are not trained in reading architectural drawings. The architect must be aware that what seems clear and self-evident might be unclear for the audience to which it is being presented. Graphics should be presented in a way that is clear to both the facility users and the architect. Three-dimensional graphics, especially those prepared as "virtual fly-by" models, can be particularly useful communication tools, which help non-designers visualize the attributes of the intended space. New software applications enable designers to create Building Information Models (BIMs) composed of intelligent attributes that can model building performance, such as lighting conditions, spatial conflicts, and acoustics, and thus accurately communicate these attributes to facility users.

Language, whether written or spoken, can be confusing. Jargon and acronyms may convey confusing or double meanings of which we are sometimes unaware. Terms that are universally understood within their respective professions of architecture and radiology may be unknown or take on an entirely different meaning within others. For example, most architects understand the acronym *CAD* to stand for "computer-aided design" or "computer-aided drafting." But for many medical professionals, the term may signify "coronary artery disease" or "computer-assisted detection." Similarly, interventional radiology– a subspecialty of radiology– has a precise medical scope. However, the types of rooms used for interventional procedures vary from fairly basic to highly sophisticated, and it cannot be assumed that the vision of an interventional room is the same for everyone.

Vague terms such as "square footage" or "dollars per square foot" often are used without precise clarification. For example, if a hospital wants to expand its existing radiology department by 800 square feet into adjacent space that was just vacated, how much new space is actually required? The question cannot be answered without more precise information. If the department is to expand by 800 net square feet (NSF) of program area, additional space will be needed for departmental corridors and wall thickness. However, if the department will expand by 800 departmental gross square feet (DGSF), including internal corridors and walls, then only about 500 square feet of net program area will be accommodated.

As another example, if an entire building–such as a freestanding imaging center–contains 8,000 square feet of net program area, the overall building size is estimated by factoring in both a net-to-department-gross multiplier (described above) and a department-gross-to-building-gross multiplier (which accounts for exterior walls, public corridors not within the department, and such building systems components as shafts, elevators, stairs, etc.). A typical net-to-department-gross multiplier for imaging services ranges from 1.5 to 1.6. A typical department-gross-to-building-gross multiplier for a freestanding imaging center is 1.3 to 1.35. Therefore, 8,000 net square feet (NSF) of program area requires approximately 15,600 ($8,000 \times 1.5 \times 1.3 = 15,600$) to 17,280 ($8,000 \times 1.6 \times 1.35 = 17,280$) building gross square feet (BGSF). As a general rule of thumb, the overall amount of BGSF is often double the programmed NSF area.

The problem becomes more complicated when discussing cost. Unit costs, such as $300 per square foot, generally refer to the construction cost per BGSF. However, if an imaging department is being renovated within an existing building, the unit cost of that of building would likely refer to de-

Figure 4-1 Defining units of area. Courtesy of Anshen + Allen, Architects.

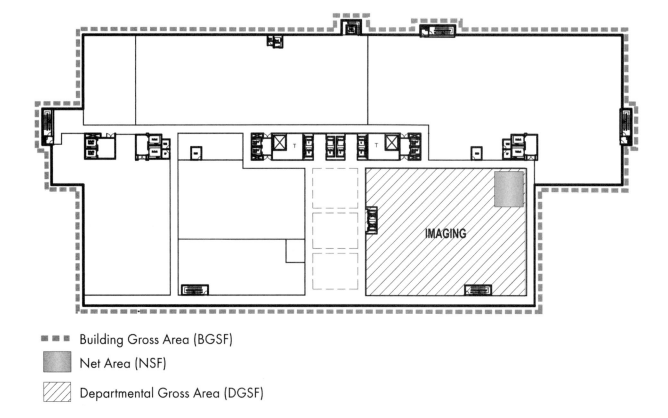

IMAGING

■ ■ ■   Building Gross Area (BGSF)

▨   Net Area (NSF)

▨   Departmental Gross Area (DGSF)

partmental gross area (DGSF) plus the additional costs associated with up-grading building systems beyond the department's boundaries. Therefore, interior "tenant improvement" costs represent only a portion of overall construction cost. The type of area measurement (NSF, DGSF, or BGSF) being discussed should always be identified; it is important to not simply refer to square feet or dollars per square foot. (Figure 4–1 illustrates the relationships among NSF, DGSF, and BGSF.)

With that in mind, assume that an 18,000–BGSF freestanding facility has a budget of approximately $5 million. A problem arises when the owner refers to a $5 million project budget and the architect refers to a $5 million construction budget. Although both may think they are in agreement, the project budget (which includes the cost of financing, the cost of land, professional fees, permitting, furniture, equipment, and so on) may be 60 percent (or more) higher than the construction budget, for a total budget of $8 million. To avoid confusion, it should be stated that the 18,000–BGSF facility costs about $280 per BGSF to build, excluding project costs, and therefore requires a construction budget of $5 million.

Project Phases

Whether the final product is a renovated department in an existing hospital or an entirely new freestanding building, the design and planning process parallels that of diagnosing and treating a patient (figure 4–2). In both cases, the early stages provide the most opportunity for determining future needs and developing a course of action that will yield an optimal outcome. Opportunities to rechart the course become both limited and costly as the process progresses.

Of course, new information will come to light and complications may arise during the course of the design and construction processes, just as may happen during the treatment process. Thus, it is important that the

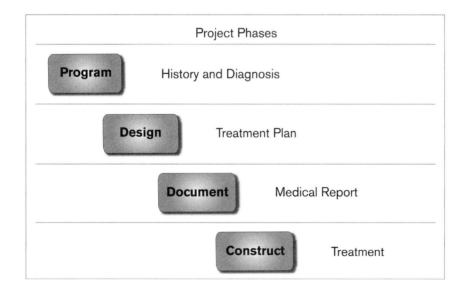

Figure 4-2 The design and planning process parallels that of diagnosing and treating a patient.

project team establish a means for incorporating new information and remedying problems as soon as they occur.

One solution is to involve the key decision makers early and continuously in the project. In this way, individual team members do not bring new ideas to the table halfway through the process, causing costly repetition of previous efforts. It is best to structure the process so that global issues are addressed initially and details are discussed during those subsequent project phases that are most appropriate for specific matters. In this way, fundamental decisions will not be overlooked because the team becomes sidetracked by specific issues less critical to that particular stage of the project.

Finally, a policy requiring user groups and administration to formally sign off at the conclusion of each phase (prior to commencing the next phase) will help the process move forward. The sign-off process is not intended to hold individuals responsible for the conclusions arrived at during each phase; rather, its goal is to document consensus on critical issues and to provide a baseline against which subsequent developments of the design can be assessed. In addition, a formal sign-off process provides clear documentation summarizing each of the project's phases.

Although the terms "planning for change" and "changing the plans" sound similar, the two have very specific meanings. The former should be an integral component of any project that is undertaken. (A variety of methods for designing flexibility into the project are discussed in chapter 8, "Design Concepts.") Although it may not be possible to predict exactly how imaging facilities will need to change in the future, it is both possible and necessary for the design to accommodate life-cycle changes that will take place. Conversely, changing the design at an inappropriate time can trigger critical events that will cost money, delay schedules, and sacrifice both functionality and appearance.

Understanding the kinds of decisions that need to be made in each project phase helps reduce the frequency and magnitude of unnecessary changes. A brief description of project phases follows.

Feasibility Study

The basic questions asked in a feasibility study for building an imaging facility are not unlike those asked by an individual in deciding whether to seek medical care. The first issues to be examined are:

- What is the need for taking action?
- What are the consequences of doing nothing versus taking action?
- Can I afford (physically and financially) to take action?
- Can I afford not to?

The feasibility study is simply a commitment to examine the go/no-go decision more closely. It is an effort to gain more knowledge of the situation but not yet a commitment to design or construct a building. Usually it is money well spent, even if the resulting conclusion is not to proceed with the project.

Programming

The programming phase for an imaging facility may begin with a process similar to that of recording a patient's history. This is the point at which the true nature of the project is identified and a plan is developed for address-ing additional needs that may emerge in the future. Program information is typically obtained through analysis of demographic and workload data and a forecast of future trends and volume projections. Interactive work sessions with programmers and facility end users are structured to identify how space and operations can be improved based on benchmarking and best practices in medical imaging (or other industries). Often a process called "visioning" takes place prior to programming and design in order to collectively raise the bar for reengineering opportunities.

> [V]isioning helps get our clients and our design team on the same page . . . visioning has helped us understand our clients' highest as-pirations for what might be their once-in-a lifetime opportunity to build their "ideal facility" . . . the visioning process allowed the client's key stakeholders to hear each other's ideas and hopes for the future and helped them get aligned around a unified goal.[1]

The programming phase concludes with a "diagnosis" in the form of a functional and space program report describing proposed space alloca-tions, adjacencies, and environmental features that should be considered for current and future conditions. Appropriate issues to be addressed dur-ing programming include:

- Flow of patients, staff, visitors, and equipment
- Space requirements of each room
- Adjacencies of one functional area to another
- Staffing projections
- Workload projections
- Operational concepts (including opportunities for reengi-neering specific operational practices)
- How technology is (and will be) utilized
- Quality of the built environment
- Relative cost of construction
- Projections for future expansion and development of new service lines

Programming provides an opportunity to identify rooms that might be used initially for one function and then converted to another at a later date. For example, a storage area might be transformed into a new image acquisition area after patient volumes increase, and so the space should be considered strategically for both its current and future uses. Taking future circumstances into account can influence the amount of space allocated for that function.

Concept Design

If programming is compared to the process of recording a patient's history and developing a diagnosis, then concept design is similar to the initial development of a course of treatment that follows the diagnosis. Concept design typically begins with a series of block diagrams (figure 4-3). These are generalized sketches that test the space program to verify whether all the rooms and departments can be arranged to provide both the required functional adjacencies and a reasonable form. The required adjacencies and circulation patterns, which were identified and tested during programming, should remain intact as the written program report is translated into three dimensions.

Circulation and flow patterns are essential elements of block diagrams. A clear conceptual diagram of spaces and travel paths will help ensure that

Figure 4-3 Example of a block diagram. Courtesy of Anshen + Allen, Architects.

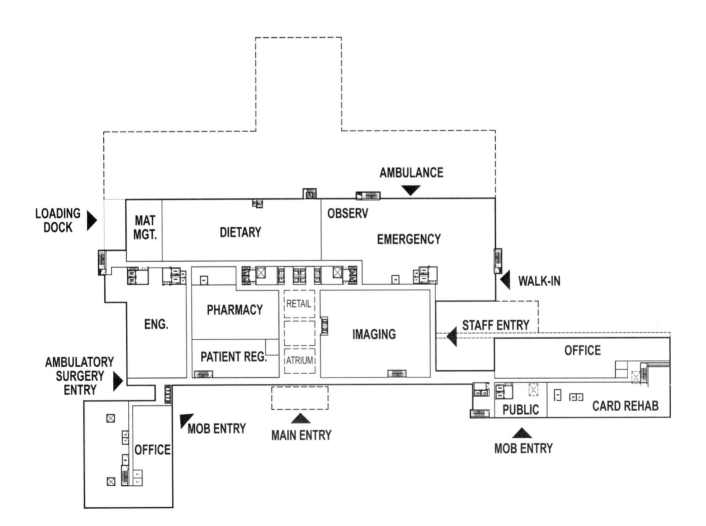

wayfinding routes are direct, so patients and visitors can easily find their destination points. Identifying how traffic patterns might change when new technologies are employed (such as the impact of digital image and information management systems on the flow of medical information) should be addressed during this early design phase. Envisioning flexibility as a key element of the concept design will allow an effective and affordable response to future change, whereas unplanned forced changes usually result in functional compromise. A variety of alternative design concepts should be explored and evaluated before beginning schematic design.

Schematic Design

During schematic design, block diagrams evolve into single- or double-line drawings in which every room identified in the program is represented. This is the time to explore a variety of forms within which the functional and space program can be realized. Alternative layouts should be developed and analyzed for their comparative strengths and weaknesses. Throughout schematic design there is constant interaction among the architects, engineers, and facility users. Schematic design work sessions reveal how people, equipment, and materials flow through the facility.

During the schematic design phase, the words and numbers previously developed to describe individual spaces during programming become more visually understandable. As the plans take form, the project seems to become more real. Sometimes, as the design becomes more tangible, there also is a desire to reconsider earlier fundamental decisions. Strong leadership, coming from both facility users and design consultants, is needed to prevent the process from becoming sidetracked.

By the end of schematic design, a preferred plan is selected from among the various alternatives (figure 4-4). Schematic design concludes with drawings, and sometimes study models, that depict the size, configuration, and arrangement of each space or room. Major medical equipment has a significant influence on room size, configuration, and arrangement within imaging facilities. Therefore, preliminary equipment selections for fixed imaging devices and other fixed equipment should be made during the schematic design phase. Each room is to be identified with a name and number; this provides a framework from which the equipment planner can develop an equipment list or database. The construction cost estimate also is updated at the end of schematic design to ensure that it remains aligned with the budget.

Design Development

Design development—the final design phase—refines schematic design and serves to both verify the previous "diagnosis" and build upon it in detail. It is the time to develop the design by evaluating finishes and materials, refining equipment requirements, examining furniture arrangements, and confirming the needs of structural, electrical, data, mechanical, security, and

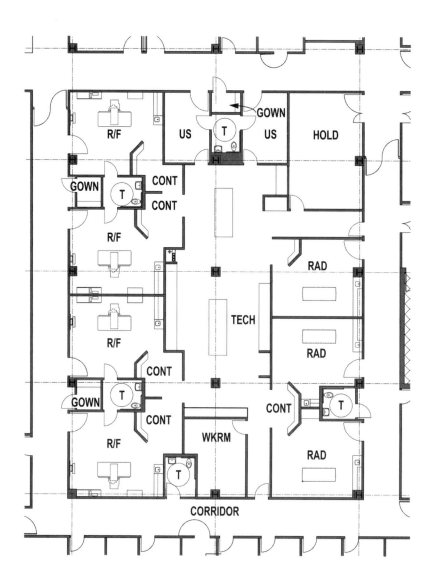

Figure 4-4 Example of a schematic design partial plan. Courtesy of Anshen + Allen, Architects.

communications systems. It also allows the team to confirm the requirements of architecturally significant medical equipment.

Design development is not the time to be adding new rooms to the program or relocating rooms, just as a physician would not want to rediagnose a patient well after a treatment plan for an initial diagnosis had been developed. Therefore, circulation patterns and required adjacencies for staff, patients, materials, and medical data should remain fixed.

Design development is the time to refine the internal and external facility design and reinforce the initial project design goals, such as articulating interior design solutions that provide patients with privacy, dignity, and positive distractions that help alleviate stress (see chapter 8, "Design Concepts"). All major design decisions should be made before the contract documents phase, in which design solutions will be documented. One useful technique employed at the beginning of design development is to fill out a series of data sheets, one for each room. The room data sheet lists specific requirements, such as floor, wall, and ceiling finishes. It also identifies electrical, ventilation, plumbing, communications, equipment, and furnishings requirements. The information contained in the room data sheets will later be incorporated into the contract documents, drawings, and specifications. Special attention must be given to coordinating architectural, engineering, equipment, and interior design information to prevent information from being overlooked or documented twice. It is important to note that so much detailed information exists in the equipment list that it usually is advantageous to keep this document separate from, but coordinated with, the room data sheets. Rooms where architectural, engineering, and equipment requirements are highly interrelated may require equipment, architectural, engineering, and interior design user group meetings to occur together. Although this demands more of the equipment consultants' time and may require longer user group meetings, it can eliminate future coordination problems.

A code compliance plan should be developed prior to finalizing the design development documents. This plan should be reviewed with the building official for compliance with applicable codes and other regulatory requirements. Confirmation from the building official at this stage is especially useful for renovation and building expansion projects, which tend to involve a greater degree of code interpretation than do new construction projects.

A cost estimate should be developed during design development to ensure that the project is aligned with the budget. Large or complex project may require two estimates; if two are prepared, the first is typically done at the midpoint of the design development phase, and the other is done at the end.

Contract Documents

Just as the programming and design phases document communication between owner and architect, the purpose of the contract documents phase is to document information needed by the contractor. In a sense, contract documents (which include construction drawings, specifications, and other exhibits) report in detail the proposed "treatment plan" for building the facility. Although the contract documents describe the desired results or outcome, they do not dictate construction methods.

It is necessary to ascertain which equipment items are to be furnished and installed by the contractor and identify them separately from those items for which the owner or vendor is responsible. Contractor items are described in detail in the contract documents, but owner and vendor items are not (although they sometimes are identified on the drawings and referred to as "owner-furnished-owner-installed" (OF-OI) or "owner-furnished-vendor-installed" (OF-VI) in the specifications). Owner- and vendor-installed equipment is not a contractor responsibility and is usually not described in detail within the contract documents (although vendor-installed equipment drawings are sometimes referenced in the contract documents). Utility lines, piping, anchorage assemblies, and couplings–which provide power, water, and so on to the owner-furnished equipment–are contractor responsibilities and must be clearly documented in the contract documents.

Drawings and specifications that convey the physical requirements of the facility to the contractor are prepared during the contract documents phase (figure 4-5). These documents should provide enough detailed and coordinated information for the contractor(s) to develop a comprehensive bid or negotiated fee. Otherwise, areas in which the documents are vague provide the contractor with opportunities to ask for additional funds, or change orders, during construction. Two cost estimates are typically prepared during the contract documents phase, one midway and another when the documents are 90 percent complete.

Figure 4-5 Example of a contract document partial plan. Courtesy of Anshen + Allen, Architects.

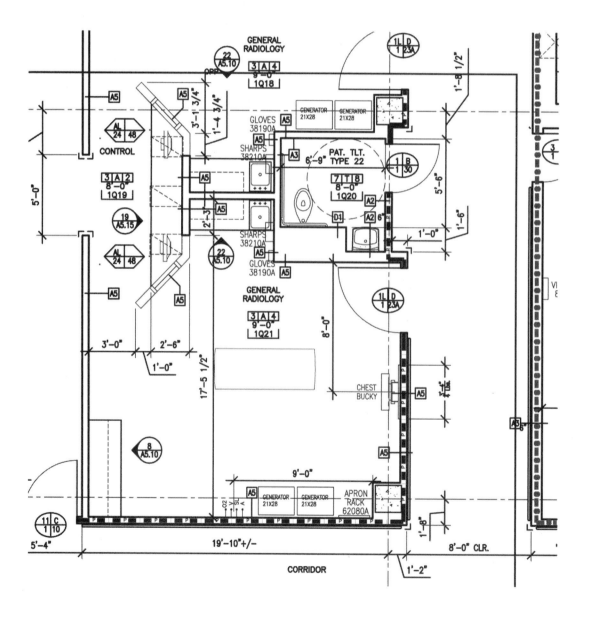

Regulatory Agency Review

Depending on the project's scope and the jurisdiction in which the project resides, the duration of regulatory agency review(s) may be as short as a few weeks or as long as a year or more. An approximate duration for the review process can usually be established by going over the project scope with the reviewing agency. An estimate of the review period should be factored into the project schedule.

The type of review process required also may be determined by the project's occupancy classification and its location. For example, in some locales hospital imaging projects are reviewed by the state, whereas nonhospital outpatient facilities are handled by the local reviewing agency. Some projects may be reviewed by multiple agencies. In addition to the building permit review, some projects also will require neighborhood approvals, an environmental impact report (EIR), licensing, and other formal regulatory reviews.

Bidding and Negotiation

The bidding and negotiation phase is determined by the owner's preferred project delivery method. Examples includes the traditional design/bid/build method in which multiple contractors bid on a project after the bidding documents have been prepared, and a guaranteed maximum price (GMP) method in which a contractor, who is selected prior to completion of design, will negotiate a construction fee instead of competitively bidding the project. Design/build project delivery–where the owner seeks a single point of responsibility for both design and construction–is an alternative to the traditional design/bid/build approach and is growing in popularity. The preferred method of project delivery should be identified at the outset of the project because each delivery method has a unique impact on the contract, schedule, budget, and document preparation.

Construction

The architect's role during the construction process is described as "administering" the contract documents. This means the architect will clarify questions initiated by the contractor to ensure that the design intent is met and code compliance is achieved. The architect has no authority to supervise the contractor because there is no direct contractual arrangement between the two.

Additional architect responsibilities include verifying payment requests and visiting the site as specified in the owner–architect agreement. The architect and consultants issue a certificate of substantial completion after the constructed work has been inspected and approved by building officials.

The Project Schedule

The project schedule is a tool that charts the various activities of the project in relation to time and each other. In addition to being a project management tool, the schedule is a communication tool. It identifies who is responsible for each activity and what will be affected as each activity is carried out or delayed.

Usually there will be one or two key drivers of the schedule. For example, the cost of money may be a key driver—as the schedule lengthens, the finance charges for funding the project increase. If the project is funded by publicly approved bonds, the conditions of funding may require that a substantial portion of the funds be spent by some predetermined date. The need to vacate existing space and occupy the new facility by a specific date may be another. Possibly the project is one of a series of projects—all of which are tied to a master schedule—in which space becomes available for one project only when another is completed.

Tasks—the basic element of any schedule—include all activities that must be completed throughout the duration of a project. For each of the project phases described earlier, a series of tasks can be identified. Each task will have a relationship to others. Some tasks must precede others, some will succeed others, others may occur simultaneously, and still others will be independent.

The duration of a given task is based upon such factors as the time required to prepare technical or equipment drawings and the task's sequential relationship to other tasks, including the need for a vendor's technical drawings before that information can be integrated into the design. The schedule tracks the various interdependent relationships among tasks; when the duration of one task is changed, all related activities must be adjusted.

Milestones are interim deadlines that are either self-imposed or stipulated beyond the control of the project team. Self-imposed milestones include planned presentations to executive committees; external milestones include deadlines for filing an application for public funding. Critical-path activities involve sequences of events that will have a negative impact on milestones if their duration slips too far; non-critical-path activities may slip without having a major negative impact on the overall schedule.

Each activity requires resources or staff to get the job done. For some activities, such as the preparation of construction details, adding staff may decrease the task's duration. Adding more staff resources, however, might not reduce the task's duration for activities that depend on the completion of other tasks.

The appropriate duration for each project phase depends on the project's scale and complexity. An approximate duration range for each phase of a moderate-size newly constructed hospital imaging department project is shown in figure 4–6. Numerous variables such as decision-making structure, regulatory review requirements, and the sophistication of equipment will influence each phase's duration.

The schedule can be presented in a variety of forms, such as a Gantt view, bar chart, PERT (program evaluation and review technique) view, or critical–path chart. A Gantt view (named for its inventor) displays each activity's name with a corresponding time line that represents duration and location within the schedule (figure 4–7). A PERT view uses lines and boxes to represent the relationships of tasks to other tasks (figure 4–8).

Programming phase:	6-8 weeks
Schematic phase:	8-12 weeks
Design development phase:	8-12 weeks
Contract documents phase:	20-24 weeks
Permit review phase:	8-24 weeks (duration varies with regulatory review process)
Bidding/negotiation phase:	6-10 weeks
Construction phase:	26-78 weeks
Subtotal:	82-168 weeks = 19 - 39 months = 1.5 - 3.25 years

Figure 4-6 Approximate duration of project phases for a newly constructed hospital imaging department.

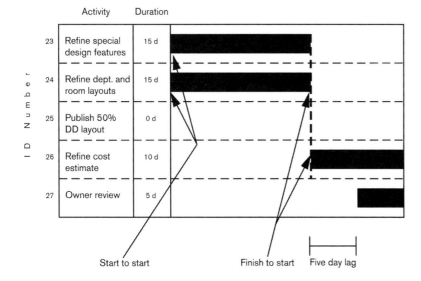

Figure 4-7 Project schedule: Gantt view.

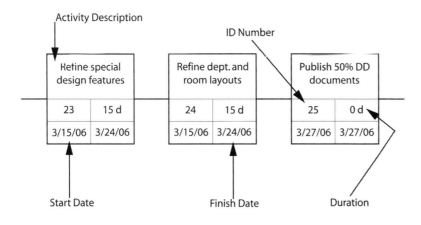

Figure 4-8 Project schedule: PERT view.

Project Budgets

Construction costs are only a part of overall project costs. The cost of land, financing costs, operating expenses, and maintenance expenses also must be considered.

A budget estimate form (figure 4–9) identifies the major elements of project cost. These elements are organized into three distinct categories: direct construction costs, indirect construction costs, and project development costs.

Direct construction costs

- Building structural components such as walls, floors, partitions, and finishes, and their associated labor costs
- Site development and site improvement costs such as grading, excavation, backfill, and the installation of utilities throughout the site
- Landscaping elements and arrangements of foliage, walkways, benches, and so on
- Fixed nonmedical equipment and systems such as permanent building–related equipment
- Utility systems and equipment (structural, electrical, plumbing, HVAC, and fire protection systems) either inside the building or extending just beyond its external limits (usually 5 feet or less)

Confusion between fixed and movable equipment can lead to misinterpretation of project cost estimates. For example, built-in paging systems are fixed equipment, whereas desk telephones are movable equipment. The cost of fixed equipment (usually referred to as group 1 equipment) is generally carried as part of the construction budget, whereas the cost of movable equipment (usually referred to as group 2 equipment) is generally carried as part of the equipment budget. (See chapter 5, "Equipment Planning," for further discussion of this subject.)

Indirect construction costs

- Site acquisition or the purchase price of land and associated expenses such as the cost of mitigating environmental hazards
- Contractor's profit and overhead
- Escalation
- Furnishings
- Movable equipment and other non–building-related equipment that is typically not considered to be a part of the building construction
- Allowances and contingencies for unforeseen conditions such as undesirable subsurface site characteristics or

Figure 4-9 Budget estimate form.

BUDGET ESTIMATE FORM

Project name _____   Building gross square feet _____
Location _____   Net square feet _____
_____   Net/gross ratio _____
_____   Total project cost/ _____
Owner _____   square foot _____
Job number _____   Direct construction cost/ _____
                                     square foot _____
                                     Site area square feet _____

DIRECT CONSTRUCTION COSTS
Building cost (gross area 3 unit cost/square foot) _____
Site development   _____
Landscaping   _____
Fixed equipment   _____
Utilities:
    Heating/ventilating/air-conditioning   _____
    Plumbing, fire protection   _____
    Electrical systems   _____
                    Subtotal   _____

INDIRECT CONSTRUCTION COSTS
Site acquisition   _____
Contractor's profit and overhead   _____
Furnishings   _____
Movable medical equipment (and fixed
imaging equipment)   _____
Allowances and contingencies   _____
Miscellaneous (describe):
    _____   _____
    _____   _____
    _____   _____
                    Subtotal   _____

PROJECT DEVELOPMENT COSTS
Professional fees
    Architectural   _____
    Consultant (_____)   _____
    Consultant (_____)   _____
    Consultant (_____)   _____
Site survey   _____
Insurance   _____
Legal   _____
Accounting   _____
Financing:
    Interim   _____
    Long-term   _____
Permit fees   _____
Taxes   _____
Miscellaneous (describe)
    _____   _____
    _____   _____
    _____   _____
                    Subtotal   _____
TOTAL PROJECT COST   _____

fluctuating costs that might increase by the time the project is bid (these amounts can be reduced as the project progresses and documents become more developed)

• Miscellaneous items including artwork, signage, and so on

Project development costs

• Professional fees for architects and consultants
• Site surveys
• Insurance
• Attorney and accountant fees
• Postconstruction leasing and advertising (if applicable)
• Financing, including interim construction financing as well as long-term financing expenses
• Permit fees for regulatory reviews, building permits, and so on
• Taxes
• Miscellaneous development costs

Some items, such as landscaping quantities, may be controlled by the project team; others, such as prevailing interest rates, are beyond the team's control.

Development of Construction Cost Estimates

Cost estimates become more complex as the project progresses and more information becomes available. Broad-brush estimates are adequate at preliminary stages, but later phases should include estimates with enough detail to enable the project team to compare the value of alternative designs. At the completion of each design phase, either a new construction cost estimate should be developed or a previous estimate should be revised.

The sections below describe cost estimate strategies that can be applied at certain phases of the project.

Conceptual Cost Model (Programming Phase)

Based on the program documents and an understanding of the intended quality of construction, the conceptual cost model assumes a unit rate of a specific number of dollars per square foot ($/SF) of construction cost for each major component of the facility. For example, high-tech spaces, such as procedure rooms and interventional areas, are assigned one unit rate, whereas general use areas, such as offices and storage areas, are assigned a different unit rate. In addition, an allowance should be assigned for furniture, fixtures, and equipment. If possible, the equipment allowance should be based on a preliminary list of proposed medical equipment rather than an average $/SF rate. The conceptual cost model is most often prepared by the architect's cost-estimating consultant using equipment costs provided by the equipment consultant.

Outline Subsystems Estimate (Schematic Design Phase)

Alternative layouts need to be compared during the schematic design phase when the conceptual or schematic drawings are developed. Options for major elements of each building subsystem (structure, HVAC, and so on) should be examined and tentative selections should be made. For example, a steel structural frame may be more expensive than concrete, but it also may provide more flexibility in its ability to accommodate future changes. Another example is the selection of building subsystems that are influenced by materials availability, applicable building codes, regional conditions (such as seismic activity), and prevailing wage rates. The outline subsystems estimate breaks the line items and their alternatives down into individual components so that each can be more easily evaluated.

Expanded Subsystems Estimate (Design Development Phase)

As more detailed information becomes available, various scenarios can be tested during the design development phase. An expanded subsystems estimate compares alternative building components and assemblies by assigning unit costs per square foot of area or other unit of measure (for example, precast concrete versus aluminum wall panels). The estimate is detailed enough to provide reasonably accurate predictions yet still allow for design flexibility. If the resulting construction cost estimate exceeds the project budget, it may be reconciled by substituting more cost-effective building components rather than having to redefine the entire project scope.

Unit Rate Estimate (Construction Documents Phase)

While the final details for construction are being assembled into the contract documents package, the project team needs to be aware of the impending cost ramifications. Previously developed subsystems estimates should be analyzed in even greater detail. The unit rate estimate incorporates costs of the individual elements that make up each subsystem. For example, the construction cost of basement walls should be calculated using the individual costs of concrete, formwork, waterproofing, and dampproofing.

Material quantities multiplied by the respective unit costs plus the cost of labor yields the total direct cost of construction. Indirect costs, such as the contractor's profit and overhead, must be included to make this figure meaningful. Additional items include cost escalation contingencies and allowances for the requirements specified in the general conditions of the construction contract. Sometimes a detailed cost estimate is provided in stages when the contract documents are 50 and 90 percent complete.

Notes

1. A. Coull, "That vision thing," *Healthcare Design*, November 2004, 28–33.

CHAPTER 5

Equipment Planning

E quipment planning is an essential and often complex process integral to the development of any imaging facility. Coordination of architectural and equipment planning activities becomes complex, in part, because imaging facilities are affected by medical equipment more directly than are other types of healthcare facilities. For instance, medical imaging equipment has unique requirements for structural, electrical, mechanical, and communications systems that play an important role in architectural design.

This chapter describes the equipment planning process, from the selection and tracking of equipment, to the various classifications for equipment (which indicate both the type of equipment and the responsibility for purchasing and installation). Also discussed are the scope and responsibilities of both the medical equipment consultant and the owner during the equipment selection process.

Most imaging projects warrant the involvement of a medical equipment consultant. Medical equipment consulting should not be confused with architectural medical planning. Medical equipment consulting (typically provided by an equipment consultant) focuses on the specific requirements of medical equipment, while architectural medical planning (typically performed by the architect) involves planning spaces used for medical functions. The medical equipment consultant provides detailed specifications for the clinical medical equipment and other technology contained within the new spaces being designed. This information is used by the owner's staff to help identify and select specific medical equipment for the project and by the architectural and engineering team to inform the design of the facility.

Some architectural firms specializing in the design of healthcare facilities offer medical equipment consulting capabilities from within their own organizations, primarily as a design support function. Others look to medical equipment consultants for this service since the technological and clinical expertise required to remain current with continuous developments is scarce. In some instances, the owner may want to contract with the equipment consultant directly as an owner's consultant; in other cases, the equipment consultant is a subconsultant to the architect. Any one of these arrangements is acceptable provided the equipment consultant is knowledgeable about equipment currently available, trends in medical imaging, and the specific needs of the owner. Ideally, the architect, engineers, and equipment consultant have previous experience working together on medical imaging projects. If design-related equipment planning services are provided by a consultant retained by the architect, they are typically considered to be additional services, as defined in AIA document B141.

Equipment consulting services provide more than just design specification support for architectural drawings. Technological advancements in medical equipment and information management devices continue to proliferate throughout the healthcare enterprise. Similarly, the scope of medical equipment consultants' work has extended to include more information management devices. For example, integration of information technology (IT) and clinical devices into a comprehensive clinical information system has led many medical equipment planning firms to add clinical engineers and communications systems designers to their staff in order to address integrated technology issues. Most medical devices perform multiple tasks, including communicating–directly or wirelessly–with other clinical devices or to hospital information systems. Patient information is captured and stored electronically, and patients are offered more technological conveniences than ever before. Traditional medical equipment consulting services have, therefore, transformed into comprehensive medical technology consulting services, involving greater integration with IT systems. Timely acquisition and distribution of medical equipment data to the team are essential to efficiently manage the design and documentation process. With imaging equipment typically accounting for a significant portion of the project's total equipment budget, its planning warrants proper attention.

Medical equipment consultants are responsible for managing the second highest budgeted line item for a project, second only to the cost of facility construction. Combined medical equipment and IT systems budgets can account for upward of 30–50 percent of total construction costs, depending on the type of project. In some instances, the cost of advanced medical imaging equipment can exceed the cost of the facility it is housed in. Because the medical equipment consultant is responsible for managing such a large portion of a project's cost, it is important that the equipment consultant remain objective with respect to which equipment vendors are chosen to provide the equipment. The equipment consultant should not have any fiduciary relationships with equipment vendors that might compromise the process of selecting appropriate equipment to match the owner's needs.

Although equipment vendors provide information to the architect that is necessary for design and planning, their role is different from that of medical equipment consultants. The equipment vendors' planning information generally is provided in support of their primary goal (selling equipment) and their planning information usually is specific to their own line of equipment. It is the medical equipment consultant's responsibility to objectively assist the owner in the evaluation and selection of equipment that best meets the owner's clinical objectives and budgetary capabilities. The vendors' primary relationship is with the owner, not with the architect. While information from equipment vendors must be provided for the architect's use, equipment vendors should not be considered consultants of the architect.

Scope of Equipment Planning Services

The responsibilities of the medical equipment consultant vary depending on the requirements of each project. Basic equipment planning services typically include:

- Assisting the owner in making equipment selections
- Establishing and tracking the equipment budget
- Compiling an "equipment book" that includes manufacturers' installation data and equipment specification sheets, and obtaining other relevant data from equipment vendors
- Developing room–by–room equipment lists indicating the general location of equipment
- Obtaining installation data from vendors and forwarding it to the architect (via the owner) in order to design related architectural and engineering components of the building
- Organizing and directing equipment user group meetings in which the specific equipment needs of clinical users are identified

Additional services, which may be beyond the scope of primary equipment planning services, include:

- Negotiating a purchase agreement with the vendor
- Additional user group equipment meetings
- Coordinating tours to visit facilities where similar equipment is in operation, and presentations by equipment vendors

Although many healthcare providers are affiliated with some type of group purchasing service, the equipment consultant can assist with negotiating competitive prices. The difference between an aggressively negotiated price and list price is considerable. Negotiated pricing should also include extended service contracts and future software upgrades to the devices (where applicable), which in themselves can eventually add up to a considerable sum.

Medical equipment consulting services that include equipment acquisition and procurement should be separate and distinct from the equipment planning consultant's work related to informing the architect and engineers about the equipment's impact on design. The architect should not be put in a position involving owner–vendor negotiations for purchasing imaging equipment. If the architect, equipment consultant, and clinical users need to meet with equipment vendors in order to clarify the equipment's space or utility requirements, that team should make it clear to the vendor that the meeting is solely for planning purposes and that similar meetings are being held with other vendors. If a vendor assumes that the owner has already selected its brand of equipment, the owner's negotiating capabilities may be compromised. Equally important is the partnering relationship between the owner and strategic technology solution vendors, who provide data and communication systems for the facility. The involvement of strategic technology solution vendors early during the process of establishing a technology strategy will contribute to the success of the facility.

Each piece of fixed and movable equipment that has an architectural or engineering impact should be identified and documented as part of an interactive user group work session. Clinical end users should be aware of the budget within which they may select their equipment, and also should verify that the proposed equipment budget supports their clinical needs. Although the medical equipment consultant may be developing and tracking the equipment budget with the architect, the allocation of funds among various departments rests with the owner. Developing wish lists instead of reasonable equipment selections that fit within the limitations of the budget can destroy the intention of the user group meetings, thereby initiating redesign and causing additional work and schedule delays.

One way to learn about the advantages and disadvantages of available equipment is to visit similar facilities that have recently opened. In most cases, the department staff will be more than happy to share their opinions and observations. When conducting such a tour, it is best to select a facility that has a scope and types of equipment similar to the one being designed. Additionally, the facility selected should be one that has been operational long enough for the staff to develop more than just first impressions, but not one that is so old that the equipment does not compare with what currently is on the market. It is important to keep in mind that the process of facility design and construction takes a few years at best; therefore, even a brand-new facility may contain equipment that already is a few years old. As part of their sales efforts, equipment vendors also may organize tours of their own showrooms and of current facilities showcasing their equipment. Such tours can be both educational and economical. However, vendor-organized tours tend to be less objective than those organized by the architect or equipment consultant.

Trade shows are another good source to learn about current equipment as well as staffing, management, and business issues relating to the operation of imaging facilities. For example, each year the Radiological Society of North America holds the world's largest gathering of medical personnel and equipment. The conference, which occurs in Chicago during the week after Thanksgiving, includes the largest display of medical imaging equipment assembled under one roof, and is typically a catalyst for many vendors to announce their latest technological developments. The Society for Computer Applications in Radiology annual meeting is a good place to learn about information technology aspects of medical imaging.

Equipment Classifications

The way that equipment is classified often determines whether its cost will be associated with the building construction budget or a separate equipment budget. Although equipment usually is divided into fixed, major movable, and minor movable categories, no single universally accepted rule for specific equipment classification exists. As a result, equipment classifications often cause confusion regarding both budgetary issues as well as procurement and installation responsibilities. In particular, medical imaging equipment (and some physiological monitoring equipment) seems to cause the most confusion regarding the way it is classified. This is because imaging equipment usually is fixed or physically attached to the building, fixed equipment usually is furnished and installed by the contractor, and the cost of fixed equipment is usually carried in the construction budget. However, imaging equipment is typically furnished by the owner, installed by the equipment vendor, and its cost is carried in an equipment budget.

As noted above, equipment is traditionally grouped into three classifications (table 5–1):

Group 1: fixed equipment
Group 2: major movable equipment
Group 3: minor movable equipment

Group 1 equipment is further subdivided into three subcategories: (a) fixed plant equipment (such as boilers, chillers, air handlers, and so on); (b) fixed medical equipment (such as fume hoods, sterilizers, medical gas headwalls, and so on); and (c) fixed nonmedical equipment (such as walk-in refrigerators, kitchen cooking equipment, built-in casework, and so on).

Group 1 equipment is typically installed by the contractor and its cost is included in the constriction budget. Although most medical imaging equipment has the characteristics of fixed medical equipment, it is usually classified as Group 2 equipment because it is not usually installed by the contractor, and its cost is not included in the construction budget. Imaging equipment is typically installed by the equipment vendor and is thus referred to as being owner-furnished–vendor-installed (OF-VI).

TABLE 5-1: EQUIPMENT CLASSIFICATIONS

Group 1 Fixed Equipment	Group 2 Major Movable Equipment	Group 3 Minor Movable Equipment
Permanent connection	Plug-in connection	No physical connection
Usually part of construction budget	Usually part of equipment budget	Usually part of owner's operational budget
Usually furnished and installed by contractor	Usually not furnished or installed by contractor	Usually does not require installation
Usually specified in the contract documents	Usually referenced in the contract documents (contractor may be responsible for necessary utilities and anchorage, but not for the equipment itself)	Usually not specified or referenced in the contract documents because it has no impact on the facility design
	Exceptions included in Group 2 equipment: Fixed medical imaging equipment Fixed physiological monitoring equipment	
Examples:	*Examples:*	*Examples:*
Fume hoods	Movable ultrasound devices	Surgical instruments
Sterilizers	Exam tables	IV stands
Medical gas headwalls	Fixed imaging equipment and physiological monitoring equipment	Pots, pans, and kitchen flatware

Architectural and engineering documents should reference architecturally significant OF–VI equipment that requires electrical, mechanical, and structural components, because these utility components are furnished and installed by the contractor as part of the construction contract. One way to reference OF–VI equipment is to indicate its outline on the construction drawings and to identify it as OF–VI in the specifications. In this way, the contractor provides the physical environment that must adhere to unique requirements determined by the equipment vendor, but the vendor–not the contractor–is responsible for installing the equipment itself.

The contract documents also should include a detailed equipment schedule, often included as part of the specifications. For each piece of equipment, the schedule identifies (1) an equipment number, (2) an equipment description, (3) whether the contractor or owner is responsible for its purchase and installation, (4) equipment width, depth, and height, (5) weight, (6) heat output, (7) mounting details, and (8) room location number (table 5–2).

TABLE 5-2: PARTIAL EQUIPMENT SCHEDULE FOR MRI

Number	Description	Responsibility	Width (in.)	Depth (in.)	Height (in.)	Weight (lbs.)	BTU/ HR	Mounting Detail	Room Number
XR-1	Control desk	OF-VI	48.25	30.25	27.50	126	NA	W-14	1-153
XR-2	Image monitor	OF-VI	21.25	17.50	18.25	44	273	C-23	1-153
XR-3	Patient monitor	OF-VI	17.50	16.25	14.75	33	171	C-23	1-153
XR-4	Patient couch	OF-VI	117.25	26.75	35.25	770	1,023	F-07	1-153
XR-5	Electronics cabinet	OF-VI	19.25	15.75	18.75	220	685	W-12	1-153

(Continues …)

Group 2, major movable equipment, includes medical equipment that may have architectural or engineering impact, although it customarily is moved from place to place without disrupting the physical components of the facility. Equipment that has the following qualities may be considered to have architectural or engineering impact:

- Draws in excess of 120 volts (alternating current)
- Draws more than 2 amperes
- Requires a dedicated electrical circuit
- Requires emergency power
- Is of a size, weight, or configuration that may affect room design, dimensions, or casework

Most movable equipment rolls on wheels, and if it requires electro–mechanical services, the connection is made with a simple plug–in receptacle. As noted above, fixed imaging equipment is an exception to the rule, as it usually is classified as Group 2 equipment even though it is not movable. Group 2 equipment also includes movable ultrasound and electrocardiography machines, patient beds, exam tables, medication carts, and movable monitors, as well as fixed imaging and physiological monitoring equipment. The cost of this equipment is typically listed in the equipment budget.

Group 2 nonmedical equipment include tables, chairs, desks, and miscellaneous furnishings. The cost of these items is more appropriately listed in the furniture budget than in the equipment budget. However, it is a good idea to verify which equipment items (such as an MRI operator's console) routinely come with matching furniture (such as an operator's chair). The cost of furniture that is part of a medical equipment purchase is usually listed in the equipment budget.

Some types of medical furniture and furnishings may be considered Group 2 equipment if they require electricity or otherwise affect facility design. If the cost of medical furniture is to be carried in the equipment budget, a clear distinction between medical and nonmedical furniture must be made so that it is neither counted twice nor unintentionally omitted.

Often the Group 2 equipment budget is divided into two distinct categories: one for medical equipment and one for furniture, fittings, and (nonmedical) equipment (FF&E). Care must be taken to accurately define each category and to assign responsibility for each item in the contract documents and the budget. For example, office furnishings usually are the responsibility of the interior designer, whereas medical furnishings are often the responsibility of the medical equipment consultant. Thus, a table lamp and secretarial desk are listed in the furniture budget, but an exam light and an exam table are listed in the equipment budget.

Casework can be another source of confusion. Built-in casework (which can be either custom-built or premanufactured) is considered part of the facility, rather than equipment. The architect is responsible for documenting and budgeting built-in casework. However, premanufactured exam room casework that is not physically attached to the facility may be considered medical equipment and thus may be the responsibility of the equipment planner. Premanufactured office-type casework that is not physically attached to the facility is considered furniture and is the responsibility of the interior designer.

Group 3, minor movable equipment, consists of miscellaneous equipment and instruments (such as surgical instruments, pots, pans, and kitchen flatware) that have no physical connection to the physical plant and are small enough that they have little or no effect on facility design. Minor movable equipment often is purchased by the owner out of an operating budget and therefore may not appear in either the construction budget or the equipment budget.

A system of classifying equipment is found in Guidelines for Construction and Equipment of Hospital and Medical Facilities. This document is written by a special task force of the American Institute of Architects/Academy of Architecture for Health (AIA/AAH) (www.aia.org). It is a revision of a series of periodically updated documents that began in 1947 as part of the implementation regulations for the Hill–Burton program, and it serves as an aid in the design and construction of hospital and medical facilities. Revisions to the document reflect dramatic changes to health facility planning that have occurred in subsequent years. In addition, the document is referenced by the federal government's Department of Health and Human Services and sometimes is referenced by certain state licensing agencies.

Chapter 4 of the AIA Guidelines refers to equipment. The nomenclature for equipment classifications is slightly different from that described above, although the intent is similar.

Equipment Selection Timeline

A key factor upon which the success of the entire design process depends is the ability of the equipment consultant to facilitate timely decision making for equipment selections. Since imaging equipment is unique in size and complexity, it affects the architectural design and construction process more dramatically than does medical equipment in most other departments. Decisions regarding imaging equipment selection fall on the critical path earlier than do selection decisions for other types of equipment.

During the programming phase, every room in the proposed facility is identified. For most imaging exam rooms, the type of equipment (for example, computed radiography versus direct radiography) is identified. Although specific makes and model numbers are still unknown, a fairly accurate budgetary range can be established, and appropriate room dimensions can be determined.

For most healthcare projects, equipment selections are far from being made during schematic design. However, because specific requirements for major fixed imaging equipment have such a dramatic impact on facility design and documentation, preliminary selections for imaging equipment should be made during this phase.

Once the equipment is identified, it usually takes a minimum of six to eight weeks for the equipment vendor to develop technical drawings needed for the architects and engineers' further development of the building design. These technical drawings are essential for the architects and engineers to have before design phase services are completed.

The suggestion that preliminary selections for imaging equipment be made during schematic design, some three to four years before the building is ready for occupancy, will cause understandable resistance from the radiology staff. The intent here is not to order equipment this far in advance, but rather to obtain necessary information required to continue with facility design.

Balancing the timing of imaging equipment selection with the development of engineering and architectural design is one of the most difficult predicaments inherent in the design of medical imaging facilities. On one hand, facility users will want to postpone equipment selections until the last responsible moment to ensure that the latest technology is installed. On the other hand, delaying equipment selection significantly hinders the development of architectural and engineering systems needed to support the equipment. Detailed information, which varies from one equipment unit to another, is needed early in the design process.

The following approach helps minimize potential equipment coordination and documentation problems. During schematic design, the radiology staff should be asked what specific equipment they would select if the facility were to open tomorrow. A future date should then be identified to revisit equipment selections and modify the contract documents if necessary. In this way, equipment identification decisions are not simply delayed but are made on a preliminary basis using the limited information available. This method allows architectural and engineering design to proceed on the basis of the identified equipment selections, while also establishing a later date when equipment decisions may be reexamined.

An alternative is to defer further design of portions of the project until equipment in those areas is selected. However, this approach can lead to substantial delays for the entire project. In either case, the architect should advise the owner to establish an equipment reconciliation contingency for out–of–sequence equipment changes that force a redesign.

A concept known as "universal room design" can help accommodate various types of routine imaging equipment (such as a general radiographic room) and thus allow the identification of specific makes and models of some basic equipment to be deferred for a short period of time. However, universal room design is less effective for rooms that require more specialized equipment (such as an angiography or MRI room), as the differences between vendors' siting requirements contain an increased number of variables.

PART THREE

IMAGING
TECHNIQUES

Steven C. Horii, MD, FACR, FSCAR

CHAPTER 6

Imaging Techniques

M edical imaging serves a central role in healthcare. Along with the patient history, the physical examination, and laboratory data, various imaging techniques are used to:

- Establish or confirm the presence or absence of disease
- Monitor the effectiveness and progress of treatment
- Guide diagnostic and therapeutic procedures
- Help communicate information about the patient's disease and treatment to the patient and other physicians
- Provide evidence in medico–legal situations

It is the role of the radiologist and other specialists who perform and in-terpret the imaging studies to help their referring physician colleagues se-lect the imaging techniques that will give the most information with the least discomfort and risk to the patient. All of the imaging methods have advantages and disadvantages for imaging certain anatomy. Some meth-ods show very fine anatomic detail but cannot determine organ function. Other techniques may do just the opposite. An important consideration is also the cost of the examinations. The different types of imaging studies vary widely in what the costs are to the facility performing them and, as a result, what the patients (or their insurance carriers) are charged.

In the quest to provide better, faster, and safer imaging of anatomy, a large section of the electromagnetic spectrum is employed. At the long wavelength end, radio–frequency signals are generated and detected as part of the magnetic resonance imaging (MRI) process. Very short wave-lengths constitute X–ray and gamma ray energies, used for a large major-ity of medical imaging. Some nonelectromagnetic mechanical energy is also used in ultrasound.

This chapter introduces the different types of imaging equipment used in radiology. It describes briefly the physics and technology of the equipment and how it is used. Because of the rapid development and evolution of medical imaging equipment, the emphasis on the fundamental principles involved is intended to be less vulnerable to obsolescence than the engineering and implementation aspects. This rapid pace of development in imaging equipment also makes it important for readers to consult the site- and equipment-specific information available from imaging equipment vendors in addition to the material presented in this chapter. Readers are also advised to consult chapter 12, "Room Design," for a further discussion of the functional, human, and technical issues to be considered when planning for the equipment described in this chapter.

Radiography and Fluoroscopy

Aside from direct observation, radiography is the oldest medical imaging technique. It was first employed by the discoverer of X-rays, Wilhelm Conrad Roentgen. By accidentally exposing a photographic plate with some coins on it to the high-voltage tube he was studying, he discovered that an unknown radiation was causing the plate to react as if light had struck it. He later went on to take the first anatomic radiograph, of his wife's hand.[1] The potential to reveal bones within the soft tissues was clear, and radiography was born.

Radiography

In modern radiography, the source of X-rays is a much-refined tube (figure 6-1) that is supplied with a high voltage. Electrons coming off a filament are accelerated and strike an anode. As the electrons are slowed within the metallic structure of the anode, they give up their energy as X-rays. X-rays can be thought of as very energetic light–energetic enough to penetrate human and animal soft tissues. However, as they pass through anatomic structures, they encounter the various atoms that make up those structures and are attenuated. What makes radiographs possible is that various tissues attenuate X-rays differentially, with soft tissue having much lower attenuation than bone. The attenuation is directly proportional to atomic number, so calcium (atomic number 20), a major constituent of bone, attenuates X-rays much more strongly than do carbon (atomic number 6), hydrogen (atomic number 1), oxygen (atomic number 8), and nitrogen (atomic number 7), the principal atoms that make up most soft tissues. This is also why heavy metals such as lead (with very high atomic numbers) stop X-rays so well and can be used as X-ray shielding.

Radiographs are basically shadowgrams. The X-rays passing through the body are captured by a piece of film, as in Roentgen's example, or in more recent radiography by a fluorescent screen. The fluorescent screen, in turn, exposes the film. The use of these fluorescent, or intensifying, screens was a major contributor to reducing the patient dose of radiation

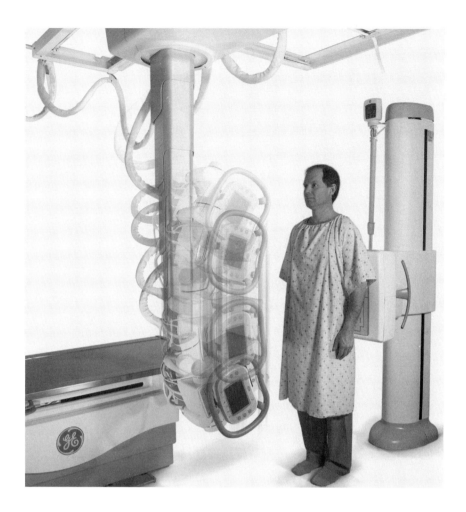

Figure 6-1 Basic radiography. Image courtesy of GE Healthcare.

used in imaging. More recently, film and intensifying screens have been replaced by digital detectors.

In what has become commonly known as computed radiography (CR), the film is replaced by a phosphor plate. This plate has the property of storing the image produced by X-ray exposure as a high-energy state of the atoms of the phosphor. When given a little more energy, typically by a laser scanned precisely over the plate, the atoms are pushed out of their high-energy state and give off light as they return to their low-energy state. The number of atoms in the high-energy state, and so the amount of light given off, is proportional to the X-ray exposure received. This light is detected by a sensitive detector, and the detector output signal is digitized. The result is a digital form of the image originally recorded on the plate. The plate is erased with a flash of bright light to make sure all the atoms have returned to their low-energy state, and the plate can be reused.[2] An important design consideration for CR systems is that the plates are housed in devices very similar to conventional film-type cassettes. These will fit into existing cassette holders, so in most cases conventional film-based radiographic rooms can be converted to CR use fairly simply. The plates are scanned in

Figure 6-2 Portable radiography. Image courtesy of GE Healthcare.

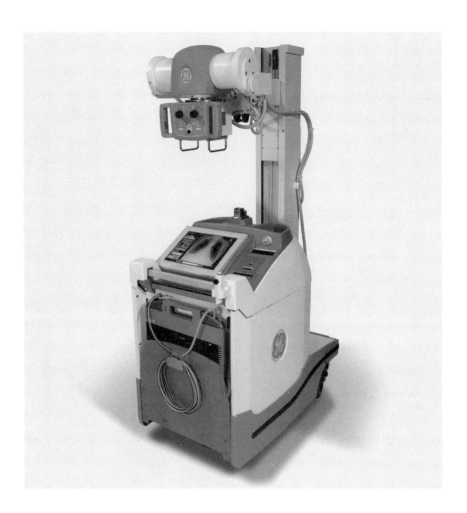

a plate reader. Associated with this is usually a workstation at which the X-ray technologist can view the images taken to make sure they are sufficient before dismissing the patient. In some CR systems, the plates have to be placed into a plate identifier that associates the plate number (from a bar code on the plate) with the patient whose image is on the plate.

A newer form of digital radiography is called direct–capture digital radiography (sometimes simply "digital radiography," or DR).[3] There are two basic types of these systems. In one type, a phosphor plate much like an intensifying screen is exposed and the fluorescent image is captured by a digital camera. The second type uses a flat–panel transistor array. This array (much like that found as part of a flat–panel display screen) either has a phosphor layer on it or is made on a semiconductor material that is sensitive to X-rays. The phosphor layer type converts the incoming X-rays to light, which is detected by the transistors. In the semiconductor detector type, the semiconductor material itself converts incoming X-rays into electron "holes," which results in a small charge difference that the transistors detect. The signals generated by the transistor array are digitized, and a digital representation of the image results. Unlike CR, DR devices are generally stationary equipment. The detector systems are built into the patient table or, for upright radiographs, a wall-mounted unit. In some designs, the detector assembly is in a head that can be moved into a number of positions. An important design note is that these systems do not require that technologists take plates to a reader; the output of these DR systems is a digital image (hence the term "direct capture"). This usually means that the equipment in a radiographic room will have to be replaced. However, it also means that planning should account for both reduced technologist walking and potentially shorter examination duration, and thus potentially more imaging exams per room.

Since many radiographs are taken at the patient bedside (figure 6–2), usually for patients too ill to be transported to radiology, some digital solution for these studies is needed. Computed radiography systems simply replace the film cassettes with CR plates and use existing portable X-ray machines, but the technologist usually has to be careful to keep track of the plates and the patients whose images are recorded on them. The plate identifiers are not generally available outside of the radiology department, so the technologist has to put the plates through the identifier after she or he returns from performing portable studies. The images are then sent from the storage system either to a printer or to an image management system (see Chapter 7, "Image Management Systems") when the technologist returns to the radiology department. There are now DR-based portable systems. In most configurations, a detector plate is connected by a long cable to a portable X-ray machine. In this case, the machine contains a computer and storage system to download and store the images from the detector.

Film Compared to Digital Detectors

Conventional film and intensifying screens (commonly referred to as a "screen–film" combination) evolved over many decades and have achieved a high level of refinement. Unlike consumer film, X-ray film is coated with emulsion on both sides, which partly explains its high cost–there is a large amount of silver halide in X-ray film.

Medical images, and radiographic ones in particular, are often described as having two types of resolution. One is the ability to represent grayscale well. In a chest radiograph, the range of X-ray exposure is very large. The air of the lungs offers little attenuation to the X-ray beam, so the portion that traverses the lungs emerges from the body with a considerable fraction of its original intensity. In contrast, the portion of the beam that passes through the spine encounters many more atoms with a high atomic number (particularly the calcium of bone) compared to those of the air and the soft tissue of the lungs, so that portion of the beam emerges at a much lower intensity. This range of intensity is large enough that film cannot capture the full range of it. Typically, chest radiographs are exposed for the lungs, as they are the major subject of interest. Imaging the heart requires more specialized techniques, as on a chest radiograph the chambers and the blood appear superimposed. How subtle a grayscale (hence X-ray attenuation) difference a particular screen-film combination can display is the contrast resolution.

Spatial resolution describes how fine a detail can be recorded on an image–that is, how close together two small structures can be and still be seen as separate. Screen-film combinations vary considerably in spatial resolution capability. Films capable of the very finest detail (highest spatial resolution) are used for mammography, where microcalcifications that may indicate the presence of tumors can be on the order of 0.1 mm. In general, the more sensitive to X-rays a screen-film combination is, the lower its spatial resolution. This is because one factor that increases sensitivity to X-rays is the size of the phosphor and film grains–larger ones yield higher X-ray sensitivity but lower spatial resolution. The spatial resolution of screen-film combinations is usually given as some number of line pairs per millimeter (a line pair being a dark line adjacent to a bright line). Most screen-film combinations used for chest radiographs have resolutions in the 5 line pairs per millimeter (lp/mm) range. For mammography, this can increase to 15–20 lp/mm.

Digital detectors for radiography, whether computed radiography plates, flat-panel detectors, or fluorescent screens with CCD cameras, are usually characterized in terms of contrast and spatial resolution, much as film is. Film, however, is both detector and display, whereas these functions are separated for digital imaging. The contrast resolution of a digital detector is based on the minimum and maximum X-ray exposure the detector can capture and how many different values it can represent between those limits. The latter is usually expressed as some number of shades of gray. This is determined by how many binary digits (bits) of information the detector captures. Most CR plates can express ten bits of exposure information between their minimum and maximum values. Ten bits can represent 2^{10} (1,024) shades of gray. Direct capture systems can express more with a larger exposure range (one advantage of direct capture detectors), typically expressing 12 bits between minimum and maximum–4,096 shades of gray. A natural question is whether or not this range is useful to a human observer since human perception is limited. To a large extent, how many different shades of gray can be discriminated is dependent on the circumstances (brightness, for example, having a very large impact on this value). The often-cited value for human gray-scale perception is between 16 and 64 shades of gray, though this is for rather artificial experimental conditions. Human perception of brightness levels is a complex phenomenon and highly dependent on what is being observed and its surroundings.[4] Film can typically represent between 256 and 1,024 shades of gray.

Spatial resolution is more simply considered. A digital detector consists of a number of discrete sensitive elements in an array. The number of those elements distributed over a given size will determine the spatial resolution of the detector. To represent a line pair, two elements, or pixels, are necessary. For CR plates, the spatial resolution is determined by how finely the plate is scanned. For fluorescent screens and CCD cameras, it is the size of the screen and the number of pixels in the CCD camera array. For DR systems, it is the number of pixels in the panel and the size of the panel. CR plates typically capture 2.5 lp/mm, though newer systems double that to 5 lp/mm (note that this quadruples the size of the resulting image array because the number of pixels is doubled in both dimensions). CCD cameras vary widely in spatial resolution capability but are often limited by the grain of the fluorescent screen and the optical elements between the screen and detector. Final resolution of such systems is on the order of 2.5–5 lp/mm. Direct capture detectors are fabricated much as CCDs are, though resolutions are limited by the ability to fabricate physically large arrays of transistors without too many bad ones. The drive to produce high-quality flat-panel displays (for laptops and televisions) has directly resulted in improvements in production of flat-panel detectors since the production is very similar.[5] Resolutions of 2.5–5 lp/mm are typical.

Digital image capture needs to be coupled with a display system to be useful. The first method for viewing images captured by CR was to print them on film. Laser film printers were (and still are) used for this. Unlike laser paper printers, however, they typically expose conventional silver halide photographic film rather than use a xerographic process. These laser film printers impose their own contrast and spatial resolution limits on the image, typically restricting contrast resolution to 8 bits (256 shades of gray) but having spatial resolution at least equal to the spatial resolution of the capture detector.[6] More recently (as will be discussed further in Chapter 7) display of digital images is done on "soft copy" devices such as cathode ray tubes (CRTs) or flat-panel displays.

Fluoroscopy

Conventional radiography is probably most familiar to readers and is still widely used for imaging of bones, joints, and the chest. However, radiographs of this sort are still pictures. Movement is not desired for these images, as it blurs detail. Much about imaging anatomy and disease involves motion of organs, so some method for producing radiographic images of moving objects is needed. Fluoroscopy provides a real-time view of moving structures.

Fluoroscopy was an early development in radiology.[7] The earliest systems were fluorescent screens mounted in front of an X-ray tube (see figure 2–1 in chapter 2). The patient was placed between the screen and X-ray tube, and when the X-ray beam was turned on, a fluorescent (and usually phosphorescent) image was visible on the screen. A radiologist or other specialist could then observe the motion of structures such as the diaphragm and beating heart. Structures that are transparent to X-rays, such as the stomach and intestine, could be made visible by having the patient ingest radio-opaque material. Barium sulfate was found to be ideal for this

Figure 6-3 Basic radiography/fluoroscopy. Image courtesy of Siemens Medical Solutions.

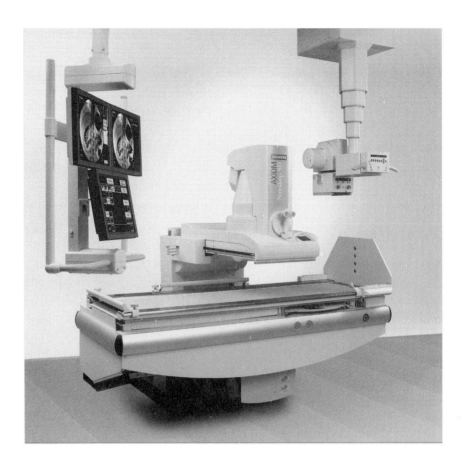

application; it has a high atomic number, so it attenuates X-rays well and could easily be followed through the gastrointestinal (GI) tract, and it is well tolerated by patients.

As simple and useful as this method sounds, a major drawback was that fluorescent screen fluoroscopy required a very high radiation exposure. Also, the resulting image was very dim, so the radiologist had to work with dark-adapted vision. This was a problem, as the radiologist would emerge from the fluoroscopy room into brightly lit surroundings. To preserve their dark-adapted vision, early fluoroscopists wore red-colored goggles when they left the fluoroscopy room temporarily.

Modern fluoroscopy uses the same principle, but in place of the fluorescent screen is an image intensifier. This device is a large vacuum tube (figure 6-3) with a phosphor face that receives the X-rays. This phosphor releases electrons as the phosphor molecules are struck by the incoming X-rays, and these electrons are then accelerated by a high voltage. At the output end of the tube a second phosphor screen converts these electrons into light. The resulting image is very much brighter than the input image would be on the phosphor alone. Effectively, the X-ray image has been "amplified" both by the acceleration of the electrons and by the smaller size of the output phosphor than the input. The output phosphor was directly viewed in early image intensifier systems, but this was rapidly replaced first

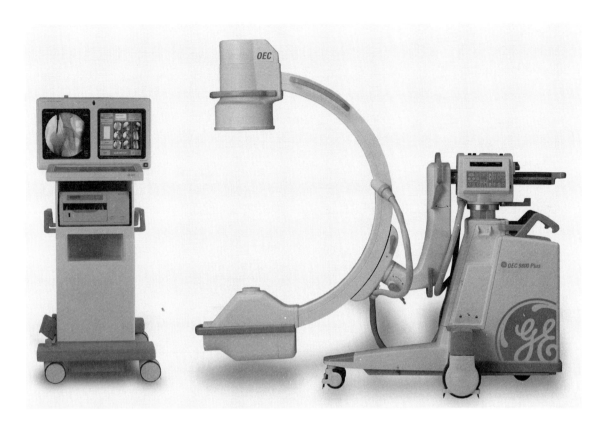

by a television camera and later by digital cameras. The output of these cameras was viewed on conventional displays, mostly cathode ray tubes (CRTs). More recently, flat–panel displays are replacing the CRTs. The dynamic aspect of fluoroscopy could be captured on film motion picture cameras (in early systems) or on video recording equipment.

The great advantage of the image intensifier is much reduced patient X-ray dose. This has made it practical to use fluoroscopy for lengthy procedures, and fluoroscopic systems are part of interventional suites. Portable fluoroscopic systems, often called "C–arm" units because of their mechanical shape, are often used in operating rooms where permanent fluoroscopic equipment is not justified (figure 6–4).

Just as flat–panel digital detectors are used in DR, similar detectors with a fast enough response time are now being used as replacements for image intensifier tubes. The image quality from these direct capture digital fluoroscopic systems is very high, and it is likely that many new fluoroscopic rooms will incorporate them.

Rooms referred to as "radiographic/fluoroscopic" (R/F) rooms have an image–intensifier or DR fluoroscopic system that uses an under–table X–ray tube and an overhead X–ray tube on a set of rails. The overhead tube can be pushed out of the way when fluoroscopic studies are being done, and the image intensifier or DR system can be moved off the center line of the

Figure 6-4 Portable fluoroscopic C-arm. Image courtesy of GE Healthcare.

table for radiographic imaging. The table usually has a Bucky (a moving grid device used to reduce the effect of scattered radiation on the image) cassette holder that slides into position for radiography and out of the way for fluoroscopy.[8] A wall–mounted Bucky allows for radiographs with the patient standing. The table itself can be tilted, in many cases to full upright position in one direction. All of this equipment is put into use for certain barium studies. While decreasing in frequency because of the growth of upper gastrointestinal (GI) endoscopy and colonoscopy, and most recently because of CT colonography (see the section "Computed Tomography" in this chapter), barium studies of the upper and lower GI tract are still performed and use these R/F rooms. For barium enemas (used to examine the colon) a fluoroscopic examination is followed by a series of radiographs (often called "overhead images") taken in multiple positions. During the fluoroscopic portion of the study, still images may also be obtained. These take two forms: either an image is recorded from the image intensifier (called a "photospot image") or a cassette is placed into a film holder built into the image intensifier and a "spot image" is obtained. These photospot and spot images are usually taken by the radiologist, and the subsequent overhead images are done by a technologist. With a DR fluoroscopic system, there is no difference between a photospot image and spot image, though the systems may have the equivalent of these–typically the photospot is a lower-resolution image, but with a shorter exposure time to stop motion, and the spot image is of higher resolution, but with a longer exposure time. The movement of the table, the presence of an overhead tube, taking cross–table lateral images, and the wall–mounted Bucky all have implications for design. Besides equipment and personnel space requirements, having the X–ray beam projected against the walls instead of the floor or ceiling creates shielding requirements and may also dictate what facilities may be located on the other side of the walls of an R/F room.[9]

While barium sulfate works well for making the gastrointestinal tract radio–opaque, it cannot be used to opacify other anatomic structures such as blood vessels because it is a suspension of fine particles that would obstruct the small capillaries. Imaging blood vessels is of great interest for diagnostic and therapeutic work, so some method of increasing the contrast between blood vessels and surrounding tissues is needed. An ideal material would have a high atomic number, be nontoxic, and cause no side effects. Unfortunately, no such ideal material exists. However, the need for such contrast agents is so important that a number of them have been developed over the years. Most of the contrast materials for radiography are based on organic iodine compounds. Iodine provides the high atomic number, and the organic part of the molecule reduces toxicity and determines how the material is metabolized or excreted by the body. A major revolution in contrast agents was the development of non–ionic materials. These have molecular structures that do not have ionic groups on them and have fewer side effects than the ionic agents. When contrast agents need to be injected rapidly, they cause less discomfort if they are warmed to body temperature. A planning consideration if the department uses contrast is that warming cabinets for the contrast materials need to be provided.

Contrast agents are typically used in the procedures that require imaging of the blood vessels (angiography and many interventional procedures), bile ducts (cholangiograms), kidneys (intravenous urography), bladder (cystography), and the fluid spaces around the spinal cord (myelography). The use of contrast in these procedures makes it possible to visualize anatomic structures that would otherwise not be visible on radiographs because of a lack of attenuation difference. Iodine–based contrast agents are also used in computed tomography, and non–iodine–based agents are used in magnetic resonance imaging (see subsequent sections).

In spite of the proliferation of newer modalities, radiography remains the mainstay of diagnostic imaging. In many healthcare facilities, radiography accounts for some 50–70 percent of diagnostic examinations.[10] For conventional radiography, chest and bone imaging have remained relatively constant. The use of CT and increased use of endoscopy have reduced the number of radiographic and fluoroscopic imaging procedures. The use of fluoroscopy in interventional radiology is increasing rapidly, and in many departments space previously used for gastrointestinal fluoroscopy is being redeveloped for interventional work. Fluoroscopy is not used only by radiologists, as gastroenterologists use it to take radiographs of the structures into which they place endoscopes and inject contrast materials, and gynecologists may use fluoroscopy for hysterosalpingography (the imaging of the uterine cavity and fallopian tubes). The volume of such examinations is such that the R/F rooms are often shared between radiology and GI or GYN specialists. Eliminating such rooms as interventional radiology expands may create problems for these other specialists, and this needs to be taken into account as facilities are designed or redesigned.

Mammography

A particular form of radiography is mammography, or radiography of the breast. Despite recent controversies, large studies have shown that screening mammography remains the single most effective tool in the early detection of breast cancer (figure 6–5). Breast cancer is unfortunately common; in the United States, approximately one in fifty–four women will develop the disease before the age of fifty, and women have one chance in eight of developing the disease at some point in their lifetime. Early detection and treatment have been shown to be effective, with survival rates now in excess of 80 percent. Early detection and treatment have also been responsible for an approximate 2.5 percent per year decline in breast cancer deaths since 1990 (for white women; for African American women the decline is smaller, approximately 1 percent per year since 1990).[11]

The great majority of mammographic examinations done in the United States are still performed using film. Special films and intensifying screens

Figure 6-5 Upright mammography unit.
Image courtesy of Siemens Medical Solutions.

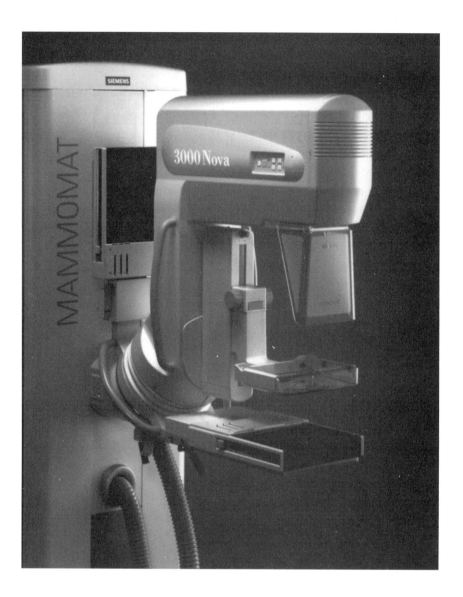

have been developed to minimize the radiation dose from the examination (as radiation itself is a risk factor for breast cancer). Special mammographic machines are also used. These have an X-ray tube with a small focal spot (this means the resulting beam is capable of producing very finely detailed images) and a device to compress the breast. As any woman who has had a mammogram knows, this compression is uncomfortable. However, it is necessary both for better visualization of the breast tissue and to view parts of the breast close to the chest wall. Since different views of the breast are taken (for screening mammograms, typically two views of each breast) the mammographic machine has a mount that allows the tube, compression device, and film holder to rotate together to make it easier to obtain these views. The height of the whole assembly is also adjustable to accommodate women of different stature. There are two major classes of mammographic examination done: the screening mammogram, which is done in the asymptomatic patient, and the diagnostic mammogram, which is directed at an abnormality seen on a screening mammogram or felt by the patient or referring physician. Screening and diagnostic mammographic examinations are sometimes performed in the same facility, though some imaging centers separate them. A planning note is that if both screening and diagnostic mammography are done at the same facility, the waiting areas for patients undergoing these two types of mammograms should be separated. The psychology behind this is that the screening patient generally believes herself to be well and thinks of the examination as a checkup. The diagnostic patient, however, already knows that something has been found and is likely to be more anxious about having cancer.

The diagnostic mammogram supplants the screening mammogram with additional views, magnified views of particular areas, or additional (spot) compression of particular areas. It may also include views of the axillary area to look for enlarged lymph nodes.

For film-based mammography, either screening or diagnostic, the mammographic area may need a darkroom and film processor. Because dust on the film or intensifying screen will result in artifacts that mimic abnormalities (white spots that can look like microcalcifications) mammographic technologists are more scrupulous about cleaning the cassettes and screens. They may need space to do this and an ultraviolet light to help check the screens for dust (the ultraviolet light causes the screens to fluoresce). The physical environment and air handling systems of the mammography room and suite should also be designed to minimize the accumulation of dust.

Increasingly, diagnostic work in mammography has been extended through the use of biopsy devices. Biopsies of suspicious lesions can be done with a fine needle aspiration procedure, or larger amounts of tissue can be obtained with a core needle biopsy. These are now most often done with a device that allows the mammographer to place the needle precisely in the lesion. The systems that do this are larger than standard mammographic units, though needle biopsy attachments are also available for standard mammographic machines. These automatic needle positioning systems are stereotactic biopsy machines (figure 6–6). The machines are usually arranged so that the patient lies prone with the breast to be biopsied passing through an opening in the table. The biopsy needle guide is located under the tabletop. To make localization feasible, these machines capture images of the suspect area of the breast with a digital detector. By taking two images at an angle, the abnormality is imaged in a stereo view. The radiologist identifies the center of the abnormal area on the images displayed on a workstation, and the machine then computes the location of the abnormality with respect to the position of the needle guide on the machine. After appropriate patient preparation, the radiologist advances the biopsy needle to the determined depth and takes the biopsy. Usually several biopsies of an abnormal area are taken.

Figure 6-6 *Stereotactic mammogrqphy concept.*

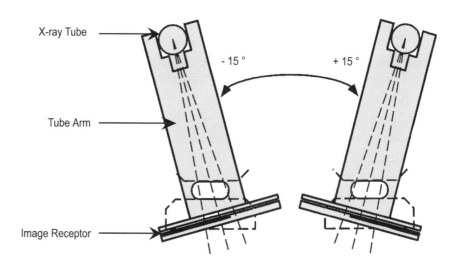

An important planning consideration for these stereotactic biopsy systems is that the machines are larger than conventional mammography devices–they have a long table, a pedestal under the table along with the needle guiding equipment, X–ray generator electronics, and an associated workstation. The workstation is usually located in the control area adjacent to the machine. It is also important to provide a private and direct route of travel between the stereotactic mammography room and a surgical procedure room, because during a procedure known as a "needle location," the gowned patient may be wheeled from the mammography room to the procedure room with the needle in its precise location within the breast.

The use of the digital detectors for the stereotactic biopsy application, and the interest in the advantage that digital detectors have over film, has led to the development of whole–breast digital mammographic systems. These systems are very similar to film–based mammographic machines except that the film holder is replaced with a digital detector. Digital detectors, with their much wider exposure latitude, are expected to offer some advantages over film for the detection of masses and distortions of the breast structure (referred to as "breast architecture" by mammographers).

An advance in computer processing that is beginning to have an impact on mammography is computer–aided detection (CAD). These systems scan film mammograms (or take digital mammograms directly) and process them to yield maps of potentially abnormal areas. The importance of this is rooted in the fact that even the best mammographers miss some cancers. CAD systems detect everything that matches the computer model of "suspicious." However, they produce a great many false positives (normal structures that look like lesions). These are readily dismissed by the radiologist, so what is left are lesions that are either suspicious or definitely abnormal. These systems are coming into wider use, as some studies have shown that they can reduce false negative diagnoses (when an abnormality is present but incorrectly dismissed).[12]

Many freestanding women's imaging centers incorporate screening and diagnostic mammography along with breast biopsy. Diagnostic ultrasound, used for both breast and gynecological imaging, is also often made available in these centers. A number of mammographic sections within radiology departments will also include ultrasound, as it forms an important adjunct to mammography for differentiating cystic from solid masses in the breast. An architect may, for these reasons, also be asked to include space for ultrasound in the mammography area.

As a result of a very large study (49,528 patients) of digital mammography that showed an advantage to digital mammography for women under fifty, women with radiographically dense breasts, and pre- or peri-menopausal women, it is likely that the next several years will show a shift of some film mammography to digital imaging.[13] For planning purposes, the digital mammographic systems are similar in size to their film-based counterparts, but space for workstations and design for computer networking need to be taken into account.

Radiographic and Fluoroscopic Procedures: Interventional Imaging

Unlike conventional or "plain" radiographic examinations, studies that involve radiographic and fluoroscopic imaging to guide complex diagnostic and therapeutic procedures fall into the category of special procedures. Distinguishing these, in addition to the involved nature of the procedures, is the use of anesthesia, imaging equipment that may be moved in many directions, moving examination tables, and many more personnel in the room. This may include technologists, nurses, anesthesiologists or nurse anesthetists, and other specialty radiologists. All of these differences dictate that rooms used for special procedures be larger than conventional radiographic or fluoroscopic rooms.

The study of the body's vascular system (with the exception of the heart) used to be done by vascular radiologists. However, these specialists began to carry out other procedures involving positioning catheters, guiding the placement of devices, opening vessels narrowed by disease (or the opposite–closing holes in vessels or closing the vessels themselves off), draining deep abscesses and other fluid collections, and more. These procedures often supplant conventional surgery and, since they are done through very small incisions or punctures of the body wall, are considered minimally invasive. Interventional radiology has become a subspecialty of vascular radiology (figure 6–7). These techniques have also found use in other radiology subspecialties, including neuroradiology, mammography, genitourinary radiology, and others, depending on the training and interest of the subspecialist. Cardiology also uses these techniques, with vascular stenting (opening up narrowed vessels) replacing some coronary artery bypass procedures. Vascular surgeons have begun using interventional radiology techniques for some of the procedures that formerly required open

Figure 6-7 Interventional radiology. Image courtesy of Siemens Medical Solutions.

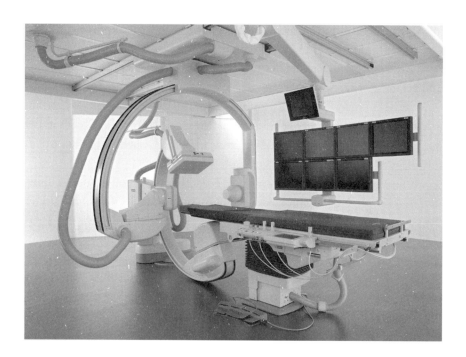

surgery. In general, there has been a blurring of the boundaries between surgery and imaging, with much surgery now image-guided (for example, laparoscopic procedures) and much imaging interventional (see chapter 15, "Imaging Beyond the Radiology Department"). This has led to some turf battles between specialists, and the architect needs to be aware of the potential for political entanglements as specialists vie for their share of the procedures. These struggles tend to vary considerably by locale, specialty makeup of the healthcare facility, and the willingness of the various parties to compromise. (This topic is discussed further in chapter 15.)

Interventional radiology suites can generally be divided into those for general body procedures and those for neuroradiology. The reason for the difference is related to the nature of the fluoroscopic systems used. Interventional neuroradiology rooms generally require biplane imaging systems. These use two movable (usually on C-arm devices) fluoroscopic imagers and X-ray tubes. This is so that images can be obtained simultaneously (or nearly so) in two planes, usually a frontal view and a lateral view. The image intensifiers of these systems, as opposed to those used for body procedures, are generally smaller since they usually have to encompass only the patient's head or a portion of the spine. The rooms for interventional neuroradiology may need to be larger than those for interventional body procedures because of this biplane requirement. Body interventional rooms usually have a single, movable fluoroscopic detector system and X-ray tube, but the image intensifier of the fluoroscopic system may have a large diameter (14 inches), so the fluoroscopic head will be large and heavy.

A major change in these systems has resulted from replacement of image intensifier tube systems with flat-panel detectors (see the section

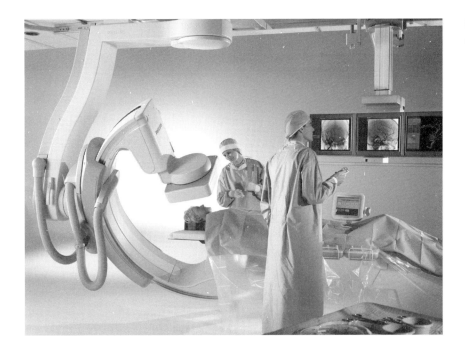

Figure 6-8 Interventional cardiology. Image courtesy of Philips Medical Systems.

"Film Compared to Digital Detectors" in this chapter). These are generally smaller (in terms of height above the imaging plane) than tube–based systems, so designing a biplane system, or a more movable single–plane system, can be easier. The move to the flat–panel detectors has also resulted in flexible rooms that can be used for either biplane or single–plane imaging with large enough detectors to accommodate body or neuroradiology cases. There are biplane systems in which the two detectors are fixed at a 90–degree angle and others with independently positionable X–ray tube/detector components. The latter tend to be larger, as they need space for both device positioners.

Ultrasound imaging, with its real–time capability, provides an important adjunct for interventional radiology. Many modern interventional suites include built–in ultrasound imaging equipment, or small units kept in the room. For some ultrasound–guided procedures, a larger ultrasound machine is brought in and may be accompanied by a technologist and a specialty radiologist. This reinforces the need for appropriate space in an interventional suite. It is certainly important for the architect to ask about the use of ultrasound when planning an interventional suite.

Cardiac catheterization involves placing small–caliber catheters into the heart and its vessels (figure 6–8). These catheters are typically inserted into the vascular system quite remote from the heart–usually at the groin or in the arm. Contrast can be injected through these catheters to follow blood motion, and physiological measurements (e.g., pressure) can be monitored through them as well. In addition to delivering contrast and measuring pressure, the catheters can be used to draw blood samples from particular areas in the heart and great vessels. The cardiologist should be able to view not only the images of the heart and vessels but also the electrocardiogram and pressure tracings from the catheter. Cardiac catheterization rooms need not just imaging equipment but also physiological monitoring and display equipment (though some of this is also needed for interventional work, especially since anesthesia is involved). For adult cardiac catheterization, single-plane fluoroscopic systems are usually employed. The situation is different for pediatrics. Because of higher heart rates in children, images need to be acquired at a higher rate as well. Also, for pediatric cardiac catheterization, biplane fluoroscopic imaging is often used, as it makes it easier to correlate cardiac motion and anatomy. Pediatric cardiac catheterization laboratories usually employ biplane fluoroscopic imaging with smaller-size image acquisition devices than those used in adult laboratories. However, the positioning systems, X-ray tubes, and electronics are not much different in size from the larger equipment used for adults.

Occasionally, the normal electrophysiological mechanism that results in regular contraction of the heart muscle is disturbed. The result is an arrhythmia—an abnormal rhythm of the heart in which the beats can be too fast, too slow, or irregular. Special catheters with sensing electrodes in them can be placed into various locations in the heart to try to find the source for these arrhythmias. If a focus, or several foci, are identified, they can be ablated to end the abnormal rhythm. This is done through another type of catheter with a special tip that allows for radio-frequency energy to be delivered at a small point. The goal is to ablate only the minimum amount of tissue needed to stop the arrhythmia. These procedures—cardiac electrophysiology (EP) and RF ablation—are typically done in cardiac catheterization rooms and are discussed further in chapter 15, "Imaging Beyond the Radiology Department."

A common design requirement for body, neuroradiology, and cardiology interventional rooms is storage for devices. The physicians who practice these specialties use a large array of catheters, guide wires, and other ancillary devices and require access to them quickly. This argues for device storage in the room rather than in a central facility some distance away, and it is important for the architect to consider this. A second requirement that the three interventional room types have in common is the need for anesthesia equipment. While the procedures are minimally invasive, they may require sedation or anesthesia for patient comfort and to minimize patient motion. This means that either the rooms have to accommodate anesthesia equipment and have the necessary gas lines available or the equipment has to be built in. Thorough consultation with anesthesiologists who work in such interventional areas is important in planning for the equipment needed and where it should be located. A third critical requirement of these room types is immediate access to resuscitation equipment, especially for EP procedures. Because anesthesia and sedation are used for many interventional procedures, an important planning consideration is the inclusion of space for preprocedure preparation by the anesthesiologist and a recovery area for patients coming out of anesthesia. These spaces will be similar to preparation and postanesthesia care areas designed for surgery, and the number of patients that can be accommodated will depend on the number of interventional rooms, the duration of the procedure and the associated observation/recovery periods, and the anesthetic agents being administered.

There is some impact on vascular imaging with the increasing use of multidetector CT machines and pulse sequences in MRI that produce images with enhanced vessels.[14] These images, often viewed as three-dimensional solid models on workstations, give such detail of vessels that they have replaced many diagnostic vascular imaging studies and are supplanting imaging for interventional procedures. Many interventional rooms are experiencing a greater percentage of interventional procedures, as diagnostic volumes are relocated to CT and MRI suites. Cardiovascular imaging is an emerging subspecialty, with both radiologist and cardiologist practitioners. Generally, the image viewing will be the same as for CT and MRI, but the reading room will have to include space for a 3-D workstation. Some vendors of PACS workstations are moving to incorporate 3-D viewing functions into the conventional 2-D workstations, so the requirements for additional hardware and space may be reduced.

Digital Subtraction Angiography

The high sensitivity of digital detectors and their larger dynamic range (minimum to maximum exposure) compared to film results in systems that allow visualization of vessels without having to place catheters in them for direct contrast injection. The idea is to inject contrast agents intravenously and, while they remain in the circulation, subtract an image taken prior to the contrast injection from one taken after. The resulting image should enhance the structures that contain the contrast, namely, the vessels. By adjusting the timing of when the postcontrast image is taken, the technologist can emphasize venous or arterial structures in the resulting image. This method relies on the digital detector's ability to capture the subtle difference in X-ray attenuation between the pre- and postcontrast anatomy.[15] Digital subtraction angiography, or DSA, was popular in the mid–1980s to 1990s. However, improvements in computed tomography, magnetic resonance imaging, and 3-D reconstruction began to replace DSA.

DSA is still used as a replacement for conventional subtraction images in interventional imaging. With film, an initial exposure was made prior to injection of contrast (typically via a catheter in a vessel of interest) and then a rapid sequence of films was taken as contrast was injected. From the film with no contrast, a negative was made, then matched and optically added to the contrast images. The resulting images showed the vessels of interest against a faint background (since a negative was made from the initial film, adding the negative mask and the positive contrast images is the same as subtracting the non–contrast-containing structures).

DSA as part of angiography has replaced this film–based subtraction process with an electronic one. The steps are the same, but the making of the negative mask and subsequent subtraction are done electronically on the digital images.

As described previously for interventional procedures, multidetector CT and vascular–enhanced MRI imaging are replacing much of digital sub-traction angiography.

Radiographic Tomography

Radiographic tomography is the radiography of sections (the word is de-rived from the Greek *tomos*, "section"). If, during a radiographic exposure, both the X–ray tube and film (or other detector) are moved, structures out of the plane of their common center of movement will be blurred. By vary-ing the ratio of the tube movement to detector movement, the position of this common center can be changed, so the location of the plane can be changed. This principle is used when it is desirable to blur structures that are outside a particular plane of interest. The simplest form of this is linear motion tomography, where the X–ray tube and detector are moved in a single plane relative to each other. This is most often used in combination with intravenous contrast in intravenous urography (or pyelography). The idea is to blur out structures anterior and posterior to the kidneys. Since much intestine is situated anterior to the kidneys, with muscle and bone posterior to them, radiographs taken without such tomography superim-pose these structures over the kidneys (figure 6–9).

Figure 6-9 *Principles of tomography.*

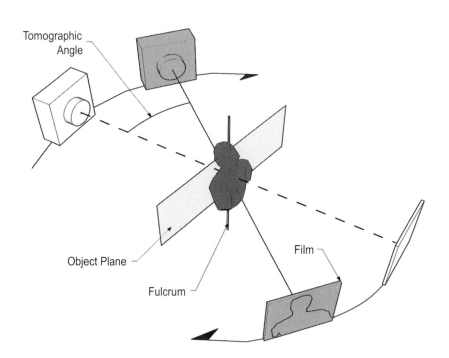

Tomographic Angle

Object Plane

Fulcrum

Film

Complex motion tomography, developed to provide even thinner sections of anatomy by using machines that make the tube move in circular, cycloidal, or even more complex patterns, was rapidly made obsolete with the development of computed tomography.

Linear tomography, however, persists and is still used with intravenous urography, though CR plates typically replace film as the detector. Many radiographic/fluoroscopic rooms are capable of performing linear tomography, so some allowance for a swinging X-ray tube needs to be made if linear tomography is to be done. The use of linear tomography is declining as more multidetector CT is used.

Computed Tomography

Though the late Sir Godfrey Hounsfield is regarded as the inventor of computed tomography (then called computerized axial tomography, giving rise to the acronym CAT, which is occasionally still used), the method of reconstructing the cross section of an object from projections of it has a history that goes back much further than Hounsfield's 1972 announcement of the method. The mathematics can be traced back to J. Radon, who in 1917 showed that an object could be mathematically reconstructed from its projections.[16] No one at the time thought to apply this to X-ray imaging, though an astrophysicist used the method for research.[17]

If you rotate an object while passing X-rays (or light, for transparent objects) through it perpendicular to the axis of rotation and capture what is transmitted on a moving piece of film, the result will look like a series of sine curves. Those curves are called "sinograms," and, together with information about the angle of the object along the direction of film movement, contain the information necessary to reconstruct a cross section of the object. This method was proposed in 1940 by Gabriel Frank, who patented the idea.[18] His method passed light back through the film sinograms and then summed the result, yielding a somewhat blurry rendition of the cross section of the object.

Others followed, often with little knowledge of what their predecessors had tried. However, the late Allan M. Cormack derived a theory for mathematical image reconstruction from projections in 1956 and tested his theory with an object made of aluminum, aluminum alloy, and oak.[19] Using a beam from a radioactive source, he was able to determine the correct attenuation coefficients (how much a material attenuates gamma or X-rays for a given thickness) for the three materials. He later did similar experiments with more complex phantoms (the term used to describe these test objects) and published his work in 1963 and 1964. However, the work received little attention, likely because the calculations were formidable in an era before the wide availability of computers. Nonetheless, the pioneering work he did was recognized along with that of Hounsfield, and the two of them were jointly awarded a Nobel prize in 1979 for the development of computer-assisted tomography.

The first clinical computed tomography (CT) machines were built by EMI, the British company for which Godfrey Hounsfield worked. These were specifically designed to accommodate a patient's head; to keep the detectors from being swamped by X-rays when the beam passed through the air around the patient's head, a rubber bag of water surrounded the head. These first machines were "rotate-translate" designs. The X-ray beam was scanned across the opening for the head, then the gantry was rotated and the beam again scanned. This process took about a minute per slice and the computer reconstruction time was several minutes more. The images were quite coarse, with a size of 80×80 pixels. Despite what now seems like great disadvantages, the views of the brain provided by the method dramatically changed radiology. Prior techniques of brain imaging were largely indirect, and most were quite uncomfortable for the patient. Pneumoencephalography involved injecting air into the spinal canal and moving it up into the ventricles of the brain. This was done by having the patient strapped in a chair that could be rotated in several directions. Tumors caused distortions of the ventricles, which the air would make visible. Subsequent to this procedure, patients usually had such severe headaches that they were confined to bed for a day or more. Pneumoencephalography disappeared very rapidly, often with the room used to house the pneumoencephalographic equipment being converted to the CT room.

CT evolved rapidly, and the technology used to be described in terms of generations, with the first generation being the rotation–translation scanner (figure 6–10A, B). Later designs used a fan–shaped X-ray beam instead of the thin "pencil beam" of the rotate–translate machines. These had either an arc of X-ray detectors or a ring of them. The machines also quickly went from being able to scan only a patient's head to scanning any part of the body.[20] During this time, computers increased in speed and decreased in cost. The original CT machines used specialized array processors to do the computations. These were dedicated high–speed processors that could increase reconstruction performance by an order of magnitude or more. As computer performance increased, the need for these processors decreased, though some current machines again require special processors to keep them fast.

For a number of years, the third–generation scanner was the mainstay of CT. This used an X-ray tube generating a fan–shaped beam and an arc of detectors. These were fixed to a large plate that rotated around the scanning aperture. Early versions used long, coiled cables and would rotate in one direction for one scan, then back the other way for the next. Later scanners had gantries (as the scanning mechanism became known) that rotated continuously. Power was sent to the equipment on the gantry and signals sent back over slip rings. These are metal rings that rotate with fixed brushlike contacts to carry power and signals.

A problem that CT machines had was that the scans took a long enough time that normal motion of the heart or bowel would cause these structures to be blurred, or to result in artifacts across the images. There has been continual pressure for faster scanners to reduce these problems. Moving mechanical parts work more quickly, but this requires larger motors and bigger X-ray tubes to handle the load of being on for a relatively long time. With slower scanners, there was time for the X-ray tube to cool down between scans. The quest for high-speed scanning resulted in an innovative device in which there are no mechanical moving parts other than the patient bed. Instead of a rotating gantry, the machine is essentially a giant X-ray tube that the patient moves into and out of. An electron beam is scanned across an arc-shaped anode, and an X-ray beam emerges where the electron beam strikes the anode. By setting the shape of this anode ring correctly, the beam emerges perpendicular to the scanning aperture. Since there are no mechanical parts to move the beam (it is deflected, much like the beam in a television's cathode ray tube) the scans can be done very quickly. Scan times are on the order of 50 milliseconds.[21] This technique is known as electron beam CT (EBCT) and has found use in determining whether or not a patient has calcium deposits in the coronary arteries (indicating atherosclerotic narrowing).

More conventional CT machine designs evolved to the current helical scan machines. In these systems, not only is the gantry continuously rotated, but the patient is moved through the scan aperture continuously as well. The fan beam of X-rays traces a helical path through the body. Computer algorithms can take the resulting helical projection data and reconstruct it into slices. It was recognized that this sort of scan method could also take advantage of a different X-ray beam shape. Instead of a thin fan, the fan could be expanded into a cone, and multiple rows of detectors could be used to take advantage of this. The most modern CT machines, multidetector or multislice CT machines, use a helical scan geometry, but with each gantry rotation they scan from four to (currently) sixty-four slices simultaneously. A few 256-slice CT scanners are beginning to emerge for limited applications. This multislice capability results in very short overall scan times–on the order of less than a minute to scan a patient from neck to pelvis.

The very short scan times have implications for room design and departmental layout. Logistics of patient transport now figures heavily in throughput, since the time to transport a patient to the machine and get the patient on the machine, off when done, and out of the room is far longer than the time to do the scan itself. As a result, it is not uncommon to provide additional prep/injection rooms per CT scan room in order to improve patient throughput. The impact of these scans has also been to reduce dependence on film even further. It is not unusual for a multidetector CT study to contain hundreds to thousands of images, whereas single-detector helical CT had studies with image counts in the hundreds at most. Also, because of the nature of the scanning geometry, the resulting images are nearly isotropic in resolution. With conventional and helical CT, the resolution in the cross-sectional plane is in the 0.75 mm range, but the slice thickness in the body's long axis (head to feet) was typically 5 mm to 1 mm.

Figure 6-10A Computed tomography.
Image courtesy of GE Healthcare.

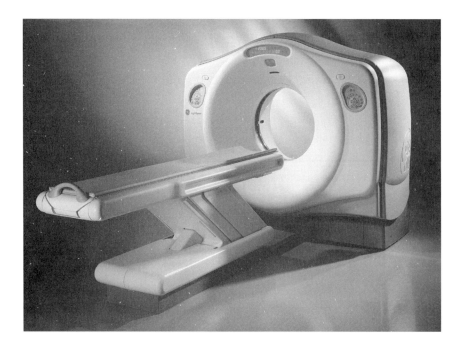

Figure 6-10B Principles of computed tomography. ECRI, *Healthcare Product Comparison System* (Plymouth Meeting, PA): ECRI, 2005.

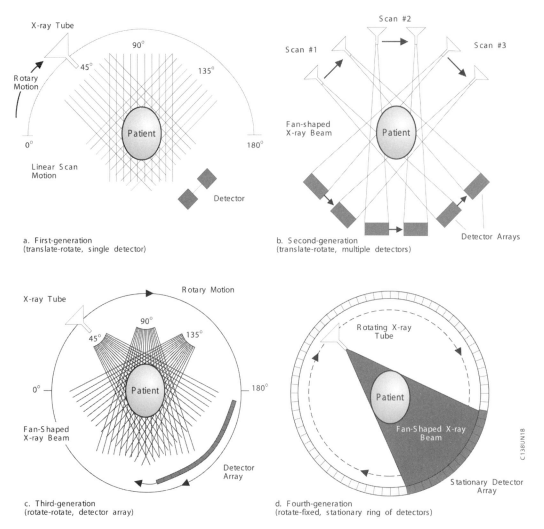

a. First-generation
(translate-rotate, single detector)

b. Second-generation
(translate-rotate, multiple detectors)

c. Third-generation
(rotate-rotate, detector array)

d. Fourth-generation
(rotate-fixed, stationary ring of detectors)

With multidetector CT, this "z–axis" slice thickness is now submillimeter, so the resulting image has equal resolution in all three axes. This has enabled very high–quality three–dimensional reconstruction to be done.

The large number of CT images per study and the ability to do 3–D and multiplanar reconstruction (reconstructing planes other than those in which the scan was done) have resulted in increased pressure to move from film to computer workstations for interpreting these studies. In fact, it is not practical to film these examinations, at least not all the images. A one–thousand–slice study, even filmed at fifteen images per sheet, would require sixty–seven sheets of film. There is no way to display that many films and be able to view them in a reasonable fashion.

Multidetector CT is now fast enough that CT scanning can be used like fluoroscopy, but to provide cross–sectional (or other plane) images in real time. CT fluoroscopy is likely to find its way into interventional suites as an adjunct to or replacement for digital fluoroscopy. An interventional suite built around CT fluoroscopy will likely need to be a large space, though the current multidetector CT machines have gantry enclosures that are smaller than those of earlier systems. The electronics supporting the machine has also gotten smaller. Unlike noninterventional CT rooms, however, the interventional CT room, or a CT room designed for occasional use in CT fluoroscopic interventional procedures, will have to accommodate personnel around the patient table. The interventional specialist and support people are also likely to be in the room for a much longer time than they would be for a diagnostic scan. For many patients undergoing interventional procedures, anesthesia is important. Accommodation of anesthesia equipment and personnel in the CT room is also important, so gas connections and room for anesthesia machines (often behind the scanner gantry) should be considered.

The fine detail resolution possible with multidetector CT has also made it possible to study the large bowel. CT colonography is done by distending the bowel with air or carbon dioxide and using the gas to provide contrast. The bowel will have been prepared the day prior to the study and so should be empty, but some patients may still want to have access to a toilet room just before or following the procedure.

Ultrasound

Unlike X–ray–based imaging, ultrasound uses only mechanical energy. X–ray photons are energetic enough that they can cause ionization of atoms, so X–rays are in the class of ionizing radiation. The ionization process can alter the way atoms interact, so the proteins and nucleic acids of the cell can be damaged by ionizing radiation. Mechanical energy, unless at extremely high intensities, does not cause ionization or other chemical changes in biological molecules. The intensities used by ultrasound are well below the levels at which physical effects, mostly from heating or shearing larger molecules, is known to occur.[22] Ultrasound transducers are piezoelectric materials–they give off mechanical energy when subjected to an electrical pulse, and they generate an electrical pulse when they are bent or squeezed.

Ultrasound as a medical diagnostic tool has its roots in post–World War II research. Sonar had been used successfully during the war for location and ranging of submarines and ships, and as a spin–off, researchers wondered if it could be used for medical purposes. The first medical ultrasound systems were little more than echo–ranging units. They sent out a pulse of high–frequency sound and determined how long it took to come back (and how strong the reflection was). Human and animal tissues propagate sound at different velocities depending on the tissue type. Also, the impedance to sound varies with tissue density and composition. A sound pulse traveling through tissues will be partially reflected when it encounters a change in tissue impedance. So in moving from the fluid surrounding the brain, for example, to the brain tissue itself, a sound pulse will be reflected at the boundary. This reflection phenomenon is what was exploited in these early A–mode (amplitude–mode) ultrasound machines. Chiefly, the use was in the brain. By placing a transducer–the device that changes an electrical pulse to a sound one and back again–on the side of the head, sonographers could plot echoes showing the various reflecting structures in the head. Since the brain consists of two connected halves, there is a thin gap between the two hemispheres in the middle of the skull. There is normally a small amount of cerebrospinal fluid (CSF) in that gap, and as a result, the brain-to-fluid transition results in sound reflection. If the patient had a blood clot between the brain and inner wall of the skull, it would displace the brain, pushing the structures normally in the middle off to one side. Consequently, the A–mode ultrasound would show the echoes corresponding to the midline structures displaced away from the midline. Before the invention of CT, ultrasound was a noninvasive way to look for this gross evidence of internal head injury.[23]

Later ultrasound developments turned to scanning the beam instead of just having it travel out and back in a single sonic "ray." Moving the beam allowed a cross–sectional image to be built up. By knowing how fast sound travels in soft tissues (it averages around 1,540 m/sec) it is possible to build up information along the depth direction, since the position of reflectors could be determined from how long it took the sound to get to a reflector and back. Early cross–sectional ultrasound imaging machines used an articulated arm that continuously computed the position of the transducer attached at one end. Combined with a display of the reflected amplitude of the returning sound, the machine would build up an image based on how the beam was moved across the patient. To get good scan results required a very skilled practitioner, and, just as for other imaging methods, technologists were trained to perform the studies.

The major advance in ultrasound came with the development of real–time scanners. The first real–time machines consisted of a single transducer element mounted on a motor shaft, or located in front of a sound reflector that was attached to a motor. The transducer generated and received the ultrasound beam, and the motor changed the beam direction. Newer real-time scanners use a transducer array that has multiple transducer elements (as many as 128) in it rather than a single one. By scanning these sequentially and rapidly, a two-dimensional image is built up in real time. Inside the machine, a scan converter changes the imaging rate of the transducer (from 2 frames per second to 20 or more) to video rate. Most ultrasound machines can output video that can be recorded on a standard video recorder for later playback. Techniques from radar design are directly applicable to ultrasound, even though radar is electromagnetic. Modern radar uses multielement antennas, much as transducers have multiple elements in them. It is possible to design circuits that will steer a beam and focus it electronically; a motor to move the transducer is no longer needed. These techniques of electronic beam steering and focusing are direct spin-offs of radar design.

Ultrasound for diagnostic work ranges in frequency from about 1 megahertz (MHz) to 20 MHz. In general, the higher the sound frequency, the finer the spatial resolution of the ultrasound transducer. A limitation of the physics of ultrasound, however, is that the higher the frequency, the higher the attenuation of the sound by the tissue. As a result, higher frequencies are limited to structures that are relatively close to the skin surface. The ultrasound machines generally have interchangeable transducers, as different ones are made to suit particular types of examinations.

Almost everyone is familiar with the Doppler effect, if not the physics of it. If you are standing still and a car approaches with its horn blaring, the pitch will sound higher to you as the car approaches and lower as it leaves. Fortunately for diagnostic ultrasound, moving blood is a very good sound reflector. Blood moving in vessels toward an ultrasound transducer will raise the frequency of the ultrasound beam in proportion to its velocity. Similarly, the frequency will be lower if the blood is moving away from the beam direction. This Doppler frequency shift, if plotted over time, is an analog of blood flow velocity over time. Doppler "stethoscopes" have been used for some years at the patient bedside. These devices are nonimaging ultrasound systems that process the Doppler signal only from vessels under the probe. Diagnostic ultrasound can combine imaging with Doppler measurements to indicate not only blood flow properties but also where in the body the flow is taking place. If multiple beams are used to generate a Doppler signal, the result is a two-dimensional Doppler "map." Many machines can now do this and display the resulting map in color. Color flow Doppler is widely used by radiologists examining abdominal and pelvic blood vessels, by cardiologists looking at blood flow in the heart, by vascular surgeons examining the carotid arteries and the arteries and veins of the extremities, and by obstetricians checking blood flow in the umbilical cord of a fetus. Color flow Doppler is often combined with pulsed Doppler so that the color flow map can be used to guide placement of the sample volume of the pulsed Doppler system. Pulsed Doppler, unlike the continuous-wave Doppler of the ultrasound stethoscope, can be set to interrogate structures at specific depths. Continuous-wave Doppler has no depth sensitivity—it will yield a Doppler signal from any vessel in the path of the beam.[24]

Ultrasound until now has been largely a two-dimensional imaging technique, as limitations on electronics and cost made three-dimensional ultrasound mostly a research topic. However, with the price of powerful microprocessors falling, 3-D ultrasound is now available on many machines. In the most commonly used mode, a 2-D transducer is scanned manually across a structure. The processing electronics then take this series of 2-D frames and generate the 3-D image from them. This method works well but requires skill on the part of the sonographer or radiologist, as well as a cooperative patient who can remain still during the time needed to acquire the set of images (typically about ten seconds). Another version of 3-D equipment has a motor-driven 2-D transducer. It is manually positioned initially, and the motor then moves the 2-D transducer uniformly. This system is somewhat easier to use, though it requires a special transducer, whereas the other system can work (usually) with any 2-D transducer. Since the 2-D transducer is motor-driven, there is no reason it could not be swept back and forth continuously, generating a series of 3-D images. Only processing power is needed for this, and many "four-dimensional" machines are now available. These do generate frames relatively slowly—on the order of one to two frames per second. However, it is very useful for moving subjects (provided they are not moving too fast), as motion can be seen in 3-D. It is also possible to build a transducer that is a square array of elements instead of a linear or curved one. In this case, 3-D and 4-D scans can be done all electronically, with no motor needed to move the transducer. These machines are relatively uncommon at present, as they use a large amount of processing circuitry and so are expensive. It is not yet clear that 3-D and 4-D ultrasound are cost-effective, though they generate impressive images of fetuses and so very likely do have a place in the diagnostic armamentarium in cases of complex fetal anomalies. These techniques, much as for multiplanar reconstruction in CT, can also be used to generate 2-D image planes that are not possible to acquire with conventional scanning.

Ultrasound machines also have the advantage of being mobile. Though not small, and weighing about 400–600 pounds (180–270 kg), virtually all the commercial ultrasound machines are equipped with wheels and can be rolled about. Newer machines incorporating lightweight electronics and power supplies and with large-diameter wheels (which make it easier to roll over door thresholds, power cords, elevator cab entrances, etc.) are purpose-built for mobile operation (figure 6-11).

Because of the biological safety of ultrasound, it is used for a wide array of imaging, literally from head to toe. The normal apertures in the neona-

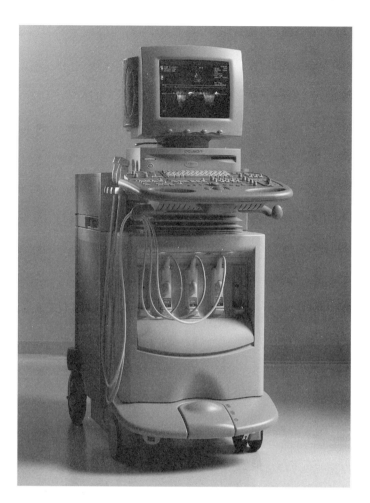

Figure 6-11 Ultrasound. Image courtesy of Siemens Medical Solutions.

tal skull provide a "window" through which ultrasound can pass, so the neonatal brain can readily be imaged by ultrasound. Cardiac ultrasound, or echocardiography, is commonly used for heart imaging. Ultrasound does not pass through air to any significant degree, so it is not useful in imaging the lungs. However, it can be used to find fluid in the chest. In the abdomen, all of the organs can be imaged, and evaluation of the gallbladder for stones is one of the well-known uses. Gas in the intestine stops the ultrasound beam, which is one limitation in abdominal scanning. Gynecological imaging is another widely performed ultrasound procedure. For the pregnant woman, ultrasound of the fetus is commonly done, as there is no ionizing radiation exposure. For nonpregnant women, visualizing the uterus and ovaries is readily accomplished. Because pelvic ultrasound is often done through a filled urinary bladder, ultrasound room designs typically include an attached toilet room, or there should be toilet rooms in close proximity. In men, ultrasound is used to image the prostate and to guide biopsies of it. Detection of arterial and venous problems in the arms and legs is easily and quickly accomplished with ultrasound. In the feet, ultrasound can be used to look for some causes of foot pain.

Ultrasound is used in the operating room to provide diagnostic imaging and guidance. Radiologists, cardiologists, gastroenterologists, gynecologists, and vascular surgeons all use ultrasound for guiding interventional procedures. There are ultrasound transducers that are designed to fit through a laparoscope, allowing ultrasound to be used for guiding laparoscopic surgery. Other specialized ultrasound transducers are those on the ends of an endoscope, allowing a gastroenterologist to both view the lining of the GI tract and scan through it. Cardiologists use an ultrasound transducer that can be placed down the esophagus, where it can be positioned against the back of the heart to give additional images. Interventional radiologists, urologists, and vascular surgeons can use very–small–diameter transducers (on the end of a spinning catheter) to perform intravascular ultrasound (IVUS) or to scan the ureters from within.

Though less heralded than CT or MR imaging, ultrasound has gone through the same sort of revolutionary technological advances that the other imaging techniques have. Ultrasound at very high power can be used therapeutically. It can be used to heat tissues for physical therapy, but the most interesting developing use is very–high–power focused ultrasound, which can deposit enough energy in tissues to destroy them. Since this ultrasound is focused, the out–of–focus portions of the beam do not have enough concentrated energy to damage tissues, so the beam can be passed through normal tissue to reach tumors. The current approved use for therapeutic focused ultrasound is to treat uterine fibroids, one of the most common benign tumors that occur in women. In this use, the fibroids are "targeted" with MR imaging and a robotic system positions the transducer and adjusts the focus to treat the lesions. Initial results are very promising, as the procedure is effective and well tolerated by patients.[25] This system is an add–on to an MRI system, and manufacturers should be consulted regarding any added planning or siting requirements.

Magnetic Resonance Imaging

Magnetic resonance imaging, or more correctly nuclear magnetic resonance (NMR) imaging, relies on a technique that was known for years prior to being used for imaging.[26] The phenomenon of nuclear magnetic resonance was described independently by Felix Bloch and Edward M. Purcell, who shared a Nobel prize in physics in 1952 for their work. Nuclear magnetic resonance is a property of certain nuclei that have a magnetic moment (that is, the nuclei themselves behave like very small magnets when placed in an external magnetic field). If nuclei are placed in a high–strength magnetic field, they tend to align with the magnetic field. The right radio-frequency (RF) pulse is absorbed by the nuclei and can be used to "flip" them from their aligned state to the unaligned state (effectively with the magnetic vector pointing in the opposite direction of the static magnetic field). When the nuclei return to their aligned state, they give off energy as a weak but detectable field. The electron cloud around the nuclei acts, to some extent, like a shield for the nucleus against the applied RF pulse. Since it is the electron cloud that is responsible for chemical interactions, it is affected by the way the atoms are attached in a molecule. This will have an effect on the behavior of the nucleus in response to the applied RF pulse, so the response of the nucleus provides some information about the environment of the atom. Different nuclei that have a magnetic moment will have a characteristic radio frequency at which they absorb energy and can flip over. This frequency varies in a predictable way with the strength of the magnetic field.

The work of Paul Lauterbur and Sir Peter Mansfield was to devise a way in which the NMR phenomenon could be used to generate images. Working independently, they determined that by adding a gradient (uniformly spatially varying) magnetic field to the apparatus, the position of the emitted NMR signal could be determined. Since the frequency at which a susceptible nucleus flips is proportional to the magnetic field strength, the local magnetic field strength could be determined from the frequency information. If the local magnetic field strength is known, then the position of the population of nuclei that generated the signal can be determined. Mansfield further evolved the gradient methods and developed the mathematical techniques for rapid reconstruction of images. For their work on NMR imaging, Lauterbur and Mansfield were awarded the 2003 Nobel prize in physiology or medicine. In the history of MR imaging, Dr. Raymond Damadian also figures prominently. He investigated, and patented, NMR as a way to differentiate malignant from benign tissue. He also constructed the first operational whole–body MRI system in 1977.

How NMR imaging became MRI is a story of public opinion. Early researchers in NMR imaging were sharply divided over what the procedure should be called. While more properly termed "nuclear magnetic resonance imaging," many had serious concerns that leaving the word *nuclear* in the name would bias the public against the technique, giving them the false impression that radioactivity was somehow involved. In the end, those who thought the public was too ill–informed to understand the difference between the meaning of *nuclear* in the context of NMR and in that of nuclear radiation won out, and the technique has been called "magnetic resonance imaging" since.

To perform MRI, a large magnet is needed. There are both high–field-strength (1 tesla and greater) and low–field-strength systems. These are further subdivided into ultra–low–field (0.06–0.4 T), low–field (0.2–0.4 T), midfield (0.5–1.0 T), high–field (1.5–2.0 T), and very–high–field (> 2.0 T) categories, though the major distinction is at approximately the 0.5 T field strength. Because of improved image quality and scanning speed with higher field strengths, 3 T magnets, which were research instruments, are increasingly being used as routine clinical systems, and many believe they will replace 1.5 T magnets as a clinical standard (figure 6–12 A–C). Research magnets of 4 T and higher are also becoming more common and are used

Figure 6-12A High-field superconductive magnet (front view). Image courtesy of Siemens Medical Solutions.

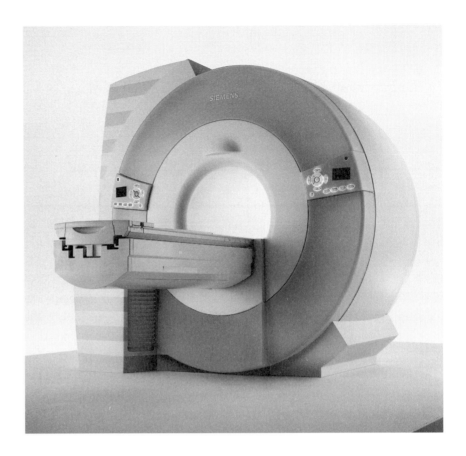

to image patients under research protocols. High–field–strength systems produce images with less noise and can usually do so faster. However, the mid– and high–field–strength MR magnets are fat cylinders with a long central tube. The anatomy of interest has to be positioned near the center of that tube. This is a significant problem for patients who are claustrophobic, and some never realize that fact until they are put into an MR magnet. Low–field–strength units can be made with an open design that obviates much of the claustrophobia–inducing feeling of being enclosed (figure 6–13). The trade–off is the somewhat lower image quality of the low–field–strength images. Commercial 1 to 1.5 T open–design and large–bore magnets have become available, making it possible to provide mid– to high–field–strength imaging for those who are too claustrophobic or obese for small–bore magnets.

The MRI scanning process is also noisy due to pulsation of the various coils needed for the RF and gradient pulses. Many centers provide either earplugs or music systems that use tubing to conduct sound to the patient.

To give a sense of how strong a high–field–strength MRI magnet is, a typical magnet used to hold notes or children's drawings to a refrigerator door generates about 0.1 tesla at its surface. One tesla is equal to 10,000 gauss, and the magnetic field of the earth is about 0.5 gauss. Magnetic fields of the strength used for MR imaging are dangerous if not respected. The

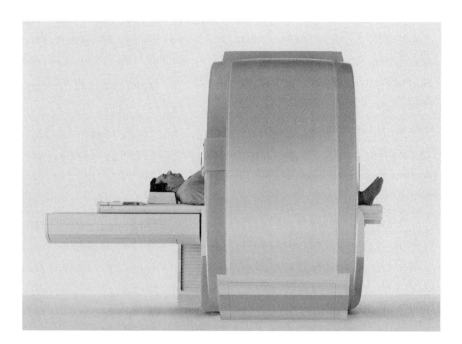

Figure 6-12B High-field superconductive magnet (side view). Image courtesy of Siemens Medical Solutions.

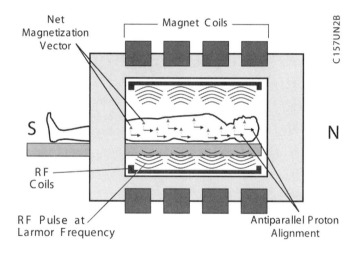

Figure 6-12C Principles of MRI. ECRI, *Healthcare Product Comparison System* (Plymouth Meeting, PA): ECRI, 2005.

need for safety regarding MRI has prompted the American College of Radiology to issue guidelines for MRI sites and procedures. These guidelines are included as an appendix of this book. A field of this strength can turn a magnetic item, such as a paper clip, into a projectile that moves fast enough to injure a person. Larger objects, such as chairs, gas cylinders, or even floor sweepers, have inadvertently been drawn into MR magnets.

Low–field–strength MR magnets are either permanent magnets, like those used on your refrigerator door, or resistive magnets that are large electromagnets. Permanent magnet units have a great advantage in their much lower cost of operation and acquisition. Resistive magnet units are somewhat more expensive, and the coils need a cooling system because of the heat generated during their operation. The typical field strength of a

Figure 6-13 Low-field open magnet. Image courtesy of GE Healthcare.

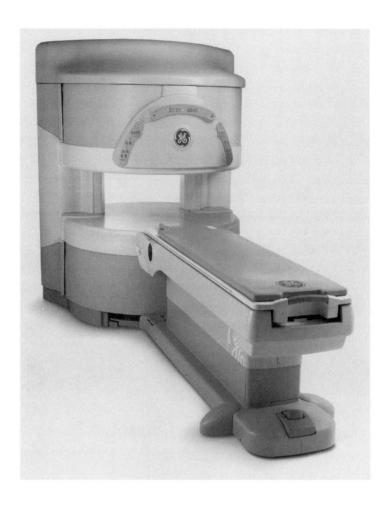

permanent magnet MR system is a maximum of about 0.35 T. For a resistive system, the maximum is about 0.15 T.

Mid- and high–field–strength MR magnets use superconducting technology. The coils of the magnet are wound with superconducting wire. If this were not the case, the energy needed to generate the high–field strength would heat up the wire coil to the point where it would melt. This is because conventional wire has resistance, and applying enough current to generate a strong magnetic field will also generate heat. To be superconducting, the coils of the MR magnet need to be chilled down to very low temperatures, typically the temperature of liquid helium (–269°C or 4 K). Surrounding this inner superconducting core is a second outer vessel filled with liquid nitrogen (–196°C or 77 K). In some systems, the outer liquid nitrogen vessel is replaced by a refrigeration system. In any event, the liquid helium slowly boils off and needs to be replaced at intervals of several months. Liquid nitrogen boils off more rapidly and needs to be topped off more frequently. The dewar containers in which these liquefied gases are delivered are large, and a provision for getting them into the magnet room has to be provided. Also, whether the device uses a low–field–strength resistive or permanent magnet or a high–field–strength superconducting magnet, one feature in common for MR systems is very high weight. The manufacturers of the MR systems have extensive siting and installation information.

Because the high–field–strength MR systems can cause ferromagnetic items in the patient's body to move (which is potentially disastrous), most centers question patients very thoroughly about any metallic objects they may have in them. Pacemakers are a contraindication to having an MR examination. For other metallic objects (e.g., slivers of metal in welders), if the patient is in doubt, radiographs to search for metallic objects can be done prior to having the MRI study. This suggests that in planning, consider the need to take a radiograph in a location convenient to the MR area.

Some of the inks used for tattoos contain iron pigments (as very fine particles), and there is considerable controversy about whether or not tattoos pose a significant risk for a patient undergoing an MRI. Likewise, some physicians have expressed a concern about "permanent eyeliner," which is a form of tattoo and may contain metallic particles. While it is thought unlikely that there could be enough pull to cause a problem, conductors in an RF field act like antennae and may get hot as they absorb the RF energy. One article in the MR literature indicates that this concern is minimal and should neither dissuade a patient from having an MRI nor discourage the referring physician from requesting it.[27]

Besides the high weight of MRI systems and the need for cryogens for the superconducting magnet systems, the high magnetic fields accompanying them are a challenge for which to plan. Generally, a surface representing where the field strength drops to 5 gauss is regarded as an operational design envelope for MR machines. Inside this line, great caution is needed with any magnetic device carried by someone. Also, inside that limit, the field strength is typically high enough to erase the magnetic strips on credit, identification, banking, and similar cards. Most MRI facilities provide lockers for both patients and personnel so that wallets, handbags, wristwatches, and eyeglasses with magnetic frames can be securely stored. The adoption of flat–panel displays is particularly useful for MR imaging suites, as the magnetic field distorts the image on a cathode ray tube. Shielding the tubes is possible but expensive. More on the topic of MRI planning is included later in this book.

Clinical applications of MRI are extensive. All parts of the body have been studied by MRI, literally from head to toe. The images that result from MR imaging are inherently three-dimensional volumes and can be "sliced" to show conventional or specialized planes. Usually MR information is reconstructed in specific planes, and the mathematical techniques to do this very quickly are well established. Standard anatomic planes form an orthogonal set. A transverse plane is most familiar and is a cross section of the body perpendicular to its long axis (head–to–toe axis). A sagittal plane is a section of the body perpendicular to the left–to–right axis. The coronal plane is a section perpendicular to the back–to–front axis of the body. For viewing of bones and joints, planes other than the standard ones may be desirable. For this reason, as well as the ability of MR imaging to show cartilage, tendon, and joint fluid clearly, musculoskeletal MR imaging is one of the technique's major uses. Bone contains a large amount of calcium. While this provides high X-ray attenuation, the calcium nucleus does not have a magnetic moment. For this reason, bone generates very little signal on MRI. If a goal of imaging is to see bone, CT is often a better choice. MRI is largely a method to image hydrogen. Since it is one of the most common atoms in the body (fourth by weight, first by number of atoms), this works out well. Differences in the way the hydrogen atoms are chemically bound and the adjacency of other atoms to hydrogen result in the signal from hydrogen being different in different tissues. Were this not the case, MRI images would be largely featureless.

Contrast agents to improve visibility of vessels are also available for MRI. Instead of iodine, the contrast agents use gadolinium bound to organic molecules. Gadolinium-based contrast agents have fewer side effects than iodine-based ones, another useful characteristic. Because blood moves through the magnetic field during a scan, it generates a signal that is often different from the surrounding tissue, and this can be exploited to show vascular structures. In effect, for some types of imaging, moving blood acts as its own contrast agent.

This ability to image flowing blood has led to the development of MR angiography (MRA). Using this technique, blood vessels in many of the body's organs can be studied. The technique has become commonplace. In some instances, MRA has nearly replaced conventional angiography. Evaluation of the carotid arteries is an example. Studying the carotid arteries by placing a catheter in them for conventional angiography carried a significant risk of causing a stroke. Since MRA does not need catheter injection of contrast agents (though intravenous administration of contrast agents is still used with MRA) the risk of the complications caused by the catheter movement in the vessels is eliminated. MRA can be used to image veins as well as arteries, so some instances of venography are also being replaced by MRA. In addition to risk, whether or not MRA is more cost-effective than conventional angiography for a particular vascular study is still an important consideration.

Magnetic resonance imaging can also show bile in bile ducts and pancreatic secretions in the pancreatic duct. Conventional diagnostic methods for evaluating the biliary tree and pancreatic duct are mostly based on endoscopy. Using an endoscope and fluoroscopy, a gastroenterologist would guide an endoscope into the duodenum, the segment of bowel connected to the stomach. This segment of bowel contains the opening (or openings) of the bile duct and pancreatic duct and is the way bile and pancreatic secretions (which aid in digestion) enter the bowel. Once in place, the physician places a catheter through the endoscope into the bile duct opening, then, using fluoroscopic imaging, injects contrast material to fill the biliary and pancreatic ducts and records their appearance. This technique is known as cholangiopancreatography (CP). Since MR can show bile and pancreatic secretions, it can also be used to show these ducts much less invasively. The bile and pancreatic secretions are effectively their own contrast material against the surrounding tissue. Conventional CP carries risks of causing inflammation of the pancreas (pancreatitis), which can require hospitalization and can be severe enough to be fatal. However, a great advantage of conventional CP is that the physician performing it can carry out interventional procedures, for example, removing stones from the bile duct or enlarging the opening of the bile duct into the duodenum. For diagnostic work, though, MRCP compares favorably with conventional CP. An advantage of MRCP is that imaging of the surrounding organs–the liver, pancreas, and bowel–can be done simultaneously with the imaging of the bile and pancreatic ducts.

Since MR can show blood flow it is possible to use MRI to evaluate function. Most radiological imaging shows anatomy extremely well but does not necessarily tell how an organ is working. In some instances, where blood flow, motion, or the ability to concentrate contrast media indicate function, techniques such as ultrasound and CT give some information about the function of organs. Barium contrast fluoroscopy of the gastrointestinal tract can be used to show how the bowel contracts, which is an indicator of function. Functional MRI (fMRI) takes advantage of the high sensitivity of MRI to blood flow, chiefly in the brain. In the brain, changes in blood flow accompany changes in brain activity, so increased activity of certain parts of the brain will result in localized increased blood flow which MRI can detect. By having a patient perform certain tasks while being scanned, the area of the brain involved in that task can be identified. Since specific areas of the brain responsible for functions such as speech or mental computation may vary from person to person, fMRI is very useful in determining the location of such important areas prior to surgery or radiation therapy for brain tumors. Functional MRI images have to be obtained very rapidly, so spatial resolution is sacrificed to some degree to acquire these images. The fMRI information can be combined with the higher–resolution conventional MRI images for more precise localization of the blood flow changes. There are other aspects of MRI that can be used to look at function. Since MRI gets a very strong signal from water (two hydrogen nuclei per molecule) it can be used to look at water motion. To distinguish the particular use of functional MRI in the brain based on blood flow from other functional MRI techniques, practitioners have advocated using the acronym *fMRI* to refer to the brain functional MRI and *FMRI* to refer to other physiological MRI imaging. Some of these other functional techniques have their own acronyms based on the way they work.

As noted previously, the environment of a hydrogen (or other paramagnetic) atom will affect its NMR signal to a slight degree. That is, hydrogen atoms in different chemical compounds or in water in different environments (intra– or extracellular) will produce a slightly different NMR signal depending on the compound or environment. If the total MRI signal over a volume of an organ is subjected to spectral analysis (recalling that MRI signals are frequencies), the resulting spectrum can yield information about the composition of the tissue volume. Particular spectra are known for compounds in various organs, so the quantity of these can give information about the health or disease of the organ as well as its function. Again, most of this work has been done on the brain, where certain chemical spectra are used to characterize tumors, neuropsychiatric disorders, and degenerative diseases. This technique is referred to as "MRI spectroscopy."

Motion of protons, particularly as hydrogen nuclei in water, can be detected by MRI. Movement of water accompanies the normal function of cells, including neurons in the brain. By imaging the motion of water protons, it is possible to determine where neurons go–that is, where the fiber tracts that carry brain signals are routed in the brain. Determining this prior to MRI typically was a process carried out using special stains on brain specimens from human and animal cadavers. The imaging of proton motion is a particular technique called diffusion tensor imaging (DTI). Fundamentally, it relies on the fact that the diffusion of water is not uniform in a functioning brain, and the MRI signals can be mathematically analyzed to determine the net diffusion direction. The technique is increasingly being used to evaluate diseases such as epilepsy and attention deficit/hyperactivity disorder (ADHD) and in research to examine the development of neuronal fiber tracts in animals.

Similar to CT, MR imaging is regarded as one of the revolutionary imaging technologies in medicine. For radiology, MR has brought much additional research interest and has attracted many nonphysician scientists to radiology. Development of new imaging pulse sequences (the way the imaging and gradient coils are energized) requires extensive knowledge of the physics of NMR. MR image reconstruction techniques require knowledge of both physics and computer science. Research in pulse sequences and reconstruction has enabled the rapid advancement of MR imaging into new areas and to yield better images more quickly. The area of development of MRI contrast agents has also attracted chemists to the ranks of MR imaging researchers. Large academic medical centers that are conducting research in MRI are likely to need laboratory space that suits the needs of the physicist, engineer, computer scientist, and chemist. This can be a planning challenge, as it also needs to be close to both research and clinical MR machines.

Biomagnetics and Biomagnetic Imaging

Faraday's law states that an electrical current moving in a conductor generates a magnetic field. This law works reciprocally as well, so moving a magnetic field in a conductor will generate electrical current. The minuscule electric currents generated by movements of ions in nerves do generate a very small magnetic field. These fields are so small that they are not detectable by the sort of equipment used to measure even small magnetic fields, such as magnetometers used to detect buried or submerged metallic objects. Brian Josephson discovered that two superconductors in a circuit separated by an insulating layer will pass a current through the insulator. Applying a small current to the circuit changes its behavior from conducting current to oscillating at high frequency. An external magnetic field would induce a current in a Josephson junction (as the superconductor/insulator sandwich is known), so such a junction could be used to detect very small magnetic fields. Earlier work along these lines had been done by Leo Esaki and Ivar Giaever. For this novel work on superconductors, Josephson, Esaki, and Giaever were awarded the Nobel prize for physics in 1973.

There are different ways Josephson junctions can be assembled into a sensitive magnetic field detector. For detection of extremely small magnetic fields, a direct-current configuration is used. This incorporates a pair of Josephson junctions in parallel. When constructed in this way, the electrons moving between the superconductors exhibit a phenomenon known as quantum interference. Quantum interference is a demonstrable but nonintuitive phenomenon and one of the most puzzling outcomes of quantum mechanics. Essentially, in quantum interference a single particle can interfere with itself (one would normally think two particles or waves are needed for interference). In the two-junction detector, the quantum interference phenomenon serves as an extremely sensitive detector of magnetic fields. A change in an applied external magnetic field will result in a change in resistance of the detector. A device constructed in this manner is known as a direct-current superconducting quantum interference detector, or DC SQUID. The magnetic fields generated by bioelectric processes (excluding animals that have bioelectric organs, such as electric eels) in the brain, heart, and muscle are on the order of 10^{-12} T. DC SQUID detectors have been built that can detect 10^{-17} T. To keep the system in a superconducting state, SQUID detectors are immersed in liquid helium dewars. Some work with high-temperature superconductors has yielded SQUIDs that can be operated at liquid nitrogen temperature, making them simpler and less expensive to run.

The problem with operating such sensitive detectors is electromagnetic noise, which is ubiquitous in the environment. Broadcast radio and television, electrical power lines, lighting (especially fluorescent), and operating electronic equipment all generate fields that would readily be detected by a SQUID. To detect biomagnetic signals, the SQUID must be operated in a shielded room. Such rooms keep out electrical interference, but they also need to keep out magnetic interference. For this purpose, the shielding also includes a layer of Mumetal, an alloy specially formulated to have very high magnetic permeability. With such a high permeability, any magnetic field entering the shield will tend to stay in it, not pass through it. To further reduce noise from extraneous magnetic fields, a separate SQUID is kept in the shielded examination room but too far from the patient area to pick up any biomagnetic signals. It will, however, pick up other magnetic noise that penetrates the shield, and the noise it detects can be subtracted from the biomagnetic signal.

At present, SQUID systems are used for magnetoencephalography and magnetocardiography–detection of brain and heart magnetic fields, respectively. In the brain, the highly sensitive SQUID is excellent at detecting normal electrical activity and departures from it, as in patients with epilepsy. For magnetocardiography, the SQUID can detect the electrical activity of normal compared to abnormal heart muscle. Muscle damaged from myocardial infarction does not produce the same signal as normal muscle. The spatial resolution of these systems is not high, so the activity maps they generate are usually overlaid on higher-resolution MR or CT images. Biomagnetic imaging is usually not part of radiology's practices and is more likely seen in neurology, psychiatry, and cardiology. However, combination MRI and biomagnetic suites have been built so as to provide very good correlation between the activity maps generated by the biomagnetic system and the anatomic imaging (plus any added functional imaging) from MRI.[28]

Nuclear Medicine

Radioactive isotopes exist in nature and are responsible for some of the background radiation that is readily detectable anywhere on earth (cosmic rays constitute another exogenous source). Radioactive isotopes are isotopes of elements whose nuclei are unstable and decay by giving off various forms of radiation. Most interesting for diagnostic imaging are those isotopes, or nuclides, of an atom that decay by giving off gamma rays. Gamma rays are X-rays, but usually of a specific, high energy. X-rays emitted from an X-ray tube exhibit a whole spectrum of energies. Many such radionuclides can be synthesized by exposing one nuclide of an element to energetic neutrons. It is the addition of neutrons to the nucleus that results in heavier isotopes of an atom, and adding neutrons often results in an unstable nucleus that exhibits radioactive decay.

The gamma rays that are given off by radionuclides are readily detected. At high enough levels, they can expose film directly. Autoradiographs are usually made from tissue specimens that are removed, keeping the cells alive, and incubated with a substance the tissue will take up that has been labeled with an isotope. The tissue is then placed on a piece of film or fixed and coated with a photographic emulsion. When developed, the film or emulsion will reveal which parts of the tissue picked up the radioactive material. This method is clearly not useful for living patients, though a similar method is still used for diagnostic work.

One form of examination that uses isotopes as an energy source but does not require them to be administered internally is the study done for bone density determination. In this procedure, typically called a dual-

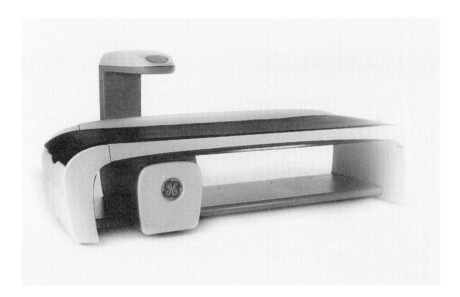

Figure 6-14 DEXA (dual-energy X-ray absorptiometry). Image courtesy of GE Healthcare.

energy X-ray absorptiometry, or DEXA, scanning, parts of the body are placed between a radiation source and detector (figure 6-14). The radiation sources are isotopes that emit at two well-defined energies. The amount of energy in these two beams that is absorbed by bone is proportional to the calcium content. There are two versions of DEXA devices. One type is fairly large, as the patient reclines on it. It examines portions of the spine and hip. The second type is small and the patient inserts an extremity into it. DEXA devices do not produce images, but because they are designed to detect osteoporosis, which more commonly affects women, they may be included in women's imaging centers.

Replacing an atom in a biologically active molecule with a radioactive isotope of that atom creates a radioactively labeled molecule. By selecting the appropriate molecule, different functions of tissues and organs can be evaluated by examining their radioactivity. The use of very sensitive radiation detectors means that the amount of such a radioactive labeled compound (or radiopharmaceutical) that needs to be administered is small. The simplest form of nuclear medicine examination is to determine an organ's uptake of a radiopharmaceutical. Evaluation of the thyroid is done this way. In this case, the radiopharmaceutical is radioactive iodine. Iodine is aggressively taken up by the thyroid gland, and comparing the amount taken up to the amount administered can reveal if the thyroid function is normal. This is a nonimaging study and is accomplished by having the patient take the radioactive iodine and then after some time placing a radiation detector over the thyroid gland and counting the radioactivity (in terms of the number of radioactive decays). The detector is usually a scintillator, a crystalline or plastic material that fluoresces when struck by the emitted gamma rays. The fluorescence is detected by a photomultiplier tube.

By scanning a very narrow aperture scintillator across the thyroid, the physician can determine the radioactivity of small areas of the gland. The amount of activity can be used to expose a spot on a piece of film in proportion to the number of counts seen in a given time. In this way, a map of the radioactive iodine distribution in the thyroid is produced. Tumors in the thyroid may take up more iodine than normal thyroid tissue and will show up with more radioactivity (a "hot" nodule). There may also be tumors in the thyroid that are composed of cells that do not function like normal thyroid cells and do not take up the radioactive iodine (a "cold" nodule). Malignant nodules of the thyroid tend to be cold (though this is not always the case).

Because radiopharmaceuticals can be tailored to organ functions, nuclear medicine examinations are more often functional than purely anatomic. There are, for example, radiopharmaceuticals that are taken up by the liver and excreted in the bile made by the liver. Bile travels through the bile ducts to the gallbladder, then through a duct to the intestine. If the bile is radioactively labeled, whether it gets into the gallbladder (it does not when the gallbladder is inflamed) or the intestine can be determined by imaging the radioactivity.

The amount of radioactive material administered for nuclear medicine studies has to be safe, so it is quite small. Film is not nearly sensitive enough to detect this radiation. A scintillator, though, is very sensitive and will produce a small light flash for every gamma ray that hits it. Nuclear medicine relies on "gamma cameras" that consist of a large scintillator and a number of photomultiplier detectors (figure 6–15A). Circuitry allows the camera to determine where the gamma ray hit the scintillator, so position can be determined. Because the gamma rays may come out at many angles, a collimator is placed in front of the scintillator. The collimator typically consists of a lead plate with many holes in it. Gamma rays coming in at an off angle will be stopped by the lead. While this decreases the efficiency of the gamma camera, it also very much improves the resulting image. The gamma rays coming in at off angles do not carry any useful position information. For example, a gamma ray may have been emitted from the radioisotope in the left lobe of the liver but cross all the way over to the right before striking the scintillator. Without a collimator, that gamma ray would have been counted among those actually coming from the right lobe of the liver.

Typical nuclear medicine studies done currently are cardiac, thyroid, bone, liver, and lung scans. In the latter, usually two radiopharmaceuticals are used. One (usually xenon–133) is inhaled and shows whether the lung is ventilated; such processes as pneumonia and collapse of lung segments will prevent the radioactive xenon from getting into them. The second radiopharmaceutical (usually technetium–99m tagged to microaggregated albumin) is injected intravenously and is carried to the lungs in the bloodstream. The small particles of albumin carry the radioactive isotope through the lung circulation. A gamma camera records the activity of the ventilation and perfusion aspects of the scan. Since the isotopes emit gamma rays of a different energy, they can be differentiated by the gamma camera, so a ventilation image and perfusion image are made. Mismatches, particularly sections of the lung that are ventilated but not perfused, are suspicious for pulmonary emboli. These will block blood flow to segments of the lung but not the airflow. Nonventilated but perfused mismatches are more likely to represent an air space problem, such as a pneumonia. Recently, the availability of high-speed helical CT is reducing the number of lung scans done, as the CT scan can directly image the blood vessels of the lung and show emboli in them.

Cardiac nuclear medicine scans are used to examine both the heart muscle and motion of the heart. The perfusion of the heart muscle can be evaluated by using thallium-201 (usually as thallous chloride). Thallium is a potassium analog, and potassium is taken up by myocardial cells. Damaged heart muscle will not take up the thallium at the same rate as normal heart muscle. By using the electrocardiogram to determine when data are collected from the heart, a series of frames can be constructed at different points in the cardiac cycle. By playing these back as a movie, the multiple gated (MUGA) scans can show wall motion (which is abnormal in a number of cardiac diseases), and measurements can be used to determine the sizes of the heart chambers and how much of the blood is ejected with each contraction (the ejection fraction). Another type of cardiac imaging is done with a dose of radiopharmaceutical given very rapidly. Imaging is then done over the heart with fast data acquisition. As a result, the action of the right and left sides of the heart can be seen separately, something that is difficult to do with a MUGA scan.

The methods of computed tomography can be applied to radionuclide imaging. The same sort of projection data can be acquired by rotating the gamma camera head around the patient, and reconstructed into cross sections. The reconstruction is more difficult because the radiopharmaceutical is usually not uniformly distributed, so the emitted gamma rays are attenuated differently depending on that distribution. Data acquisition is more efficient if more than one gamma camera is used. In this way, the emitted gamma rays can be simultaneously acquired. Typically, two, three, or four gamma camera heads are used. This method is known as single photon emission computed tomography, or SPECT. When SPECT cameras are combined with a CT scanner, it is known as SPECT/CT (figure 6-15B).

The area of nuclear medicine currently generating the most interest is positron emission tomography, or PET (figure 6-16). Positrons are anti-electrons–that is, they are like electrons but with a positive charge. Some unstable nuclei emit positrons as they decay. A positron travels through tissue but very quickly encounters an electron. When the two collide, they annihilate each other and the energy is given off as two photons (these could also be called gamma rays). An important property of this positron–electron

Figure 6-15A Principles of nuclear medicine. ECRI, *Healthcare Product Comparison System* (Plymouth Meeting, PA): ECRI, 2005.

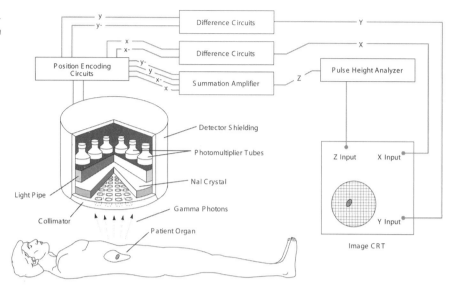

Figure 6-15B SPECT/CT. Image courtesy of Philips Medical Systems.

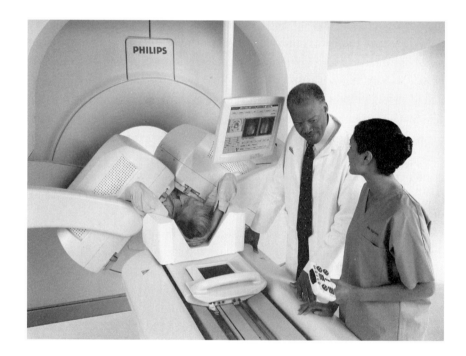

annihilation is that the two photons are emitted exactly 180 degrees apart. A pair of radiation detectors on either side of the body will detect these two photons simultaneously (they travel so fast—at the speed of light—that the slight differences in position in the body do not make for a significant departure from being detected simultaneously). The pair of radiation detectors use a circuit called a coincidence detector that rejects any events that are not simultaneously seen by both. The fact that these photons are emitted 180 degrees apart helps simplify the reconstruction process since an event detected simultaneously must have come from somewhere along the straight line between the two detectors.

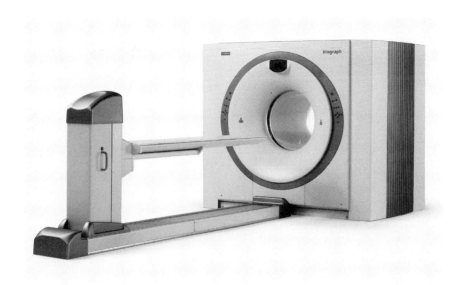

Figure 6-16 PET/CT. Image courtesy of Siemens Medical Solutions.

There are a number of useful isotopes that are positron emitters. Oxygen-15, carbon-11, and nitrogen-13 are readily incorporated into sugars or amino acids. Fluorine-18 is frequently made into fluorodeoxyglucose, which can be used for imaging brain function since glucose is the neurons' "fuel." All of these isotopes have short half-lives (oxygen-15, for example, has a half-life of 2.1 minutes), which places some requirements on PET imaging facilities. Either very large amounts of the isotopes have to be delivered for use, or a way to make the isotopes has to be nearby. To make the positron emitters is not trivial and typically requires a cyclotron to bombard stable nuclei with helium-3 or helium-4 nuclei. This adds considerably to the space requirements and cost of a PET facility. Newer cyclotrons are reasonably compact, and the low-energy types (which operate around 11 MeV) can be installed with reasonable shielding. The shields (often called "surface shields") are multilayer composite devices on tracks. The shields are closed for normal operation and can be opened for maintenance. Even these "lightweight" systems have weights in the 85,000-pound (39,000 kg) range. Larger, research-type cyclotrons, such as high-energy radiotherapy machines, require very heavy shielding. This shielding usually has to be built in and is often referred to as a "vault" since the construction is similar to an explosion-resistant bank vault. Some facilities have moved to placing cyclotrons off-site with a pneumatic tube or other fast delivery device for the radionuclide. Such delivery systems will have their own shielding and safety considerations.

Operation of a cyclotron and the PET scanner itself requires experienced, expert personnel. Medical physicists who have trained in cyclotron and PET scanner operation, safety, and quality assurance are needed, as are nuclear medicine technologists who can operate the scanner. A radiopharmacist or radiochemist familiar with synthesizing positron-emitter-labeled radiopharmaceuticals is a must.

Despite these difficulties, there is great interest in PET imaging because the isotopes are easily used to label tumor antibodies and substrates that organs or glands metabolize. PET scans can be very sensitive at detecting malignant metastases that are too small to see even with high-resolution CT. Detecting solitary, small metastases in the liver or lymph nodes may prove to allow for early surgery that aims to be curative, or follow chemotherapy to determine effectiveness.

The most recent development in PET is a combination of the functional imaging of PET with the high-resolution anatomic imaging of CT. Combined PET–CT machines are now commercially available, and a few PET–MR devices are beginning to appear for limited applications. While expensive, this combination is proving to be very powerful in the detection and evaluation of malignancies since tumors and metastases can be very accurately localized. The future for PET and PET–CT is also very promising as molecular medicine and molecular imaging provide more specific and more accurate ways to detect and localize disease and dysfunction. PET–CT does add an additional level of complexity in operation, as most nuclear medicine experts who are trained to interpret PET scans likely have little training in reading neuro and body CT. Similarly, most neuroradiologists and body CT specialists do not have enough training to read PET scans. Some centers with PET–CT have resorted to the obvious solution: joint reading sessions are scheduled and experienced specialists from both domains interpret the studies together.[29]

Film Processing

Until relatively recently, and to some degree still, most medical imaging was recorded on film, to both display and store the results. For radiography, film is also the acquisition device. With digital imaging equipment in film-based practices, the images are typically filmed using a laser printer. The resulting film is processed and viewed as other films are. Over the past few years, some laser printers have been replaced by "dry" laser systems. These use film that has a single emulsion layer (as is the case with many laser printer films), but conventional processing is replaced by a waterless development process.

Film-based departments and practices had, to a large extent, the handling and movement of film as a major design factor. Aside from the film library, there were the darkrooms and processors, motorized film changers for viewing, and many light boxes around the hospital. The darkroom and associated labor were eliminated with the introduction of daylight processing systems. These systems allowed cassettes to be unloaded into a processor or holding magazine in daylight.

Early automated film processors needed water within a specific temperature range for the wash. Later machines could take cold water (though filtering was used for both), as they had heaters that could raise the water's temperature. The processor wastewater used to be drained into a facility's sewer lines. However, changes in many state and federal regulations meant that the silver had to be removed prior to allowing the wastewater into public sewers. Silver recovery systems are now used on the waste lines of X-ray film processors that use a conventional water wash.

As many imaging techniques became digital, the image capture and recording processes were separated. This meant that to make film, the images had to be exposed onto film. Early film recording cameras used a cathode ray tube and optics to transfer the image on the tube to film. Because of resolution requirements, these film recorders (or multiformat cameras) were usually used for small image matrix modalities (CT, ultrasound, MRI, nuclear medicine). The development of computed radiography included laser film printers. These could reproduce the resolution of the CR plate onto film. Laser film printers became a standard item in most hospitals, and many are still in operation. They were manufactured by most of the firms making film and imaging equipment. To improve throughput from laser film printers, they could be coupled directly to a film processor. If this was not done, the laser film printer could stack the exposed film in a magazine that could be unloaded into a processor in a darkroom. As described in the beginning of this section, dry-processing laser film printers have replaced many conventional laser printers with wet processors attached. The advantage is that they can be located without having to provide a source of water, a drain, or a wastewater treatment (silver recovery) unit.

The next chapter will discuss image management systems and the reasons for replacement of film with electronic viewing will be described in more detail. Recent changes in practice have seen an accelerating transition from film to electronic imaging. Despite this, it is not certain that all medical imaging use of film will disappear, much as electronic documents have not replaced books.

Notes

1. A. B. Wolbarst, *Physics of Radiology*, 2nd ed. (Madison, WI: Medical Physics Publishing, 2005), 1–2.

2. H. K. Huang, *Elements of Digital Radiology* (Englewood Cliffs, NJ: Prentice-Hall, 1987), 83–86.

3. Wolbarst, 386–88; H. Oosterwijk, "CR and DR detector technology," in *PACS Fundamentals* (Aubrey, TX: OTech, 2004), 102–7; J. A. Rowlands and J. Yorkston, "Flat panel detectors for digital radiography," in J. Beutel, H. L. Kundel, and R. L. Van Metter, eds., *Handbook of Medical Imaging*, Vol. I: *Physics and Psychophysics* (Bellingham, WA: SPIE, 2000), 223–44.

4. T. N. Cornsweet, *Visual Perception* (New York: Academic Press, 1970), 365–83; P. G. J. Barten, *Contrast Sensitivity of the Human Eye and Its Effects on Image Quality* (Bellingham, WA: SPIE, 1999); E. H. Adelson, "Lightness perception and lightness illusions," in M. Gazzaniga, ed., *The New Cognitive Neurosciences*, 2nd ed. (Cambridge, MA: MIT Press, 2000), 339–51.

5. J. Jiang, S. Lim, and M. Oh, "Technology development and production of flat panel displays in Korea," *Proceedings of the IEEE* 90, 4 (2002): 501–13.

6. Huang, 313–23.

7. M. J. Dennis, "Following time-dependent processes with fluoroscopy," in Wolbarst, 371–82.

8. Wolbarst, 315.

9. National Council on Radiation Protection and Measurements, *Structural Shielding Design and Evaluation for Medical Use of X-Rays and Gamma Rays of Energies Up to 10MeV*, Report No. 49 (Bethesda, MD: NCRP, 1976).

10. B. Partik and C. Schafer-Prokop, "Digital radiology in chest imaging," in W. Hruby, ed., *Digital (R)evolution in Radiology* (Vienna: Springer-Verlag, 2001), 189–203.

11. L. L. Humphrey, M. Helfand, B. K. Chan, and S. H. Woolf, "Breast cancer screening: A summary of the evidence for the U.S. Preventive Services Task Force," *Annals of Internal Medicine* 137 (2002): 347–60; S. W. Fletcher and J. G. Elmore, "Mammographic screening for breast cancer," *New England Journal of Medicine* 348 (2003): 1672–80; Institute of Medicine, *Saving Women's Lives: Integration and Innovation: A Framework for Progress in Early Detection and Diagnosis of Breast Cancer* (Washington, DC: National Academies Press, 2005).

12. Y. Jiang, R. M. Nishikawa, R. A. Schmidt, C. E. Metz, M. L. Giger, and K. Doi, "Improving breast cancer diagnosis with computer-aided diagnosis," *Academic Radiology* 6 (1999): 22–33.

13. E. D. Pisano, C. Gatsonis, E. Hendrick, M. Yaffe, et al. (for the DMIST Group), "Diagnostic performance of digital versus film mammography for breast-cancer screening," *New England Journal of Medicine* 353 (2005): 1773–83.

14. E. Chesson, "1.5T MRI: Friend to physician and patient alike," *Health Imaging and IT* 3, 10 (2005): 40–42; F. V. Coakley and B. N. Joe, "MDCT: How many rows is enough?" *Decisions in Imaging Economics* 18, 5 (2005): 25–28.

15. K. K. Shung, M. B. Smith, and B. M. W. Tsui, *Principles of Medical Imaging* (San Diego: Academic Press, 1992), 55–58.

16. A. C. Kak and M. Slaney, *Principles of Computerized Tomographic Imaging* (New York: IEEE Press, 1988).

17. R. H. Bracewell and A. C. Riddle, "Inversion of fan beam scans in radio astronomy," *Astrophysical Journal* 150 (1967): 427–34.

18. S. Webb, "Historical experiments predating commercially available computed tomography," *British Journal of Radiology* 65, 777 (1992): 835–37.

19. A. M. Cormack, "Early 2-dimensional reconstruction and recent topics stemming from it," Nobel lecture, December 1979, available at http://nobelprize.org/medicine/laureates/1979/cormack-lecture.pdf.

20. Wolbarst, 399–415.

21. D. J. Goodenough, "Tomographic imaging," in Beutel, Kundel, and Van Metter, eds., 511–54.

22. J. A. Zagzebski, "Ultrasound imaging IV: Biological effects and safety," in Wolbarst, 508–10.

23. J. A. Zagzebski, "Ultrasound imaging III: Image production and image quality," in Wolbarst, 496–507.

24. W. J. Zweibel, *Introduction to Vascular Ultrasonography* (Philadelphia: W. B. Saunders, 1992); M. Hennerici and D. Neuerburg-Heusler, *Vascular Diagnosis with Ultrasound* (Stuttgart: Georg Thieme Verlag, 1998).

25. J. Hindley, W. M. Gedroyc, L. Regan, et al., "MRI guidance of focused ultrasound therapy of uterine fibroids: Early results," *American Journal of Roentgenology* 183 (2004): 1713–9.

26. Z.-P. Liang and P. C. Lauterbur, *Principles of Magnetic Resonance Imaging* (New York: IEEE Press, 2000).

27. F. G. Shellock and J. V. Crues III, "Commentary: MR safety and the American College of Radiology white paper," *American Journal of Roentgenology* 178 (2002): 1349–52.

28. V. Pizzella, S. Della Penna, C. Del Gratta, and G. L. Romani, "SQUID systems for biomagnetic imaging," *Superconductor Science and Technology* 14 (2001): R79–R114.

29. Wolbarst, chapters 13, 41, 42; S. Bacharach, "Gamma ray imaging IV: Nuclear cardiology, SPECT, and PET," in Wolbarst, 442–49.

CHAPTER 7

Image Management
Systems

Almost twenty years ago, Dr. Marvin Haskin asked attendees at the annual meeting of the International Society for Optical Engineering (SPIE) if they had any idea how many X-ray light boxes were in their facilities.[1] No one had any idea. The author of this chapter took up the challenge and began counting on the ground floor of his hospital. By the time he reached the third floor (of eighteen) he had gotten to a thousand and decided to quit, as the number was clearly quite large.

What this says is that there is a need to view medical images in diverse locations and that many healthcare providers, besides those who produce the images, need to see the images as a part of patient care. In the early days of radiology, before there was even a specialty of radiology, most of the images were of great interest to physicians, as they provided a novel view of a patient's anatomy and disease. Since film was the image capture, display, and storage medium, there was usually only one copy of a film. If the film was displayed on the radiologist's light box for reading, it could not simultaneously be on a light box in the operating room, where a surgeon might want to see it to guide a surgical approach. This led to systems that were used to track the location of films and who borrowed them. Film libraries were established, and these rapidly consumed space in a department as the number of film jackets grew steadily.[2] Personnel were hired to staff the library, often for at least two eight-hour shifts per day to provide support for evening and emergency department needs.

The demand for imaging meant that a first-come, first-served manner of determining order of examinations to be done by radiology would not work. Increasing specialization in radiology also meant that some examinations would be performed only on certain days or at certain times. The earliest scheduling systems were pencil-and-paper-based and involved schedule books similar to those used by many physicians' offices.

Specialization, though, made this more complicated, as resources had to be scheduled as well. As a result, many departments had multiple schedule books, one for each specialty area. The problem with this was cross–coordinating studies. Since it is common for patients to need more than one imaging study, scheduling them so that they could be done on the same day was advantageous for the patient, the referring physician, and the radiologist. Accomplishing this with multiple scheduling books was difficult and required, typically, that the patient or referring physician keep track of what examinations had been scheduled, so as to avoid conflicts. Besides date and time, some examinations also had to be done in a particular order, or could not be done on the same day as another examination. For example, an upper or lower gastrointestinal study involving barium (see the "Fluoroscopy" section in chapter 6) could not be done prior to an abdominal CT study because the high–density barium used for GI work interfered with the CT study. Similarly, the very dilute barium used for abdominal CT could cause problems if an upper GI study was to follow.

Examination scheduling had to interact with the film library functions also. When a radiologist interprets a study, one of the most important things to have is the prior examination (if one was done) for comparison.[3] If a different examination of the same anatomy (for example, an intravenous urogram for the kidneys done prior to a CT of the abdomen) had been done, the radiologist would ideally also want to correlate the results of that study. While this could be done ad hoc–that is, the radiologist would call the film library to retrieve the prior studies for each study being read–this is cumbersome and adds a delay that most radiologists find unacceptable. If the schedule is known by the film library, the clerks can retrieve the prior studies ahead of time and make them available when the new examination is read.

The studies on patients are done by technologists. Typically, they take the patient into the examination room, perform the study, check the films/images for completeness and correctness, and then either perform additional imaging or dismiss the patient. On occasion, if the patient was scheduled for multiple studies, they would send, or take, the patient to the next section of the department. They would usually complete a log sheet noting which patient had been done and what the start and end times were. They then would take the films to the film library, where the library clerks would create a new examination folder and add that to the master jacket (if the patient did not have a master jacket, the library clerk would create that). The study films, relevant other films, and paperwork would then be put together and taken to the radiologist for interpretation.[4]

The "product" of diagnostic radiologists is the radiology report. It is the description of findings and the interpretation of them that gives important information to the referring physician, typically answering the clinical question posed. Over the years, the basic mechanism of producing the radiology report has been for the radiologist to dictate it and have a transcriptionist type it. One transcriptionist per radiologist is wasteful of transcription effort, as the transcriptionist can usually type a report more quickly than a radiologist can interpret a study. For this reason, various dictation systems were developed.[5] The first systems were based on the dictation systems used by businesses and evolved as that technology did. Various magnetic belts, cassette tapes, and digital storage systems have been, and are still, in use. The use of these systems allows for transcription services to be kept continuously busy typing reports. The disadvantage of these systems is the turnaround time. Usually reports were transcribed overnight and returned to the radiologist for signature (needed since the radiology report is a legal document) the next day. The dictation/transcription information had to be correlated with both scheduling and the film library—the former because it is important to know when an examination was performed, and dictation of the results provides a positive indication that the examination was done and was interpreted. If the referring physician called scheduling wanting to know the status of a patient's studies, the schedulers would know the status if they had information from the technologists (examination done) and dictation/transcription system (examination read). The film library needed to know about dictated studies because these would then be put in a "dictated" area and, when the report was finalized, a copy of the report would be put in the master jacket and the jacket returned to storage.

No radiology department would work if its personnel could not be paid. The revenue a radiology department generates is typically based on two things: the actual performance of the examination and the radiologist's interpretation of it. For this reason, most departments issue two bills for any given examination. In a hospital setting, when the hospital owns the radiology department equipment and space and pays the technologists, schedulers, and film librarians, the hospital usually collects the technical component of the bill, and the radiologists collect the professional component separately. To bill for an examination, a number of pieces of information are needed: what examination was done, for what reason, when it was done, by whom it was interpreted, and the results. For some examinations, insurance carriers may require specific information about the equipment used to perform the examination. Usually the technical component of a bill is generated when the examination is completed. The professional component is billed when the radiologist finalizes (signs) the report. So information from the technologists, film librarians, transcriptionists, and schedulers is all needed for billing.

Radiology Information Systems

As should be apparent, much information flow is necessary if a radiology department is to function both clinically and fiscally. With small examination volumes, many of these management functions could be accomplished with paper-and-pencil methods. However, as radiology became more integrated into medical care, management of the information by paper–and–pencil methods began to require increasingly large numbers of personnel. Fortunately, the growth of the radiology's management needs paralleled the developments in computer engineering.

Until the advent of time–shared computing and then distributed computing, computer operations were typically batch–oriented.[6] Large accounting jobs, billing generation, and even scientific computing were accomplished by submitting jobs to a large computer center, having the job run and output created, then retrieving the output. Time sharing meant that users could access the computer directly, allowing jobs to be submitted and results obtained very quickly. In addition, some computer languages (e.g., BASIC) were designed to be run in real time. A user could enter a program and data and get results nearly as quickly as the data could be entered. A major break from the large central computer paradigm came about through the introduction of the minicomputer. These small computers moved computing from large data centers to offices and laboratories.[7]

The availability of the minicomputer meant that significant computing power could be had for a reasonable price (tens to hundreds of thousands of dollars, as opposed to millions for large mainframe computers). The relatively low cost of minicomputers meant that computing power could be had at the departmental, rather than hospital, level. The specialized needs of radiology (and other departments that moved large amounts of information, such as clinical laboratories) opened a market for software that could run on minicomputers and automate at least some of the manual procedures. The other aspect of minicomputers that was important is that they often had real-time operating systems. That is, the computer's software could accept and process data in a nearly continuous manner; no batching was needed.[8]

Not long after the introduction of the minicomputer, early pioneers began to develop computer systems to help manage radiology departments.[9] This led the way for an industry based on software supporting radiology management. It was evident to the early radiology information system (RIS) vendors that the basic functions of a radiology department–scheduling, film library, report management, and billing–were amenable to solution with a minicomputer and software. One major push for the development of radiology information systems came about through interested radiologists and computer scientists developing a set of functional specifications for what an RIS needed to do.[10] This eventually led to one of the major (and still widely used, though much modernized) radiology information systems.

Radiology information systems were accepted relatively quickly, as their value was obvious to both radiologists and managers. Instead of moving information between the sections of a department using handwritten log sheets, memos, or forms, information could be moved electronically. Another advantage of radiology information systems is that they use a database for the various data they manage. This makes it possible to search the database for trends and other information useful to managers. A report generator either is built into an RIS or is available from third-party vendors. In paper-and-pencil operations, such reports would often be too cumbersome to generate. For example, to determine if a particular examination type was showing an increase or decrease over time, the daily log sheets would have to be searched for that examination type and the results tabulated–all by hand.

Most radiology information systems now use existing database software rather than re-creating the functions widely available there. What the RIS developers do is to create their own database structures and tables using commercial software. The advantage of this is that third-party database tools can be used to perform searches and generate reports. The RIS vendor does not have to create these tools.

Early RISs used character-based computer terminals to provide functions to users. These terminals usually consisted of a cathode ray tube monitor and a keyboard with most of the electronics built into the monitor case. They communicated with the central computer over serial communications interfaces. Typically, they used the RS–232 standard to send the bits representing text characters as a sequence of bits and to receive a sequence of such bits into a character displayed on the screen.[11] These were often referred to as "dumb terminals" because they had no processing capability on their own–they relied on the computer to which they were connected to provide text handling.

The only advantage of serial communication is that it was readily adaptable to telephone lines. For sending data from the terminal to a computer, a device called a modem (short for "modulator–demodulator") turned the serial string of bits into tones that could be handled by a telephone system. On the receiving end, the modem turned the tones back into bits at the computer. These were bidirectional devices, so the computer could send and receive data. Modems are still used, but they operate at much higher speeds than the early RIS terminals.

With the development of computer networks and the Internet, communication became fast enough to transmit sufficient data to enable graphics to be sent and received. When Tim Berners-Lee developed the World Wide Web, a key piece of that invention was the development of a language that could specify how information would be coded for display.[12] The language, called Hypertext Markup Language (HTML), allowed programmers to specify in what font, what size, what color, and where on the page text should appear. For graphical elements–drawings or pictures–the language also allowed for them to be positioned and sized on the display page. Critical to this was the standardization of HTML so that different computers could all interpret it correctly. Browsers such as Mosaic, followed by Netscape, Internet Explorer, Mozilla, and Firefox, took user input in the form of typed text, clicks on buttons, and clicks on links and translated them into actions by the computer.[13] The browser would then translate the output of the computer back into an updated display. Hyperlinks were one important facet of the World Wide Web; HTML provided an easy way to create a text display that, when clicked on by a user, would link to another Web site. This allowed for very complex, nested Web environments.

The RIS vendors gradually began to take advantage of the Web functions and created systems that replaced terminals with personal computers and ran the user interface to the RIS on a Web browser. While this seems to be an expensive change, the computer could be tasked to do several things, so communicating with the RIS became only one of the things it did. Rapid developments in microprocessors, memory, disk storage, and displays rapidly brought the cost of personal computers down to the level at which "dumb terminals" originally sold. Even if an RIS still needs a terminal for users, software that emulates a terminal in the computer is widely available and, when run, gives the user a window on the computer screen that looks, and operates, like a terminal.

From a planning standpoint, hardware implementation of a radiology information system varies widely. For smaller RIS implementations, the entire system may be in a single electronics rack (typically 72 inches high, 24 to 30 inches deep, and 19 inches wide) and sited within the radiology department. There may be supporting hardware needed, however, mainly connections to the network to which the various personal computers are attached. Since the RIS is a critical system, it usually has backup power and, to stay on through a transition from normal to backup power, may also be on an uninterruptible power supply. The RIS vendor will have specifications about the space needed for the computer but may refer an architect to the computer vendor for specifics of heat load, maximum operating temperature, and power quality.

A larger RIS may occupy several racks, typically because it may have redundant computers and storage, or the storage component is large and fills a rack by itself. With the increasing capacity and decreasing size of disk drives, very large amounts of storage (several terabytes) may occupy only 5.25 inches of rack height.[14] There are reasons besides space for siting an RIS computer system in a larger computer room, particularly if it is in a data center that the hospital already uses. Such centers tend to have strict access control for security, emergency or uninterruptible power, HVAC designed for the equipment, raised flooring to accommodate cabling, and easy access to the hospital's communications networks. An important aspect is also that such computer rooms are usually staffed twenty-four hours per day, every day, because of the critical nature of the hospital's information systems.

Image Management Systems

With most of radiology's image-producing equipment generating digital images, the development of low-cost computing and communications hardware also meant that film could be replaced with electronic means of capturing, displaying, and storing images. The first efforts at trying to do this were in the early 1980s.[15] The first scientific meeting on the subject of filmless medical imaging was held in 1982.[16] The term most commonly used to describe these systems is an acronym, *PACS*, which stands for "picture archiving and communications systems." This term has been criticized for not including the management of the images, but efforts to change to a more descriptive acronym have been unsuccessful.

The early idea behind PACS was to capture digital images from the imaging equipment, communicate it to where it was needed, display it electronically (another function missing from the acronym), and store the images on electronic media. The earliest published paper that this author knows of is from 1979, and it describes much of what modern PACS do.[17] Implementing these systems, however, turned out to be more complicated than the early pioneers thought. Affordable communications networks were barely able to handle the load of digital data that radiology departments produce. Storage was also expensive, though most studies showed that it was cheaper than handling, processing, and storing film.[18] Recall that in the 1980s, memory in a minicomputer was usually far less than a megabyte (typically 64 kilobytes) and that the common storage medium, an 8-inch floppy disk, held some 256 kilobytes. A top-end digital display had a resolution of 1024×1024 pixels (a 1-megapixel display) and cost about U.S. $20,000. Computer hard disk drives had capacities of several megabytes each. How small this amount of storage is becomes evident when image sizes are considered: a single CT image in digital form needs about 0.5 megabyte, while a CR image uses 6 to 10 megabytes.

Despite these formidable obstacles, a number of institutions developed prototypes that showed the concept was viable.[19] Very rapid advances in computer processing power combined with exponentially falling prices made PACS increasingly practical. In a now famous paper written in the very early days of integrated circuit electronics, Gordon Moore (a co-founder of the Intel Corporation) stated that the number of transistors on an integrated circuit chip would double every eighteen months to two years.[20] The paper was published in 1965, and what is now known as "Moore's law" has held nearly true for the past thirty years. What this means is that modern microprocessor circuits consist of millions of transistors, all on a piece of silicon about $\frac{3}{8}$ of an inch on a side.

Moore's law affected more than just the computer. Faster, cheaper processors drove communications speeds up and costs down; memory was made of transistors, so it also increased in capacity and fell in cost; storage devices matched this trend as well. Consumer electronics helped drive this movement (no one reading this book would likely be able to afford a personal computer, CD player, or high-definition television if the cost per transistor were at 1970s prices).

The end result of this real revolution in electronics was that the hardware to build a PACS was affordable. This was largely true in the late 1980s, so it is interesting to ask why actual systems did not appear until about ten years later.

The Need for Standards

The first digital imaging equipment, mostly nuclear medicine and CT systems, stored their images in proprietary formats. Before systems were connected by networks, CT machines were often sold with "independent consoles." These allowed the images to be viewed in "soft copy" so that they could be reviewed quickly; the patient would not have to wait until the films were printed to be told they were done. Radiologists discovered that they could also perform functions on these consoles that could not be done easily with film. Such things as measurements could be done with film, but adjusting the gray scale of the displayed image could not. The importance of this is that CT images have more information than can be displayed (or perceived) on a CRT or printed film, so either images have to be printed with different gray-scale settings (this used to be done routinely) or the image has to be displayed electronically so the gray scale can be adjusted. What manufacturers wanted to avoid was having these independent consoles used to view images from a competitor's imaging equipment. They believed that enabling this would cut into their sales of both imaging equipment and independent consoles.

Users of imaging equipment, particularly radiologists and researchers in radiology, saw these proprietary formats as an impediment to their work and academic pursuits. They had to either agree to nondisclosure or "break" the formats and use the unauthorized results. The problem with the latter approach was that updated versions of software would usually result in changes in the storage formats and render obsolete any custom software developed by the users. From the earliest PACS meeting there were papers arguing that a standard format for images should be developed and that such a standard should be open and publicly available.[21] About a year later, radiologists, engineers, and physicists representing imaging equipment users convinced the American College of Radiology and the Bureau of Radiation Health (now the Center for Devices and Radiological Health) of the Food and Drug Administration to discuss potential standards efforts with the manufacturers. The ACR and FDA approached the National Electrical Manufacturers Association (NEMA), which represented imaging equipment manufacturers, about developing standards for digital images and interfaces to imaging equipment. From meetings between these organizations, the ACR-NEMA Digital Imaging and Communications Standards Committee (DICOM) was established. The first meeting was held in November 1983.[22] Within two years, the ACR-NEMA Committee published its first standard, "Digital Imaging and Communications in Medicine." This defined both the format of digital images and a point-to-point interface so that equipment from disparate manufacturers could be connected and could exchange information. An updated version of the standard was published in 1988, but by that time, advances in networks for computers and computers themselves had advanced tremendously. Other specialties in medicine, notably ophthalmology, dentistry, cardiology, and pathology, were increasingly interested in using digital images.[23] Many manufacturers outside of the United States were also participating in the ACR–NEMA Committee, but users could not because of the committee's established rules. A decision was made to expand the committee to other nonradiological professional organizations and non–U.S. manufacturers. The ACR–NEMA name no longer represented the makeup of the committee, and so its name was changed to the DICOM Standards Committee. DICOM was the acronym adopted for new standards that the Committee would produce. In 1992, the first portions of the new standard were published and defined the network interface and protocol to be used. Rather than define a new network standard, the decision had been made to use existing communications standards. The most ubiquitous standard (still true as of this writing) is that used for most local area networks (LANs): IEEE 802.3, commonly known as Ethernet. For the protocol, nothing was more widely used than the transmission control protocol/Internet protocol (TCP/IP), so this was adopted as well.

Since that time, DICOM has become the dominant standard for communication of medical digital images. It is in use worldwide, and all the major imaging equipment manufacturers employ it.[24] This made a large difference to PACS, since the data structure of digital images became vendor–independent, and mass–market LAN interfaces were used. DICOM has expanded what it standardizes, and DICOM storage media exist along with a standard so that display devices can be uniformly calibrated. Images from other specialties using digital imaging are now supported.[25]

For planners and architects, the importance of DICOM is not so much what it does, but that sites will employ it and that it does not require any specialized communications hardware. Local area network designs for hospitals and other healthcare facilities can support DICOM if they use the TCP/IP protocol and IEEE 802.3 (and its compatible variants, including wireless).

What Does a PACS Do?

Fundamentally, a PACS replaces the functions of film management. Images generated by equipment are captured by the PACS (where DICOM is most frequently used), moved over networks to where they are needed, displayed on workstations to be interpreted, and stored in a digital storage facility. However, these basic operations need a number of support functions to work as film does. For example, how does a radiologist know what studies are to be read? With film, the answer was usually self–evident: studies to be read were put up by film library clerks on motorized film viewers together with prior studies if needed, or were placed into carts from which the radiologist would pick. With workstations and no film library clerks, what replaces the functions performed by those clerks?

Technologists identified film studies by flashing the name on the films. The film flash cards are generated by the RIS as a result of at least some typed input by radiology schedulers or receptionists, but in a PACS environment, the technologists have to type this identifying information into the machine. This is effectively a shift of work, and in this case a detrimental one. There are other examples of work shifting because of PACS.[26] For example, film library clerks often learned how radiologists liked to have films displayed–that is, where they wanted current and prior studies placed on light boxes, which views in which locations, et cetera. Since radiologists often differ in these preferences, the film library clerks would put up (or "hang") films based on who would be reading them. How is a PACS workstation to do this? Without the ability to do this automatically, the radiologist will have to spend time moving the electronic images around.[27] For technologists, radiologists, and staff, even small amounts of time added to tasks can be significant because of the large volume of examinations that most radiology departments perform. For example, just ten seconds added to a task that is needed for 500,000 examinations per year amounts to nearly 174 eight-hour workdays.

This inability to automate functions when moving from film to PACS is one of the factors that held back the proliferation of the systems. It is difficult to make a good business case for PACS if the lack of automation increases workload rather than decreases it. While DICOM made it possible to get images from imaging equipment to workstations and storage equipment, it did not fully address the issue of moving needed information between systems.

The RIS and hospital information system (HIS) domains also have standards. HL7 is a standard widely used by such information system vendors.[28] It enables information to be moved between patient registration, billing, scheduling, and other systems or system components. One of the first working groups of the DICOM Standards Committee to be chartered was one directed at HIS–RIS–PACS interfaces. Visionaries in this working group began looking at, and developing information models of, the information exchange that would be needed between a PACS and RIS or HIS.[29] What this working group accomplished was not widely implemented, mostly because users were not requesting RIS–PACS interfaces. As more sites installed PACS, however, the need for standards to cover the interchange of information became more apparent. Eventually, organizations representing the users and manufacturers of PACS (the Radiological Society of North America, RSNA) and HIS and RIS (the Health Information Management Systems Society, HIMSS) decided to help with the standardization efforts. The resulting effort, known as Integrating the Healthcare Enterprise (IHE), began by planning demonstrations of integration functions at major radiological and information systems meetings. The IHE decided not to write standards themselves, but to rely on the existing DICOM and HL7 work. The various IHE committees developed clinical scenarios and what was needed from the standards to support automation of such scenarios. The resulting needs were turned into "profiles" that described how DICOM and HL7 data structures and functions could be used to implement a solution that would replace manual processes. An example familiar to most hospitals is what to do about the patient seen in the emergency department who is unconscious and unknown. Imaging and laboratory studies cannot wait until the person is identified, so they are often done using a pseudonym (e.g., "unknown male"). Once the person is identified, the problem is how to go back in the RIS and PACS and change the identification. For the most part, patient identification functions are handled by an HIS, which, through established HL7 protocols, passes the information to an RIS. What the IHE defined was how to then pass the information to a PACS. Prior to this, the update of PACS information from an RIS was typically done through manual data entry, a process known to introduce errors (name misspellings, transposed identification number digits, etc.). The IHE effort is ongoing and is steadily expanding the profiles needed for integrating PACS and RIS. A full discussion of IHE work, the profiles, and downloadable versions of the profiles themselves may be found at the RSNA Web site.[30]

Integrated Systems

Studies by the author and colleagues and others have shown that there are a number of often complex steps needed to schedule, perform, interpret, report, and store imaging studies and that the number of these steps can range from thirty-nine (in a department with RIS and PACS, but not integrated) to fifty-nine (in a film- and paper-based department).[31] With implementation of just the basic IHE profiles, these counts decrease to between nine and eleven steps. Since each step involves personnel and time, it should be clear that such reductions in steps are of major importance for operating efficiency. Eliminating manual steps also reduces errors. While it is commonly said that images "cannot be lost" in a PACS, in fact, if an examination is misidentified, it may be impossible to retrieve it subsequently. Much has been discussed regarding medical errors, and eliminating potential sources of error has had increasing importance as a result.[32]

As noted previously, one issue is how to know what studies are to be read and how to display images in the manner desired. In the film and paper environment, work lists consisted of paper lists of examinations on the motorized viewers (called "multiviewers" or "alternators"). With integrated systems, the daily schedule that the RIS has can be sent to the PACS. As examinations are done, the PACS can use that information to build lists for display at the workstation. For radiology departments or practices that are specialized, the examination type known from the RIS request and sent to the PACS can be used to build work lists for specialists (e.g., the head CT studies would go onto a list for neuroradiology, etc.). When examinations are to be dictated, the PACS can send the order number to the dictation system so that the radiologist does not have to enter patient information into it. Once dictated, this information can be automatically sent to the RIS and PACS so that the status of the examination is updated. A referring physician looking at a study on a PACS workstation can see that the examination has been reported and, if the report has been transcribed, can read the report at the same workstation.

The examination type sent from the RIS to the PACS can be used to automate the way the images are displayed. When the radiologist logs into the PACS workstation, the PACS can invoke his or her preferences for display of various examination types. As the examinations are displayed, the images usually are put in the desired locations with the manipulation tools that the radiologist prefers. The arrangement of images as the radiologist prefers to see them is known as a "hanging protocol" or "default display protocol" and is considered an essential workstation function.[33]

A most important aspect of PACS is how the function of image distribution is accomplished. Recall Dr. Haskin's question about the number of light boxes in a hospital. How does a PACS meet the requirement of distributing images to those who need them? One solution would be to install workstations at every location where a light box was installed. With the number of light boxes in an average hospital, this solution is far too expensive to implement. Printing film for image distribution means having to retain film printing, processing, and distribution capability, even if physicians can be convinced to store and manage the films themselves–also not a practical solution.

Most hospital information systems started with terminals installed at many locations in the hospital–typically at every nursing station, in all operating rooms, and in all outpatient clinics. As these systems moved to the distributed computing design, the terminals were replaced with personal computers. Support of these was greatly simplified if they ran on commercial software rather than a fully custom application, so most of these PCs run a standard operating system. Access to the HIS is via an application that runs on the PC. With the advent of the World Wide Web, HISs (like RISs) have moved, or are moving, to using a Web browser as the client and a server to support the application. A PACS that supported Web-based image access could take advantage of the PCs deployed for HIS use. Most PACS vendors now support a Web-based image and report viewer, so the problem of how to distribute images widely has a potential solution.[34] There are several vendors of PACS whose entire system is Web-based, so the practicality and feasibility of this idea has a commercial foundation.

A disadvantage of having multiple information systems in a hospital is that physician access to them becomes cumbersome. Besides radiology for reports and images, there is the clinical laboratory (sometimes several laboratories), order entry, pharmacy, surgical management, and specialty consulting (specialty departments often have their own information systems).

Many HISs support access to a number of these other information sources, but not all of them do. So a physician may have to log in to several information systems to order tests or studies and to track progress on patients. To help reduce the burden of this, many institutions have moved to "physician portals" or "single log-on systems" that at least allow access to multiple information sources with a single log-on. The next step in this integration would be the electronic medical record (EMR). A true EMR would include functions analogous to the radiologist's work list. A physician would log on to one system, would be shown his or her current list of patients, and after selecting a patient would then be shown all of the relevant information in the manner the physician desires. In many ways, this is superior to the paper chart, as an EMR could search reports and notes for particular phrases, plot laboratory values, warn of abnormal trends, and provide decision support for calling in consultants or deciding on the best diagnostic tests to order.[35] For radiology, computerized physician order entry (CPOE) would help physicians determine not only when a study could be done but also the most appropriate examination. There are some prototype EMR systems, but full EMRs are not yet widely deployed.

Planning Considerations

An important aspect of the increasing speed of imaging equipment, such as multidetector CT, is that the high cost of these systems dictates that they be kept busy. As noted in the previous chapter, scan times are now far shorter than the time required to move patients to the scanner, get them on and off the table, and move them out of the scanner room. A departmental plan that puts such machines far from major transport routes will create a logistical disadvantage.

For PACS planning, it is important to determine where the image archive computer hardware will be sited. Because of the volume of image data stored, the storage component of a PACS will be much larger than that of an RIS. Radiology's long-term storage, if separate from the hospital's electronic archive, may also be a large device, typically an automated magnetic tape library. These automated libraries can range from single-rack size to room size, so it is important to know what the facility has planned. Some newer PACS are designed without a separate archive; all information is stored on "spinning disks"–large-capacity magnetic disk arrays.[36] If this is the case, most facilities will not purchase more than two years' worth of storage capacity at a time, as the trend to progressively decreasing costs for storage is projected to continue. The facility will simply add more disk storage as it is needed. However, this means that space must be allocated for such expansion, probably for at least as many years as the facility is required to retain images. If this is not planned for, the storage system may have to be moved to a larger space, and this will mean at least temporary downtime. Planning needs to include not only the space but support services (HVAC, electrical power, etc.) as well. To avoid even brief interruptions in power, such backup power will usually include uninterruptible power supplies and emergency generators.

The Health Insurance Portability and Accountability Act has provisions that are projected to require that facilities have a disaster recovery plan. For many hospitals with RIS and PACS, this can mean a solution as simple as storing updated sets of backup tapes off-site, though most facilities are considering plans that will allow them to continue operating, not just recover, after restoring the backed-up data; this latter process can take from days to months. Such plans usually consist of storage in an off-site facility and range from completely redundant systems to complete redundancy for some interval of storage with a long-term, lower-cost archive for the rest of the retention time. For example, for a facility that has a disk-only primary storage system, the disaster recovery storage might consist of a disk array to hold one year's worth of data with an automated tape library to store information for as long as they are legally required to do so. The need for disaster recovery also means planning for the off-site facility and will require that high-speed communications to the facility be included in such planning. The potential costs for operating and managing a disaster recovery facility may drive some healthcare facilities to consider outsourcing the disaster recovery operation. There are vendors who provide such solutions.

The network infrastructure is vital to RIS and PACS, so appropriate plans for it should be made. Facilities should be encouraged to pull extra cabling for future expansion, as the cost of pulling cable is usually much higher than the cost of the cable itself. Besides having adequate wiring and wall terminations, wiring closets and the location of them need to be considered carefully. The wiring closets may contain electronics (the various network switches and routers) as well as cable connection points, so adequate power (with backup power) and HVAC are important to consider. Many commercial users of large computer networks have network operations centers where the various network elements can be monitored. This concept is not yet common in hospitals, though it perhaps should be. Since the network is so important to hospital operations, a good design case could be made for the inclusion of such a facility in the hospital planning.

Information Security

Aside from the provisions of HIPAA, protecting patient privacy has always been considered a part of good medical practice. Electronic systems may make it more difficult to protect patient information, as the various systems and databases they use are on local area networks that may have indirect or direct connections to the Internet. Most hospital information technology departments are well informed about protecting their networks from snooping or malicious attacks, though protecting networks and providing access tend to be conflicting goals.

A comprehensive discussion of information security is beyond the scope of this chapter. There are a number of excellent publications on the subject, and one by the Society for Computer Applications in Radiology serves as a good introduction.[37] There are planning considerations that may not be obvious. If there are displays that show any patient information, they should not be viewable from public areas. This may have implications for the layout of public corridors that pass by patient care areas, particularly technologist control areas in radiology. These are usually replete with many display screens for the HIS, RIS, and PACS. As an example, in the author's institution, a retrofit of reflective glass film had to be made to prevent a patient scheduling board from being visible from a semipublic corridor.

Architects and planners are well advised, if they are not familiar with the patient privacy and confidentiality aspects of current practice, to consult with those whose specialty is implementing HIPAA provisions. Many healthcare facilities developed detailed HIPAA compliance plans and formed expert teams to develop these, so there may be local resources that can be used.

Conclusion

Most healthcare facilities, especially for new construction, are moving to electronic systems for information and image management. These technologies replace film, the support hardware for film and its storage, and some of the paper-based management with electronic systems. The increasing costs of healthcare and the demand for imaging studies are driving hospitals to be more efficient, but trying to meet this demand with operations that require many manual steps will likely fail.

Understanding how the technology of electronic information and image management systems evolved and how it works should help the architect and planner to be ready when clients call on them.

Notes
1. M. E. Haskin, P. H. Haskin, P. A. Laffey, et al., "Data versus information: Which should we exchange?" *Proceedings of SPIE* 536 (1985): 37–42.
2. W. G. Scott, *Planning Guide for Radiologic Installations*, 2nd ed. (Baltimore: Williams and Wilkins, 1966); H. W. Fischer, *Radiology Department Planning, Operation, and Management* (Ann Arbor, MI: Edwards Brothers, Inc., 1982).
3. D. R. Haynor and A. O. Saarinen, "'Old study' and the correlative study: implications for PACS," *Proceedings of SPIE*, Medical Imaging III, 1093 (1989): 10–12; D. C. Rogers, E. E. Johnston, B. Brenton, et al, "Predicting PACS console requirements from radiologists' reading habits," *Proceedings of SPIE* 536 (1985): 88–95.
4. B. Reiner, E. Siegel, and J. A. Carrino, "Workflow optimization: Current trends and future directions," *Journal of Digital Imaging* 15, 3 (2002): 141–52.
5. R. G. Jost, J. Trachtman, R. L. Hill, B. A. Smith, and R. G. Evens, "A computer system for transcribing radiology reports," *Radiology* 126 (1980): 63–66.
6. S. Augarten, *Bit by Bit: An Illustrated History of Computers* (New York: Ticknor and Fields, 1984).

7. C. G. Bell, "Toward a history of (personal) workstations," in A. Goldberg, ed., *A History of Personal Workstations* (New York: ACM Press, 1988), 4–36.

8. C. P. Thacker, "Personal distributed computing: The Alto and Ethernet hardware," in Goldberg, 267–89; B. W. Lampson, "Personal distributed computing: The Alto and Ethernet software," in Goldberg, 293–335.

9. R. G. Jost, S. S. Rodewald, R. L. Hill, and R. G. Evens, "A computer system to monitor radiology department activity: A management tool to improve patient care," *Radiology* 145 (1982): 347–50.

10. Society for Computer Applications in Radiology (SCAR): "SCAR Background and History," available at http://www.scarnet.org/history.html.

11. Electronic Industries Alliance, *EIA232E–Interface Between Data Terminal Equipment and Data Circuit-Terminating Equipment Employing Serial Binary Data Interchange, revised from EIA232D* (Washington, DC: Electronic Industries Alliance, 1991).

12. K. Hafner and M. Lyon, *Where Wizards Stay Up Late: The Origins of the Internet* (New York: Simon and Schuster, 1996).

13. Wikipedia: "Web browser," available at http://en.wikipedia.org/wiki/Web_browser.

14. T. Chunn and J. Honeyman, "Storage and database," in Y. Kim and S. C. Horii, *Handbook of Medical Imaging*, Vol. 3: *Display and PACS* (Bellingham, WA: SPIE, 2000): 365–401.

15. S. J. Dwyer III, "Early PACS papers: Laying the foundation for the future of digital medical imaging," *Journal of Digital Imaging* 16, 1 (2003).

16. A. J. Duerinckx, ed., *Proceedings of the SPIE*, Vol. 318: *Picture Archiving and Communication Systems (PACS) Part I and II* (Bellingham, WA: SPIE, 1982).

17. H. U. Lemke, H. S. Stiehl, N. Scharnweber, and D. Jackel, "Applications of picture processing, image analysis, and computer graphics techniques to cranial CT scans," *Proceedings of the Sixth Conference on Computer Applications in Radiology and Computer/Aided Analysis of Radiological Images* (New York: IEEE Computer Society Press, 1979), 341–54, reprinted (with new introduction) in *Journal of Digital Imaging* 16, 1 (2003): 11–28.

18. S. J. Dwyer III, A. W. Templeton, N. L. Martin, et al., "Cost of managing digital diagnostic images for a 614–bed hospital," *Proceedings of SPIE* 318 (Part I) (1982): 3–8, reprinted (with new introduction) in *Journal of Digital Imaging* 15, 4 (2002): 255–60; B. Reiner and E. Siegel, "Digital storage: A clinical perspective," in B. I. Reiner, E. L. Siegel, and E. M. Smith, eds., *Archiving Issues in the Digital Medical Enterprise* (Great Falls, VA: SCAR, 2001), 17–30.

19. E. V. Staab, J. Anderson, E. L. Chaney, D. J. Delaney, et al., "Medical image communication system: Plan, management and initial experience in prototype at the University of North Carolina," *Proceedings of SPIE* 318, Part I (1982): 19–22; S. J. Dwyer III, A. W. Templeton, W. H. Anderson, et al., "Salient characteristics of a distributed diagnostic imaging management system for a radiology department," *Proceedings of SPIE* 318, Part I (1982): 194–204; S. Nudelman, M. P. Capp, D. Fisher III, D. Ouimette, T. W. Ovitt, and H. Roehrig, "Photoelectronic–digital radiology (PE–DI–R) at the University of Arizona," *Proceedings of SPIE* 318, Part I (1982): 205; G. Q. Maguire, M. P. Zeleznik, S. C. Horii, J. H. Schimpf, and M. E. Noz, "Image processing requirements in hospitals and an integrated systems approach," *Proceedings of SPIE* 318, Part I (1982): 206–13; N. J. Mankovitch and H. K. Huang, "An architecture for a comprehensive radiological image processing and communication facility," *Proceed-*

ings of SPIE 435 (1983): 187–91; S. K. Mun, H. Benson, S. Horii, et al., "Completion of a hospital-wide comprehensive image management and communications system," *Proceedings of SPIE,* Medical Imaging III, 1093 (1989): 204–13; B. M. ter Haar Romeny, J. Raymakers, P. F. G. M. van Waes, et al., "The Dutch PACS project: Philosophy, design of a digital reading room, and first observations in the Utrecht University Hospital in the Netherlands," *Proceedings of SPIE* 767 (1987): 787–92.

20. G. E. Moore, "Cramming more components onto integrated circuits," *Electronics* 38, 8 (1965).

21. R. H. Schneider, "The role of standards in the development of systems for communicating and archiving medical images," *Proceedings of SPIE* 318, Part I (1982): 270–71; B. Baxter, L. Hitchner, and G. Q. Maguire Jr., "Characteristics of a protocol for exchanging digital image information," *Proceedings of SPIE* 318, Part I (1982): 273–77.

22. S. C. Horii, introduction to "Minutes: NEMA ad hoc Technical Committee and American College of Radiology's Subcommittee on Computer Standards," *Journal of Digital Imaging* 18, 1 (2005): 5–22.

23. W. D. Bidgood Jr. and S. C. Horii, "Modular extension of the ACR–NEMA DICOM Standard to support new diagnostic imaging modalities and services," *Journal of Digital Imaging* 9, 2 (1996): 67–77.

24. J. Honeyman–Buck, ed., special issue on DICOM, *Journal of Digital Imaging* 18, 1 (2005).

25. National Electrical Manufacturers Association, *Digital Imaging and Communications (DICOM) PS 3-2004, Parts 1–18* (Rosslyn, VA: NEMA, 2004).

26. S. C. Horii, H. L. Kundel, B. Kneeland, R. Redfern, et al., "Replacing film with PACS: Work shifting and lack of automation," *Proceedings of SPIE* 3662 (1999): 317–22.

27. K. M. McNeill, G. W. Seeley, K. Maloney, et al., "Comparison of a digital workstation and film alternator," *Proceedings of SPIE* 914 (1988): 929–37; R. L. Arenson, D. P. Chakraborty, S. B. Seshadri, and H. L. Kundel, "The digital imaging workstation," *Radiology* 176 (1990): 303–15, reprinted (with new introduction) in *Journal of Digital Imaging* 16, 1 (2003): 141–62.

28. Health Level Seven, Inc., *HL7 Version 2.5* (Ann Arbor, MI; Health Level Seven, Inc., 2003).

29. D. E. Best, S. C. Horii, W. Bennett, B. Thompson, and D. Snavely, "Review of the American College of Radiology–National Electrical Manufacturers Association standards activity," *Computer Methods and Programs in Biomedicine* 37, 4 (1992): 305–9.

30. Radiological Society of North America and the Healthcare Information and Management Systems Society, http://www.rsna.org/ihe.

31. S. C. Horii, "The role of workflow modeling and analysis for image–guided interventions," in H. U. Lemke, K. Inamura, K. Doi, M. W. Vannier, and A. G. Farman, eds., *International Congress Series 1281: Computer Assisted Radiology and Surgery,* 2005, 381–86; R. O. Redfern, C. P. Langlotz, S. B. Abbuhl, M. Polansky, S. C. Horii, and H. L. Kundel, "The effect of PACS on the time required for technologists to produce radiographic images in the Emergency Department Radiology suite," *Journal of Digital Imaging* 15, 3 (2002): 153–60; E. Siegel and B. Reiner, "Work flow redesign: The key to success when using PACS," *American Journal of Roentgenology* 178 (2002): 563–66; B. Reiner, E. Siegel, and

J. A. Carrino, "Workflow optimization: Current trends and future directions," *Journal of Digital Imaging* 15, 3 (2002): 141–52; K. P. Andriole, "Productivity and cost assessment of computed radiography, digital radiography, and screen-film for outpatient chest examinations," *Journal of Digital Imaging* 15, 3 (2002): 161–69.

32. L. T. Kohn, J. M. Corrigan, and M. S. Donaldson, eds., *To Err Is Human: Building a Safer Health System* (Washington, DC: Institute of Medicine, 2000).

33. K. Levin, S. Horii, S. K. Mun, et al., "Analysis of data assembling activities for radiologists and its implications for clinical acceptance of PACS," *Proceedings of SPIE* 1234 (1990): 670–75; J. C. Honeyman, R. L. Arenson, M. M. Frost, et al., "Functional requirements for diagnostic workstations," *Proceedings of SPIE* 1899 (1993): 103–9; S. A. Hohman, S. J. Johnson, D. J. Valentino, et al., "Radiologists' requirements for primary diagnosis workstations: Preliminary results of task-based design surveys," *Proceedings of SPIE* 2165 (1994): 2–7; K. T. Leung, B. K. T. Ho, W. Chao, et al., "Image navigation for PACS workstations," *Proceedings of SPIE* 2435 (1995): 43–49.

34. P. J. Chang and E. Hoffman, "Multimodality workstation featuring multiband cine mode and real-time distributed interactive consultation," Radiological Society of North America Annual Meeting 1993, infoRAD exhibit 9507WS.

35. L. A. Fratt, "State of the EMR: Gaining traction, showing results," *Health Imaging and IT* 3, 10 (2005): 20–24.

36. B. I. Reiner, E. L. Siegel, and E. M. Smith, *Archiving Issues in the Digital Medical Enterprise* (Great Falls, VA: SCAR, 2001).

37. S. J. Dwyer III, B. I. Reiner, and E. L. Siegel, *Security Issues in the Digital Medical Enterprise*, 2nd ed. (Great Falls, VA: SCAR, 2004).

PART FOUR

DESIGN AND PLANNING

CHAPTER 8

Design Concepts

A well-planned facility cannot replace good medicine or the efficient management of an imaging department. Designed creatively, however, it can enable radiologists and their staff, administrators, technologists, and other healthcare providers to perform their jobs to the best of their abilities. A soothing, healing environment comforts fearful patients and reduces their apprehension of the unknown. Such an environment also can help lower the staff's level of stress. A poorly planned facility, on the other hand, can compromise the abilities of all who use it, and as such can be expensive to staff and operate.

This chapter discusses the design challenges for a successful medical imaging facility. Chief among these challenges are those posed by the psychosocial needs of patients, the importance of flexibility, an expression of local identity through design, governmental regulation (such as HIPAA), as well as designing for sustainability.

Evidence-based design–a process similar to evidence-based medicine, which supports clinical decisions and methods with documented proven outcomes–has become a critical method of ensuring that appropriate design decisions are made. Evidence-based design can help designers and planners identify appropriate planning concepts and determine the impact of design decisions on patient outcomes, operations, and economics. For example, design decisions can be studied to determine if the initial cost of a specific operationally based planning concept can be amortized through life-cycle clinical cost savings, such as savings associated with reduced nosocomial infection rates or reduced staff injuries.

The Martinez, California–based Center for Health Design (CHD), a not-for-profit healthcare design research organization, has been instrumental in identifying and disseminating relevant healthcare design evidence. CHD's focus is to scientifically measure the impact of healthcare facility design on hospitals' and other healthcare facilities' medical outcomes and costs.[1] The Coalition for Healthcare Research (CHER) is also involved in correlating health facility design with medical outcomes.

Design Basics

Four key ingredients of good facility design are convenience, image, flexibility, and economy. Although some of these factors may be more prominent than others in certain projects, all of them must be considered in order for a design to be truly successful.

Convenience

How easy is it for a patient arriving at a facility for the first time to find and drive to the front door (figure 8-1)? How visible is the facility from a distance? How simple is it to navigate through the site to find a parking space or a drop-off zone? For many patients and visitors, convenience is the most

Figure 8-1 Visibility from a distance.
© Mark Luthringer. Architect: Anshen + Allen.

important factor contributing to their impression of how well medical services are delivered, even if the convenience (or inconvenience) they experience is not directly related to the quality of the services they receive. For staff and referring physicians, convenience can have direct economic and operational benefits.

Convenient wayfinding begins beyond the building's boundaries. For example, the building site must be easily accessible to pedestrians, private automobiles, and public transit. Directional signage should clearly identify site entrances and parking areas. Whether a facility has a single entrance or separate entrances for inpatients and outpatients, ample patient and visitor parking should be located within 200 feet of the appropriate entrance, according to accessibility codes, and should be clearly identified (figure 8–2). Parking designated for disabled persons must be located adjacent to these entrances. Additionally, the paths of travel from the parking areas to the building should be level and protected from adverse weather conditions.

Once patients have found their way to the site and identified the building's main entrance, architectural cues should guide them to their destinations (figure 8–3). Graphics and directional signage inside the building

Figure 8-2 Convenient site accessibility. Courtesy Anshen + Allen, Architects.

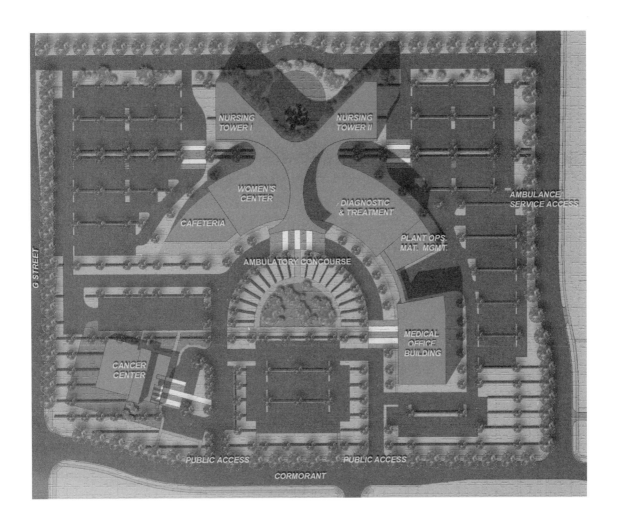

Figure 8-3 Entry sequence: architecture as directional device. © Mark Luthringer. Architect: Anshen + Allen.

should support and enhance architectural wayfinding cues but should not be the sole source of guidance. From the moment patients arrive at the site to the time they depart, their path of travel should be obvious to them without their having to ask for directions along the way. Healthcare designer Barbara Heulat describes how patients and visitors navigate through healthcare facilities:

> As patients and visitors embark on their journey to and through healthcare facilities, they bring previous experiences with them, they look at what they see and evaluate it in context. The wayfinders will try to understand the spatial characteristics of the environment. With this information, they consider the signs, maps, landmarks and other indicators to understand the place, and then examine their options and determine the best route to their destination.[2]

Figure 8-4 Landmarks help orient patients and assist in wayfinding. © Richard Barnes. Architect: Anshen + Allen.

Architectural form and pattern can aid patients in wayfinding or orienting themselves to their destinations. For example, a repeating pattern of columns might identify a wayfinding decision point, such as a major corridor or other directional transition. The use of special materials at intersecting corridors can direct patients to turn instead of continue ahead. Public circulation can be further directed by patterns created with light fixtures, skylights, or atria. Often a distinct landmark, such as a statue or another form of artwork, can help orient patients and visitors (figure 8–4).

A message of patient convenience can be conveyed by the built environment as much as by operational routines (such as extended hours and service-oriented personnel). Sensitive design can reinstate a measure of dignity for patients experiencing discomfort as part of an imaging exam. For example, a layout that minimizes the distance patients must travel through corridors in their gowns helps reduce their stress and discomfort.

A reception desk can either be inviting or become a barrier between staff and patients. Details such as the relationship of counter height to the receptionist's seating height influence patient and staff communication. A multilevel counter, where staff can talk face-to-face with either seated or standing patients, is both convenient and required by accessibility codes. An area for confidential discussions about medical procedures, billing status, or other concerns is both convenient and a necessity to be compliant with the Health Insurance Portability and Accountability Act (HIPAA).

MRI control rooms and PACS reading areas are often unintentional sources of HIPAA violations. In some instances, previous patients' medical images linger on the MRI operator's console and can be seen by the next patient entering the exam room. At times, control rooms double as reading areas. When radiologists use the control room to read images, they frequently dictate while viewing images. If the control room is not acoustically isolated, dictation can be overheard.

Architects Robert Junk and Tobias Gilk identify strategies that can be employed to mitigate MRI control room HIPAA violations. They recommend controlling the line of sight to control room monitors and view boxes from adjoining rooms, providing visual screens if necessary; removing patient information as soon as it is no longer being used; keeping patients out of the control room; acoustically separating the control room from adjoining areas; and providing dedicated consulting, charting, and dictation spaces that are designed for acoustic privacy.[3]

An imaging facility that offers convenience to staff helps retain and recruit qualified personnel. After all, as Texas A&M professor Dr. Leonard Berry writes, employees spend more time in the building than do customers.[4] He notes:

> A well-designed physical environment has a positive impact on employees as well, reducing physical emotional stress—which is of value not only to employees, but also to patients because visible employee stress sends negative signals.[5]

Staff amenities include short distances for frequently traveled paths, ample natural lighting, and lounges or break rooms where staff members can momentarily leave their highly active work areas. Long travel distances to and from staff toilets is one of the most common complaints among staff. Many radiology practitioners consider it convenient to have a reading area designed to accommodate both virtual and face-to-face consultations with referring physicians.

Facility Image

Like people, buildings have unique personalities. Each projects a distinct and powerful image. A building's public face serves as its calling card. Berry points out that a facility's architectural image reflects the quality of care provided within.

Ideally, the design of a medical facility tells a compelling story about the service that the service cannot tell by itself. The facility communicates a torrent of clues about the service; it is a physical reflection of the core values and quality of care offered by the institution.[6]

Thus, architectural detailing, both interior and exterior, can be a powerful tool. A positive image that is clearly visible and skillfully articulated has a profound effect on all who use or pass by the facility.

The skill with which architectural imagery is articulated is as important as the kind of image conveyed. In such buildings as medical imaging facilities—where services rely on modern medical technology—various approaches to projecting an image can be successful, including softening technology, emphasizing technology, neutralizing technology, incorporating regional imagery, and creating an identity for special groups of patients.

Softening Technology

For some patients, the cold, impersonal feeling of medical equipment compounds fears and feelings of helplessness in the face of the unfamiliar procedures they are about to undergo. Artwork, indirect lighting, quality fabrics and finishes, and landscaping can help comfort fearful patients and relieve their sense of alienation. An institutional policy that emphasizes patient education, combined with a dedicated space for teaching patients, also reassures those who are intimidated by the unknown.

Softening technology should begin long before patients come in contact with medical machinery. The tone should be set outside the front door and continued through the waiting, reception, and dressing areas. If no attempt has been made to ease patients' fears before they reach the procedure room, the benefit will be lost.

Many patients undergoing imaging procedures are conscious and well aware of their surroundings. Patients on gurneys and those on tables during imaging examinations spend much of their time staring at the ceilings of corridors and procedure rooms. Thus, special effort should be made to improve and enhance these often harsh and uninteresting surfaces (figure 8–5).

Acoustic damping of walls and ceilings softens the environment and provides an extra measure of comfort. Proper acoustic design reduces both ambient airborne noise and transmitted noise traveling through walls, partitions, and floors. Special sound treatment should be provided in business offices and consultation rooms where conversations must be contained, as well as in excessively noisy procedure rooms.

Interior designer Cynthia Leibrock cites a number of recommendations for effective acoustic design. Carpeting (where appropriate) can reduce ambient noise and mitigates the impact of noise transmitted from floor to floor. Cut pile absorbs more sound than does loop pile. Equipping doors with silencers reduces unnecessary noise. Long rectangular rooms increase sound reflectivity and thus increase noise levels. Sound panels are effective

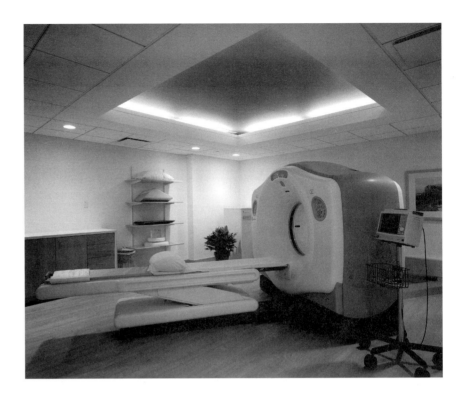

Figure 8-5 Patients often spend more time looking at the ceiling than they do looking at walls. © Desroches Photography. Architect: Anshen + Allen + Rothman.

in absorbing low-frequency noise generated within the space; these should be placed on two adjacent walls rather than on opposite walls. Irregularly shaped rooms or recessed areas along walls and ceilings diffuse sound waves, whereas hard surfaces facing each other produce reverberation. Staggered doors along corridors control noise better than doors directly facing each other. Overhead paging systems are a common source of noise-induced stress.[7]

While some materials are ideal for controlling noise, they may not be well suited for infection control, and their use in healthcare facilities may not even be permitted in some jurisdictions. Thus, designers must ensure the appropriateness of each material for both acoustic and hygiene concerns.

Some procedures, such as magnetic resonance imaging (MRI), are inherently noisy. Special audio and video systems are available to mask the noise and distract patients from thinking about either the machinery or the medical procedure. In addition, some magnets (usually lower-field-strength magnets) are designed with an open bore to improve access and reduce patient claustrophobia, which is a common problem with this procedure. A study published in *Administrative Radiology* found that a significant number of MRI patients fail to keep their appointments for fear of the noise and the claustrophobia induced by the equipment.

> In [some] reports, as many as twenty percent of individuals attempting an MRI scan could not complete it secondary to claustrophobia.

It has been noted that the rate of unfinished scans varies from unit to unit and changes with the experience of the MRI technologist. The most striking sources of patients' anxiety involve the physical condition and setting of MRI: not being able to move and hearing the unbearable noise. Many patients have already discussed the exam with family and friends; unfortunately, the context is usually negative. Statements like "MRI is the worst experience they've had" [and] "It's like being in a coffin or tomb" are common.[8]

Psychologist S. R. Evers has noted a number of psychological factors that contribute to patient responses to MRI:

First, MRI's reputation has created a set of expectations in patients' minds. Second, MRI taps into a patient's more primitive emotional responses because of its design and how it is used. Third, MRI usually is part of a diagnostic workup that involves an increase in stress, making a patient more vulnerable to developing psychological symptomology. Finally, the psychological responses it elicits in patients are more diverse and complex than the oversimplification that all responses are "mere" claustrophobia. . . . Stress always seeks the system's weakest link. In the MRI patient, that weakest link is often susceptibility to claustrophobically induced anxiety, which may have lain dormant until the patient is confronted with the procedure.[9]

Ironically, compared to other methods of diagnosis and/or treatment, MRI is not painful, just frightening. For many people, fear can be mitigated by the surrounding environment and the way care is administered within the environment. Providing such mitigations can potentially reduce the amount of missed appointments and incomplete scans. Soft indirect lighting also helps temper the imaging environment.

Emphasizing Technology

Many patients place confidence in technological advances in modern medicine. For this reason, a strategy of highlighting the technical components of the physical environment also may be appropriate. An image that emphasizes technology might begin on the exterior and continue through public spaces into procedure rooms, where patient/provider interaction can be either intimate or stressful. This not only creates an opportunity for articulating the architecture but also tends to create a feeling of strength and confidence (figure 8–6). Furnishings, lighting fixtures, and finishes that echo advances in technology may diminish patient fears by reinforcing the quality and capabilities of medical imaging. With this approach, it is important that human scale and comfort are well integrated into the design.

Figure 8-6 Highlighting the technical components of a building can help patients place their confidence in modern medicine. © Richard Barnes. Architect: Anshen + Allen.

Neutralizing Technology

Another alternative is to neutralize technology, allowing medical equipment to blend into the background. Equipment manufacturers are improving the appearance of their products, which in turn enables designers to neutralize the equipment's visual impact.

Procedure rooms that conceal medical equipment from view often tend to mitigate the massive appearance of the machinery. Careful selection of floor and wall coverings, colors, and lighting can further humanize the imaging environment. Additionally, positive distractions–design elements such as special lighting or artwork strategically placed to take the patient's attention away from the medical procedure at hand–often have the effect of reducing tension and apprehension, thus improving the patient's compliance and ultimately improving the experience for both staff and patient (figure 8-7).

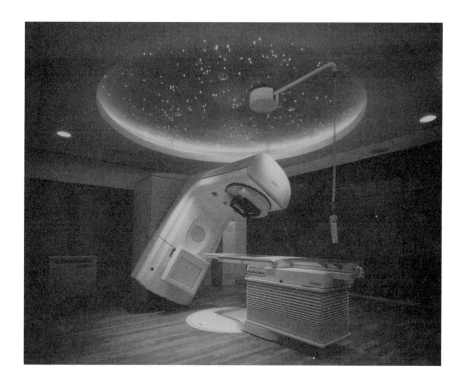

Figure 8-7 Strategically created positive distractions can take patients' attention away from their immediate troubles, and thus reduce their stress levels and anxiety. © Michael O'Callahan. Architect: Smithgroup.

Incorporating Regional Imagery

Regardless of whether technology is softened or emphasized, local context can be incorporated into the building's exterior and interior image. Local materials that are indigenous to the region (such as masonry, wood siding, stone, and cement plaster) can be used, perhaps in a more playful way than they have been assembled historically.

A sense of local context can have both marketing and recruiting benefits. Patients and staff are often attracted to facilities they perceive as good neighbors. A British study that examined how a building's design affects recruiting, retention, and performance of staff notes that nurses place importance on how a building's design engages with the local community. This is something they refer to as a facility's "civic value."[10]

Regional imagery can be expressed through form as well. For example, the facade of a large building can be subdivided into smaller elements that echo the forms of adjacent residential structures. Other references to regional style can be expressed through the articulation of window and door openings and roof forms (figure 8-8).

Creating an Identity for Special Groups of Patients

Special patient populations provide design opportunities for yet another form of architectural imagery. As the number of diagnostic and therapeutic imaging procedures performed on ambulatory patients increases, many providers elect to differentiate inpatient and outpatient settings. In some cases, one department may have both an inpatient and outpatient zone; in others, there may be two separate imaging facilities or departments.

Figure 8-8 Regional imagery can be expressed through forms found elsewhere within the vicinity. Image courtesy of Anshen + Allen, Architects.

The distinction between inpatient and outpatient areas can be addressed both architecturally and operationally. Architecturally, each area can be differentiated with special lighting, furnishings, and finishes. Operationally, streamlining outpatient registration paperwork–perhaps by verifying patients' medical history and insurance coverage prior to the day of treatment–can reduce lengthy waiting periods and thus further strengthen the facility's image. Paperless admitting and registration systems are a common way that imaging and other services are being reengineered to improve work flow and efficiency.

Within the outpatient zone, special populations can be further accommodated. For example, if ultrasound and mammography rooms are clustered together and separated from other traffic, a women's health area with its own entrance can be created within the department (figure 8–9). Ideally, this area would be located either toward the front or off to the side of the department so that these patients do not have to travel through the entire facility. Dressing rooms and toilet rooms can be placed inside the suite, with a separate waiting area for gowned patients to maximize privacy. A dedicated area for patient education also should be considered.

When children make up a significant percentage of the patient workload, a separate pediatric waiting area is appropriate (figure 8–10). This area might have a more playful feeling and be designed in brighter colors than similar adult areas. Furnishings can be scaled for kids, and murals and graphics can appeal to children. Pediatric areas, however, should be designed for both children and parents. Special acoustic treatment should contain noise within the immediate area, and choices for both interaction and quiet should be provided.

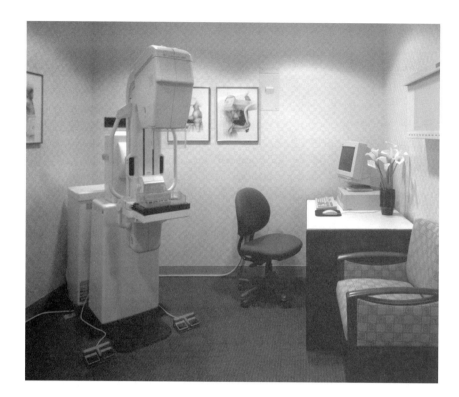

Figure 8-9 A women's health screening center. © Robert Canfield Photography. Architect: Anshen + Allen.

Figure 8-10 Pediatric areas are often best designed for both children and their parents. © Peter Eckert. Image courtesy of Anshen + Allen.

An imaging exam can be a frightening experience for both children and their parents. Visual cues can help children better understand the experiences they are going through and reassure them. In some children's facilities the imaging process is architecturally themed as both a positive distraction and an educational story. For example, at the University of

Figure 8-11 Prior to their MRI exam, each child and parent is given a storybook about "Magneto" the monkey and his MRI exam. Image courtesy of NBBJ.

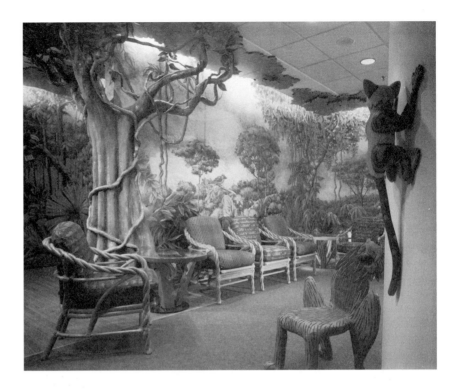

Figure 8-12 When the child and patient arrive at their appointment, they are greeted by "Magneto" in the familiar jungle setting they just read about. Image courtesy of NBBJ.

Washington in Seattle, an MRI suite has been designed to look like a jungle hut. Prior to the exam, each child and parent is given a storybook about Magneto the monkey and his MRI exam. When the child and parent arrive at their appointment, they are greeted by Magneto in the familiar jungle setting they just read about (figures 8–11 and 8–12).

Researcher V. L. Tyc notes that parents need reassurance as well:

Approximately 30% of children and their parents reported that [MRI procedures] produced significant distress. However, parents' ratings of their child's distress were significantly higher than the children's self-ratings, and agreement between child and parent pairs was poor. Insertion of an intravenous line was identified as the most aversive component of [MRI procedures] by both parents (55%) and children (38%).[11]

In both the women's and children's areas, recognition of these special patient groups strengthens the facility's image and enhances the branding of these distinct service lines.

Flexibility

One of the most challenging aspects of imaging facility design is providing flexibility for future changes. During the several years often required for design, documentation, regulatory review, construction, and occupancy of a new facility, both technology and medical practice will have changed considerably. Unfortunately, for this reason it is possible that a new facility could be partially obsolete on opening day if the design does not provide ample flexibility. Although it is difficult to predict exactly what will change in the near future, it is both possible and necessary to build flexibility into the facility's design. Imaging facilities can be extremely expensive to modify if flexibility is not integrated into the project from the outset.

Every design solution should enable change to occur in two distinct ways: external expansion and internal conversion. Expansion implies both a building that will grow and a site that will accommodate such growth. Structural, mechanical, electrical, and communications systems also must be planned to accommodate such expansion. In addition to accommodating a larger building footprint, the site also must be able to expand its parking capabilities and related circulation space. Conversion implies a building that will change from within. As with expansion, building systems, department locations, and even room configuration should be planned to maximize flexibility. Both approaches–expansion and conversion–can occur simultaneously (figure 8-13).

In each case, the planning team must first determine which building elements are fixed, or hard, and which ones are flexible, or soft (figure 8-14). Fixed elements include stairs, elevators, mechanical rooms, and major structural elements. Major nonmovable medical equipment with special plumbing, electrical, or structural connections also is considered fixed. Fixed elements should be arranged so as not to impede future modifications to the facility. In contrast to hard space, offices, lounges, and conference rooms are flexible and can be more easily designed to accommodate future change. Infrastructure systems (electrical, communications, and ventilation systems) must be flexible enough to accommodate change even though many elements of the systems are fixed or permanent.

Figure 8-13 The imaging facility should be designed to accommodate both external expansion and internal conversion with minimal disruption. Courtesy of Anshen + Allen, Architects.

Figure 8-14 Flexible elements (and soft space) can be changed easily, while fixed elements (and hard space) cannot. Courtesy of Anshen + Allen, Architects.

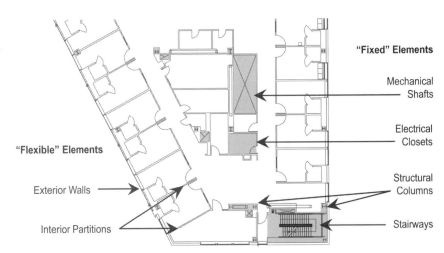

Proactive planning allows future expansion to occur without disrupting existing services. Imaging (and other) departments should be located and designed with a future expansion zone identified at the time the initial construction phase is being planned. Expansion of mechanical and structural systems, as well as extension of exit paths and parking areas, also requires preplanning.

If external expansion opportunities are limited, conversion might be a more appropriate means of accommodating future operational needs. This, too, should be preplanned because conversion requires soft space, such as administrative offices or unfinished shelled spaces, to be modified later to accommodate internal growth.

However, some risk is involved in determining the amount of soft space that must be reserved initially to accommodate future needs. For instance, adequate space must be available to accommodate functional activity clusters, or groups of spaces that grow as a functional unit. As an example, the addition of two radiology rooms requires additional dressing areas to be provided and may require a larger holding area for nonambulatory patients. The seating capacity of waiting areas also would need to increase, particularly if the additional procedure rooms are intended for high-volume, short-duration examinations. Converted space that is too small or of the wrong configuration may result in the inefficient use of that space. Converted space that is poorly located may result in staffing inefficiencies.

One approach to preplanned conversion involves relocating an entire section of the imaging department once additional space becomes available. For instance, in some facilities, nuclear medicine is a part of radiology. If the two functions are combined initially, it may be feasible to relocate the nuclear medicine component in the future, thus vacating internal space that could be converted for additional radiology functions already within the department boundary. This arrangement can provide useful expansion opportunities, particularly in small departments.

The Integrated Building System

The rigorous systems approach, often used in designing research laboratories, has also been applied to healthcare facility design. The internal use of space in research labs continually changes or "churns" in response to the ongoing iteration of research grants. Once a grant has expired, the space previously used for research activities is replaced by new occupants conducting new research and requiring modifications to their space and equipment. Imaging facilities–which also change over time as equipment and clinical practices evolve–benefit from a systematic design approach that anticipates and enables such change to occur.

The integrated building system (IBS) is a systematic planning and construction concept developed to maximize life-cycle or long-term flexibility while minimizing both the cost and disruptive nature of equipment and facility changes. Developed initially as part of the Department of Veterans

Affairs (VA) Hospital Building System, the IBS also has been successfully incorporated into many healthcare facilities that are not part of the VA system. Because it offsets initial construction cost premiums with a potential for reducing overall construction duration, it was more widely deployed in the 1970s and 1980s, when interest rates were high and the benefit of a shortened construction period could be more easily translated into cost savings. However, the design concepts upon which it is based still serve as valuable tools for providing flexibility over the life of a building.

Objectives of the integrated building system include ease of construction, ease of maintenance, and ease of facility modification. The concept utilizes a series of three-dimensional modules, where each module is organized into three distinct zones: service bay, service zone, and functional zone. Each module is approximately 10,000 departmental gross square feet (DGSF) in size and is self-contained and independent from adjacent

Figure 8-15 Distinct interstitial mechanical floors enable renovation to take place with minimal disruption to ongoing services below.

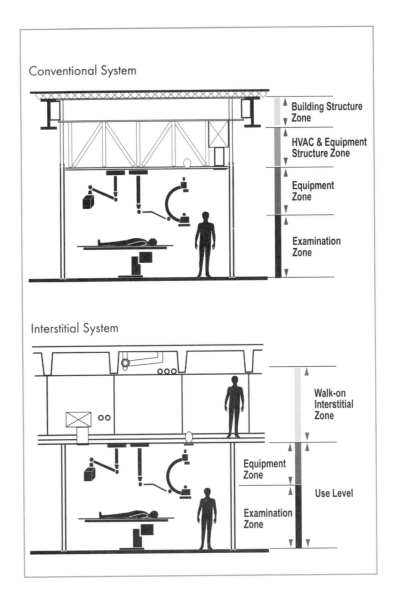

modules. The functional zone extends from the floor to the ceiling below the interstitial space and is where public circulation and medical treatment occur. The service zone is the interstitial space above the functional zone, extending between the ceiling of the functional zone and either the roof or the floor above (figure 8–15). This is where mechanical and electrical services are distributed and where maintenance of the utility systems occurs. Each service element–lighting fixtures, power distribution lines, medical gas piping, HVAC ductwork, fire protection systems, and so on–has a specific location within the service zone. The service bay is located at the building's perimeter and is as tall as the functional and service zones together. The service bay houses mechanical and electrical rooms, service shafts, and stairways.

Because the integrated building is divided into modules–each with its own mechanical and electrical system–one module can be modified without disrupting other portions of the building. Changes can be made to building services with little disruption to medical functions, because the functional zone within each module is physically separated from both the service zone and the service bay.

The interstitial floor can simplify renovation projects: work can take place on the interstitial floor with minimal disruption to occupants below. However, workers should not occupy the interstitial floors above or near any radiation–emitting equipment when it is in use unless adequate radiation barriers are in place.

Separating functional and service areas provides another important advantage: it allows multiple building trades to work simultaneously. For example, workers can work in the interstitial and functional zones concurrently. This offers the potential to shorten the construction schedule, compared to conventional approaches in which most building trades work sequentially.

The IBS can provide another measure of flexibility. When each module is designed with long–span structural bays, flexibility in the functional zone will be enhanced because there will be fewer columns to restrict facility layout. The additional depth required for long–span trusses can be incorporated into the interstitial space. Additionally, using the IBS, building components can be mass–produced and repeated from one module to the next.

Offsetting the flexibility benefits of the integrated building system, however, is the massiveness of most IBS buildings. The large unobstructed footprints of most IBS floors often make it a challenge for designers to incorporate natural daylight and can become confusing for patients with regard to wayfinding and orientation.

In many facilities, a fully integrated building concept is integral to the entire structure. However, alternative hybrid solutions may include either interstitial floors without the IBS approach to modular design or interstitial floors only on equipment-intensive floors (such as radiology, surgery, interventional procedure suites) and not on less equipment-intensive floors (such as those housing general nursing units or other functions unlikely to be converted to equipment-intensive diagnostic and treatment space in the future).

Flexibility for Future Technologies

Preplanning today's buildings to accept tomorrow's technology requires that department and room design must be flexible enough to accommodate equipment enhancements without necessitating major physical changes to the facility. Three types of technological enhancements are likely: software upgrades, hardware upgrades or replacement, and integration of comprehensive data and communication systems.

Software Upgrades

In many instances, software upgrades can extend the usefulness of existing imaging equipment by either increasing its speed or enhancing its diagnostic capabilities. For example, enhancements for magnetic resonance angiography can add angiographic capability to certain MRI equipment not initially purchased or designed for that purpose.

The upgrade may not be as simple to install as some equipment manufacturers claim. Such new capabilities often require additional space for electronics cabinets, consoles, and patient holding areas or other support space as procedural capabilities increase. Furthermore, as a result of the equipment's extended capabilities, other medical specialties (such as neuroradiology, interventional radiology, and cardiology) may want to use the equipment, thus changing traffic patterns and politics within the department.

Hardware Upgrades or Replacement

Replacing outdated imaging equipment is usually more complicated than upgrading software. To simplify replacement, universal room design, a strategy that results in a generic room layout for certain procedure room types, can be employed where appropriate. In addition, procedure rooms, computer equipment rooms, and building systems (such as electrical, HVAC, and structural) should be designed to be larger than their minimum acceptable dimensions. This "loose-fit" approach provides reserve capacity to accommodate both future equipment and still-undeveloped procedures. However, planners should be careful not to provide too much space. A room that is too large for its function not only is unnecessarily expensive but also may be functionally inefficient if equipment and supplies are not easily within reach when needed.

Electrical and HVAC reserve capacity also is important. However, the mechanical engineer must be careful not to provide so much reserve air-handling capacity that it will become difficult to control humidity.

Some consultants suggest providing a minimum of 20 percent reserve capacity for HVAC systems and 50 to 100 percent reserve capacity for electrical systems.

Finally, accommodations for removing or replacing large, heavy equipment (some of which can be broken down into smaller components) need to be considered. The building's structural capacity, as well as doorway and corridor clearances, must be able to accommodate this equipment along an entire route connecting the room where the equipment is housed to the location outside the building where it will be placed onto or removed from a truck or trailer. Potential obstacles along this route should be anticipated and eliminated during detailed planning. For example, it is common for a door and door frame to be dismantled in order to bring a large equipment component into a room because the doorway is too low or narrow.

If corridors are not designed for the weight of the equipment, temporary load-bearing supports may need to be added as the equipment is delivered, installed, and eventually removed and replaced. For example, MRI components and the materials used for magnetic shielding can each weigh many tons. Before design solutions are finalized, it is advisable to review maintenance and access requirements with equipment vendors and installers. Each vendor should be walked through building plans and sections in order to identify a preferred access route and verify that each specific piece of equipment can, in fact, be installed and removed.

Comprehensive Data and Communication Systems

The one component of imaging that has the greatest impact on facility design is the continuous refinement of electronic picture archiving and communication systems and image management and communication systems. Federal mandates are now in place to develop an interoperable electronic health record nationwide.[12] PACS and IMACS have become a necessary prerequisite for this to happen.

Many circulation and adjacency requirements for spaces that previously relied on manual transmission of images and written information are rapidly disappearing as electronic transmission systems become more prevalent. As comprehensive networks of fiber-optic cable and Internet-based communications systems link remote sites to others across campus, throughout the community, and even around the world, physical adjacency is becoming less important for imaging professionals.

Electronic storage of images and information enables a greater volume of data to be stored in less space, and diagnostic images represent most hospitals' largest component of data storage. Researchers Lucier and Wanchoo describe several key data storage challenges for healthcare providers, such as gathering, storing, and managing ever-increasing volumes of clinical data; providing clinicians with secure access to clinical data, anywhere and anytime; securing data against loss and/or inappropriate access; and reconciling the cost of efficient data management with limited capital and operational budgets.[13]

The amount of electronic data that must be stored is increasing at an astronomical rate. For example, CT and MRI may generate thousands of images of a given anatomical region. How these images will be generated, viewed, postprocessed, and stored is still a challenge, as the standard unit of measure for data has rapidly evolved from megabytes to gigabytes to terabytes and beyond.

New, sophisticated imaging techniques that generate larger quantities and sizes of files add to the challenges of data storage. As Lucier and Wanchoo note, "Even hospitals with PACS systems in place are challenged as they prepare to manage not gigabytes, but terabytes and even petabytes of radiology data.... A typical [multibeam computed tomography] exam may consist of many thin slices, ultimately producing thousands of images per exam."[14]

Although it may be difficult today to anticipate all the forms that an imaging department might take in the future, it is both possible and necessary to plan now for the continuous evolution of integrated electronic information management. For example, a decision to archive images on-site instead of at a remote location determines whether archive space needs to be built within the facility and, if so, what type of space is needed. Lucier and Wanchoo outline some of the considerations:

> Some hospitals prefer to archive data on site, storing the files in the hospital data center and providing redundancy by manually storing a duplicate to a vault or electronically transmitting it to a data center at a geographically separate location, such as an affiliate institution across town.

Others prefer the application service provider (ASP) model that provides the additional redundancy of a remote data center. Today's ASP solutions for radiology enable the rapid, seamless transfer of information to remote sites. For example, one ASP provides a direct, broadband, fiber optic connection that carries data from the hospital to a secure data center. Personnel at that location can create a duplicate data set for storage in a secure vault or bunker.... This allows the hospital to avoid significant investments in IT infrastructure.[15]

On-site image archives today are able to store more data in less space than they could several years ago. Requirements for heavily air-conditioned space and raised access flooring–although sometimes still encountered–are also becoming more flexible and less restrictive.

The installation of empty conduit or cable trays and accessible ceiling space throughout imaging areas and at other strategic locations (between the imaging department and intensive care, emergency, medical records, and registration, for example), as well as the systematic and coordinated provision of amply sized communications closets throughout the facility, will enable wires, cable, and even wireless systems to be installed in the future without demolishing existing walls and ceilings. It should be noted that wireless systems are not entirely wireless. Most of the cable is merely eliminated at certain portions of the communications network, usually at the final run, connecting point-of-use devices to a router or hub.

Technology Docks

Another approach to adaptable facility design involves planning for relocatable, mobile, or "plug-in" imaging environments. For example, a technology dock–a simple structure that connects a mobile trailer or building module to the main facility–can be built to facilitate mobile technology that enables multiple users to share expensive equipment for providing special imaging services. The technology dock affords a unique measure of flexibility because it provides a means of housing short-lived technologies, or those in the midst of development, without the same capital investment required of permanent structures. (See the section "Technology Docks" in chapter 15, "Imaging Beyond the Radiology Department.")

Economy

The cost of healthcare is escalating at an astonishing pace, in parallel with rising construction costs. At the same time, medical reimbursement rates are shrinking. Among all healthcare services, imaging involves some of the most expensive construction because of its extensive structural, electrical, and mechanical requirements. With multimillion–dollar imaging equipment, expensive facilities, and diminishing reimbursement, imaging facility design and construction must be efficient as well as functional. Yet in spite of the expense of equipment, staff labor costs can easily exceed the value of capital equipment purchases. In fact, facility construction and equipment acquisition costs represent only a small fraction of the cost of healthcare salaries and operating expenses.

Therefore, the economic value derived from facility design must be measured in two ways simultaneously: the initial cost of space and the recurring value of space. The initial cost of space includes the price of construction, furniture, and equipment as well as associated costs for professional fees, land acquisition, and financing. These costs are generated only once, although they may be paid in increments throughout the facility's functional life span.

The recurring value of space is measured by the ratio of the value–or revenue generating potential–of medical services provided in a space relative to the combined recurring costs for staffing, utilities, and maintenance associated with that space. Maintenance costs include cleaning, repairing, and replacing construction components, finish materials, and equipment.

The initial cost of space is directly influenced by plan efficiency as well as by the quality of construction components and finish materials. The recurring value of space is influenced by a multitude of variables (such as staff travel distances) that affect operations and work flow.

Initial construction cost, which usually is the simplest of the cost indicators to quantify, often is the one most closely analyzed. However, initial construction cost should not be the sole determinant of economy; operational and staffing costs and the ability to provide services efficiently have a greater financial impact than does initial construction cost. For example, an inexpensive HVAC system might lower the cost of construction, but that saving could be negligible compared to higher heating and cooling bills or the need to replace the system in the near future. Equipment downtime and the associated lost revenues due to HVAC failure also are significant expenses. In addition, poor planning that causes inefficient staffing or an unpleasant working environment also adds a financial burden for the life of the facility. Sustainable, energy-efficient facility design can save money over the life of a building.

Several documents provide guidance for designing sustainable healthcare facilities. For example, "The Green Guide for Healthcare" can be found at www.gghc.org, and the U.S. Green Building Council's "LEED Application Guide for Healthcare Facilities" is discussed at www.usgbc.org.

> The common fear of many embarking on a capital project, when faced with the question of whether to pursue high performance design, is the notion that it will increase costs. While there are as of yet insufficient numbers of green health care facilities from which to gather historic cost data, early indicators from the few completed projects to date don't support that fear.[16]

Recent evidence on the ability of life-cycle cost savings to offset the initial cost of high-performance sustainable-design features is favorable. Leaders at the Center for Health Design familiar with both the literature and pioneering sustainable healthcare projects note, "The evidence indicates that the one-time incremental costs of designing and building optimal facilities can be quickly repaid through operational savings and increased revenue and result in substantial, measurable, and financial benefits."[17]

Plan Efficiency

Facility size directly influences construction cost. Overall building size relative to the number and size of individual rooms programmed into a building indicates how compact the layout is. While floor plans are being developed, a plan efficiency ratio can be easily determined (figure 8-16). The efficiency ratio identifies the amount of net assignable area relative to departmental gross area.

Net assignable area is equal to the sum of all the individual rooms and spaces (excluding wall thickness) within each department or tenant space.

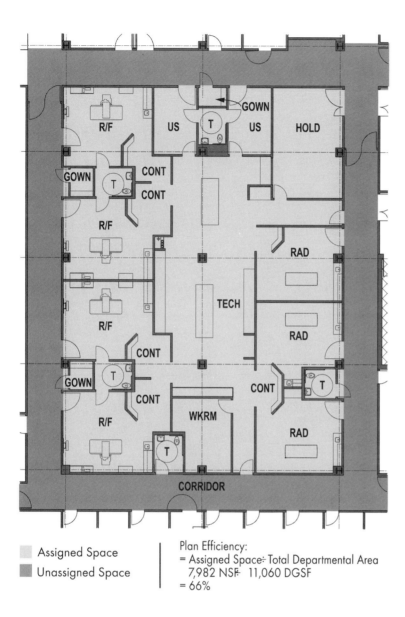

Figure 8-16 Plan efficiency is determined by the ratio of assigned space relative to the quantity of overall space. Courtesy of Anshen + Allen, Architects.

Assigned Space
Unassigned Space

Plan Efficiency:
= Assigned Space ÷ Total Departmental Area
  7,982 NSF   11,060 DGSF
= 66%

This includes procedure rooms, dressing rooms, waiting areas, utility rooms, offices, and so on. Excluded from net assignable area are spaces such as departmental corridors, structural columns, walls, and partitions. These spaces usually are considered net unassignable area and are accounted for in the net-to-departmental-gross multiplier.

Rooms housing equipment required to support imaging procedures, such as X-ray transformers and computer rooms, are considered part of net assignable area, whereas rooms housing equipment serving the entire building, such as telecommunication closets necessary for building-wide communications systems, are considered to be part of net unassignable area.

Departmental gross area is equal to the sum of net assignable area and the corridors, walls, and partitions that serve a given department or tenant space. Building gross area is equal to the departmental gross area of each

Figure 8-17 Space can be classified as either activity space, support space, or administration space. Courtesy of Anshen + Allen, Architects.

■ Activity Space

□ Support Space

■ Administrative Space

department plus nondepartmental stairs, elevators, exit corridors, mechanical rooms, electrical closets, shafts, and the thickness of exterior walls.

Plan efficiency is expressed as a percentage and can be defined as net assignable area divided by departmental gross area. The higher the number, the more efficient the plan is in terms of the amount of usable space it provides relative to the amount of overall space it occupies. For example, a hospital radiology department that has a plan efficiency greater than 65 percent is usually considered to have an efficient layout. However, the term "plan efficiency" can be a little misleading, because a plan that is too compact may provide inadequate circulation space or be uncomfortable to work in. Plan efficiency is not necessarily an indicator of flexibility or operational efficiency and thus should not be the sole economic criterion for planning. In fact, a tendency to pack too much functional space into a small, compact area usually will decrease operational efficiency and limit flexibility.

One way to preserve future flexibility is to strategically place "soft" office, storage, or administration space in a location and configuration where in the future it can be converted into revenue–generating space such as a procedure room. Ironically, this approach will decrease the quantitative plan efficiency of the layout in order to accommodate qualitative operational efficiency and flexibility.

Too often procedure rooms are programmed at their minimum dimensions, or even below. This may result in a small department footprint, but it severely limits the types of procedures that may be accommodated in each room. This limitation may be compounded in the future as more complex procedures requiring additional equipment and personnel become common.

Plan efficiency can be measured by analyzing the program and plans in terms of their revenue–generating potential. Each room can be classified as either "activity space," "support space," or "administration space (figure 8–18)." The number of activity spaces, such as examination and procedure rooms, is directly related to workload potential and thus to the revenue–generating capacity of the facility. Conversely, support and administration spaces, such as offices, waiting areas, and utility rooms, contribute indirectly to workload and revenue–generating capacity.

The proper amount of support and administration space enables each activity space to operate at its maximum potential. For example, if there are not enough dressing rooms for each radiography room, patient throughput will be constrained, negatively influencing work flow and potentially revenue. However, if too many dressing rooms are constructed, they will not be fully utilized and initial construction costs will be higher than necessary.

By labeling activity space on a floor plan with one color or tone and support and administration space with another, a pattern will emerge, indicating both revenue–generating and non–revenue–generating space. This graphic comparison of space allocation illustrates the proportion of revenue–generating space relative to the overall department size. However, it should be kept in mind that at many facilities, basic imaging procedures (such as general radiography) represent a high volume of moderate–cost and moderate–revenue workload, whereas special imaging procedures (such as angiography) represent a lower volume, yet each procedure has a significantly higher cost and generates potentially higher revenue.

It is essential that space programming be comprehensively completed and the final space program be reviewed, approved, and signed by both administration and all appropriate user groups before schematic design begins. If for some reason the net assignable area in the program changes during schematic design, the projected departmental gross area should be modified proportionately, because it has significant budget implications. Too often, there is a tendency to add net program area during schematic

Figure 8-18 Economic efficiency can be determined, in part, by the amount of revenue-generating space and how efficiently it is used. Courtesy of Anshen + Allen, Architects.

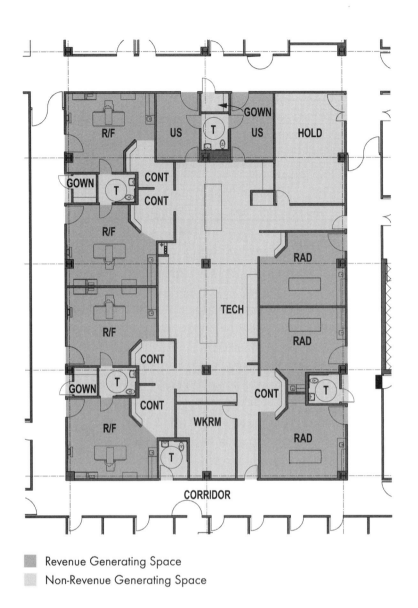

Revenue Generating Space
Non-Revenue Generating Space

design without increasing the gross area because there is no contingency in the budget for the additional space. This results in undersized rooms, insufficient support space, and storage areas that are likely to end up being used as offices. Attempts to increase net area without also increasing gross area create a congested plan, which may result in operational inefficiencies in one form or another. Area increases without corresponding budget increases will similarly create an inadequately budgeted building design.

Notes

1. M. Pederson, "The fable hospital," *Metropolis* 24, 5 (2005): 92–93.

2. B. Heulet, "The elements of a caring environment," *Healthcare Design* 4, 3 (2004): 18–23.

3. R. Junk and T. Gilk, "HIPAA compliance strategies for MR control rooms," AuntMinnie.com (Web site), October 26, 2004.

4. L. Berry, "Communicating without words," *Healthcare Design* 2, 1 (2002): 15–18.

5. L. Berry and N. Bendapudi, "Clueing in customers," *Harvard Business Review* 81, 2 (2003): 100–6.

6. Berry, 16.

7. C. Leibrock, *Design Details for Health: Making the Most of Interior Design's Healing Potential* (New York: John Wiley and Sons, 2000), 264–65.

8. M. Depies, S. Balint, M. Guell, J. McGovern, and C. Towle, "MRI anxiety reduction," *Administrative Radiology* 10, 7 (1991): 43–48.

9. S. R. Evers, "Psychology: Anxiety of MR patients extends beyond claustro-phobia," *Diagnostic Imaging* 21, 7 (1999): 41–43, 45, 48.

10. D. Armstrong, M. Kane, D. Reid, M. McBurney, and R. Aubrey-Rees, "The role of hospital design in the recruitment, retention and performance of NHS nurses in England," Commission for Architecture and the Built Environment (CABE), London, 2004, Executive Summary, 3.

11. V. L. Tyc, D. Fairclough, B. Fletcher, L. Leigh, and R. K. Mulhern, "Children's distress during magnetic resonance imaging procedures," *Child Health Care* 24, 1 (1995): 5–19.

12. D. Brailer, *The Decade of Health Information Technology: Delivering Consumer-centric and Information-Rich Health Care* (Washington, DC: Department of Health and Human Services, 2004), iii.

13. G. Lucier and V. Wanchoo, "Intelligent solutions for radiology data management and storage," *Health Management Technology* 23, 11 (2002): 20–23.

14. Lucier and Wanchoo, 21.

15. Lucier and Wanchoo, 22.

16. G. Roberts, "Green value," *Healthcare Design* 4, 4 (2004): 10–12.

17. L. Berry, D. Parker, R. Coile, K. Hamilton, D. O'Neill, and B. Sadler, "The business case for better buildings," *Frontiers of Health Services Management* 21, 1 (2004): 3–24.

CHAPTER 9

Work Flow
and Circulation

Facility design begins with circulation. Work flow patterns and the highly repetitive movement of people, objects, and information among different activity areas are major drivers of department layout. Several important factors influencing imaging facility work flow have changed dramatically in recent years. As a result, today's imaging facility layout and composition respond to different design drivers than did facilities of recent years. The most significant new rules influencing work flow design are those influenced by digital image and information management, which has radically altered the flow of data and noticeably altered technologist and radiologist traffic patterns.

This chapter identifies the work flow and circulation principles that affect medical imaging facility design and layout. Work flow constants are described to illustrate the primary functional needs of imaging facilities. Variables illustrate the numerous variations to work flow that must be accommodated through flexible design.

The Impact of Technology on Work Flow

While the single most important design driver of yesterday's film-based facility was the desire to reduce technologists' travel distances by locating film processors near the point of image acquisition, this driver of layout and work flow no longer applies to today's digital department. The efficient flow of images and information today depends more on data infrastructure than on the physical adjacency of spaces.

According to Osman Ratib, MD, PhD, a practicing radiologist and cardiologist and a pioneer in radiologic informatics at UCLA (who is now based in Geneva, Switzerland), "Film-based radiology was a very sequential process and one that was allowed to unfold over time. The resident or fellow would read the film, and then show it to an attending physician, and next to a subspecialist. We don't have time for that any more. Now, I get the image, read it, and get it out in less than an hour. If I don't do that in an hour, the doctor in the ER will be upset and call someone else."[1]

Radiologists today are more dependent on efficient image and information management systems, but technology alone will not improve radiology work flow. Says Paul Chang, MD, professor of radiology at the University of Pittsburgh School of Medicine and director of radiology informatics at the University of Pittsburgh Medical Center, "The real challenge is not the technology itself. PACS is just an enabling technology. . . . [T]he challenge is in changing people's attitudes. It's a classic change–management situation. . . . If we refuse to re–engineer ourselves, these systems will actually make more glaring the deficiencies in radiology services and can be seen as a threat to us."[2]

Thus, well–designed film–based imaging departments–with comprehensive infrastructure systems and an accompanying reengineered culture–will likely function effectively in today's digital environment, and even departments that have been fragmented over time due to piecemeal modifications may function better as digital departments than they would have in a film–based practice.

The pace of patient flow has also changed for many modalities. Compared to the historically slow image acquisition speed, which used to cause work flow bottlenecks, today's high–speed CT and MRI scanners result in work flow capacities so high that additional staff (such as technologists) and support spaces (such as prep and injection rooms) must be available in order to realize maximum throughput.

Finally, the growth of interventional radiology requires the flow of patients, staff, instruments, and material through interventional suites to be controlled–in a manner similar to that of surgical flow–in order to reduce the spread of infection. As a result, many interventional radiology suites are being decanted from diagnostic imaging departments (where work flow is less restricted) and co–located within the surgical suite (where work flow is more carefully monitored). Interventional patient flow also requires pre–procedure holding areas and postprocedure observation or recovery stations similar to those required for surgery. This is true even for minimally invasive procedures (such as CT–, MR–, and ultrasound–guided biopsies), which are likely to remain in the diagnostic imaging department.

Interdepartmental Work Flow

The numerous activities surrounding an imaging examination intertwine to form a complex, almost choreographed sequence of events. For hospital-based imaging services, department location must be coordinated with the hospital-wide flow of patients, staff, supplies, and material to and from other nearby departments. For freestanding imaging facilities, issues of location will differ from those for hospital-based departments (although issues of configuration may be similar). Because the movement of people, informa-

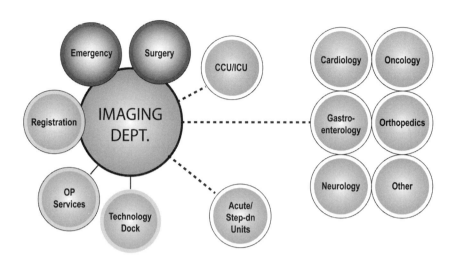

Figure 9-1 Interdepartmental functional relationships.

tion, and equipment involves peaks and lulls in workload, a variety of patient types, and a range of procedures, both the imaging department and freestanding imaging facilities must be adaptable and capable of change.

Certain adjacency requirements between a centralized hospital–based imaging department and other patient services are critical (figure 9–1). These include:

- Outpatient registration and clinic areas
- The emergency department (ED)
- Surgery
- Nursing units (both intensive care units and acute care units)

The relationship between imaging and the emergency department, the intensive care unit, and surgery are described in more detail in chapter 15, "Imaging Beyond the Radiology Department."

Work Flow Between Imaging and Outpatient Services

Because many imaging patients are outpatients, an inpatient imaging department should be conveniently accessible to ambulatory patients, regardless of whether they are also seen in a separate outpatient facility. In many cases, outpatients will be required to have a chest X–ray, blood work, and an electrocardiogram (EKG) in conjunction with other forms of outpatient treatment. Therefore, basic X–ray services should be near each of these functions, which often are located in the vicinity of an outpatient entrance or main hospital entrance.

Imaging services also should be easily accessible to specialty clinics, such as orthopedic clinics (which frequently utilize general radiography, MRI, and CT), obstetric/gynecological clinics (which use ultrasound), and oncology clinics (which use many imaging modalities such as MRI, CT, radiography, fluoroscopy, mammography, ultrasound, and nuclear medicine).

Imaging services in freestanding centers may be either the sole occupant of a facility or one of many outpatient-oriented tenants of a building or group of buildings. For instance, a medical office complex is likely to have imaging, laboratory, pharmacy, and other medical support services located convenient to medical offices and clinics. However, an outpatient orthopedic, cardiology, or oncology center might have specialized imaging services to support only its needs.

For facilities that house only imaging services, there will be fewer types of traffic and circulation, and so flow patterns will likely be simpler. In comparison, for centers with multiple functions, it may be necessary to separate staff work flow from patient traffic and to segregate users of imaging services from other areas. The degree to which separate traffic routes are needed depends on the size of the facility, the extent to which digital technology has been implemented, and the extent to which the various functions within the facility are compatible. However, in any freestanding facility it is a good idea to:

- Allow staff to arrive and leave without having to pass through patient areas
- Separate service vehicular traffic from patient traffic
- Provide emergency access and egress routes for patients who may become unstable before, during, or after a procedure

Although freestanding facilities usually provide services to outpatients, some states allow a percentage of nonambulatory patients to be examined and treated in nonhospital settings which meet certain code requirements. In addition, some ambulatory patients become temporarily nonambulatory during certain procedures due to either the invasiveness of the procedure or the type of sedation administered. Finally, not all ambulatory patients are in good health. As complex medical proceedures continue to move outside the hospital, more patients who are treated in nonhospital settings will require some form of supervision or visual observation.

Work Flow Between Imaging and the Emergency Department

Emergency patients often need immediate access to many imaging services, especially radiography, ultrasound, CT, interventional radiology, and interventional cardiology. Many large EDs have some imaging capabilities within the department. However, even when dedicated imaging capabilities are provided within the ED, close proximity to the imaging department is desirable to facilitate additional staff and patient traffic and to improve access to additional imaging services that are integral to emergency medicine.

Work Flow Between Imaging and Surgery

Imaging is becoming an increasingly important adjunct to surgery, and surgical procedures are becoming increasingly more reliant on image guidance. Therefore, data, personnel, and equipment may frequently travel between the two areas. Presurgical planning that utilizes three-dimensional CT and MRI as well as other sophisticated imaging modalities is necessary for the preparation of complex surgical procedures. Various forms of image guidance, such as ultrasound, fluoroscopy, and even CT, also are significant tools used within the operating suite to track surgical progress and location. Imaging itself is becoming more interventional. Surgical procedures such as biopsies may be performed within ultrasound, CT, and MRI suites. Hybrid surgical suites with integral MRI (and other forms of imaging) may be specially configured for stereotactic neurosurgery and other complex procedures.

Many imaging procedures are invasive, and thus some imaging procedure rooms now require a high level of sterility and support spaces for additional personnel as well as patient observation and holding. Imaging's integral role in surgery suggests that (1) radiologists and technologists need access to surgical suites and (2) surgeons will be performing more procedures in conjunction with radiologic personnel. Therefore, both proximity and advanced communication systems between the two departments are desirable. Imaging's interventional nature suggests that some patients may need surgical backup in the event of a medical emergency. In addition, observation of imaging patients prior to and after their procedures can sometimes be efficiently combined with perioperative prep, observation, and recovery areas.

Work Flow Between Imaging and Nursing Units

As the emphasis of healthcare shifts to outpatient diagnosis and treatment, the patient population remaining in the hospital generally is more critically ill than was true in the past. Imaging plays a pivotal role in the management of inpatients. In the intensive care unit in particular, rapid turnaround of images and image interpretation is essential to the effective care of patients because their medical condition is likely to change quickly and current diagnostic data have a direct impact on their course of treatment.

In addition, it is important to minimize the transport of these patients. One approach is to acquire ICU patients' images at bedside and review them on adjacent PACS workstations in the unit. Another alternative is to acquire the images in the ICU and interpret them in the radiology department or other remote location and report diagnostic findings back to the ICU via the PACS network. Therefore, many imaging procedures are performed using portable imaging equipment at the patient's bedside. Patient rooms must be sized and configured appropriately to accommodate bedside imaging.

The imaging department should have direct access to and from elevators used for inpatient transport. In some hospitals, an X-ray (or other procedure) room is decentralized and located near either critical care or acute care inpatient units. Generally, a cluster of approximately 100 beds is required to justify a decentralized imaging procedure room within or adjacent to the nursing unit.

Figure 9-2 Intradepartmental functional relationships.

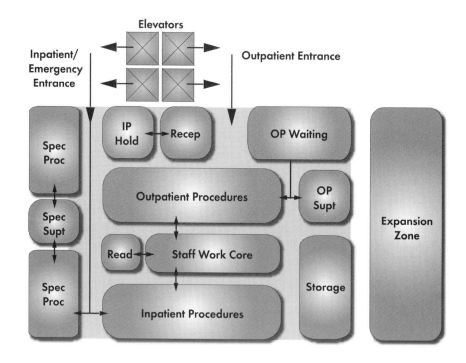

Intradepartmental Work Flow

In order for an imaging department to operate efficiently, it must accommodate various internal interrelated–and sometimes conflicting–circulation needs (figures 9–2 and 9–3). Traffic patterns to consider include the following:

- Patients must be afforded convenience, privacy, and confidentiality. Work flow should minimize patient travel distances, separate inpatient and outpatient traffic, and visually screen gowned patients from other patients. Where appropriate, circulation routes should provide patients (and staff) with natural daylight and views to the outdoors.
- Technologists must be able to travel efficiently between procedure rooms, patient preparation areas, supply rooms, and other staff areas. Room layout and adjacencies should enable unobscured visibility of the imaged patient while also providing acoustic containment, radiation safety, and protection from other physical forces, such as radio–frequency and electromagnetic emissions.
- Radiologists spend much of their time reading images and preparing reports in a reading room or office, but they must also be accessible to technologists and other clinical staff. Reading rooms should be located where radiologists can work undisturbed, but they should also provide radiologists

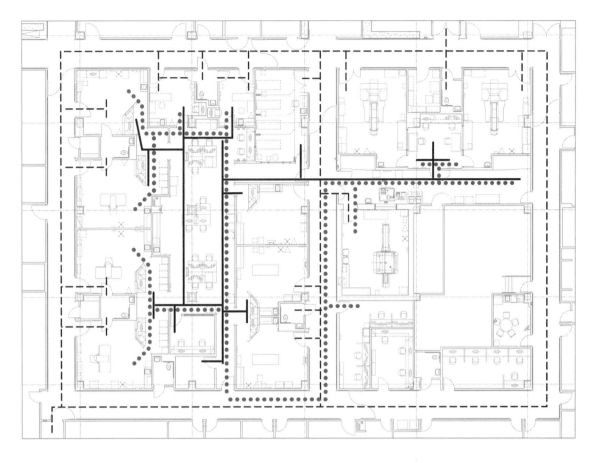

--- Patient
••••• Radiologist
——— Technologist

with convenient access to procedure rooms where interventional procedures are performed. Those radiologists involved in teaching and research activities may also need to travel between the imaging area and a remote office.

- Radiologic nurses require circulation routes that enable them to observe patients in holding areas but which also provide patients with acoustic privacy.

- Other support staff require circulation that separates the flow of materials and supplies from the flow of people. Additionally, the flow of clean supplies should be separated from the flow of soiled goods.

- Medical image and information transmission no longer requires that image acquisition and processing be physically adjacent. As noted previously, image and information management is the most rapidly changing aspect of imaging facility work flow.

Figure 9-3 Traffic and circulation within an imaging facility. Courtesy of Anshen + Allen, Architects.

Work Flow and Circulation Principles

In 1977 B. G. Brogdon, MD, of the University of New Mexico School of Medicine, described a work flow organizational concept for radiology departments that placed rooms for short-duration, high-turnover procedures toward the front of the department while locating rooms for more complex, longer-duration procedures in the back of the department (figure 9-4). In doing so, he underscored the importance of radiology department planning that was sensitive to the various traffic patterns inherent to medical imaging. Although his description concerned an older, film-based imaging environment, the concept remains relevant today.[3] The same planning philosophy had been implemented by Dr. Thure Holm of Lund, Sweden, in 1963. Dr. Holm also helped the Swedish government update requirements regarding imaging department design in 1978.

Since the time of Brogdon's description, image and information flow has become ubiquitous and instantaneous. As a result, digital images can now be viewed by referring physicians (and others) from within an office and from other key locations, such as the ED, operating rooms, nursing units, conference rooms, remote offices, and even homes, thus minimizing the need for referring physicians to physically travel to the radiology department (although some radiologists still prefer that a consult area be provided near or within their reading room). Referring physicians can consult with radiologists and other clinicians while each simultaneously views the same digital image from different locations.

For purposes of both efficiency and convenience, circulation routes should be short and direct. Dressing areas should be adjacent to both waiting and procedure areas to eliminate (or at least minimize) the need for patients who have already changed into gowns to travel through the

Figure 9-4 Conceptual layout diagram based on work flow and circulation.

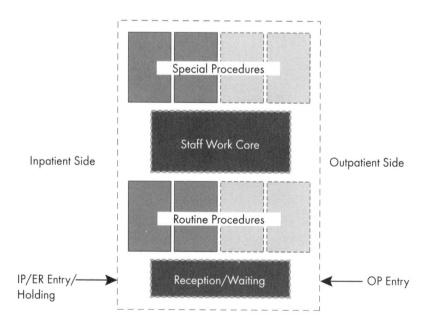

corridors, and patient examination and dressing areas should be screened from the view of waiting patients.

Patient and staff traffic should be separated to the extent practical. For example, staff areas can be segregated into "off-stage" zones, where confidential and HIPAA-compliant conversations can take place without being overheard, and "on-stage" zones, where technologists and nurses can escort and observe patients without having to travel far from their workstations. Inpatient and outpatient traffic also should be separated, however, procedure rooms should be able to be used by either group when necessary. In addition, traffic patterns should be established in such a way that they can support facility growth and expansion without having to be altered significantly or losing their inherent clarity. For example, perimeter corridors can be configured to become double-loaded, and corridor ends can be extended to accommodate predetermined incremental expansion.

It may be desirable to segregate rooms for special groups such as women's services (including mammography or ultrasound) into separate activity clusters to provide additional privacy and a special identity. Similarly, in practices where pediatric patients are seen frequently, a separate children's waiting alcove removed from heavy traffic areas may improve work flow. For many imaging examinations, children will be sedated. As a result, prep and holding areas should be located convenient to procedure rooms.

Some imaging modalities have unique traffic requirements. For instance, circulation in and near an MRI suite must be restricted for safety reasons to prevent unauthorized personnel from approaching the magnet room. Following a fatal 2001 incident in which a ferrous oxygen tank was mistakenly brought into a MR scan room, the American College of Radiology (ACR) established planning guidelines for MR safety.[4] These draft guidelines (which are included as an appendix of this book) suggest that any MR imaging facility be divided into four distinct zones, each having specific security access restrictions:

- Zone I is unrestricted and is limited to areas outside of the MR suite.
- Zone II is a restricted zone that must be supervised by authorized MR personnel. This zone includes reception, waiting, dressing, and toilet areas.
- Zone III is a highly restricted area where serious injury may occur. This zone includes the MR control room, entry vestibule, and computer room.
- Zone IV is the most highly restricted zone, where all non-MR personnel (including facility administrators and non-MR physicians) must be within direct visual supervision of at least two authorized and specially trained MR personnel. This zone consists of the MR scanning room.

There is debate among radiology and allied professionals about many of the specific recommendations contained within the draft ACR guidelines. For example, some of the recommendations may conflict with life-safety exiting requirements in some jurisdictions because the ACR guidelines focus on limiting access into the MR suite, while life-safety codes focus on emergency egress. While the guidelines are only recommendations, not requirements, it makes sense for MR facilities to comply with their intent to restrict access, while also complying with all other code requirements.

MR scanners must also be separated from objects that can degrade the MR image and from other equipment whose images can be degraded by the MR scanner. For example, MR scanners should be located away from power transformers, elevators, moving cars, and other large moving metal objects. Exact distances will vary by make and model of the equipment and can be provided by the equipment manufacturer or shielding consultant. (See chapter 13, "Physical Properties Influencing Design.")

Nuclear medicine suites also require special planning considerations for reasons of radiation safety and for ensuring proper image quality. For example, corridors where radioactive materials are handled must be controlled to prevent food and other materials from being exposed to radiation. Also, gamma cameras, which are susceptible to magnetic and radio-frequency interference, should be located away from MRI systems to avoid image degradation. As another example, nuclear medicine patients often leave the department after being given a low-level radioactive dose and return a short time later for their examination. Therefore, nuclear medicine functions should be organized so that dose administration rooms are easily accessed from the waiting area and are near the dose preparation room. In addition, "hot" patients who have been radioactively dosed should not walk alongside gamma camera rooms that are in use, to prevent active images from being distorted by the traveling patient. Therefore, nuclear medicine procedure rooms, and uptake rooms should be isolated from the hot lab and isotope waste holding areas to prevent low-level radiation in these areas from disturbing procedure results. Similarly, the hot lab and isotope waste areas should be located together. Often, nuclear medicine functions are organized as a distinct department, separate from other medical imaging services. Traffic patterns can be mapped on preliminary plan drawings to identify potential areas of congestion or conflict.

Traffic patterns for diagnostic radiography and fluoroscopy areas are often determined by the need to maximize technologists' ability to both increase patient throughput and observe patients during the examination from behind a radiation-shielded barrier. One planning concept, known as functional zoning (described in chapter 10, "Department Location and Configuration"), suggests a staff control corridor running parallel to a patient corridor (also known as an exam corridor). This arrangement enables separation of staff and patient traffic yet allows the technologist to greet the next patient in the exam corridor once the previous exam is completed.

In many practices, a radiologic technologist accompanies the patient into the procedure room. This will depend, in part, on the degree of invasiveness of the imaging procedure. Typically, for basic radiographic and R/F imaging procedures, the technologist greets patients at the reception area, escorts them to the dressing room and procedure room, positions them on the table, proceeds with the examination, assesses image quality, and either takes additional images or directs the patient back to the dressing or waiting area. For interventional procedures, however, a gowned patient will likely be brought into and out of the procedure room on a gurney. The patient may also pass through a prep room before the procedure and a recovery room following it.

Work Flow Variables

The work flow of a basic imaging examination is subject to many variations. However, almost all imaging procedures involve the following steps in one form or another:

1. The need or indication for the examination is determined.
2. An appointment is scheduled unless the clinical problem is of an emergency nature.
3. The patient's prior records are prepared or retrieved.
4. The patient is received in the radiology department or imaging center (or staff and portable equipment are transported to the patient).
5. The examination is conducted.
6. The images are processed and reviewed for quality and completeness.
7. The patient is sent home, sent to an inpatient nursing unit or another department, or asked to wait for further instructions.
8. The images are interpreted, a diagnosis is made, and findings are reported.
9. Results are reported to the referring physician and integrated with the patient's medical record.
10. Follow-up imaging evaluation or treatment is scheduled as necessary.

Although these steps may appear to be a simple linear succession of events, many complex subsets of activities are involved in each step. For some activities, patients are intimately involved; for other activities, patient involvement is limited or nonexistent. Some procedures require detailed interaction among patient, radiologist, radiologic nurses, and support personnel, whereas other procedures may be performed entirely by the technologist. Figure 9-5 illustrates the relationships between space

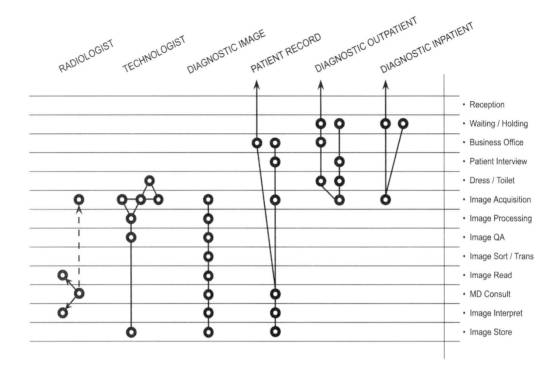

Figure 9-5 Work flow activity matrix.

and personnel for each of the basic steps that are part of medical imaging work flow.

Regardless of how each step is carried out, the basic activity can be referred to as a constant, whereas the various means by which it is carried out can be referred to as variables.[5] Each activity will vary according to the operational philosophy of the institution, the type of institution (teaching hospital, community hospital, freestanding imaging center, physician's office, and so on), the type of examination and equipment involved (routine versus special procedure), and the type of patient (emergency, acutely ill, stable, inpatient, or outpatient). For each constant, hundreds of variables may exist, all of which have architectural implications. For example, in the case of an emergency patient, it is desirable to have dedicated imaging equipment in the ED or for the ED and imaging department to be located near each other and connected by a dedicated circulation route that is short and direct, with a minimum of nonessential traffic traveling through it.

Many of the following work flow variables may exist for each of the constants listed above.

1. Constant: The Need or Indication for the Exam Is Determined

Variables

- A patient is rushed to the emergency department (ED). If the ED has radiographic capabilities, imaging staff are based there or will be called in. If comprehensive radiographic capabilities do not exist in the ED or if more sophisticated imaging capabilities are needed, the ED staff will have the patient transported to the main imaging department. Scheduled imaging patients may be delayed because of the emergency patient. Based on the results of plain radiographs, computed tomography (CT), ultrasound, and so on, the patient may be returned to the ED or brought to other locations such as the operating room, the ICU, or the medical nursing unit.

- An inpatient is identified as needing an imaging examination. The referring physician requests the next available examination time slot.
- An outpatient is identified as needing an imaging examination. An outpatient clerk or manager schedules an appointment when it is convenient for the patient and imaging department.

Architectural Implications

Adjacency between emergency and radiology departments is desirable; the circulation route should avoid busy public areas such as lobbies and waiting areas. To some degree, the importance of this adjacency depends on the extent of radiographic capabilities in the ED. Radiology staffing also will be affected by the extent of radiographic capabilities in the ED. It should be assumed that many emergency patients will require CT or other special exams, which might necessitate transporting patients to the radiology department or a special imaging unit if those capabilities do not exist within the ED.

2. Constant: An Appointment Is Scheduled

Variables

- Appointments are scheduled manually.
- Appointments are scheduled via an automated scheduling system.
- Some appointments are accepted on a drop-in basis.
- Billing and payment methods may be determined during appointment scheduling.
- The patient is given preparation instructions.

Architectural Implications

If a large percentage of appointments are unscheduled (as on a drop-in or emergency basis), room utilization may be inefficient. This should be considered when calculating the number of procedure rooms, waiting areas, and dressing booths to be provided and determining overall space requirements.

3. Constant: The Patient's Record Is Prepared

Variables

- This is the patient's first imaging exam. The patient's record needs to be assembled if possible. Transmitting (electronically or manually) the patient's most recent clinical examination and the indications of other tests may be adequate.
- The patient has been seen before but for a different medical problem. The old record is retrieved and held until the exam.
- The patient has been seen before for the same medical problem. The old record is retrieved and held until the exam. Just prior to the exam, previous images are displayed for comparison with the new image.

Architectural Implications

Computer workstations will be used throughout the enterprise, and their associated work environment requires special acoustic and lighting design.

4. Constant: The Patient Is Received in the Department

Variables

- An acutely ill patient is brought from the ED to the radiology department; his or her family members arrive later in the ED. The patient is accompanied by the medical team and is brought directly into the procedure room once it is available and has been prepared.
- An inpatient, already dressed in a hospital gown and accompanied by his or her medical chart or EMR, is transported from the nursing unit and kept in the inpatient holding area prior to the procedure. He or she may require monitoring, oxygen, and supervision prior to and during the exam. The transporting supervisory team may transfer its monitoring responsibilities to the radiology monitoring team, which includes radiologic nurses.
- An outpatient accompanied by family and/or friends arrives in a registration and waiting area. Registration and waiting areas may be either within the radiology department or combined with other outpatient functions. Outpatient waiting areas should be separate from inpatient holding areas. Individual waiting areas may be designated for special populations such as women's health or pediatrics.
- Co-payment may be required when the patient arrives. In that case, the billing representative may be needed to determine the amount of co-payment required.

- A patient requires pre-exam preparation. With a nuclear medicine exam, for example, the patient receives a low-level radioactive dose and returns later for the exam.
- A patient dons a gown and remains in a gowned waiting area or goes directly to a procedure room. His or her valuables and street clothes are stored in a locker area or remain in a locked dressing room.
- Educational information may be provided while the patient is waiting. Television and video may be used to facilitate patient education.

Architectural Implications

Waiting areas should be provided for inpatients, outpatients, and friends and family members. An area should be designated where patients, and those accompanying them, can ask questions confidentially. Consideration also should be given to providing an education alcove near the waiting area. Additionally, secure places should be made available to store patients' valuables and, in the event that cash payment is required upon arrival, to temporarily store money that has been collected. For MRI exams, metal objects, magnetic data storage media, and other similar items need to be separated from the patient and staff and temporarily stored away from the procedure room. The flow of people through an MRI suite must be controlled to prevent unauthorized individuals from approaching the MRI scanning room (see appendix for ACR MRI safety guidelines). Dressing areas should be located so that gowned patients can move discreetly to and from the examination room.

5. Constant: The Exam Is Conducted

Variables

- Exams may be simple and brief or complex and lengthy. A patient may require considerable assistance to be properly positioned for an exam. In some cases, young children might be accompanied by a family member as long as his or her presence does not pose a safety hazard.
- Young children may be sedated.
- Patients may undergo one exam or a series of exams. In the event of a series, some exams may need to take place before others. For example, if the patient has had a barium enema and is then referred for a gallbladder examination, the exam may not be possible because residual barium is likely to obscure the region of interest. The next examinations may be delayed for days because of this error in sequencing.[6]
- An exam may cause considerable or no discomfort to the patient.

- An exam may involve considerable or no risk to the patient.
- A patient may become nauseated, vomit, or develop a skin rash or anaphylactic shock in response to the required radiologic medication or contrast media. Immediate medical treatment must be available.
- Some imaging procedures, such as a virtual colonoscopy, barium enema, or abdominal ultrasound, require that a toilet room be directly and immediately accessible from the procedure room.
- A patient may require monitoring, life support, and medical supervision. In the case of MRI exams, only ancillary equipment made of special MR–safe or MR–compatible materials may be brought into the procedure room.
- Exams may be conducted by a technologist, a radiologist, or by a team of healthcare professionals.
- An exam may need to be repeated if the quality of the acquired image is not acceptable.
- Some procedure rooms may accommodate various imaging procedures; others may be equipped only for specific procedures (for example, a dedicated chest room).
- Some exams may yield single images that are fixed in time; others may yield a series of images taken over some period of time. Some images represent a two–dimensional view; others are manipulated to form three–dimensional or four–dimensional (3–D plus time) models.
- The facility layout may provide imaging control areas within the procedure room or may separate the two.
- Facility organization may include one large, centralized imaging department or may provide multiple imaging areas located throughout the enterprise.
- Inpatient and outpatient exam areas may be combined or separate.
- Some modalities may be provided via mobile trailers. These may be permanently located at one campus or may be shared and travel among numerous institutions.

Architectural Implications

Special facility requirements for different imaging modalities are discussed in chapter 12, "Room Design."

6. Constant: The Images Are Processed and Reviewed for Quality

Variables

- Images may be static or dynamic.
- Images may be reviewed on–site or from a remote location.

- Some imaging techniques, such as MRI, CT, and digital sub-traction angiography (DSA), involve complex manipulation of the image as part of image processing.
- Images may be stored on–site or at a remote location.

Architectural Implications

A postprocessing room with advanced computer workstations may be de-sirable within the imaging department.

7. Constant: The Patient Is Sent Elsewhere

Variables

- A patient is held for further observation. Usually this occurs somewhere other than in the imaging department, for ex-ample, in the nursing unit or the ED.
- A patient is rushed to surgery.
- A patient is returned to the ED.
- A patient is returned to the nursing unit.
- A patient returns home.
- Payment at the cashier/billing office may be due prior to departure, or the patient or his or her insurance carrier or health plan may be billed later.
- A follow–up appointment may be scheduled prior to departure.

Architectural Implications

A direct path of travel should be provided between the radiology depart-ment and the emergency, surgery, and nursing units. If possible, the route of travel should avoid busy public areas. Inpatient, outpatient, and emer-gency traffic should be separated where practical. Family waiting areas should be located so that they can be supervised but screened from pa-tient areas.

8. Constant: The Images Are Interpreted and a Diagnosis Is Made

Variables

- Some diagnoses will appear obvious; others will require collab-oration and consultation among various specialists to develop.
- Some imaging diagnoses will be defined in terms of anatomical to-pography. Others, such as nuclear medicine studies, will present information in terms of metabolic activity. Molecular imaging studies may present information related to cellular growth. Simi-larly, some diagnoses will relate to what has already happened to the patient; in other cases, future risk can be of greater thera-peutic importance.

Architectural Implications

Image reading areas and devices should be provided within radiologists' offices and/or in reading rooms, based on the particular requirements of the institution. In addition, group viewing areas should be provided for radiology staff and physicians from outside the department. In general, indirect variable lighting and acoustic control are needed for viewing images. (See the section entitled "Reading Rooms" in chapter 12, "Room Design.")

9. Constant: Results Are Transmitted, Reported, and Stored

Variables

- The reporting, transmission, and distribution of information may be automated, manual, or some combination of the two.
- Digital image viewing stations located in the ICU, the operating rooms, or the ED will allow rapid transmission of images when time is of the essence.
- Hospital information systems may be integrated with, or separate from, comprehensive radiology information systems.
- Information may be stored on film, paper, magnetic disks, optical disks (within electronic jukeboxes), or magnetic tapes, or as a combination of archival media. Film and paper image storage has declined with the advent of PACS archival systems.

Architectural Implications

Physical requirements for image transmission, distribution, and storage will vary greatly depending on the medium.

10. Constant: Follow-up Imaging Consultation or Treatment Is Scheduled

Variables

- An infinite number of variables exist.

Corridors and Exitways

Circulation corridors have an unfortunate way of becoming a home for equipment and supplies whose assigned storage space is either inadequate or poorly located. Sometimes corridors inappropriately become temporary holding areas for patients prior to and after imaging procedures. Such use of corridors is both unsafe and visually unpleasant. Additionally, life-safety codes have strict requirements limiting the use of corridors and exitways for medical equipment holding or storage. Additionally, in many jurisdictions, nonenclosed alcoves directly off inpatient corridors (where fire/smoke-rated construction is required) may not be used to store medical devices such as plate readers or even portable X-ray equipment. Thus, enclosed equipment and device storage must be provided to prevent instruments from ending up along corridors or in unassigned alcoves. Ideally, supply and equipment storage rooms should be located convenient to all patient and staff areas.

While hospital corridors generally are required to be at least 8 feet wide, the required width of corridors in outpatient imaging facilities is not so clearly spelled out and may vary by jurisdiction. Although life-safety codes usually require that exit corridors in a medical office building or clinic be at least 44 inches wide, this is too narrow for maneuvering patients and equipment within an outpatient imaging facility. In medical office buildings, dedicated staff passageways with no patient or equipment traffic should be at least 4 feet wide (although 5 feet is preferable and may be necessary in order to accommodate ADA clearance requirements); outpatient corridors with ambulatory patient traffic but no gurney traffic should be at least 5 feet wide (although 6 feet wide is preferable), and outpatient corridors with some equipment or stretcher traffic should be at least 6 feet wide (although 8 feet wide is preferable). The installation and replacement of large pieces of equipment may also influence corridor width and door sizes. In many cases, removable access panels or door panels are selected to allow for installation of large equipment components. For MRI (and other large and heavy equipment) installations, the entire route of travel required for equipment placement and removal may need to be structurally strengthened and spatially enlarged in order to accommodate the equipment's weight and size.

Some jurisdictions have special occupancy classifications for outpatient facilities, depending on the type of procedure performed and the degree to which the patient may become temporarily nonambulatory or "incapable of self-preservation" during the course of an emergency, such as a fire. Each classification has special exiting requirements, including minimum corridor widths. In addition, licensing agencies often have their own requirements. Although these requirements may not appear in the building code, they must be adhered to if the facility is either to be licensed or certified or to receive certain levels of reimbursement.

Additionally, the facility should be provided with a back door or service door, especially if deliveries are scheduled during patient treatment hours. A back door also allows staff to come and go without passing through the waiting area and may provide a direct route if emergency transport of medically unstable patients becomes necessary. Both the size of the facility and its occupancy classification will determine the minimum number of required exits. Exit requirements often are subject to interpretation by various regulatory agencies.

Material Management Transport Systems

The delivery, disposal, and reuse of supplies and equipment for imaging services is part of a larger system of enterprise-wide material management if the imaging service is hospital-based. If the facility is freestanding or independent, the material management service may be less complex. In either case, the flow of material and the space required for its storage, staging, and holding must be considered.

A number of supply systems–exchange carts, topping-up carts, just-in-time delivery, or any combination of these–may be used. Each system has its own space, scheduling, staffing, cost, and work flow implications. It is important to identify the material needs of the imaging services provided in the facility in order to select the appropriate supply systems and to understand their associated space and work flow requirements.

Linens, reusable supplies, and disposable items will all be used. Generally, a linen cart is preferred over fixed shelving for holding clean linens. The cart should be located in a clean supply room or at its point of use. Soiled linens must be stored in a separate area, preferably near a service corridor and away from the main entrance. Typically, ultrasound and interventional procedures are heavy users of linen.

Clean reusable and disposable supplies are typically stored on movable carts, which can be located in a central clean supply room, at their point of use, or within a series of decentralized storage areas. Secured holding areas for biohazardous waste and contaminated linens should be provided, ideally near a service corridor away from unauthorized traffic. Some interventional imaging procedures will require sterile instruments similar to those used in the surgical suite. Initial cleaning of these instruments may be performed in cleanup rooms in the imaging department, whereas terminal sterilization will likely take place in a central sterile department. The initial cleaning area should be located convenient to the interventional imaging procedure rooms.

Nuclear medicine services have special requirements due to their use of radioactive substances. Typically, a hot lab will be used for the receipt, preparation, and storage of radioactive substances. A cold lab, which is usually adjacent to or part of the hot lab, is where these materials are later processed and prepared prior to administration to the patient. In addition, a locked isotope waste room, adjacent to the hot lab, is where radioactive waste and linens are held until they decay to a safe level, after which they can then be safely transported and removed. Nonabsorbent, seamless, impervious, easily cleanable surfaces should be specified for corridors and procedure rooms throughout the nuclear medicine area.

Notes

1. M. Hagland, "Reshaping radiology: Change management and workflow optimization give PACS new punch," *Healthcare Informatics*, November 2004, 26–30.

2. Hagland.

3. B. G. Brogdon, *Planning Guide for Radiologic Installations* (Chicago: American College of Radiology, 1977), 32–45.

4. E. Kanal, J. P. Borgstede, et al., "American College of Radiology White Paper on MR Safety," *American Journal of Roentgenology* 178 (2002): 1335–47.

5. R. Lindheim, *Uncoupling the Radiology System* (Chicago: Hospital Research and Education Trust, 1971), 57.

6. G. S. Lodwick and E. Kovisto, "Radiology space requirements in the computer age," in M. Kormano and F. E. Stieve, eds., *Planning of Radiological Departments* (Stuttgart: Georg Thieme Publishers, 1974), 112.

CHAPTER 10

Department Location and Configuration

The location of an imaging department (or freestanding imaging facility) is one of the first design decisions that must be made, yet it is also one of the most important. Its location will determine how accessible imaging services are for patients, visitors, staff, faculty, and all who directly or indirectly are involved in imaging functions. Location will also affect the department's (or the facility's) configuration by either accommodating or restricting an optimal geometry, and thus will affect work flow (as described in the previous chapter).

This chapter considers criteria for the location and configuration of imaging departments and facilities relative to both interdepartmental traffic and intradepartmental work flow. It also discusses special considerations for freestanding imaging facilities. Additionally, the chapter illustrates various layout typologies.

Department Location

Historically, imaging departments were frequently located on basement levels of hospitals, often without access to natural daylight. The weight of imaging equipment and the need for radiation protection are reasons that typically have been cited for a basement location. However, imaging departments are usually better located on grade-level floors (or above) to improve access, to accommodate future expansion, and to provide access to daylight.

The ability to expand the department or to allow for future conversion of areas within the department should be a primary consideration when determining the imaging department's location and configuration. Departments located below grade can be difficult to expand unless ample unfinished space or "soft" space also is provided, or unless major expansion (in which expansion of the imaging department is one component) is planned. Additionally, most basements contain industrial-type activities, such as material management and central processing, that are incompatible with patient activities. It is desirable to have those spaces remote from patient traffic routes.

Another advantage to a grade-level location is access to natural daylight, even where imaging procedures take place within darkened rooms. Natural daylight can be helpful in brightening and softening of interior spaces, particularly in facilities planned with perimeter patient corridors. A perimeter corridor also allows light into the department and provides a direction for future expansion. In addition, a grade-level location is advantageous for equipment delivery, installation, and replacement, as equipment will not need to travel via cranes or elevators.

The imaging department should be located for convenient access to and from other departments that are functionally related to imaging activities and for convenient transit of patients and staff between these departments. Most users of the imaging department are located at grade level or above. Interdepartmental adjacencies have been described in chapter 9, "Work Flow and Circulation."

Location Considerations for Freestanding Imaging Facilities

Criteria for the location of, and access to, freestanding imaging facilities will differ from those previously discussed in this chapter because freestanding imaging facilities, by definition, are not physically attached to hospital departments. Location criteria for freestanding centers relate more closely to individual healthcare referral patterns, community and regional demographic patterns, and the distribution of services among both competing and collaborating providers.

Because the perfect site may not exist or be available, a few best choices should be identified and compared to one another. In this way, the relative strengths and weaknesses of each can be analyzed and a sensible selection made. The following sections address criteria (described by Lifton and Hardy in *Site Selection for Health Care Facilities*) that should be considered when selecting a site for a freestanding imaging facility.[1]

Proximity to Patients and Referring Providers

Any service facility should be located near the people who use it. Because medical imaging services usually are the result of referrals from primary or other healthcare providers, the distance between the imaging facility and referring physicians must be considered. Similarly, the location of other facilities providing similar services can have an impact on the success of a new facility.

Major Road Access

A well-designed building is of little use if it is not easily accessible. Even a building that is well located within its projected market area must be easily accessible by private car, on foot, or by mass transit. Furthermore, these routes should be convenient for staff, patients, and equipment transport. A slow and indirect route or one with constant traffic congestion is tedious. "Generally the ideal is for a [facility] to be close enough to a major highway that access to the general area of the site is easy from all directions, yet not so close to the road that noise and congestion result."[2]

Accessibility by Public Transportation

The importance of access by public transportation depends on the general location of the site (urban versus rural) and the degree to which public transportation already exists. If the quality of the existing public transportation network in the region is marginal or if the network is not heavily used, accessibility by public transportation is less important than it would be in an area where people rely more on this type of transportation.

Direct Access

All circulation routes should be clearly visible from the street and coordinated so that they do not conflict with one another. It also is important that on-site traffic congestion and peak parking loads be anticipated. Provisions should be made to ensure that these peak loads do not complicate off-site circulation.

A site with streets on many sides will likely enable adequate segregation of various types of traffic, making it easy for special routes, such as those used primarily for patient arrival, to be directed to specific areas on the site without interrupting other routes, such as those reserved for staff circulation.

Size and Usable Area

The actual size of a site alone is not always an accurate indicator of the amount of usable area. In determining the amount of usable land needed, building configuration, parking, and circulation patterns must be considered. Local building codes often require building setbacks and may further restrict the usable area, including parking and circulation layouts. Consideration also should be given to the need for expansion, as the site might be of adequate size for present needs but not for future growth.

Configuration and Orientation

In addition to size, the geometry and configuration of a parcel of land can determine its relative usable area. For example, a long, narrow parcel might not have the depth required to efficiently arrange buildings, parking, and circulation, whereas a smaller but more regular parcel might. The site configuration should accommodate the greatest amount of design freedom in terms of building configuration, location within the site, circulation, and parking layout. Although a square or rectangular geometry is most likely to allow such freedom, other configurations can be considered. However, sites with gross irregularities or unusual topography may present unnecessary design constraints.

Zoning

Most municipalities have zoning requirements based on land use. Local codes should be reviewed to see if any restrictions exist. If they do, it sometimes is possible to have land rezoned or to obtain a conditional use permit, although this often is a lengthy and costly process.

Some zoning ordinances specify required setbacks and restrict the size, height, and type of building. Most codes specify required parking areas and loading zones, often on the basis of a building's occupancy classification. Before design begins, a thorough investigation and interpretation of applicable codes and ordinances must be completed. The existing zoning of adjacent sites also should be examined to determine if neighbors are likely to be compatible in terms of noise, character, appearance, and traffic.

Legal and Physical Restrictions

Once the site's configuration and orientation have been evaluated, it must be examined more closely to see whether any legal or physical restrictions will adversely affect its development potential. Legal restrictions may be in the form of easements, covenants, trust agreements, or previous subdivision rules. They may restrict the location of construction on the site, the type of use, or the size or height of a building.

Many of the operational disadvantages of being remote from related services located in the hospital or other freestanding facilities can be mitigated through the implementation of enterprise-wide data and communications systems. For example, scheduling and billing services can be remote. PACS, IMACS, and teleradiology systems enable images and other data to be transmitted to and from remote sites. Thus, radiologists can review images acquired in other locations, and referring physicians can re-

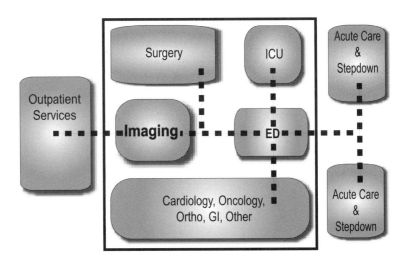

Figure 10-1 Centralized models for imaging services enable staff to work efficiently without having to duplicate imaging equipment.

view images and reports sent to their homes and offices. Additionally, remotely located archive images can be digitized and sent on an as-needed basis. Finally, special teleconferencing and interactive communication capabilities can allow real-time consultations to take place and procedures to be observed from remote facilities.

Centralized Versus Decentralized Imaging Department Configurations

Imaging departments can be centralized, decentralized, or some combination of both. Proponents of centralized imaging claim that in a centralized department, quality control is better, radiology personnel are utilized more efficiently, and equipment is not duplicated unnecessarily (figure 10-1). On the other hand, advocates of decentralized imaging cite reduced patient transport, decreased waiting time, a streamlined imaging work flow, and flexibility as beneficial outcomes of decentralizing these functions.

While in a film-based department decentralized imaging was previously the bane of radiology managers, it has been made easier through the use of digital image and information management systems (figure 10-2). Therefore, more hospital imaging functions are now becoming decentralized and organized around specialty programs. Decentralized imaging, however, can result in a costly duplication of imaging equipment if each decentralized device or cluster of devices is not heavily utilized. For example, nursing units and diagnostic and treatment functions may be organized by individual organ-specific or medical subspecialty program floors, such as musculoskeletal programs (providing orthopedic, rehabilitation, and radiology services), neuroscience programs (providing neurology, neurosurgery, and neuroradiology services), and cardiopulmonary programs (providing cardiac and thoracic surgery, cardiology, pulmonary, and radiology services). Organization based on decentralized programs often is found in large teaching hospitals, where patients, staff, residents, interns, and

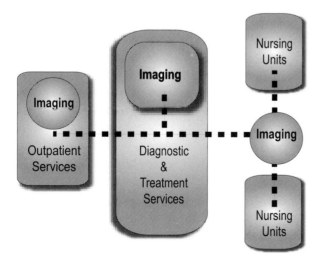

Figure 10-2 Enterprise-wide digital image and information management systems enable imaging services to be more decentralized and thus come to the patient.

medical students would otherwise frequently need to travel long distances between related areas.

Another form of decentralized imaging services occurs when outpatient imaging is separated from inpatient imaging. Outpatient services may be provided within a separate zone of the hospital imaging department, a separate outpatient imaging department within the hospital campus, or a physically separate outpatient facility.

Department Configuration: The Functional Zone Concept

Numerous systems based on repetitive planning modules have been used to develop the layout of imaging departments. One notable example is a detailed system of modular radiology planning described in 1972 by Dr. Thure Holm of the University Hospital in Lund, Sweden, at the International Symposium on Planning of Radiological Departments (ISPRAD) in Finland.[3] This concept, sometimes referred to as the functional (or concentric) zone concept, was further described in 1982 by Dr. Harry Fischer of Strong Memorial Hospital at the University of Rochester Medical Center.[4] It comprises the following activity zones:

- Patient zone, where waiting and patient preparation occur.
- Examination zone, where the primary activity of imaging examination occurs.
- Central staff zone (previously called the central image processing zone by Holm and Fischer), where image processing and quality assurance occur. Even though image processing is now performed mostly through digital technology, hard copy in some form may still be required for records and reports sent to referring physicians outside the facility, who may not yet have PACS systems. In addition, the placement of imaging examination rooms around a central core remains an effective organizing tool to separate staff and patient activities.
- Personnel zone, where staff offices and support spaces are located.
- Image archive zone (previously called the long-term file zone by Holm and Fischer), where inactive files are stored. A central film file room is no longer necessary, as digital images can now be stored anywhere.

Although the details of Holm's and Fischer's descriptions of modular planning are somewhat dated (for example, room sizes will not necessarily apply to today's equipment, and electronic image management was not considered because it was not yet available), the philosophy behind the concept is worthy of review. Their identification of separate functional zones led to a clear planning logic that has since been incorporated into many contemporary design solutions. While the flow of information has changed radically since this concept was first developed, the separation and coordination of the various flow patterns of people remain applicable.

Patient Zone

The patient zone includes space for patients prior to and after their imaging procedure. Patients have their first contact with the imaging department and staff in this area. First impressions should be positive ones. If both inpatients and outpatients are seen in the department, the patient zone can be separated into two distinct areas, each adjacent to the examination zone. Functions found in the patient zone include:

- Patient and visitor waiting areas
- Dressing rooms
- Toilet rooms
- Lockers
- Education space
- Reception and registration areas
- Patient corridors
- Patient preparation and holding areas

Reception and registration areas should be located in such a way that clerical staff can easily supervise waiting areas and have easy access to patient records and administration areas. A room or alcove screened from the waiting area should be provided for confidential medical or financial conversations and/or as an education space.

Sometimes dressing areas are clustered together, with each cluster serving a series of procedure rooms, rather than locating a dressing room near each procedure room. A clustered arrangement tends to accommodate variations in work flow and thus more effectively maintain a high volume of patient examinations. The cluster arrangement also facilitates those patients who need to be seen in more than one examination room. In addition, clustered dressing rooms may accommodate the accessibility requirements of the Americans with Disabilities Act (ADA) more efficiently than do segregated dressing rooms. Patients and visitors in the waiting area should not be able to see into examination or dressing areas. If clustered dressing rooms are used, the design should preclude patients from having to travel far through public corridors to and from procedure rooms.

Examination Zone

The examination zone consists of two primary elements: examination or procedure rooms and control areas (figure 10-3). Patient access is limited to the procedure room; they are not permitted in the control area. The control area is where technologists' consoles and other equipment used to control the imaging procedure are located. The control area should be carefully designed with both visual and acoustic barriers preventing patients from

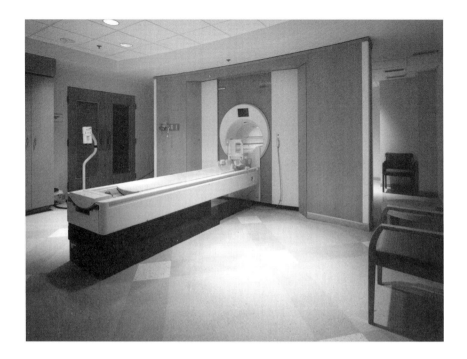

Figure 10-3 The examination zone–the point where care is administered–should be designed for patient and staff needs, not just the physical requirements of equipment. © Michael Dersin Photography. Architect: Anshen + Allen.

seeing or hearing confidential information about other patients.[5] Where two procedure rooms share one control room, windows between the control room and the procedure rooms should be configured to prevent patients in one procedure room from being able to see patients in the other procedure room.

In the functional zone concept, all control functions were removed from the procedure room and placed in a control corridor, running parallel to a series of procedure rooms. In many instances, however, the preferred location for X–ray control alcoves is within the procedure room. This occurs more often in general radiography and fluoroscopy rooms than it does in special procedure rooms, such as those used for interventional radiology and interventional cardiology. Special procedure rooms often have an enclosed control room directly adjacent to the procedure room, rather than within a control corridor. (Advantages and disadvantages of control corridors, control alcoves, and control rooms are discussed in the section entitled "General Considerations for Control Corridors, Control Alcoves, and Control Rooms" in chapter 12, "Room Design.")

As mentioned previously, the imaging department should be arranged so that rooms for procedures that are of short duration and high frequency are located near the waiting area and the department entrance. This configuration will reduce the amount of traffic congestion in the patient corridor.

Central Staff Zone

Imaging departments that have been planned using the functional zone concept often have a staff work core in the center. If the control corridor approach is used, the work core abuts the control corridor. If the control corridor approach is not used, the work core abuts procedure rooms that

Figure 10-4 The staff core can be designed as an interactive work core, promoting collaboration among various medical specialties. © Michael Dersin Photography. Architect: Anshen + Allen.

have internal control alcoves and control rooms adjacent to the procedure rooms. While the staff core is no longer required for processing and organizing films, it still provides the important functions of enabling technologists to access multiple examination rooms from one location and separating staff traffic from patient traffic. A central core can be designed as an interactive work area/conference area, and it also allows technologists to quickly back each other up in case of an emergency (figure 10–4).

Personnel Zone

The personnel zone includes office space and staff support areas such as lockers, toilet rooms, lounges, and conference space. Sleep rooms and showers also may be desired. If a staff lounge and conference areas are to be shared by other departments, these spaces should be located along the perimeter of the department to keep nondepartmental traffic away from busy work areas. Some department managers prefer to locate the lounge near the work area for the convenience of the technologists. Many radiologists review and interpret images in their offices; others review and interpret them in dedicated reading rooms, which should be located in a quiet area that is also close to interventional procedure rooms that radiologists need to access.

Image Archive Zone

Most imaging files are stored electronically, and those procedures for which images are still captured on film will soon become digital. Similarly, if previous film images are needed for comparison to current digital images, they are usually digitized as needed. While it is not cost–effective to digitize entire film file rooms for archival storage, it is appropriate to digitize individual images as a specific previous film is needed.

Several options exist for digital image archiving. Some multifacility organizations provide long-term archiving in one remote location, where one central archive stores data from various facilities, each located in a different city. Medium-term storage can be provided via server racks located within each facility's main data room. Short-term storage can be part of each imaging device. Alternately, file storage can be outsourced through companies known as application service providers (ASPs) (see chapter 8, "Design Concepts"). In each case, a long-term central file room is no longer required within the facility.

Plan Typologies

Over the years, the size and configuration of imaging facilities have evolved in parallel with the evolution of healthcare facilities and imaging equipment. This section discusses a variety of common plan typologies. Many corridor-based typologies, which lack flexibility, reflect the configuration of early hospitals, with long single- and double-loaded corridors. Core and cluster plans improve on their more linear predecessors and reflect an approach to planning that is appropriate for both contemporary hospital-based departments and freestanding imaging facilities.

Single-Loaded Configurations

Many single-corridor imaging department layouts developed as a result of long, narrow hospital wings, which were common in the first three-quarters of the twentieth century (figure 10-5). Although these layouts may be usable for small departments with low workload volumes, the single-corridor plan has many limitations.

First, inpatient, outpatient, staff, and service traffic are combined. In addition, there often is little separation between departmental traffic and through traffic, which some codes do not allow. Expansion is inconvenient and usually limited to one end, and travel routes are long, by definition. Many old single-corridor departments needing renovation are better off if they are relocated and configured more efficiently, especially if they were initially designed with short structural bays (and therefore numerous structural columns), inadequate infrastructure, and floor-to-floor heights that are incompatible with current imaging facility requirements.

Double-Loaded Configurations

The traditional double-loaded corridor plan is a slight improvement over the single-corridor arrangement (figure 10-6). Although there is potential for some traffic segregation, travel distances still tend to be long. Communication among staff and the mixing of different types of traffic remain problems. In addition, space utilization tends to be inefficient because the increased amount of corridor space is disproportionate to the limited functional advantages it provides.

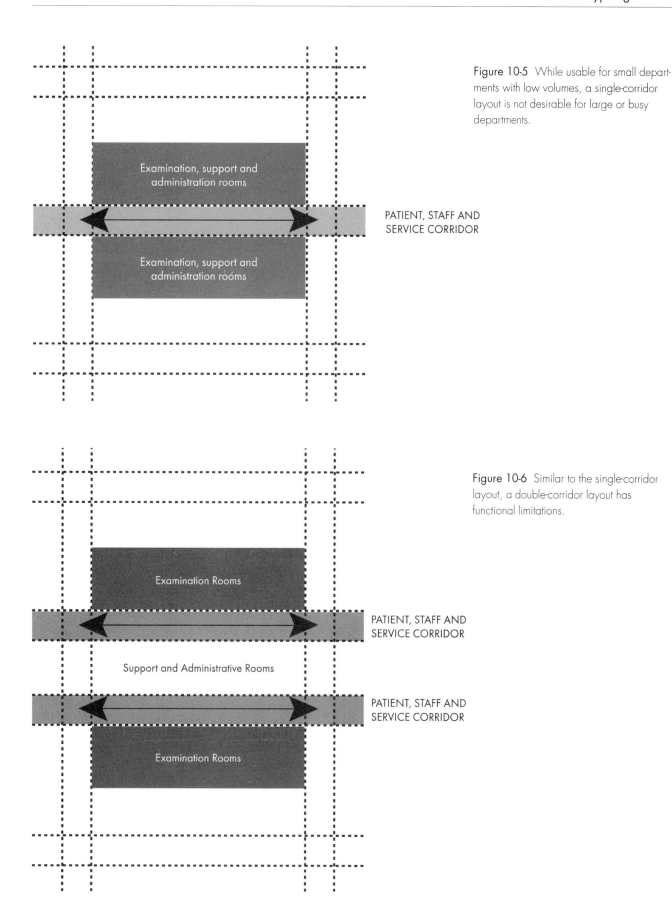

Figure 10-5 While usable for small departments with low volumes, a single-corridor layout is not desirable for large or busy departments.

Figure 10-6 Similar to the single-corridor layout, a double-corridor layout has functional limitations.

Figure 10-7 A core layout separates patient and staff traffic.

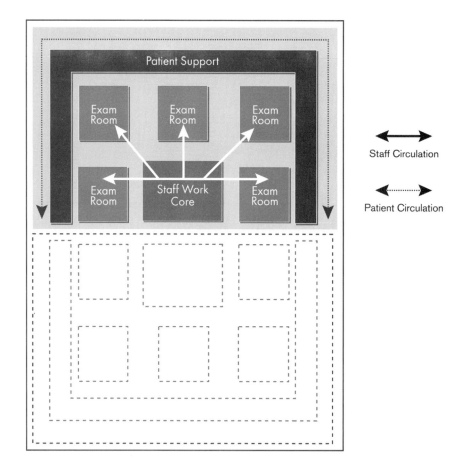

Figure 10-8 A cluster layout–with multiple staff cores–can be ideal for large departments or facilities with numerous types of patients.

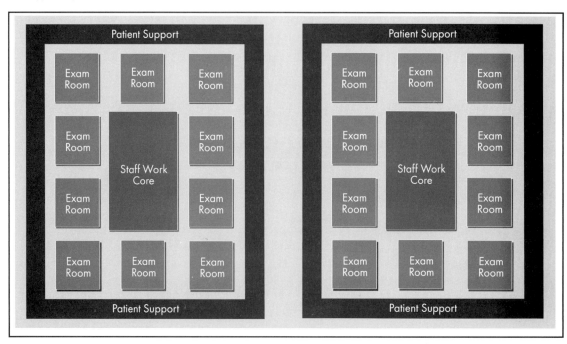

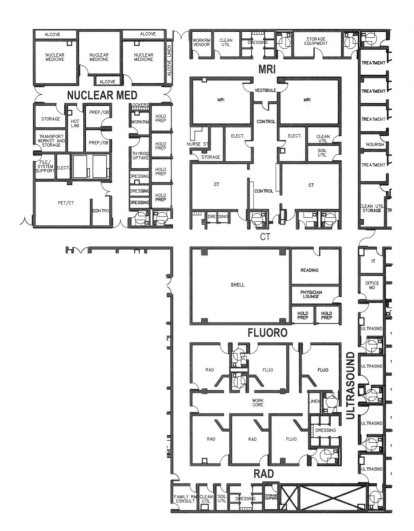

Figure 10-9 In a cluster plan, each modality group can have its own work core and support space. Courtesy of Anshen + Allen, Architects.

Core Configurations

The core plan solves some of the inefficiencies found in the single- and double-corridor layouts (figure 10–7). Based on a concentric arrangement of activity zones, the core plan separates staff and patient areas and allows for the separation of inpatient and outpatient traffic. The core layout allows a discrete division between patient, examination, and personnel zones, as previously described in the functional zone concept. A core arrangement circumscribed by a patient corridor can take advantage of natural daylight if it is located along a building's perimeter. At least one edge of the department should remain unobstructed for future expansion. A single-core plan can work well for small- and medium-size departments (fewer than ten or twelve procedure rooms).

Cluster Configurations

The cluster plan is a modified form of the core arrangement (figures 10–8 and 10–9). It is appropriate for most medium- and large-size departments where procedure rooms can be arranged into several modality zones or clusters. For example, basic radiography, fluoroscopy, and ultrasound rooms might constitute one cluster, with CT and MR in another. This approach is also beneficial when separate zones for special patient populations are desired, such as a women's imaging cluster, a pediatric imaging cluster, and a general imaging cluster.

Notes

1. J. Lifton and O. B. Hardy, *Site Selection for Health Care Facilities* (Chicago: American Hospital Association, 1982).

2. Lifton and Hardy.

3. M. S. Lapayowker, H. L. Kundel, and F. J. Shea, "Planning of a vertically oriented radiology department in a program–floor hospital," in M. Kormano and F. E. Stieve, eds., *Planning of Radiology Departments* (Stuttgart: Georg Thieme Publishers, 1974), 97.

4. H. W. Fischer, *Radiology Departments: Planning, Operation, and Management* (Ann Arbor, MI: Edward Brothers, 1982).

5. R. Junk and T. Gilk, "HIPAA compliance strategies for MR control rooms," AuntMinnie.com (Web site), October 26, 2004.

CHAPTER 11

Space Requirements

Planning for too much space costs a lot of money; planning for too little costs even more! With all the complexity and continually changing variables associated with medical imaging, how is it possible to determine the size of an imaging facility, the number and size of procedure rooms, and their optimum configuration? Because all facilities are unique, there is no single answer to such a question as "How big is a radiology department?" any more than there is an answer to "How big is a house?"

Determining space requirements is a rigorous and complex process that depends on the outcome of other related studies, such as strategic analysis, demographic research, and functional programming. However, some individuals tend to look for quick solutions for identifying space needs. Although a broad-brush approach might be acceptable at a project's inception (when no more than order-of-magnitude information is needed to see whether it is financially viable), to continue detailed planning without verifying preliminary guesstimates is inappropriate. The penalty paid for bypassing detailed functional and space programming is the creation of a facility that either cannot operate efficiently or will soon require costly renovation.

This chapter illustrates a general methodology for determining space requirements for any imaging facility and identifying the variables that may influence the size of a specific project. The discussion includes how to forecast the type, number, and size of procedure rooms required, as well as the amount and size of support space needed. Space requirements for any particular imaging facility can be most accurately determined only after conducting a careful analysis of the specific facility's needs.

Space Determinant Methodology for the Imaging Facility

Two processes–functional programming and space programming–must precede the design and planning of any healthcare facility. Functional programming analyzes current and future operational models for staffing, room throughput, functional adjacencies of space, and service delivery. As part of this process, it evaluates historical and current workload data in order to calculate future space projections. Thus, functional programming is the first step in the umbrella process of programming. Its end product describes anticipated workloads (quantity, duration, and mix of procedures) in terms of staffing, equipment, and work flow. It also identifies operational procedures and the desired adjacency of spaces necessary for services to function efficiently.

Space programming follows functional programming and translates the functional program into area requirements. It identifies the size, number, and spatial characteristics of every room and department in the facility.[1] Functional and space programming begins with a series of interviews among the planners and the administrative and medical users of a facility. The following historical and existing data are typically reviewed and analyzed:

- Workload volumes in terms of procedure mix and quantity
- Staffing patterns, trends, and opportunities for cross-training
- Equipment requirements
- Degree of satisfaction with existing space, equipment, and work flow
- Assumptions regarding future trends, based on operational goals, market changes, and changes in technology
- Space requirements to accommodate future workload (number and size of rooms to accommodate anticipated patient examinations, consultations and treatments)
- Space requirements to support future staff volumes (number and size of offices, conference rooms, reading rooms and support spaces)
- Space requirements to accommodate future equipment
- Estimated space requirements to accommodate future expansion scenarios
- Functional adjacencies
- Work flow and traffic patterns

The user group interviews will disclose varying opinions from different individuals within the organization (administrators, radiologists, technologists, nurses, physicists, engineers, housekeeping personnel, clerical staff, patient advocates, and so on). Because the most vocal individuals may not necessarily be those with the most authority, recording individual requests without obtaining some degree of consensus from the group can prove misleading. The planning team will benefit from having one key individual from each user group first take responsibility for reviewing and verifying the collected data and then become part of the review process all the way through the contract documents and construction phases of service.

Key Space Generators

For each type of room or area there usually is a primary driver, or key space generator, that best determines the number, size, and shape of rooms or areas.[2] Key space generators reflect units of work (such as the number of annual CT scans), number of staff, and size of equipment. For example, one cardiac catheterization procedure room can generally accommodate approximately 1,200 to 1,500 cases per year (depending on the type of cases). It should be noted that certain equipment technology advances can have a significant impact on how key space generators influence throughput and the associated space needed. For example, while direct radiography and computed radiography are both digital X-ray processes (and devices), a DR unit can potentially accommodate more patients per day/per room as compared to a CR unit, because DR does not require a technologist to spend time physically transporting a phosphor plate cassette to and from a plate reader. Similarly, fast multidetector CT devices can accommodate more patients per day than can slower CT devices; they also may require an additional patient prep/injection room and additional staff to support their potential increased rate of throughput.

Some types of rooms are affected by more than one key space generator. For example, the optimal number of cardiac catheterization labs is determined primarily by the anticipated number of annual cases, whereas each catheterization lab's size and shape is influenced by the array of equipment and how it will be used (biplane versus single–plane equipment, amount of vascular versus electrophysiology studies, etc.). Furthermore, the size of a catheterization lab might be larger in a teaching facility, where medical students and others may participate in procedures, than in a similar type of room located in a small community hospital.

In contrast to imaging procedure rooms, which are sized according to workload and equipment requirements, offices are sized according to the number of occupants and their status within the organization, the number of people involved in consultations, how the office is used, and the size and arrangement of furniture needed within the room (for example, will furniture in the office need to accommodate a small conferencing arrangement or only individual workstations?). Workload (the number of consultations) has little influence on office size. The number of offices required is based on the number of staff, which is indirectly a result of both workload and the number of procedure rooms. In teaching facilities, the number of offices may be higher than in nonteaching facilities.

Types of Space

Most imaging facilities are composed of three types of space: activity, support, and administration. (See the "Economy" section in chapter 8, "Design Concepts.") Activity space reflects the primary activity of the facility (such as image acquisition) and is the key determinant of department area. The required number of activity spaces (for example, procedure rooms) is determined by the department's anticipated workload.

TABLE 11-1: PROCEDURE ROOM SIZE GUIDELINES

Procedure Room	Minimum Dimensions: Length × Width (ft) (Not Recommended)	Suggested Dimensions: Length × Width (ft)	Suggested Ceiling Height	Remarks
Dedicated chest room	14 × 12	16 × 14	9' 6"	Includes control alcove
General radiography—inpatient	16 × 12	17 × 15 to 20 × 16	9' 6"	Includes control alcove Can be smaller if used exclusively for ambulatory patients Can be larger if dedicated to emergency patients
Routine fluoroscopy	16.5 × 12.5	17 × 15 to 20 × 16	9' 6"	
Universal R/F	N/A	20 × 16	9' 6"	
Interventional cardiology/ interventional radiography	20 × 20	25 × 20 to 27 × 22	10' 0"	Excludes control room and electronics equipment room
CT exam room	18 × 20	24 × 19	Varies	Consider orienting scanner at a 30° angle to axis of control room
Nuclear medicine with one full-body scanning camera	18 × 16	20 × 16 to 20 × 20	9' 0"	
MRI	Varies	28 × 18	Varies	Varies significantly, based on type of magnet, field strength, and manufacturer
Mammography (upright unit)	9 × 11	10 × 14 to 12 × 12	8' 0"–9' 0"	Can be combined with prone room
Mammography (prone unit)	12 × 12	16 × 14	8' 0"–9' 0"	
Ultrasound	10 × 12	10 × 14 to 12 × 12	8' 0"–9' 0"	2 adjacent rooms at 10 × 16 can be easily converted to one R/F room
PET/CT	26 × 16	28 × 20	9' 0" or higher	Excludes control room and equipment room Varies by manufacturer

The size and configuration of imaging rooms often are determined by clearances required for the specific imaging equipment selected. Room dimensions are further influenced by patient flow, staff flow, and ancillary equipment that will be used within the room (table 11–1). It is advisable to size procedure rooms larger than the manufacturer's minimum dimensions. This is sometimes referred to as a "loose–fit" approach, as noted in chapter 8.

As an example of the loose–fit approach, computers and electronics racks that are required for MRI, angiography, cardiac catheterization, and other specialized equipment vary significantly from one manufacturer to another. Therefore, programmed space should be allocated for a worst–case scenario, at least until equipment selections are close to being finalized. In addition, while some may desire to place much of this electronics equipment within the procedure room, much of it may be better located in a separate adjacent electronics closet–which can be shared among two or more procedure rooms–in order to better utilize the procedure room floor area and wall space (wall space is often at a premium for clinical supplies, such as catheters, as some radiologists may require a hundred or more different catheters, a dozen of which may be frequently used and need to be readily accessible). From an infection control standpoint, use of a separate space for electronics reduces opportunities for dust to collect within the procedure room. Locating electronics cabinets separately will also allow better management of the often considerable heat gain without subjecting the patient to cold drafts from the air–conditioning system.

Procedure rooms in a dedicated ambulatory care facility can often be slightly smaller than similar rooms within a hospital, where patients frequently arrive via a stretcher, gurney, or hospital bed (with or without life support equipment). Conversely, procedure rooms prioritized for emergency patients should be slightly larger in order to accommodate patients on life support with a team of personnel at their side.

Support spaces and administration spaces directly assist the function of activity spaces, whose characteristics determine the number and size of the first two (table 11–2). For example, control rooms assist the function of conducting a computed tomography (CT) exam. The number and size of control rooms are determined by the type and quantity of CT procedure rooms, the anticipated CT workload, the number of personnel and ancillary equipment in the control room, and whether the control rooms will be shared among multiple scanning rooms. Similarly, requirements for administration space (office and clerical areas) are determined by the number and type of staff needed to support and operate the imaging equipment and to assist patients.

Activity Clusters

In most instances, certain types of spaces are grouped together in what can be called an activity cluster. The individual spaces in the activity cluster work together to support efficient operations. For example, a pair of utility

TABLE 11-2: SUPPORT SPACE SIZE GUIDELINES

Area	Space Guidelines	Remarks
Waiting, public	15–17 NSF per seat; allow 20 NSF per seat for areas with fewer than 10 seats	Assume 3–4 seats per routine procedure room
Waiting, gowned	15 NSF per seat	Assume 1–2 seats per routine procedure room when dressing areas are not adjacent to procedure room
Reception	60–75 NSF per position	
Dressing areas	35 NSF for wheelchair-accessible; 16–20 NSF for standard	Assume 1–1.5 dressing cubicles per procedure room for most scheduled routine procedures Assume 5–6 dressing cubicles per dedicated chest room Assume 1–2 dressing cubicles per routine fluoroscopy room Consider clustering dressing cubicles together
Control alcove	25–35 NSF (usually included as part of procedure room area)	See "General Considerations for Control Corridors, Control Alcoves, and Control Rooms," in Chapter 12, "Room Design"
Control room, cath /IR	100–180 NSF, depending on equipment and personal needs	See Chapter 12 Larger for shared control room 9 ft. minimum width
Control room, CT	100–180 NSF, depending on equipment and personal needs	See Chapter 12 Larger for shared control room 9 ft. minimum width
Control room, MRI	100–180 NSF, depending on equipment and personal needs	See Chapter 12 Larger for shared control room Also, provide entry vestibule 9 ft. minimum width
Toilet room	60–65 NSF for wheelchair-accessible, single-accommodation toilet room	Assume 1 per R/F or fluoroscopy room; also at least 1 for ultrasound, CT, and MRI Multiple doors into toilet room may require additional space
Image reading alcove/ computer workstations	60–100 NSF/workstation	See Chapter 12 Note: Referring MD PACS review stations can be smaller
Image reading room/ private consultation office	100–130 NSF/office	See Chapter 12
Group reading room with computer workstations	65–80 NSF per person	See Chapter 12
Housekeeping closet	40–60 NSF	
Clean supply room	80–140 NSF	Size depends, in part, on how clean linen is supplied and stored Can be combined with equipment storage
Soiled utility room	80–140 NSF	Size depends, in part, on how soiled linen and trash are collected

Area	Space Guidelines	Remarks
Patient prep/holding/ recovery	80–120 NSF per position; 1–4 positions per CT, MRI room, IR, cath procedure room (varies)	Provide gases and suction, nurse call, and intercom Consider grouping holding areas together for efficient observation of patients Nurse's station with medication storage is needed near holding and recovery areas Note: Faster CT and MR scanners require more positions per procedure room Enclosed spaces with doors require larger size
Conference room	20 NSF per person	
Staff lounge	10–15 NSF per person	Provide staff toilet room adjacent
Crash cart alcove	10–20 NSF	
Storage, radioactive decay	40–120 NSF	Varies; radiation protection to be determined by certified physicist
Storage alcove, portable X-ray equipment	35–55 NSF/portable X-ray unit 50–80 NSF/portable C-arm	Assume 1 portable unit or C-arm per 6–10 ICU beds Most C-arms also include separate operator console
CR reader alcove	Varies	Some countertop units need only 4–10 NSF, while others are floor-mounted and require additional operator console; this technology is changing rapidly
Hot lab	80–120 NSF	Size depends on number of nuclear medicine rooms being supported
Barium kitchen (alcove)	20–40 NSF	May not be required if premixed contrast media is used

rooms for clean and soiled material can support several procedure rooms. If the number of procedure rooms is so large that the distance between the procedure rooms and the support space becomes excessive, imaging clusters–each with its own utility rooms–can be configured. One cluster might accommodate radiography and fluoroscopy, while a separate cluster might accommodate CT and MRI. Sometimes one support room within an activity cluster can support multiple activity rooms. For instance, two dressing areas (one for men and one for women) with multiple cubicles can support a group of procedure rooms, rather than one or two dressing cubicles being assigned to each room.

Other examples of activity clusters include:

- Fluoroscopy or CT room and toilet room, so that patients can eliminate immediately following a fluoroscopic exam when barium enemas are used or a CT exam utilizing virtual colonoscopy
- Ultrasound room and toilet room, so that patients undergoing abdominal ultrasound can eliminate the large quantities of water consumed prior to the exam (see figure 12-21 on page 279)

- Radiography room, control area, and dressing area (see figure 12–16 on page 268)
- Interventional radiology or cardiology procedure room, patient prep and holding area, and control room
- Nuclear medicine scanning room, toilet room, dressing area, holding area, and dose room (see figure 12–25 on page 290)

Magic Numbers: Quick Formulas for Determining Facility Size

Over the years, numerous quick formulas or rules of thumb have been developed for calculating the optimal size of imaging facilities. Sometimes they are referred to as "magic numbers."[3] Unfortunately, many of these do not take into account the numerous variables involved in developing space requirements. Additionally, many of these formulas were developed years ago and do not reflect recent developments in medical imaging. For example, older formulas often calculate the size of an imaging department by suggesting a certain number of square feet per hospital bed. Square-feet-per-bed formulas are very misleading because the diagnostic and treatment space needed relative to the number of inpatient beds has changed dramatically in recent decades. Other formulas may be useful for undertaking feasibility studies and deriving very broad-brush estimates. However, these formulas should not be used for detailed facility planning unless their accuracy has been verified by preparing a functional and space program.

Variables Affecting Facility Size

Quick rule-of-thumb formulas do not take into account the numerous variables that affect the space requirements of any facility, such as space variations between teaching and nonteaching hospitals. The following variables also should be considered when determining space requirements:

- The number of annual operating hours differs among institutions. Workload projections must be based on stated assumptions regarding operating hours per day and operating days per year. Additionally, at most hospitals the imaging workload varies dramatically from one shift to another. The night shift has peaks and lulls, depending on the workload of emergency cases. In contrast, the day shift may be heavily scheduled and will be subject to staff efficiency and the frequency of emergency cases disrupting the schedule.
- Renovation projects are likely to require more space than would be required for a newly constructed facility with the same workload capacity, because planning may not be able to be as efficient as with new construction.
- If dedicated radiographic capabilities exist in the emergency department, they should not be counted as part of the pri-

mary radiology workload. However, radiology staffing may be inefficient if the same personnel are used to staff the two departments.

- Although some imaging equipment is getting smaller, many imaging procedures are becoming more complex, with more people and ancillary equipment involved; thus, some room sizes are getting bigger and additional patient holding areas are required. Equipment throughput capabilities are increasing, and so in some instances the number of annual procedures per examination room is getting larger. For example, direct radiography and computed radiography each have different throughput capacities, as previously discussed.

- Imaging workload is determined by the type of patient being seen, not just the number of patients. For example, a facility with a large obstetric program is likely to perform more abdominal ultrasound examinations than one without an OB specialty. Similarly, a major heart center is likely to perform more cardiac imaging than a facility that does not focus on cardiology. Magic numbers that simply convert patient beds to procedures per year do not reflect the fact that all patient beds are not equal.

- Outpatient imaging centers, as compared to hospital imaging departments, may perform many routine procedures of short duration. Thus, an outpatient facility is likely to accommodate more procedures per room per hour than a hospital. However, the outpatient facility may not be open as many days per week or as many hours per day as a hospital department, and each room might accommodate a different number of procedures per year as compared to hospital procedure rooms.

- Some facilities include nuclear medicine as part of radiology, while others do not. Some even include radiation therapy as part of the radiology department. Some facilities have MRI within the imaging department, and some have MRI in a separate area. A clear description of what is to be included in the department is necessary before determining department size.

- Some facilities have one central imaging department; others decentralize routine imaging rooms and locate them near the various inpatient and outpatient users, such as orthopedics. Special procedure rooms usually are placed within one central location. Some facilities combine inpatient and outpatient imaging; others have two (or more) separate facilities. Each of these variables will influence the amount and type of space required.

Intelligent Numbers:
Workload Analysis for Determining Facility Size

Because of the many variables that influence space requirements, a detailed analysis of workload and staffing is needed before design and planning begins. This analysis, which relies on "intelligent" rather than "magic" numbers, should include workload projections for each type of procedure presently performed, as well as the anticipated future workload.[4] Future workload volume and throughput projections might increase because of the development of technology that scans more rapidly than current devices. Other factors that will influence future workload include additional changes in reimbursement and new alternatives to imaging.

The analysis also should consider whether some rooms should be dedicated to only one type of examination or used for a variety of procedures. As an example, chest examinations usually make up a large percentage of the department's total workload. If the number of chest exams is high enough to keep one or more rooms busy all the time, a dedicated room probably will be warranted. A dedicated chest room may be able to be smaller than a general radiography room (which can be used for chest X-rays as well as other procedures), although the dedicated chest room may not be as flexible as the general radiography room.

As mentioned earlier, the purpose of the detailed workload analysis is to identify the facility's key space generators. The next steps include determining the types and number of procedure rooms, the size of each procedure room, and the number and size of support and administration spaces.

Determining the Types and Number of Procedure Rooms

After deciding what types of procedure rooms should be provided, the optimal number of rooms can be projected. The number of required rooms for each type of procedure (for example, basic radiography, angiography, ultrasound, and CT) is derived from the following basic formula:

$$\text{Projected annual procedures} \div$$
$$\text{projected annual procedures per room}$$
$$= \text{number of procedure rooms needed}$$

It is assumed that the number of projected annual procedures per room is a function of the average procedure duration, including turnaround time—which includes the procedure duration plus setup time and cleanup time—and the number of hours per day the room is used. Turnaround time is defined as the average length of time between when one patient enters the room and the next patient enters the same room.

For example, assuming that the average duration of a basic X-ray exam is 15 minutes, or 0.25 hours (including setup and cleanup) and that 70 percent of basic X-ray exams are performed Monday through Friday (250 days a year) during the daytime eight-hour shift (even though the facility is open 24 hours a day, 365 days a year), utilization projections should be based on the period of peak demand. On the basis of these figures, the average number of potential procedures per prime shift per basic radiography room is calculated as follows:

$$8 \text{ hours per day} \div 0.25 \text{ hours per procedure} =$$
$$32 \text{ procedures per prime–time 8–hour shift}$$

Even allowing for downtime, setup, and cleanup, scheduling will not be 100 percent efficient. An 85 percent efficiency factor can be used to account for time in which the room is available but not used. Therefore, the projected number of prime–time annual procedures that the room is capable of is as follows:

$$32 \text{ procedures per shift} \times 0.85 \text{ efficiency factor}$$
$$\times 250 \text{ days per year} = 6{,}800 \text{ procedures}$$

Because these calculations are based on 70 percent of the basic X-ray procedures anticipated (70 percent of the procedures occur during the peak eight–hour shift), the total number of annual procedures that one room can accommodate is as follows:

$$6{,}800 \div 0.70 = 9{,}714 \text{ procedures}$$

Referring back to the original formula, assume that 20,000 basic annual procedures are projected:

$$20{,}000 \text{ annual procedures} \div 9{,}714 \text{ procedures/room}$$
$$= 2.05 \text{ procedure rooms}$$

Therefore, two basic radiography rooms should be programmed. If the actual workload exceeds the estimate, variations in staffing or hours of operation can accommodate much of the difference.

Similar calculations should be performed for each type of procedure room. The calculations should be adjusted based on the degree to which rooms are to be used for multiple types of procedures. The variables in the formulas should be adjusted because the duration of each type of procedure will vary. Some complex procedures may last several hours; some special studies–such as those requiring that the patient not eat prior to the procedure–might always be performed in the morning. The rooms used for these special studies might be available for other types of examinations in the afternoon.

Table 11-3 shows hypothetical average procedure durations and annual workload capacities that might be used as starting points for the duration variable in the above formula. However, it should be noted that each average can represent a wide range of actual durations. Because the technology and complexity of procedures change rapidly, these figures may not be current or appropriate for some applications. Current data should be examined before factoring this information into space programming formulas. Seasonal population fluctuations should also be considered. For example, the population of Sun City, Arizona, is much larger in the winter than in the summer.

TABLE 11-3: HYPOTHETICAL AVERAGE PROCEDURE DURATIONS

Room Type	Duration Including Setup and Cleanup	Approx. Annual Procedures
Routine radiography	0.25 hours	8,000–10,000
Routine fluoroscopy	0.75 hours	2,500–3,500
Angiography/cath	2.00 hours; varies	1,200–1,500
CT scan	Varies	4,500–6,500 (varies with scanner speed)
Nuclear medicine	1.00 hour (does not include time between administration of dose and scan)	2,000–3,000
Ultrasound	0.50 hours	4,000–5,000
MRI	0.50 hours, varies	3,500–5,000 (varies with scanner speed)
Mammography (screening)	0.25 hours	6,000–8,000
Chest exam	0.10 hours	22,000–26,000

Note: These durations are rough estimates and, therefore, will not apply to all equipment or to all situations. Each should be verified with the most recent data available.

Determining the Size of Procedure Rooms

The proper size of an imaging procedure room is determined by understanding the function of the procedure, patient flow, staff flow, and equipment needs. Usually, the most important key space generator is the imaging equipment. The space required for other fixed equipment, movable ancillary equipment, the patient, and staff also must be taken into account. Additionally, consideration must be given to the area required for movement or extension of equipment, including clearances needed when the units are swiveled, tilted, or rotated.[5]

When determining the proper size of each procedure room, three trends must be kept in mind. First, some types of imaging equipment are getting smaller. In some instances, the associated electrical and data components (such as transformers, generators, and computer processors) also are getting smaller. Second, and in contrast to the shrinking size of equipment, is the tendency for imaging procedures to become more complex. This means that more people and ancillary equipment may be required in the procedure room and that additional patient support spaces may be necessary. Third, sometimes imaging equipment can be upgraded by purchasing new software and hardware packages. This means that today's equipment may be capable of more complex examinations in the future. This is likely to reinforce the second trend, of more people and ancillary equipment being present in the procedure room. Therefore, although some equipment is getting smaller, there often is a need for additional space and surplus capacity of utility systems. If the loose-fit approach is applied, these changes can usually be implemented without the expense and disruption of requiring major renovation.

Most equipment vendors list both recommended and minimum room dimensions for their major imaging equipment. Minimum dimensions should be avoided because they usually refer to the absolute least amount of space in which the equipment will function. Often, significant functional sacrifices will be made if minimum dimensions are used instead of recommended dimensions. Minimum dimensions often take into account only the space required for the major fixed imaging equipment but not the needs of ancillary equipment or even of some basic code requirements. Most equipment will require clearance for servicing and access; clearance data can be obtained from the equipment vendor.

Requirements for accessibility by disabled individuals also must be considered when determining room size and configuration. These dimensions, including those prescribed in the Americans with Disabilities Act, are often omitted in vendor-supplied data. The fact that many functions in the procedure room may not be able to be performed by individuals with mobility impairments does not eliminate the need to incorporate mandated accessibility standards. Usually, a minimum clearance of 36 inches is required in front of all fixed objects. The electrical code also specifies minimum clearance requirements for electrical equipment, such as transformers and generators. In addition, maneuvering clearances for wheelchair-bound people are required.

Vertical clearance also must be considered in procedure rooms. For many modalities, imaging equipment is designed for a finished ceiling height of 9 feet 6 inches above the finished floor, and some equipment requires a higher ceiling. A ceiling that is lower than what the equipment is designed for might not accommodate the movement or focal angles of ceiling-mounted equipment; a higher ceiling might require the equipment to be modified for proper installation. Ample space is required above the finished ceiling for primary structural beams, air supply and return ducts, lighting fixtures, fire protection piping, and in some cases a "unistrut" structural support system. These items should have their own dedicated horizontal zone above the ceiling so that they do not run into each other. (See figure 8-15 on page 170.) This requires careful coordination during the design and construction phases of the project. Usually, a clear floor-to-floor height of at least 16 feet is recommended (for buildings without interstitial floors) to provide a finished ceiling height of 9 feet 6 inches and to accommodate the various subsystems required above the ceiling with some additional flexibility for future modifications, although this varies based on many factors including the type of structural system being employed.

Notes

1. B. Rostenberg, *Design Planning for Freestanding Ambulatory Care Facilities* (Chicago: American Hospital Publishing, 1986), 26.
2. C. Hayward et al., *A Generic Process for Projecting Health Care Space Needs* (Washington, DC: American Institute of Architects, 1985).
3. Hayward et al.
4. Hayward et al.
5. S. Jenkins, *The Medical Imaging Planner* (self-published, 2003). Available at www.xrayplanning.com.

CHAPTER 12

Room Design

Room design is influenced by the staff who use each room, the patients the rooms serve (pediatric, bariatric, geriatric, and other types), the procedures the rooms support, and the equipment and accessories used therein. There are many viable design solutions for any given type of room. Room design or renovation occurs only periodically, yet medical practices and their associated technology are constantly changing. Therefore, each design solution must enable the room to be easily modified in the future, in order to accommodate changes in how imaging services are provided, who administers them, and when they take place.

Like the imaging department itself, each room must be designed in concert with work flow, as well as patient, staff, and supply traffic (figure 12–1). For example, the placement of a door between a corridor and a procedure room suggests where in the room circulating versus stationary activities should occur. It also determines if it will be easy or difficult to transfer a patient from a gurney to the equipment's patient couch. Additionally, the placement, size, movement, and access requirements of equipment will influence activities within a room.

This chapter identifies basic criteria to be considered when planning particular types of rooms. The intent is not to describe every room component in detail, nor is it to describe any single best design solution for a specific type of room; rather, it provides general guidelines for room design. The first part of this chapter describes design guidelines for various support spaces, such as control rooms and reading rooms. The second part of the chapter identifies functional, human, and technical design issues for specific types of procedure rooms.

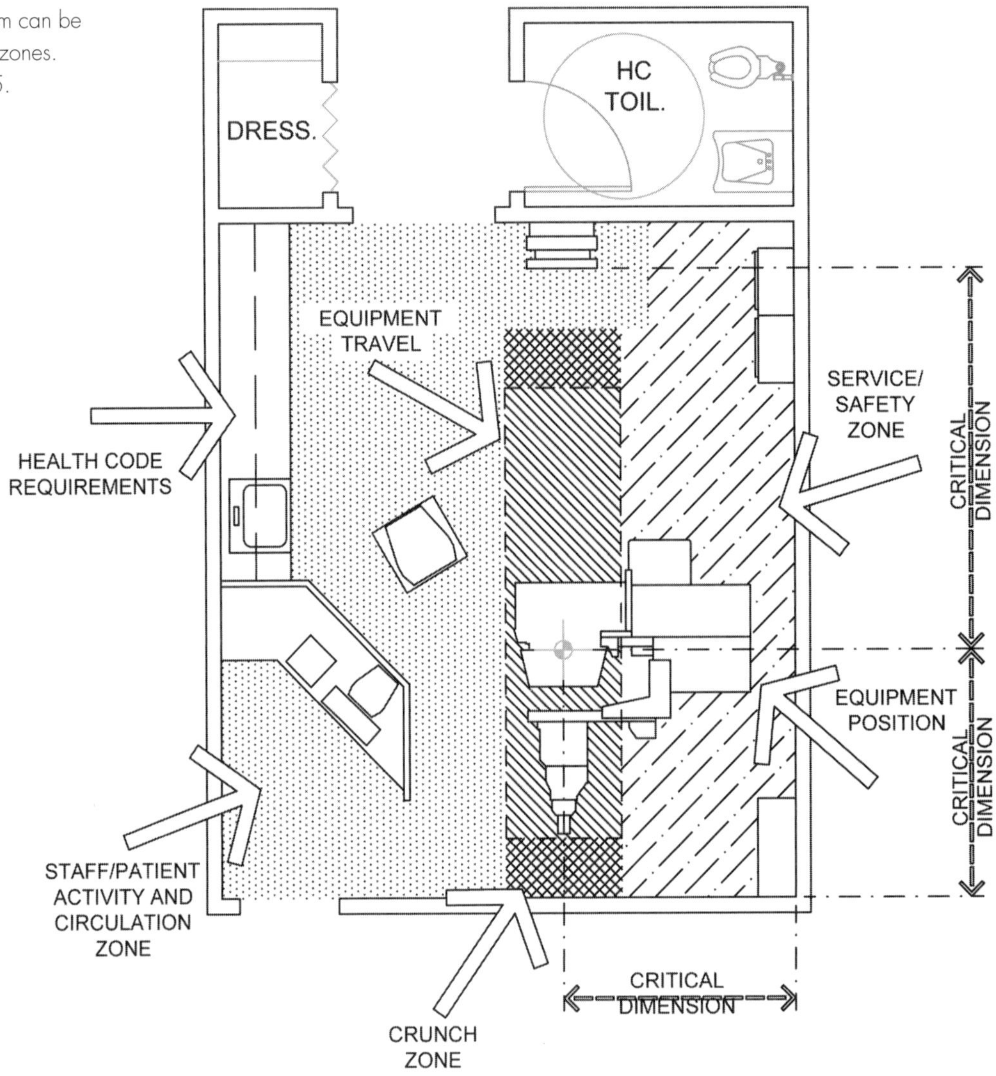

Figure 12-1 Each procedure room can be subdivided into several functional zones. Courtesy of Scott Jenkins, © 2005.

General Considerations for Procedure Rooms

Because the complexity and characteristics of many procedures are evolving rapidly, the number of personnel in many procedure rooms is increasing, and the patients in those rooms are often sicker. Because the size, sophistication, type, and quantity of equipment to be found in many rooms are changing equally rapidly, the dimensions, physical characteristics, and infrastructure requirements of these room types are not necessarily fixed.

With few exceptions, formulas for complex procedure room design are of limited value. Even those for basic procedure rooms need to be modified for single-corridor, double-corridor, core, or cluster department configurations. (See "Plan Typologies" in chapter 10, "Department Location and Configuration.") This is because single- and double-corridor layouts tend to combine patient and staff traffic (and thus suggest one door into the procedure room), whereas core and cluster plans tend to separate the two types of traffic (and thus suggest two entrances into the room). Similarly, considerable modification is needed to apply one standard room layout to both a control corridor and a control alcove planning concept, as discussed in the next section.

The ability of staff to easily observe patients (and the entire room) is another key consideration affecting room design. For example, the technologist should be able to see the patient's face from the control area at all times (although the need for this will depend on the type of room and the imaging modality). If the patient table is accessible from only one side and tilts from horizontal to vertical, this establishes a physical relationship between the placement of the control area and the placement of the patient table within the procedure room. Maximum lengths of preassembled equipment cables may limit the distances between various equipment components.

As another example, the interventional radiologist or invasive cardiologist may need to access the patient's right side, have an unobstructed view of ceiling-supported (and/or cart-mounted) monitors, and have unobstructed contact with the control room staff. Other staff may need to reach catheters and other supplies with minimal movement at the same time that the technologist in the control area needs an unobstructed view of the patient and physician.

Two trends regarding imaging procedure rooms are worth noting. The first is that the complexity of outpatient imaging procedures continues to increase. The second is that many procedures, both inpatient and outpatient, are becoming more invasive.

Design Considerations for Outpatient Facilities

Facility implications of the increasing complexity of outpatient procedures are numerous, especially for facilities other than acute care hospitals. First, floor-to-floor heights in nonhospital buildings are traditionally lower than they are in hospitals, but advanced outpatient imaging centers may require floor-to-floor heights similar to those provided in hospitals. The ability to construct functional and flexible procedure rooms without adequate ceiling height may be compromised where overall vertical clearance is inadequate. Similarly, power, HVAC, plumbing, and fire protection systems typically designed for nonhospital buildings may be inadequate for complex procedure rooms and their equipment. Separate, redundant systems may be required just for the imaging component of some outpatient facilities. Structural systems in nonhospital facilities must be able to support the dynamic loads created by imaging equipment and its movement. Additional structural reinforcing may be needed for outpatient renovation projects. Floor loading and vibration reduction capacities greater than those typically seen in other types of buildings also may be needed. The installation of some imaging equipment will require wider hallways and larger doorways than are typically found in many nonhospital facilities. Finally, much of the construction criteria that apply to complex procedure rooms may be listed in building codes that primarily govern hospital projects, whereas building permits for many outpatient buildings are issued by local agencies, which may follow other types of building codes and regulations. Therefore, some local building jurisdictions may be unfamiliar with the construction criteria (including the Joint Commission on Accreditation of Healthcare Organization (JCAHO) and the National Fire Protection Agency (NFPA) requirements) that are appropriate for complex procedure rooms and their associated building systems.

Design Considerations for Interventional Imaging

The implications of increasingly invasive imaging procedures also are numerous. Some procedure rooms require higher levels of infection control, emergency power and an uninterruptible power supply, emergency equipment, medical gas outlets, and more space than may be required for purely diagnostic imaging procedures. Special wall, floor, and ceiling finishes may need to be specified in order to meet infection control criteria. Special methods of assembling these materials to limit the growth of bacteria and to simplify cleaning procedures also may be necessary. In addition, exhaust, ventilation, and air filtration specifications may need to be upgraded for these procedure rooms. Special requirements for HVAC systems in imaging procedure rooms have also been proposed in some states in order to combat resistant strains of tuberculosis and other infectious diseases. Air-handling requirements for both interventional radiology and interventional cardiology are approaching OR standards. It is prudent to design these rooms to meet surgical standards, as interventional procedures and minimally invasive surgical procedures continue to converge.

A broad array of fixtures and accessory equipment is needed in most procedure rooms. Common examples include:

- A hand-washing fixture should be provided in the room.
- Interventional procedure rooms should have scrub sinks located immediately outside the room entrance, but they should not have sinks within the procedure room because these rooms are often used for minimally invasive surgery-like procedures. In many states a hand-washing sink is not permitted within these procedure rooms. Alcohol disinfectant dispensers, however, are appropriate for the procedure room. Plumbing for sinks in MRI procedure rooms should not penetrate the RF shield. Therefore, they may be better located just outside the entrance to the scanning room.
- Some rooms, such as interventional radiology and cardiology procedure rooms, may require an additional sink located in a nearby utility room for soiled material (but not within the procedure room) for dumping fluids and soaking reusable instruments prior to their transport to sterile processing.

- Many procedures that emit radiation require that patients and personnel be protected by lead-lined aprons or other forms of protective clothing. Therefore, apron racks (as well as gown, mask, boot, and cap cover dispensers for infection control) are required in or near those rooms. Additionally, radiation protection is integrated into the room construction itself.

Coordination of the numerous accessory items and fixtures required in the procedure room should begin early in the design development phase of the project. If it is not, last-minute decisions regarding seemingly minor items may lead to numerous design changes and even compromise a workable procedure room layout.

Wall thickness should be ample where flush-mounted accessories are used and where major conduits, pipes, or electrical floor and wall trenches pass through wall partitions, and to accommodate low wall air returns in interventional rooms. For example, wall construction should consist of heavy-gauge 6-inch studs at a minimum. As an alternative, a double-stud wall with lead-lined gypsum board between can make room modifications easier and eliminate the need to provide lead covers behind receptacles, ducts, and other penetrations. This method is most applicable where two high-tech rooms share a common wall. However, this approach does require slightly more space than conventional wall framing. Usually, it is advantageous to increase the wall thickness (using either of these methods) around the entire procedure room.

Finally, various types of special construction are required to accommodate the unique physical properties of many imaging processes. (These specialties—including radiation protection, magnetic shielding, and RF shielding—are described in chapter 13, "Physical Properties Influencing Design.")

General Considerations for Control Corridors, Control Alcoves, and Control Rooms

The control area is the space from which the technologist or physician (and sometimes other personnel) monitors and observes the patient while conducting an imaging examination. Many examinations simply involve acquiring an image while a relatively healthy patient sits or lies still. However, other procedures are much more complex.

Some procedures involve infants, young children, or elderly patients who cannot hold still without assistance or sedation. The technologist may be the only staff member in the room for simple procedures, but radiologists and other medical professionals are also in the room attending to the patient during more complex imaging examinations. Sometimes the patient's life functions are being supported by respirators, medical gases, and other equipment; sometimes the patient is injected with contrast material in order to acquire a diagnostic-quality image; and sometimes the patient is undergoing a surgery-like procedure under medical image guidance. Some procedures, such as electrophysiology, studies can last up to six hours, and the nature of the study can subject the patient to potentially life-threatening conditions. In such situations, danger to the patient must be mitigated by close monitoring and immediately accessible life support and stabilization equipment.

Three types of control areas–control corridors, control alcoves, and control rooms–are described in this section. Although each type requires specific design factors, the following should be considered when designing any one of the three types:

- Visibility of the patient from the control area (including when the patient couch travels into the equipment gantry, and when the patient table tilts in various positions). Typically the patient is positioned on the table with the patient's feet toward the control area in a general radiographic or fluoroscopic room (figures 12-3 and 12-4).
- Visibility of the entire room to ensure that no one other than the patient is in the room at the time of the exam.
- Ability to communicate with the patient from the control area (often compromised in shared control rooms).
- Ability to communicate with other staff from the control area.
- Impact of equipment on the control area location and configuration.
- Ability to quickly and efficiently carry out image acquisition and image quality assurance activities.
- Immediate access to the patient from the control area.
- Need for acoustic and visual privacy between the control area and the procedure room(s).
- Adequate space within the control area for (initial and future) personnel and equipment.
- Adequate space for circulation and maneuvering.
- Lighting, acoustic, humidity, ventilation, and temperature control appropriate for the activities that will take place and the equipment that will be used in the space. For example, lighting levels between control rooms and procedure rooms should be balanced to prevent glare on either side of the control window.
- Visual screening to prevent patients from seeing confidential data in the control area.
- Sound control to avoid disturbing personnel in the control room and the procedure room, and to prevent patients from overhearing confidential conversations.
- Protection of medical personnel against radiation and other emissions inherent in various imaging modalities.

- Proper functioning of equipment that may be disturbed by, or cause disturbance to, other equipment due to physical effects inherent in different imaging modalities, such as magnetic and RF interference.
- Provision of scrubs, lead aprons, and other items at the staff entry point to the procedure room.
- The need to provide infection control between the control room and some procedure rooms by means of a closable door.

Control Corridors

The control corridor concept is based on a planning philosophy in which the department is arranged with a series of procedure rooms, each adjacent to a continuous control corridor, rather than placing individual control alcoves within the procedure rooms. The control corridor concept has been used in European hospitals for decades but has not been as common in the United States.

Proponents of the control corridor concept claim that radiation protection is simplified by including a large leaded glass window for the technologist to see into the X-ray room, that communications among staff and work efficiency are improved because they all work together within the control corridor, and that modifications to the facility are improved due to the modular layout suggested by the concept.[1]

Critics of the control corridor concept, however, question the efficiency and functionality of a uniform room depth for all procedures, question its practical (as opposed to theoretical) benefit for flexibility and adaptability, find the control corridor to be noisy, feel that separation between the procedure room and control corridor hinders communication between patients and staff and thus leaves patients feeling isolated, and compromises patients' privacy. The concern of compromised patient privacy has become increasingly important with the implementation of HIPAA and other privacy-related legislation.

Control Alcoves

A control alcove located within the procedure room is a popular approach to providing a control area for a basic X-ray procedure room (figure 12-2A, B, C). This approach is ideal when a small and limited amount of control equipment is involved and where the technologist needs to attend to the patient directly and frequently. This often is the case for procedures that are of short duration and high volume or frequency.

The control alcove is an integral component of universal room design (described later in this chapter). Typically, lead-lined barriers separating the control alcove from the procedure room extend approximately 7 feet above the finished floor surface of the procedure room. This allows ceiling-mounted equipment to pass above the control area without its movement

Figure 12-2A Control alcove.

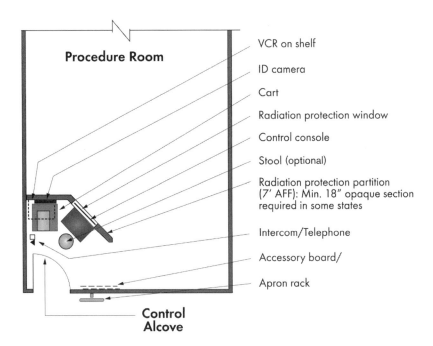

Procedure Room

VCR on shelf

ID camera

Cart

Radiation protection window

Control console

Stool (optional)

Radiation protection partition
(7' AFF): Min. 18" opaque section
required in some states

Intercom/Telephone

Accessory board/

Apron rack

Control
Alcove

Figure 12.2B Control alcove.

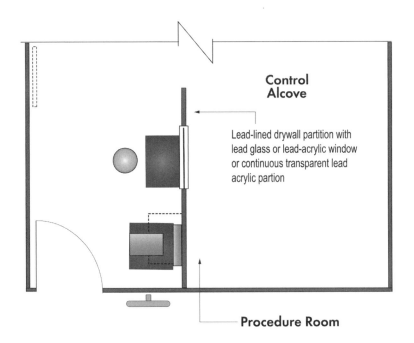

Control
Alcove

Lead-lined drywall partition with
lead glass or lead-acrylic window
or continuous transparent lead
acrylic partion

Procedure Room

being unnecessarily restricted. Control consoles are located in the alcove in such a way that the technologist can see the patient through a radiation–shielded but visually transparent window. Control alcoves should have a minimum of 18 inches of an opaque shielded barrier next to the control window, to protect the technologists' arms and sides while they are looking through the shielded window. (Some regulations specify where the X–ray

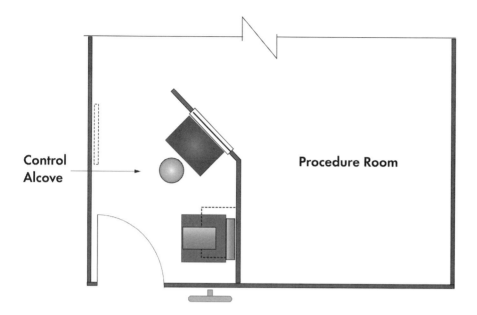

Figure 12-2C Control alcove.

exposure on–switch must be placed in lieu of specifying a minimum of 18 inches of an opaque shielded barrier.) There is a requirement in some jurisdictions that the technologist be able to see the entire procedure room. If this cannot be accomplished by visual sight lines, it may be supplemented by using a closed–circuit television camera (where permitted by code).

Some control alcoves are constructed with a door separating the alcove from the staff work core; others have a door opening but no door. The decision as to whether to provide a door (instead of just a doorway) depends on a number of factors. These include:

1. Whether radiation protection is required at the opening (which, in turn, will depend on a number of variables such as the location and movement of radiation–emitting equipment relative to the door opening, whether the control alcove itself shields the door opening, and whether there is adequate space for a radiation maze–an arrangement of protective partitions that block scatter radiation)
2. Whether noise control is determined to be more important than the ease of technologist movement into and out of the procedure room
3. The amount of equipment that will be transported between the staff work area and the procedure room
4. Whether there is adequate space to accommodate the door swing as well as both staff and equipment movement
5. Whether an infection control barrier is desired between the control area and the staff work core

Figure 12-3 One control room, or control alcove, can support multiple procedure rooms. Courtesy of Anshen + Allen, Architects.

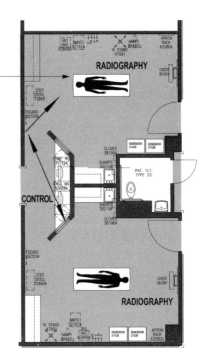

If this is a tilting table, the patient's head will not be seen from the control alcove, unless the table is designed to tilt in both directions.

With this type of shared control alcove, acoustics can be difficult to control. The voice of the technologist on the right side can be reflected off the control window and be heard by the patient on the left side.

Note that even though physically disabled individuals may not be able to perform all the tasks required of X-ray technologists, both the procedure room and the control area must meet the requirements of the Americans with Disabilities Act (ADA), which specifies minimal clearance dimensions.

Sometimes two control alcoves are placed back to back to form a double-control alcove that serves two procedure rooms (figure 12-3). Advantages of this arrangement are:

- It enables one technologist to cover two procedure rooms.
- It accommodates one shared quality assurance workstation that can be accessed directly from both control console areas.
- It may provide space for toilet rooms between the two procedure rooms.
- It simplifies staff traffic flow between the two procedure rooms.

However, double control alcove configurations often result in a pair of mirror-image procedure rooms with one "right-hand room" and one "left-hand room" rather than a consistent standard arrangement for both rooms. This is because a patient lying supine on a table is often approached from his or her right side, and some tables only tilt in one direction. There may be problems associated with mirror-image rooms that result in a mirror-image placement of X-ray equipment. The right-hand room will have good visibility between the control area and the patient table, but the left-hand room may have compromised visibility because the patient table may block the technologist's view of the patient's head when the table is tilted.

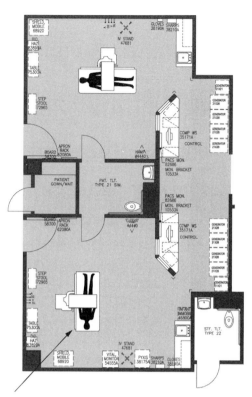

Figure 12-4 One shared control area can result in different visibility conditions in each procedure room. Courtesy of Anshen + Allen, Architects.

Tilting table must be rotated for technologist at control area to see patient's head

Thus, if planning a double control alcove, it is important to verify that the patient table and imaging equipment assembly to be installed will allow adequate view of the patient from the control area, regardless of the table's movement or positioning. Some imaging equipment does not come in right- and left-hand models and some tables tilt while others do not. The latter are called "floating" tables. Therefore, when the table tilts, the patient may be visible only if the control alcove is located to the right and at the foot of the table. To ensure proper visibility of the patient from the control area the imaging equipment may need to be rotated 90 degrees in its placement in the room (figure 12–4).

Conversely, the concept of "same-handed" procedure rooms (figure 12–5) suggests that each procedure room has its own control area and that each procedure room is identical to other rooms of the same type and use, rather than mirroring two similar rooms around one shared control area. The logic behind "same-handed" rooms is that if every room is configured, equipped, and supplied identically, staff members are more likely to know exactly where everything is, and thus will be less likely to make mistakes or contribute to medical errors. This concept also provides greater flexibility when equipment is changed, upgraded, or replaced in the future.

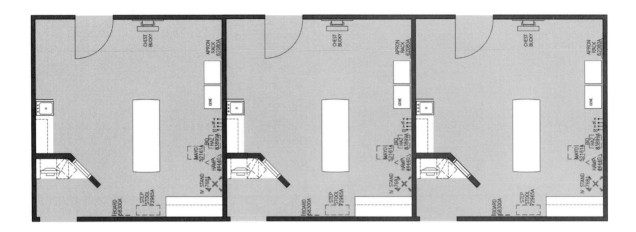

Figure 12-5 With "same-handed" procedure rooms, each room is configured the same. Courtesy of Anshen + Allen, Architects.

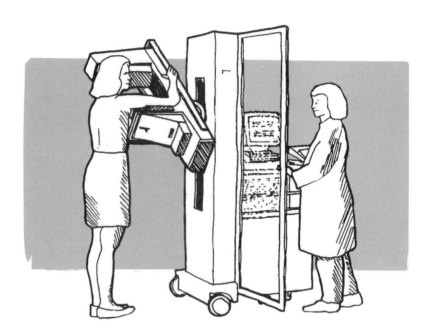

Figure 12-6 Patient positioning for routine mammography exam.

Some procedures do not require a separate control area. For example, most mammography units incorporate a radiation-protected control space into the design of the imaging equipment itself (figure 12–6). In ultrasound rooms, the control area may simply consist of a chair located near the equipment console.

Control Rooms

For special procedure rooms such as CT, MRI, PET, interventional radiography, cardiac catheterization labs, sometimes fluoroscopy, and other rooms used for interventional studies, a separate control room (figure 12–7), rather than a control alcove, usually is necessary (although in an electrophysiology lab, many of the control activities take place within the

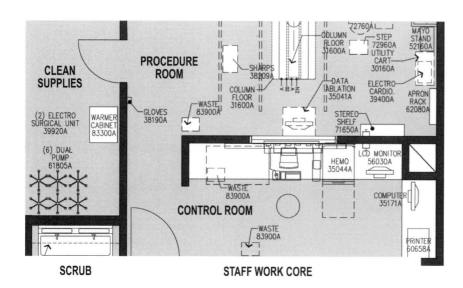

Figure 12-7 A single control room dedicated to each procedure room is preferred over shared control rooms for most interventional procedures. Courtesy of Anshen + Allen, Architects.

procedure room, at the patient's side). The separate control room is desired because of:

- The amount of equipment and personnel that need to be in the room.
- The special environmental (cooling, ventilation, and electrical power) requirements of the equipment.
- The need for acoustic control to prevent noise from a shared control room from disturbing the medical team and to prevent the patient from overhearing confidential conversations. However, electronic communications systems allowing control room staff to converse with procedure room personnel and the patient enable necessary communications to take place.
- The increasing need for infection control and surgery-like conditions in the procedure room. A separate control room enables personnel to enter and exit without passing through the procedure room. It also can allow for separate ventilation, humidity, and air filtration conditions within each space.

IR and Cath Lab Control Rooms

Proper orientation of the control room relative to the procedure room is critical for optimal visibility between personnel in both the procedure room and the control room. Orientation will also affect how easily monitors can be seen and whether or not monitors and other equipment will block lines of sight. Some radiologists and cardiologists prefer the patient to be oriented perpendicular to the control room, while others prefer a parallel orientation (figure 12–8).

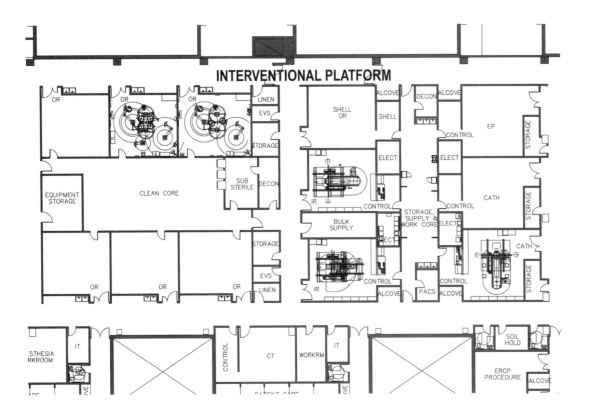

INTERVENTIONAL PLATFORM

Figure 12-8 Orientation of the control room relative to the procedure room may vary (control room parallel versus perpendicular to procedure room). Courtesy of Anshen + Allen, Architects.

Shared Control Rooms

Sometimes one larger control room is used for two (or more) special procedure rooms, such as CT (figure 12–20, page 277). A shared control room also can be advantageous for purposes of safety, by enabling one technologist to more easily view two procedure rooms (such as in a shared MR control room) and for staffing efficiency. However, a shared control room is not always preferred for interventional radiology procedure rooms because a high degree of activity in the control room can cause distractions, a need for acoustic control, and the desire to physically separate procedure rooms for infection control. Regardless of whether a control room is shared or not, scrub sinks, some supply storage, and some ancillary equipment can be shared effectively among multiple procedure rooms. These items can be located just outside the control rooms.

CT Control Rooms

Computed tomography suites typically have a control room physically adjacent to the procedure room. The electronics space requirements of these devices have become simpler than they were in the past; much of the electronics equipment is incorporated into the control console, rather than requiring a separate computer room. PET/CT and MRI scanners (and some CT scanners) may, however, require a dedicated chiller in a separate equipment room or outside the building.

Figure 12-9 MRI control room.

MRI Control Rooms

Magnetic resonance imaging (MRI) control areas must be physically separated from the procedure room because of magnetic and RF interactions (figure 12-9). In addition, the entire MR suite must be configured to prevent any materials that are not MR-compatible or MR-safe from approaching the magnet.[2] Based on the American College of Radiology's guidelines for MR safety (see Appendix B), the control room is considered to be a restricted zone and should be configured in such a way that nobody can enter the zone without being escorted by trained and designated MRI staff.[3] In addition, nobody should be able to enter the scan room without being seen by the control technologists. Therefore, the control room should provide a clear view of the entire scanning room and a security vestibule in front of the door to the scan room. Where two MRI rooms share one control room, the control room should enable multiple technologists to have an unobstructed view of both MR rooms as well as the security vestibules outside the entrance doors to either scan room.

Universal Room Design

Frequently, it is desirable to design universal X-ray rooms (figure 12-10), that is, rooms that can accommodate similar equipment from a variety of vendors with few modifications to the space. There are several reasons for this:

1. Equipment is changing rapidly.
2. Similar equipment from different vendors often requires different clearances and special infrastructure and design features.
3. Most imaging facilities are expected to outlive the current generation of equipment.
4. It often is difficult and inappropriate for radiologists and administrators to commit to a specific make and model of

Figure 12-10 Universal x-ray procedure room.

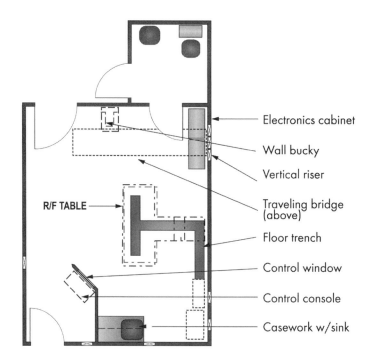

Electronics cabinet

Wall bucky

Vertical riser

Traveling bridge (above)

Floor trench

Control window

Control console

Casework w/sink

R/F TABLE

equipment well before the building is to be occupied. However, even if universal rooms are incorporated into the planning concept, there should be a preliminary equipment selection to determine baseline electrical loads, heat dissipation, and other criteria necessary for designing the building's infrastructure systems.

Universal rooms can be appropriate for general radiography or radiography/fluoroscopy (R/F) procedure rooms. That same universal room design, however, will not be appropriate for more specialized procedure rooms such as those for interventional radiology and cardiology procedures. A different room layout can be developed to enable those types of interventional procedures to be performed in a somewhat interchangeable room (although the equipment for each specialty will vary).

To provide flexibility, control costs related to equipment changes, and minimize the scheduling impact of equipment changes, universal rooms contain special ceiling systems, floor systems, and utility distribution components. In particular, the characteristics of a universal room often include:

- Slightly more space than equipment–specific rooms. The additional space accommodates the space requirements of various vendors, and often the room is sized for worst–case conditions.
- A universal ceiling support system (figure 12–11), instead of individual equipment–specific ceiling supports. Individual manufacturers and individual equipment models require

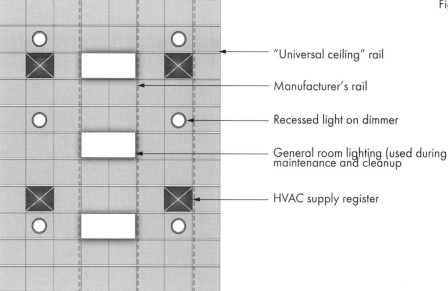

Figure 12-11 Universal ceiling.

"Universal ceiling" rail

Manufacturer's rail

Recessed light on dimmer

General room lighting (used during maintenance and cleanup

HVAC supply register

ceiling supports in specific locations. A universal system evenly spaces ceiling-mounted supports along the entire ceiling or a major portion of it (usually ±26 inches on center). Because the supports are perpendicular to the equipment rails, they can support equipment rails placed in almost any location.

• Electrical ducts and troughs provided at various locations in the wall, ceiling, and floor. Often, vertical riser ducts are located in the walls on all four sides of the room. Typically, they are placed near the control alcove, the power supply, and the likely locations of other fixed equipment, such as generators and transformers. Raceways can also be located in the floor connecting the power supply and other equipment to the table and other floor-mounted imaging equipment. For new construction, floor slab thickness should be increased throughout the imaging suite to accommodate the depth of these flush raceways set into the floor and to support the weight of the imaging equipment. This may not be practical in renovation projects with suspended floor slabs (that is, for those that are not on grade). In this case, raceways sometimes are placed beneath the floor slab, if possible. However, running cables through subfloor raceways can be difficult because longer cable runs and numerous bends and turns are required. Finally, a cable tray above the ceiling may be located along the room perimeter. Wires and cable are pulled from a power source to the various pieces of equipment. Universal raceways are designed and placed to accommodate wires and cable provided by a variety of manufacturers. In equipment–specific rooms, cables are often run through channel ducts or conduit that is specifically located by the vendor supplying the equipment. A universal cable tray or duct system will cost more initially but will likely reduce the cost of future renovations and equipment upgrades.

The universal room approach offers several advantages. These include:

- Ability to accommodate a variety of makes and models of imaging equipment. Because the universal room is designed for this flexibility, major portions of the contract documents (drawings and specifications) can be prepared even if equipment selections change later. However, universal room design does not imply that equipment selections should be deferred. It simply is an attempt to reduce the cost premium that may result if equipment selections change.
- Ability to modify and replace equipment in the future with minimal remodeling or demolition.
- Preservation of the project schedule, which might otherwise be significantly delayed by last–minute equipment changes.
- Preservation of the construction budget due to fewer architectural, electrical, and structural change orders.

Conversely, the universal room approach also has a number of disadvantages. They include:

- Cost premiums due to slightly oversized space. (However, this additional space may provide additional operational efficiencies and adequate space for future modifications.)
- Cost premiums for installing universal structural supports. (In addition, as new equipment is selected, additional structural calculations may be necessary, depending on the loading conditions of that equipment. Universal room design implies providing some excess structural capacity. It is likely that not all the excess capacity will be used. However, the alternative of having to increase structural capacity after the room has been built can be prohibitively expensive.)
- Cost premiums for excess electrical, plumbing, and HVAC capacity, as well as placement of additional raceways and ducts.
- Possibility that the flexibility provided by the universal room design will not accommodate all equipment selections and configurations. (This is particularly likely with imaging

technologies that go through significant changes within brief periods of time. Therefore, the particular characteristics of universal rooms may need to be evaluated and refined periodically. For this reason, universal room design is most appropriate for basic procedure rooms, where physical needs are relatively constant.)

- Requirements that specific equipment must be identified before the regulatory review process can begin. This might suggest that the equipment that represents the worst case for structural, HVAC, and electrical conditions should be selected for the purpose of the review process. However, the worst case may be represented in one piece of equipment for some conditions (such as structure) and in another for other conditions (such as HVAC and electrical systems).

The theory behind universal room design is that investing a little extra money initially makes sense in order to avoid greater costs that would be required by future changes. Because the likelihood of future changes is high, the advantages of universal room design for most basic imaging rooms generally outweigh the disadvantages. There should always be some reserve capacity in the building systems. The difficulty is in predicting, defining, and justifying the optimal amount. The HVAC system presents a unique challenge. If it is designed to cover the worst case for equipment heat loads, and the equipment selected and installed requires significantly less cooling, the HVAC system may not cycle often enough to adequately control humidity.

Digital Image Management Areas

Most facilities acquire and manage the majority of their medical images digitally. Those that do not yet do so are aggressively in the process of converting from film to digital image management. Yet at some facilities, film may not disappear entirely. Occasionally digitally acquired images will be printed on film. Sometimes patients' previous film images will be retained for comparison to new images (although they can be digitized into an electronic format). Many radiologists continue to request a few film illuminators in their soft-copy reading rooms for the hard-copy film images they periodically examine.

This book, however, focuses on the design of digital image management spaces—especially the design of soft-copy reading rooms—and does not dwell on how to design more traditional spaces such as darkrooms, which have declined and are rapidly disappearing. While the technology influencing digital image and information management continues to advance exponentially, the design of advanced information management environments responds to these technological developments and so lags somewhat behind. For example, in the early 1990s, when some of the first major

PACS systems were installed, a typical digital archive space supporting a single hospital might have contained close to a thousand net square feet of space, been intensively air-conditioned, and included computer access flooring throughout. Less than ten years later, that same archiving capability could have been contained in one or two jukebox devices in a small fraction of the space and required air-handling systems as basic as those used to condition a typical suite of offices. More recent designs include a single archive supporting multiple facilities within various cities; many of these archives have no physical connection (other than data connections) to the facilities in which the images are acquired or interpreted, and the operation of some are contracted out to application service providers (ASPs), rather than being maintained directly by the hospital's radiology informatics personnel. Conversely, other design issues–such as those affecting security, privacy, and confidentiality of the managed data–have become more stringent since the early years of PACS.

General radiography examinations represent more than 60 percent of all of the studies performed in a radiology department. In a digital department, these are acquired using either computed radiography or direct radiography. Computed radiography represents a transition technology that employs a reusable, light-sensitive phosphor (rather than film) in a cassette holder that can fit inside existing film-based units. Direct radiography is a technique that utilizes a digital detector such as a CCD, a selenium-based system, or an amorphous-silicon-based system. This technology does not require a cassette and thereby eliminates the cassette processing required for both film and computed radiography. Other diagnostic imaging acquisition devices such as CT and MRI also have inherent system components that capture the digital image directly. Much of the phosphor plate technology is beginning to be replaced by direct capture systems, and so the need for plate readers in the vicinity of where images are acquired may diminish, with the readers replaced by ubiquitous network design solutions.

Digital image management systems may involve a number of components, including:

- Computed image acquisition devices
- An image-viewing monitor (to verify image quality)
- Data storage devices (to provide both intermediate storage and archival storage)
- Image display workstations (located in a variety of places such as the imaging department, the intensive care unit, the emergency department, operating rooms, physicians' offices or homes, and remote reading areas)
- Some form of output device (to produce image copies on film, paper, CD, DVD, or other media)
- An image transmission network
- An RIS and/or HIS interface (to combine image data with other patient information)

- Multimedia workstations (to enable users to access and postprocess PACS images and to interface with RIS, HIS, and other information systems from one location)

Special electrical, ventilation, heat dissipation, acoustic, and space requirements are necessary. However, each is likely to change as the technology develops further.

Reading Room Design

Too often image acquisition–obtaining a CT, MR, or other scan–is considered to be the primary purpose of medical imaging, and thus the majority of design effort is frequently spent on developing procedure rooms and their associated support spaces. Image acquisition, however, is merely an intermediate process that facilitates the true purpose of medical imaging–the interpretation of images and the preparation of the accompanying report or findings, which are used by multiple care providers to inform and alter patients' courses of treatment and thus improve their medical outcomes.

Image interpretation is an instrumental component of both medical information management and the delivery of medical care. Radiologists are information sages, and the physical heart of information control is the reading room. The importance of image interpretation combined with the influence that the reading environment has on both reading productivity and accuracy make the reading room one of the most important spaces within the healthcare enterprise, and so it is essential that reading rooms be designed correctly.[4]

Medical images are viewed and read by individuals as well as groups. Properly designed reading areas are necessary for:

- Initial diagnosis
- Second opinions
- Follow-up review
- Peer discussion and consultation
- Discussion and consultation with referring physicians
- Consultation and education with patients and family members (usually done by the referring physician in a consultation room or office rather than by the radiologist in a reading room)
- Student/resident teaching

Images may be viewed in a number of different areas simultaneously or sequentially, including:

- Reading rooms
- Physician's private office or home
- Referring physician's viewing alcove, consultation room, or office

- Procedure rooms
- Conference rooms
- Auditoriums
- Various other remote locations

Additionally, images may be viewed using a variety of devices, including:

- Computer workstations
- Conventional film illuminators (sometimes referred to as light boxes)
- Motorized multiviewers (sometimes referred to as alternators). These are on the decline as are–to a lesser extent–film illuminators.
- Video monitors
- Projection screens
- Multimedia display systems
- Personal digital assistants (PDAs)[5]

The care and attention typically expended on selecting new PACS equipment stands in sharp contrast to the amount of attention typically dedicated to the design of the environment in which such equipment is used. Considering the impact that the physical environment has on both the effectiveness of PACS components and the productivity of its users, this imbalance is puzzling. In order to balance the needs of PACS users with the needs of PACS equipment, the digital environment must be seen as an integral extension of the equipment itself. This is of particular importance in the design of reading rooms. A small investment in proper design can quickly be amortized through improved reading efficiency, reduced work-related injury, and greater levels of user satisfaction.

After years of considering picture archiving and communications systems as a philosophical concept not yet ready for cost–effective implementation, digital image management has become mainstream, and many radiologists and radiology administrators have suddenly become acutely aware of how unprepared they have been for soft–copy reading without properly designed reading rooms.[6] In many cases, the absence of a properly designed reading room remains the most significant impediment to realizing the potential benefits of automated image management. A number of circumstances have led to this predicament:

- Funding for PACS implementation is frequently biased in favor of tangible capital costs, such as the purchase of image acquisition and storage systems. When image display components are considered, emphasis is often placed on selection of equipment such as computer hardware, with little consideration for designing the physical environment in which the equipment is placed. Ironically, image interpretation is arguably the most important step in the multiphase process of medical imaging. Reading an image and generating a report are the ultimate reasons an image is acquired in the first place.

- A poorly designed traditional film-based reading room (although undesirable) is less detrimental than a poorly designed soft-copy reading room. As a result, "nondesigned" reading rooms unfortunately have become an accepted practice. In contrast, reading soft-copy images in an improper reading environment can lead to eye fatigue, repetitive strain injuries, headaches, decreased reading efficiency, and even decreased reading accuracy. Ongoing pressures to read a greater number of more-complex images during longer reading sessions will exacerbate work-related injuries.

- Many designers do not fully understand the process of soft-copy reading. As a result, they are sometimes unfamiliar with the specific design interventions needed to mitigate the detrimental effects of reading in an inappropriate space. Many architects consider the reading room an office space. As such, it is often inappropriately designed with standard office lighting, furnishings, finishes, and accessories.

- Contradictory design requirements are inherent in the reading process. For example, there is frequently a need for visual and acoustic privacy (spatial enclosure), while at the same time there is a need for intense collaboration among colleagues (spatial openness).[7] Solving either need usually results in compromising the other.

- A hybrid environment—in which both soft-copy and hard-copy reading occur simultaneously—combines contradictory lighting requirements in which light emitted from film display devices (such as film illuminators) creates unwanted glare on computer monitors.

In order to comprehend the reading room's physical design requirements, the design team must first understand its functional requirements. Radiologic reading workstations serve multiple functions, including reading film-based images, reading soft-copy images, dictating, talking on the telephone, writing out paperwork by hand, entering bar codes, and manipulating images via keyboard, mouse, trackball, or other devices. Compared to nonradiologic administrative workstations, radiologists tend to use trackballs and nontraditional input devices more than keyboards for data entry and manipulation. New input devices—many of which are based on videogame user interfaces—are being applied to radiology workstations. Computer configurations vary considerably and often are based on individual preferences. For example, the number of monitors may vary from one to four, with a configuration of two monitors for images plus an additional monitor for display of HIS and RIS information being common.[8] Image dis-

Figure 12-12A Conceptual reading room designed for soft-copy reading.

Figure 12-12B Reading room modules are scalable into a variety of grouping configurations.

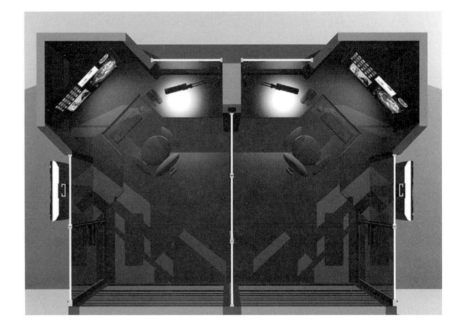

play components also are changing in response to the dynamic properties of many medical image data sets. The unique nature of radiologic work processes requires a unique approach to radiology reading room design.

In an effort to better understand the characteristics of the ideal reading room, several prototype designs have been developed (including ones by this author (figures 12–12 A, B and 12–13) as well as those developed at the Department of Veterans Affairs–Baltimore Medical Center, at the University of California, Los Angeles (see appendix A), and at the Medical College of Wisconsin (figure 12–14).[9]

Figure 12-13 Sources of light are kept away from the user's field of view, while controlling acoustics and spatial adaptability and providing optimal ergonomic design.

Figure 12-14 Prototype based on adapted commercially available components. Courtesy of Herman Miller for Healthcare, © 2005.

Much can be learned from other industries about how to best approach the design of radiologic reading rooms. For example, successful automobile designers make no distinction between machine and environment. One of the reasons a well-designed car is a pleasure to drive is because the driver is unaware of where the equipment ends and the physical environment begins. The same approach–integration of equipment and space–is appropriate for the design of reading rooms. The automobile analogy suggests five aspects of reading room design that should be considered:

- Enclosure
- Lighting
- Acoustics
- Ergonomics
- Connectivity[10]

Enclosure

How big should a reading room be? How many people should each work-station accommodate, and how many workstations should be in each room? The answers to these questions vary widely, based mostly on individual user preference. However, in contrast to the large "ballroom-style" reading rooms commonly found in film-based imaging departments of yesterday, today's soft-copy reading rooms can be much smaller, decentralized, and distributed throughout the enterprise.

Centralization was the common model for traditional film-based reading rooms because only one film existed for each image, and so one large central reading room was typically placed adjacent to the file room. In contrast, radiologists can now read images anywhere, and multiple individuals can examine a common image simultaneously from multiple locations. Noisy central reading rooms are no longer necessary or desirable.[11]

Some radiologists prefer to read in private offices, while others prefer to have a small number of reading stations clustered within one room (to encourage and accommodate face-to-face collaboration), with acoustic and light control provided between each workstation. In either case, most reading workstations should accommodate at least two or three primary users, with an option for up to four to six people to occasionally review cases together. Exceptions include teaching institutions, where larger groups may need to be accommodated, and private radiology practices, where images may be read in private single-occupancy offices.

Individual reading rooms can accommodate either single or multiple workstations. However, if a single room contains too many workstations, lighting and acoustics will be difficult to control. One approach is to place several two- or four-workstation rooms in proximity to one another. Within each room, individual workstations should be screened from the others for visual and acoustic privacy.

Irregularly shaped reading rooms–while not necessarily the most efficient use of space–can be advantageous in controlling acoustics. This is described below under "Acoustics."

Lighting

Lighting control is the reading room's single most important design requirement. Control of lighting becomes more difficult when reviewing both soft-copy and hard-copy images simultaneously in the same room.

Dr. Eliot Siegel, director of imaging at the Veterans Administration Maryland Health Care System, suggests that four primary objectives in the radiologic reading process be considered in order to properly understand ambient lighting needs in the reading room:

1. General illumination levels for computer tasks
2. Illumination for reading tasks using localized light sources
3. Balance of brightness levels in the user's field of view
4. Control of monitor reflection[12]

Two distinct types of lighting are needed in the reading room. Dimmable ambient lighting provides low levels of evenly distributed background illumination for reading soft-copy images, with higher illumination levels available for maintenance and housekeeping activities. Supplemental task lighting enables manual tasks such as writing and paperwork without disturbing others in the room. Ambient lighting should be broadly dispersed and indirect (bounced off ceilings or washed along walls) if possible, while task lighting should be narrowly focused. A ceiling height of at least 9 feet 6 inches above the floor surface will facilitate hanging indirect light fixtures from the ceiling. If this height is not available, indirect light fixtures can be wall-mounted or integrated within the workstation assembly.

Sources of light (such as light fixtures, film illuminators, and other display monitors) should be completely screened from the workstation. Veiling glare—the reflection of light sources—on the monitors' surface should be minimized. Flat-panel monitors, liquid crystal displays (LCDs), and plasma screens tend to be less glare-prone than CRT monitors (which have mostly been replaced by flat-panel alternatives). One study of mammography reading room design suggests the use of green lighting filters to help preserve radiologists' dark adaptation of their peripheral vision by providing "the most excitation of the cones and the minimum excitation of the rods" in their eyes.[13] (A similar use of green lighting filters in operating rooms to reduce glare on PACS monitors is described in chapter 15, "Imaging Beyond the Radiology Department"). The mammography reading room study also references the Mammography Quality Standards Act (MQSA) requirement that ambient light levels be kept to a minimum in rooms where mammography images are evaluated.[14]

An overlighted environment or one in which the lighting is designed for paperwork instead of computer work creates a lighting imbalance between the monitor and the work surface. Ambient lighting for computer workstations must be provided in such a way that the contrast between the screen and surrounding surfaces is not so great that it causes eyestrain, yet the room must be dark enough and free of glare for the display to be readable. In general, brighter displays permit the human visual system to discern a greater number of shades of gray, which is very important in diagnostic image interpretation.

Room lighting that is three times brighter than the display itself has been suggested for nonradiologic administrative workstations; for radiologic reading room workstations, ambient luminance equal to that of the display terminal has been recommended.[15] In addition, separate task lighting is advised for such low–light conditions. However, task lighting must be arranged so it does not result in additional screen glare.

Several studies attempting to correlate room and monitor lighting levels with radiologist productivity and accuracy have found that radiologists' fatigue increased and image interpretation accuracy decreased as background room light levels increased relative to monitor brightness. According to Drs. Siegel and Reiner at the University of Maryland School of Medicine, these studies also suggest that the use of newer, brighter monitors will likely accommodate higher levels of ambient room lighting.[16]

Screen glare not only hinders image interpretation but also causes unnecessary eyestrain. The amount of glare on the screen results from the physical properties of both the computer monitor and the surrounding environment. Thus, the reading room environment should be designed to minimize the incidence of reflected light. This can be accomplished by selecting neutral-colored surfaces with low reflectivity. In addition, surface finishes with low reflecting values for work surfaces, keyboards, armatures, and shelves also cut down on glare.[17] If an exterior window is present, it should have adjustable shades or louvers. Computer monitors should be placed away from the window, or at an angle that will reduce the amount of light reflected onto them, directly or indirectly, from the window.

The single most effective way to control glare is with proper selection and placement of artificial lighting within the room. Dimmable indirect ambient lighting fixtures should be used in conjunction with carefully placed dimmable narrow-beam task lights. As previously noted, the actual source of light itself should be completely screened from the workstation. Where indirect lighting is not practical (indirect lighting systems often require a higher–than–average ceiling height to be effective), recessed lamps with a narrow beam focus can be used. Controls should be dimmable to limit the amount of ambient light. Regardless of which lighting system is used, multiple workstation reading rooms should be zoned so that relatively small areas within the room can be illuminated independently from other areas.

Acoustics

As speech recognition systems become an integral component of soft–copy reading, acoustic control within the reading environment also grows in importance. Complete acoustic control is possible only in a private office–a solution that does not foster collegial interaction. However, some measure of acoustic control is possible through the strategic application of sound-absorbing floor, wall, and ceiling finishes. Modular systems furniture designed for nonradiologic workplace installations can be adapted to meet the acoustic needs of reading rooms. Confidential conversations should also be confined within the reading room for HIPAA compliance.

According to Alan Hedge, PhD, director of Cornell University's Human Factors and Ergonomics Laboratory, "The ceiling is the most important surface for controlling acoustics."[18] He also suggests that irregularly shaped rooms with walls that are not parallel to each other can help control acoustics by minimizing the amount of acoustic reflection from one wall to the next.

While the ability of referring physicians to view images from almost anywhere has led to reduced face-to-face consultations with radiologists, the number of radiologist phone consultations are increasing. As a result, the radiology report–often discussed over the phone–has become an even more critical element for communicating radiologic findings, frequently replacing in-person consultations.[19] Conversations in reading rooms with multiple workstations can be distracting if acoustic damping materials are not installed as part of the workstation and on the walls, floor, and ceiling of the room. Furthermore, where reading stations are placed in patient areas–such as the ED, ICU, and clinics–special care must be taken to prevent confidential discussions from being overheard, as required by HIPAA.

Ergonomics

Improper design of workstations or improper use of well-designed workstations can lead to health problems, ranging from occasional headaches to chronic orthopedic and neurological disorders. Three points of contact are the chief concerns in maintaining a healthful workplace: where the eye meets the monitor screen, where the fingers press against the keyboard, and where your body rests in its chair.[20]

Many eye problems can be avoided by proper work habits and proper ergonomic design. Eye irritation of workers using computers for repetitive tasks can often be attributed to poor ergonomic conditions, such as improper lighting and glare.[21] Refer to the guidelines under "Lighting," above, to prevent eye fatigue and related illness.

The incidence of hand- and wrist-related health problems has escalated since computer workstations have become increasingly common. One common malady, repetitive strain injury, is caused by constant repetition of the same physical motion. Multiple adjustments of seating, work surfaces, keyboards, and monitors can help reduce the likelihood of such injuries. The proper height of these workstation components, coupled with the ability to adjust workstations for different body types and sizes, can further reduce injury. As a general rule, to reduce the incidence of ergonomically preventable health problems, provide adjustable furniture specifically designed to be used with computer systems, and avoid nonadjustable, built-in casework.

Proper seating should conform to dimensions and ranges of adjustment specified by the Human Factors Society (HFS). The American National Standards Institute (ANSI) and the HFS publish voluntary national standards (such as ANSI/HFS Standard 100–1988) with recommended ergonomically appropriate dimensions and motion ranges for computer workstations. The ability of workers to occasionally modify their posture

Figure 12-15 Like a well-designed automobile, the reading room should be configured so that all frequently used devices are within easy reach.

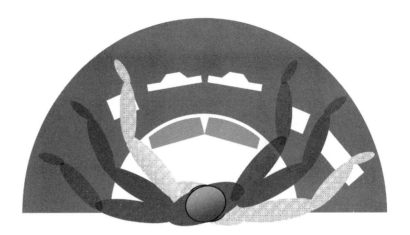

and seating position can reduce the likelihood of workplace-related discomfort. Some furniture companies have developed product lines specifically for radiology applications by modifying ergonomically designed nonradiologic computer workstations.

Furniture and devices in the reading room should provide flexibility to accommodate future changes in both reading practices and reading equipment. For example, the growing use of speech recognition systems has altered how radiologists document their findings and has similarly led to modifications to the equipment used for this documentation. Movable adjustable computer furniture and work surfaces are preferred over built-in casework to ensure flexibility and adaptability over time. One should also recognize that most reading workstations are shared by several individuals during the course of a day, and so users will vary in size, weight, age, and visual acuity.[22] Adjustability is also beneficial in single-user workstations to avoid muscle fatigue. Ideally, adjustability should range from sitting to standing positions. The height and angle of input devices and monitors should be adjustable, as should the distance between the user's eyes and the monitor surface.

Frequently used devices (such as phones and dictation controls) and reference materials should be placed within easy reach of the radiologist without having to search for them (figure 12–15). Common ergonomic situations to avoid include frequent viewing of reference materials placed at the side of the monitor and excessively high monitor placement.[23] Where possible, provide individually adjustable ventilation controls to accommodate personal comfort preferences. [24]

The ergonomic interface between radiologists and today's advanced dynamic images differs from their previous interface with static two-dimensional films. According to presenters at the 2004 annual meeting of the Society for Computer Applications in Radiology, "Dynamic image interpretation requires a sophisticated multimedia approach to interpretation, and radiology has lagged behind the entertainment and video game industry in widespread acceptance of these new tools."[25] Design solutions must look beyond just adding new devices to the reading workstation, and should include a radical reengineering of the way dynamic data sets are examined and interrogated. April McGee, a usability engineer for Siemens Medical Solutions, envisions future multimodal data interfaces that will use speech and the senses of hearing, sight, and touch; ultimately they will be capable of "affective computing," able to sense, recognize, understand, and respond to human emotions.[26] Some input devices like those used in video game interfaces combine hand and foot controls and are beginning to be applied to radiology workstations. Reading room design must respond to these new interfaces, rather than assume that traditional mouse and pull-down menu commands will remain as the dominant interface in the future. Similarly, image display will likely become a more integral component of the reading environment–perhaps becoming part of the wall or even consisting of hologram-like projections within the reading room–and the monitor as a separate device may cease to exist.

Connectivity
Wire and cable management is often an afterthought in reading areas that may otherwise be well designed. Management of telephone, data, power and other lines is often best solved by integrating raceways within modular furniture systems–a concept common in business workplace design. Wireless communications systems may solve some cable management problems; however, they may introduce security and transmission interference challenges.

Design Considerations for Support Spaces
In addition to procedure rooms, control areas, and reading rooms, imaging facilities include a variety of support spaces. These include dressing areas, patient toilet rooms, and waiting areas.

Dressing Areas
Imaging facilities must provide cubicles large enough to accommodate patients protected under the Americans with Disabilities Act. Clustered dressing areas–one for men and one for women–tend to accommodate accessibility requirements more efficiently than do separate dressing cubicles.

If dressing cubicles are assigned to specific procedure rooms and located adjacent to them, at least one cubicle within each area is to be made accessible to those with disabilities, according to ADA requirements. If dressing cubicles are clustered together, where one cluster for males and one for females serve the entire department or area, 5 percent (but at least one per cluster) are to be made accessible to the disabled. However, if dressing areas are clustered together, some gowned patients may have to travel some distance if the dressing area is not adjacent to the procedure room.

Because dressing cubicles are small, it usually is desirable to have the surrounding partitions stop well below the ceiling (but above eye level) and to have door bottoms raised 8 to 12 inches above floor level. This allows for ventilation without providing separate air diffusers in each cubicle. Curtains in lieu of doors are not desirable where the door opening leads directly to a departmental corridor or alcove.

Patient Toilet Rooms

Patient toilet rooms should be provided near certain types of procedure rooms, such as fluoroscopy, ultrasound, MRI, and CT rooms. It is desirable for patients to enter the toilet room directly from the procedure room and exit to the department corridor without having to pass back through the procedure room (except for MRI exam rooms, where it is best to keep the number of RF-shielded doors to an absolute minimum). With this arrangement, which may require more space than would a toilet room with only one door, the procedure room is available for the next patient when the previous patient is still in the toilet room. The two doors leading into the toilet room may require special hardware to prevent the previous patient from unintentionally exiting through the procedure room and to prevent the next patient from inadvertently entering the toilet room when it is occupied. Acoustic insulation and even music systems can improve the level of privacy in toilet rooms adjacent to procedure rooms. Emergency nurse call systems also should be provided and are required in many states. Specific guidelines for designing toilet rooms that meet federal requirements for accessibility are described in the ADA.

Patient Waiting Areas

Waiting areas should be located and arranged so that they can be observed by a receptionist who also can attend to other responsibilities. Additionally, natural daylight should be provided where possible, although the lighting level in the waiting area should not be significantly brighter than it is in other parts of the department. If windows or skylights transmit direct sunlight, additional shading or screening may be necessary. Seating arrangements that accommodate small groups are the most appropriate. Individual seats are preferred over couches or benches. Seat fabric and coverings should be attractive and yet durable and easy to clean. Many jurisdictions have strict requirements regarding the fire and smoke rating of materials permitted in healthcare facilities.

If the number of seats required is large, it is desirable to subdivide the waiting area into smaller sections to ensure privacy and to control noise. It also may be desirable to have multiple waiting areas to accommodate certain groups of patients, such as children or infectious patients.

If dressing rooms are not located adjacent to procedure rooms, separate waiting spaces for gowned men and women should be provided in addition to general waiting areas. Waiting areas for gowned patients should be located within the patient zone of the department, either adjacent to the dressing area or near the procedure rooms.

Because imaging procedures often are frightening and difficult for some patients to understand, an education alcove near the waiting area may be beneficial. The education alcove should provide some degree of visual and acoustic privacy, a place to read books or pamphlets, and possibly a place to view instructional videos. A consultation room adjacent to the waiting area provides privacy in which personal medical or financial matters can be discussed.

Ventilation and air filtration requirements in waiting rooms for people with infectious or communicable diseases should be considered. The AIA Guidelines for Construction and Equipment of Hospitals and Medical Facilities (section 7.10.G1) provide design criteria for situations in which infectious disease may be present. Some states have proposed special infection control design requirements that apply to waiting areas as well as other locations.

Design Guidelines for Specific Types of Imaging Procedure Areas

The first part of this chapter described general considerations for procedure rooms, such as their orientation to control rooms and how procedure rooms can be placed relative to patient corridors and staff work cores. This section of the chapter provides guidelines and considerations for the design and planning of specific types of procedure rooms. For each room type a floor plan is provided to illustrate one of many possible ways the room can be developed. In addition, design considerations for each room type are offered for three categories: functional requirements, human factors, and technical issues.

These guidelines identify design considerations for specific types of imaging procedure rooms. However, because imaging techniques and equipment change over time, the reader is advised to periodically update these guidelines with current technical information as it becomes available for each modality and room type.

For any project, site-specific and room-specific technical drawings should be provided by the selected equipment vendor, ideally during the early stages of design development. These vendor drawings must be integrated with the additional knowledge of the design team. It is important to note that each vendor's equipment—and each equipment model—will likely influence detailed design uniquely. The space and configuration requirements of similar imaging equipment from different manufacturers can and often do differ significantly. Room design based on the worst-case scenario and a loose-fit concept can avoid costly last-minute changes. In addition, vendor drawings focus mostly on the specific needs of the equipment and cannot be considered comprehensive—for example, they should not be relied upon to address building code, accessibility, or aesthetic requirements.

Design and Planning Considerations for All Procedure Rooms

Functional Requirements

- Provide adequate space for moving ambulatory (and non-ambulatory if appropriate) patients on and off the exam table, and for maneuvering people, supplies, and equipment within the room. It is not recommended that procedure rooms be programmed or designed based on manufacturer's minimum dimensions.
- Consider how the room, its operations, and its equipment might change in the future. Where possible, design the room to easily adapt to future uses.
- Provide adequate equipment access and clearances for all equipment components.
- Provide ample ceiling height for equipment movement and space above the ceiling for coordination of infrastructure systems.
- Provide a hand-washing sink in all procedure rooms except MRI and interventional rooms (such as interventional radiography and interventional cardiology); see descriptions of those rooms for additional information. Hand-washing sinks are required by code in many states.
- Consider dual-leaf corridor entrance doors (except in MRI rooms) to improve patient access. Special hardware may be required where radiation shielding, or other types of shielding, are called for.
- Visually and acoustically screen control rooms from patient areas (including the procedure room) to ensure that confidential data or conversations are not seen or heard, per HIPAA requirements.
- Provide adequate storage for equipment and supplies in the procedure room and adjacent support areas to help minimize staff travel time and reduce clutter.
- Portable or permanent oxygen and suction services may be needed in the procedure room, depending on the type of patients and procedures intended.
- Secure holding areas should be provided for biohazardous waste and contaminated linen.

Human Factors

- Design procedure rooms to help reduce patients' anxiety and to improve patient privacy and compliance. Don't limit design considerations to the technical needs of equipment.
- Minimize distances that gowned patients must travel as they enter and exit procedure rooms.

- Consider same-handed procedure rooms for similar room types to help minimize medical errors and to reduce staff time spent looking for supplies.
- Daylight in procedure rooms is controversial for some people. While many imaging techniques require that the room have low levels of illumination and be free of glare, there are also many benefits for both patients and staff to having natural daylight within the procedure room. Therefore, day-lighted procedure rooms can be desirable provided the light can be controlled when clinically necessary. Furthermore, patient and staff corridors with views to the outside and opportunities for natural light to enter are also beneficial.
- Because direct overhead lighting may cause discomfort to patients facing the ceiling, additional indirect lighting should be considered.
- The appearance of the ceiling is important. Patients may spend more time staring at the ceiling than looking at other areas of the room.
- Controlled variable lighting allows staff to adjust the lighting level and direction, minimizing glare and improving patient comfort.
- Additional high-level lighting may be needed if biopsies or other intricate procedures are to be performed.

Technical Issues

- Where appropriate, locate equipment electronics cabinets in separate but easily accessible electronics equipment rooms, rather than in the procedure room. This may enable the procedure room to be slightly smaller, be used more efficiently, be cleaned more easily, and even look better (considering that many patients are acutely aware of their surroundings during an imaging exam or procedure).
- Be aware that some equipment comes with preassembled cables that have maximum lengths, which may limit the allowable distance between specific equipment components.
- Two levels of lighting should be provided. Generally, a relatively low light level is adequate for the imaging procedure room and is more comfortable for the patient. Bright illumination is needed for equipment maintenance and housekeeping activities. In addition, a high illumination level (but a focused beam) usually is required for detailed work during biopsy procedures. The lighting in control alcoves/rooms and procedure rooms should be adjustable so the technologist (and others) in the control room can see the patient without reflection on the control room window.

Figure 12-16 General radiography room.
Courtesy of Anshen + Allen, Architects.

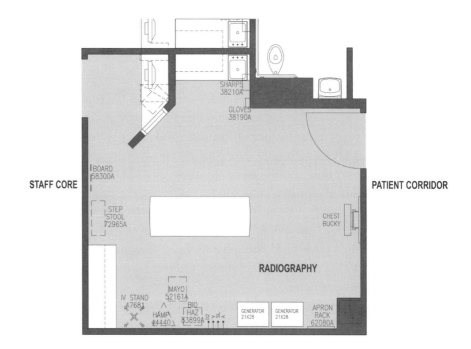

- Installation of a broadband and/or voice–over–Internet protocol (V/IP) network with a direct connection to the equipment vendor can facilitate remote systems quality assurance
monitoring and diagnostics.

Design and Planning Considerations for Basic Radiography (figure 12-16)

Functional Requirements

- Convenient direct access from the emergency department
(ED) and nursing units (where applicable) may improve ED
patient throughput.
- The control console should be arranged for direct view of
the patient's head; if the table tilts, it should not block the
technologist's view of the patient.
- Dedicated rooms should be considered for high–volume
procedures such as chest exams. Alternatively, rolling chest
stands can be used in some radiography rooms. Having patients stand instead of sit during chest exams, where appropriate, will improve throughput.
- Space should be provided for hanging several radiation
protection aprons and gloves.

Human Factors

- Locate short–duration/rapid–throughput X-ray rooms near
the front of the department (near the waiting area) to minimize traffic through the department.

Technical Issues

- Radiation protection should be provided as directed by a certified medical or health physicist. State and federal radiation protection requirements often vary. (See the section "Radiation Protection" in chapter 13, "Physical Properties Influencing Design.")
- Special structural support for floor-, wall-, and ceiling-mounted equipment should be provided per approved structural calculations.
- Adequate access space and structural capacity should be provided for installation and/or replacement of large and heavy equipment.
- A variety of methods exist for preventing unauthorized individuals from entering a procedure room during X-ray exposure, ranging from simply posting notices that warn that X-rays are in use and prohibit access of unauthorized personnel to the use of electronic interlocks that terminate the exposure if the procedure room door is opened. However, stopping an exposure before completion means that the patient has been irradiated needlessly and that the examination will need to be repeated.

Design and Planning Considerations for Radiography/Fluoroscopy (figure 12-16)

Design and planning considerations for fluoroscopy are similar to those for radiography, with the following additions.

Functional Requirements

- A barium preparation or work area should be provided within or near the procedure room. However, as preprepared barium doses become more common, a work area may consist of only a sink and a small counter area.
- Contrast agents may need to be available for injection and administration. Crash carts, contrast warmers, articulating exam lights, and emergency resuscitation equipment should be provided in areas where contrast agents are used.
- Automated contrast material injectors should be kept near the patient table and installed in such a way that they do not obstruct staff movement. They can be mounted as part of the table, from the ceiling, or on a cart.

Human Factors

- An adjacent toilet room with direct connection to the fluoroscopy room must be provided for patients eliminating enemas. This is a requirement in many jurisdictions and per the AIA guidelines.

Technical Issues

- To reduce the possibility of contamination, clean or dedicated fluoroscopic rooms should be considered for invasive procedures in which barium enemas are used.
- If a tilting table is used, orient the table so the technologist can view the patient's head, regardless of how much the table is tilted.

Design and Planning Considerations for Mammography
(figure 12-17)

Functional Requirements

- Storage should be provided for a biopsy setup cart when biopsies are to be performed in the procedure room.

Figure 12-17 *Mammography rooms (upright and prone units).*

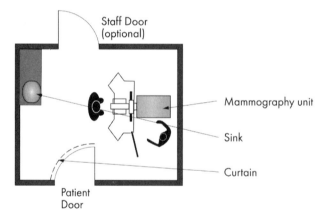

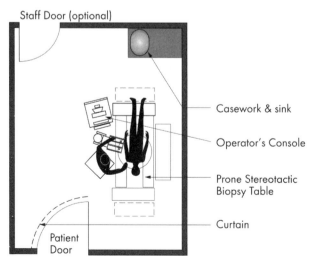

Human Factors

- A dedicated dressing area in (or adjacent to) the procedure room should be considered to maximize privacy.
- The exam room should be located so that mammography patient traffic does not need to pass through the entire radiology department. During needle location procedures—usually performed within a stereotactic mammography room—the gowned patient may need to be wheeled to a surgical procedure room while the needle remains in the patient's breast.
- The mammography procedure room could be incorporated into a women's health area, with image and branding considerations reflected in its design.

Technical Issues

- Digital mammography files can be quite large. Computer-assisted detection (CAD) systems may be employed.
- Due to the low dose of radiation emitted, mammography equipment often does not require external radiation shielding beyond that provided by the equipment itself and the standard materials used in construction of the walls. (The size of the room and the location of the equipment also are factors in determining the need for radiation shielding.) However, some states require that additional radiation protection be installed. A certified medical or health physicist should determine whether additional shielding is needed.
- Mammograms can become difficult to read if dust accumulates on the imaging equipment or on the image itself. Design the environment to be relatively dust-free.

Design and Planning Considerations for Interventional Radiology and Interventional Cardiology (Cath Lab and EP) Procedure Rooms *(figures 12-18A, B and 12-19)*

Design and planning considerations for interventional radiography and interventional cardiology rooms are more stringent that those of R/F special procedure rooms, as these spaces are typically used for minimally invasive surgery–like procedures. While many of these rooms have historically been used for both diagnostic and therapeutic procedures, new imaging techniques—such as CT angiography and MR angiography—are off-loading many of the diagnostic cases, resulting in a greater therapeutic utilization of these rooms. (A concept known as the "integrated interventional platform" co-locates interventional radiology and cardiac catheterization labs within the surgical suite. This concept is described in chapter 15, "Imaging Beyond the Radiology Department.")

Figure 12-18A Integrated interventional radiology and cardiology suite. Courtesy of Anshen + Allen, Architects.

Figure 12-18B Interventional radiology/ interventional cardiology procedure room with support spaces. Courtesy of Anshen + Allen, Architects.

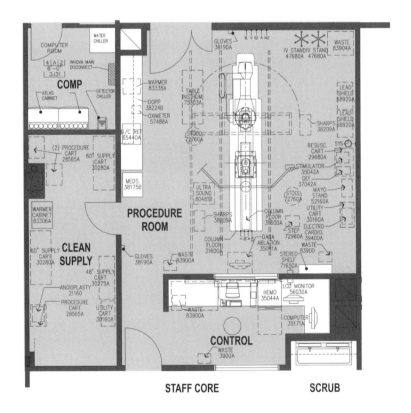

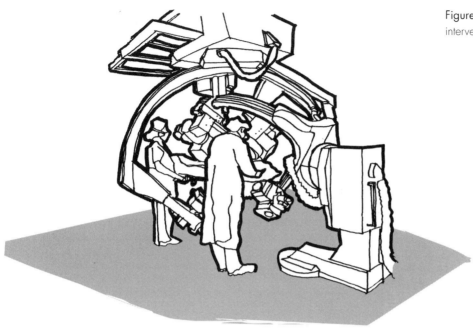

Figure 12-19 Interventional radiology/interventional cardiology.

Functional Requirements

- Generally, the procedure room is larger than it is for R/F special procedures. Room size and configuration will be influenced by types of procedures and equipment selection.
- Hand-washing and cleanup sinks should not be in the procedure room. Scrub sinks should be directly outside the entrance to the procedure room.
- Provide a dedicated and enclosed control room, sized to accommodate multiple personnel and equipment. The sharing of one large control area by two procedure rooms has become less popular for these procedure rooms because of infection control concerns, difficulties in controlling noise during procedures, and the amount of traffic that tends to flow between the control and procedure rooms. Dedicated enclosed control rooms also improve patient privacy and confidentiality.
- Orientation of the control room from either the patient's side or foot may be preferred. Control room orientation is often determined by personal preference and equipment configuration.
- The control console should be arranged so that personnel in the room have a direct view of the patient's head and the interventional team. Televised viewing of the patient may also prove valuable.

- The interventional radiologist or cardiologist usually will work from the patient's right side (although during some procedures, such as those involving pacemakers and implantable cardiovascular defibrillators (ICDs), the physician may work from the left side). He or she should be able to have direct visual and voice contact with the control room. Both the physician and the technologist at the control console should have a direct line of sight to the patient monitors. In some installations, this may be difficult to achieve, depending on equipment configuration, complexity, and physical size.

- A doorway (without a door) between the control room and procedure room is preferred. This configuration should be reviewed by a certified health physicist to ensure radiation safety.

- The control window should be made as large as practical. Vertical window mullions should not obscure the control technologist's line of sight.

- Monitors in the procedure room should be located so as not to obstruct the view from the control room.

- Ample space is needed to bring people and large portable equipment into and out of the procedure room without disturbing the imaging procedure.

- An intercom between the procedure room and the control area should be specified if one is not already provided by the manufacturer. Such systems should allow for good voice modulation to reassure the patient.

- Patient preparation and holding space (similar to that in a postanesthesia recovery unit) should be provided, with a nurse's station and lockable medication storage located nearby.

- Two work areas, one for clean materials and one for soiled materials, should be provided, with close access from the procedure room.

- An area for sterile supplies and storage of large carts and scrubs should be provided.

- Secure holding areas for biohazardous waste and contaminated linen should be provided.

- Contrast agents may need to be available for injection and administration. Crash carts, contrast warmers, articulating exam lights, oxygen, and emergency resuscitation equipment should be provided in areas where contrast agents are used. A floor pedestal for medical gases and physiological monitoring may work better than wall or ceiling outlets because cables to and from the pedestal are less obtrusive than those connected to the wall or ceiling, and a pedestal is less likely to conflict with the movement of overhead devices. The placement and configuration of medical gases will vary, based on procedure type and individual preference. Often a floor pedestal with one or two sets of gases is preferable. A gas scavenger system as well as suction and oxygen should be provided.

- Contrast media injectors should be kept near the patient table and installed in such a way that they do not obstruct staff movement.

- Space should be provided near the control room for hanging several radiation protection aprons. In addition, ceiling-mounted radiation shields should be provided in the procedure room.

- Often, foot-activated lighting controls at the tableside are needed to reduce the light level during fluoroscopy. Preset lighting levels that can be customized by the interventional team may also be desired. Focused procedural lights can be mounted on ceiling-mounted radiation shield arms.

- In addition to the procedure room, at a minimum the following should be provided:
  - Control room
  - Scrub area
  - Imaging electronics equipment room
  - Utility room for clean materials
  - Utility room for soiled materials (cleanup room)
  - Technologist work area/office
  - PACS image review room and dictation stations
  - Clean supplies storage area
  - Medication storage and dispensing devices
  - Patient prep and recovery areas
  - Patient toilet(s) grouped in proximity to prep and recovery areas
  - Staff toilet(s)
  - Staff lockers, staff lounge, patient holding area, and family waiting area

- Some states classify cardiac catheterization labs as one of two types, diagnostic or therapeutic. In some cases, building and licensing requirements governing catheterization labs are different for each of these two types of labs. As noted previously, there is a pronounced trend for cath labs to become more therapeutic, as techniques such as CT angiography and MR angiography are used for many of the diagnostic procedures. Some states place limitations on the kind of interventional procedures that may be performed

within outpatient facilities. For example, in California, cardiac catheterization labs are not permitted in B-occupancy
medical office buildings.

- Adequate space should be provided for storage of catheters,
  guide wires, and so on. A long countertop work surface and
  ample wall-mounted or movable cabinets are desirable.
  Special catheter storage units are available.
- Direct access to the ED, surgery, and the intensive care units
  should be considered.
- If the cardiac catheterization lab is used for electrophysiological (EP) studies (which address problems relating to the
  heart's electrical conductivity), room throughput may be
  decreased because of the long duration of many EP procedures. Consider a dedicated EP procedure room if projected
  volumes justify this.

Human Factors

- Many procedures are long in duration, and often the patient
  is awake and acutely aware of his or her surroundings.
  Therefore, the physical environment should be soothing
  and sufficiently interesting to take the patient's attention
  away from the procedure. This is a challenging requirement
  in a room full of technical equipment. Lighting should be
  dimmable and indirect, and special audio systems should
  be available to provide music. However, provisions for the
  high illumination levels needed to set up and begin the
  procedure should also be planned.

Technical Issues

- A separate equipment room that allows systems electronics
  equipment to be stored outside the procedure room is preferred. This enables emitted heat and noise to be isolated
  and removed. It also allows the limited wall space in the
  procedure room to be used for clinical equipment.
- Special environmental conditioning (such as temperature
  and humidity) and electronics rack cabinets may be needed
  due to additional computer equipment.
- Special air filtration and air pressure relative to adjacent
  spaces may be required.
- It should be determined whether biplane or single-plane
  capabilities are desired. Biplane equipment—which is most
  common for pediatric imaging and for neuroangiography—
  requires additional structural support components.

- Hybrid rooms with multiple imaging devices (such as MRI and cath lab equipment) may be desired. Suite planning should consider the possibility of combining multiple procedure rooms in the future to create a hybrid room. (See chapter 15, "Imaging Beyond the Radiology Department.")
- Power requirements should be verified with the equipment vendor. In most cases, the IR or cath lab should have its own main feeder line. Additional backup capabilities should be provided. Clean power should be provided to prevent surges.
- The cath lab should provide a range of lighting options, from whole room illumination to independently dimmable lighting for use during fluoroscopy. Under–cabinet lights can illuminate counter surfaces without necessarily illuminating the entire room. Fluorescent lights, if used, should not cause radio–frequency interference that can be detected by the heart's electrical conducting system.[27]
- In cases where the procedure room is used for catheter–dependent EP studies, radio–frequency interference and electrical grounding requirements should be carefully reviewed.

Design and Planning Considerations for Computed Tomography (figure 12-20)

Functional Requirements

- Provide convenient access to and from the ED. Location within the ED may improve work flow involving emergency patients.
- A patient dressing, preparation, and holding/observation area should be provided in the CT suite.

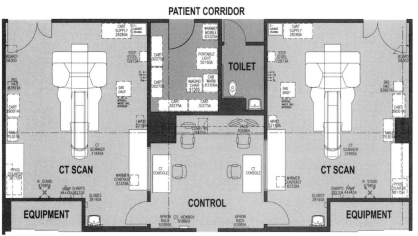

Figure 12-20 Computed tomography rooms. Courtesy of Anshen + Allen, Architects.

- The control console should be arranged so that the technologist has a direct view of the patient's head. Some equipment manufacturers may specify the angle of orientation between the table/gantry and the control console. Often, an angle of 30 degrees from the axis of the patient table is suggested so that a view of the patient's head is not blocked by his or her feet and torso when positioned within the CT gantry.[28]
- A closed-circuit camera or a mirror may be helpful to allow the technologist to see the patient behind the gantry. Some operators prefer a mirror because it provides a better indication of the patient's color and therefore a truer vision of the patient's medical condition. Others prefer television monitoring to observe the patient and ensure proper positioning.
- An intercom between the procedure room and control area should be specified if one is not already provided by the manufacturer.
- Consideration should be given to locating a dedicated physician viewing console near the control area.
- Provide a patient toilet directly adjacent to the CT scan room for use after virtual colonoscopy and other procedures.
- A ceiling-mounted IV track or a portable IV pole and hangers should be considered.
- Work areas for clean and soiled materials should be provided adjacent to the procedure room.
- Secure holding areas should be provided for biohazardous waste and contaminated linen.
- Contrast agents may need to be available for injection and administration. Crash carts, contrast warmers, articulating exam lights, oxygen, and emergency resuscitation equipment should be provided in areas where contrast agents are used.
- IV contrast storage should be provided.
- Storage should be provided for a biopsy setup cart when biopsies are to be performed in the procedure room.

Human Factors

- Large control room windows improve the technologist's comfort and allow for better observation. The windowsill should be low enough to provide good visibility while the technologist is seated at the control console.
- When two CT procedure rooms share one control room, position the control windows so a patient cannot see from one procedure room into the other room.

Technical Issues

- Radiation protection should be provided as directed by a certified medical or health physicist. Shielding requirements have increased considerably for some CT scanners.
- Special structural support for floor-, wall-, and ceiling-mounted equipment should be provided per approved structural calculations.
- Adequate access space and structural capacity should be provided for installation, maintenance, and/or replacement of large equipment.
- Special environmental conditioning (such as temperature and humidity) may be needed. In some instances, a dedicated CT chiller may be required.
- Power requirements for CT have increased considerably for some CT scanners.

Design and Planning Considerations for Ultrasound (figure 12-21)

Functional Requirements

- A blanket warmer should be provided for patient comfort.
- Ultrasound uses a large volume of linen and/or disposable supplies; adequate supply, storage, and removal systems should be provided.
- A sit-down workstation should be provided for the technologist or physician.
- Good task lighting should be provided for specialized procedures, such as biopsies and cyst aspirations.

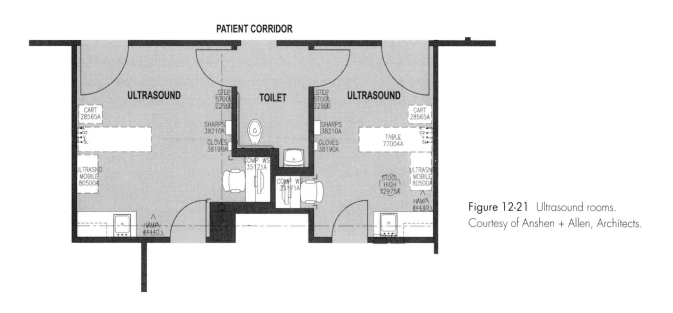

Figure 12-21 Ultrasound rooms. Courtesy of Anshen + Allen, Architects.

- Space, equipment, and staff for high-level disinfection of ultrasound transducers should be provided nearby.

Human Factors

- For obstetric and gynecological ultrasound suites:
  - A dedicated toilet room should be provided adjacent to the procedure room because patients will need to empty their bladders after examinations.
  - Consideration should be given to providing a dedicated dressing area to maximize privacy.
  - Consideration should be given to locating the procedure room so that patient traffic does not need to pass through the entire radiology department.
  - The procedure room could be incorporated into a women's health area with a special image (for example, color palette, materials, finishes, furniture and lighting), if appropriate.
- Although most patients go home and shower to remove the lubricant that was missed by the technologist, oversized dressing spaces with a hand-washing lavatory should be considered for those patients who cannot go home immediately after the exam or procedure.
- Sonographers experience frequent work-related injuries. Therefore, proper ergonomic design—for both right-handed and left-handed personnel—plays an important role in the ultrasound suite.

Design and Planning Considerations for Magnetic Resonance Imaging (figure 12-22)

The following considerations are only general comments; the manufacturer should be consulted for specific requirements, which will vary depending on magnet type, manufacturer, field strength, and specific site conditions. (See the section "Special Considerations for MRI Installations" in chapter 13, "Physical Properties Influencing Design.")

Functional Requirements

- Unauthorized access into and near the MRI suite must be prevented. A security vestibule should be placed in front of the scan room entrance. See Appendix B for excerpts from the American College of Radiology MR Safety Guidelines
- A hand-washing fixture and casework should be provided. However, plumbing lines should be routed and constructed so as not to disrupt the continuous RF shielding. This may

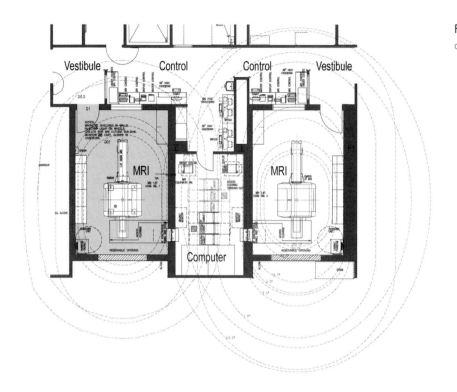

Figure 12-22 MRI rooms. Courtesy of Anshen + Allen, Architects.

suggest providing a MR–compatible alcohol disinfectant dispenser within the magnet room and placing the hand-washing sink at the entrance to but outside the room.

- A patient dressing, preparation, and toilet area should be provided within the MR suite.
- The control console should be arranged so that the technologist has a direct view of the patient's head, the entire scan room, and the entrance vestibule outside the magnet room.
- An intercom between the procedure room and the control area should be specified if one is not already provided by the manufacturer.
- Adult and pediatric holding areas with medical supervision and lockable medication storage and medical gases should be provided just outside the procedure room. If a patient requires immediate medical assistance during a scan, the medical team may choose to remove the patient from the scan room and resuscitate or otherwise assist him or her in this area.
- Adequate storage for equipment and supplies in the procedure room and adjacent support areas helps minimize staff travel time.
- Nonferrous oxygen and suction services should be provided in the procedure room. Often permanent medical gas systems are preferred over portable units because they reduce the risk of having a ferrous container carried into the mag-

net room in response to an emergency. Also, special nonferrous equipment (gurneys and crash carts, for example) must be considered.

- Work areas for clean and soiled materials should be provided just beyond the restricted MRI zone III.

Human Factors

- Often patients in the magnet's bore experience fear and claustrophobia. Every effort should be made to alleviate patient stress and anxiety. Sensitive room design, the use of natural lighting, and noise reduction through the use of sound–absorbing materials can contribute to stress reduction (figure 12–23). Often, counseling is provided to assist patients in completing an initial exam and returning for follow–up appointments. Some low–field–strength magnets are

Figure 12-23 The creative use of lighting and sound-absorbing materials can help reduce stress and improve patient compliance with imaging exams. Courtesy of the Stein-Cox Group, Architects.

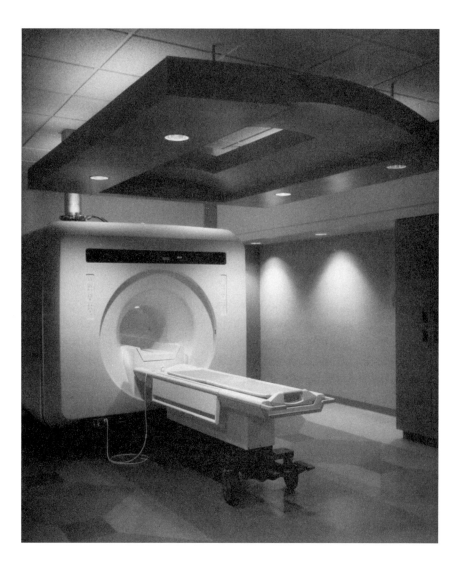

available with an open bore to reduce the incidence of claustrophobia. Magnets with shorter or wider bores are also available.

- Abrupt loud sounds originating from the gradient coils can be frightening to patients and uncomfortable for both patients and staff. Sound–damping devices can be installed as part of a suspended ceiling or applied directly onto the RF enclosure. Noise cancellation systems programmed to the appropriate frequency have been introduced.

- Audio and video systems should be considered to make the MR environment more pleasant. Various accessories are available to mask noise and combat patient fears generated by claustrophobia. Claustrophobia contributes to patient anxiety and results in a high rate of missed appointments or ineffective exams. Having patients wear prismatic glasses so they can view videos during the procedure may be helpful, as may premedication.

- Fluorescent lighting should not be used because it emits RF waves that can degrade the MR image. If incandescent lighting is used, special tungsten filaments should be specified; standard ferrous filaments may be destroyed quickly by the magnetic field. Direct–current lighting is recommended by most manufacturers.

- Consideration should be given to providing a room for video patient education prior to the MRI exam.

Technical Issues: General

See also the section "Special Considerations for MRI Installations" in chapter 13, "Physical Properties Influencing Design."

- MRI procedure rooms will consist of a "parent room" installed by the contractor and a "shielded room" installed by the shielding vendor.

- Siting requirements vary significantly by vendor and magnet type.

- Special structural support for floor-, wall-, and ceiling-mounted equipment should be provided per approved structural calculations that take into account the weight of the magnet, magnetic shielding (where provided), and accessory equipment. Magnetic shielding can weigh many tons.

- Adequate access routes and structural capacity should be provided for installation, maintenance, and/or replacement of large equipment.

- Special environmental conditioning (such as temperature and humidity) should be provided to accommodate additional computer equipment.

- An oxygen-monitoring system should be considered for superconducting magnets.
- Removable access panels should be provided in the ceiling, roof, or walls to enable equipment and magnet gantry installation and replacement.
- A computer equipment room with dedicated air-conditioning should be provided adjacent to the MRI procedure room. Reserve power and air-handling capacity for future expansion and/or equipment upgrades also should be provided.
- Adequate structural support should be provided in the MRI procedure room and along the magnet's entire installation route.
- Adequate space must be allocated for dedicated chillers or other types of cooling equipment required for some magnets. These systems are noisy, so acoustic damping should be provided.
- Adequate cryogen venting must be provided for superconducting magnets. Cryogen vent points of discharge must be clearly identified and placed where people will not be harmed in the event of a quench.
- While many MR scan room entry doors swing inward, some manufacturers suggest out-swinging doors as a safety precaution due to the pressure buildup created in the event of a cryogenic quench. Some RF door manufacturers offer in-swinging doors with emergency access panels to address this concern.
- Hybrid rooms—where MRI equipment is combined with other equipment (such as PET, PET/CT, and surgical equipment)—are described in chapter 15, "Imaging Beyond the Radiology Department."
- Magnets of higher strength, such as 3.0 T, may not easily fit into all existing environments designed for 1.5 T magnets. Common issues include:
  - Scan room size may need to be larger for stronger magnets. Even if the magnet physically fits into an existing 1.5 T room, the fringe field is larger; thus the magnet may be affected by—and affect—nearby devices that were not influenced by a 1.5 T magnet. Typically, the 5-gauss line of a 3.0 T magnet is about 1 meter farther from the magnet's isocenter than the 5-gauss line of a 1.5 T magnet; as a result, safety boundaries for 3.0 T magnets are more extensive.[29]
  - The 3.0 T magnet is more likely to require magnetic shielding (especially above and below, if floor-to-floor heights are low).

- The 3.0 T magnet will likely be noisier, be more sensitive to vibration, and cause more vibration itself.
- Devices that are MR–safe and MR–compatible with 1.5 T magnets may not be so with 3.0 T magnets (see "MRI Safety Considerations," below).
- Steel within the MR suite can become magnetically contaminated over time from the cumulative magnetic emissions originating from the magnet. When MRI rooms are vacated and the space is used for a different function, magnetic contamination can adversely affect other types of equipment, such as PET, CT, and rotational angiography devices (see chapter 13, "Physical Properties Influencing Design").

Technical Issues: Radio-Frequency Interactions

- Radio-frequency shielding must be provided.
- Wave guides or filters should be installed where the RF enclosure is penetrated.
- Fluorescent lamps or electronic light dimmers should not be used within the RF enclosure because they generate RF interference.

Technical Issues: Magnetic Interactions *(figure 12-24)*

- Refer to the equipment vendor, shielding vendor, and qualified health physicists for magnetic shielding requirements.
- External magnetic shielding may be needed to limit the fringe field. Shimming will compensate, to some degree, for inhomogeneities caused by asymmetrical fixed ferrous objects in the vicinity. However, shimming will not necessarily compensate for moving ferrous objects, such as elevators.
- The 5–gauss line (sometimes referred to as the "FDA exclusion zone") should be contained within the MRI procedure room boundary. The 1–gauss field should not encroach upon adjacent leased tenant spaces. This applies to all three dimensions. Supplemental magnetic shielding may be required to contain the 5–gauss line within the procedure room.
- Magnets of different field strength have varying siting requirements. For example, when replacing or upgrading a 1.5 T magnet with a 3.0 T unit, verify that the room enclosure and building systems will accommodate the new magnet's siting requirements and that surrounding activities and devices will not be disturbed by or cause disturbance to the new magnet.

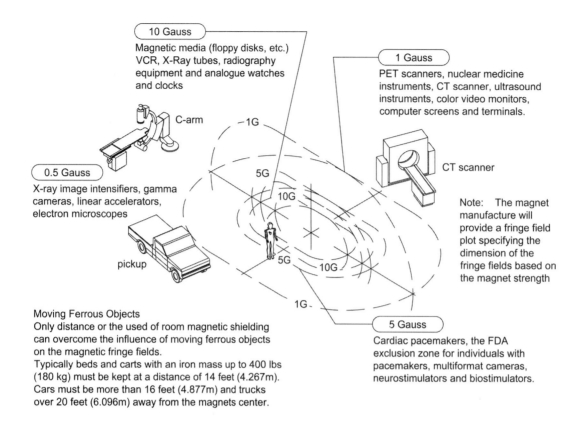

10 Gauss
Magnetic media (floppy disks, etc.)
VCR, X-Ray tubes, radiography
equipment and analogue watches
and clocks

1 Gauss
PET scanners, nuclear medicine
instruments, CT scanner, ultrasound
instruments, color video monitors,
computer screens and terminals.

0.5 Gauss
X-ray image intensifiers, gamma
cameras, linear accelerators,
electron microscopes

CT scanner

Note: The magnet
manufacture will
provide a fringe field
plot specifying the
dimension of the
fringe fields based on
the magnet strength

C-arm

pickup

Moving Ferrous Objects
Only distance or the used of room magnetic shielding
can overcome the influence of moving ferrous objects
on the magnetic fringe fields.
Typically beds and carts with an iron mass up to 400 lbs
(180 kg) must be kept at a distance of 14 feet (4.267m).
Cars must be more than 16 feet (4.877m) and trucks
over 20 feet (6.096m) away from the magnets center.

5 Gauss
Cardiac pacemakers, the FDA
exclusion zone for individuals with
pacemakers, multiformat cameras,
neurostimulators and biostimulators.

Figure 12-24 Certain objects and devices
must be kept a minimum distance away
from the magnet. Courtesy of Scott Jenkins,
© 2005.

- When siting a magnet, consider the distance between the magnet and other devices that may be affected by or affect the magnet, such as:
  - Gamma cameras, other imaging devices, especially MRIs
  - CRT displays
  - EEG and EKG monitors
  - Image intensifiers
  - Motors
  - Elevators
  - Electrical transformers
  - Moving steel equipment or vehicles
  - Mechanical equipment rooms
  - Pacemakers
  - Image processors
  - Credit cards, watches, cameras
  - Linear accelerators[30]
- For actively shielded magnets, consider the "bloom field," the additional distance to which the magnetic field will extend if the active shield fails.
- Substantial ferromagnetic objects must be avoided within a certain distance of the magnet's isocenter. It is usually

desirable to place the magnet perpendicular to major steel beams or equally spaced between parallel steel beams.

- Dense concentrations of ferromagnetic structural reinforcement in the floor and ceiling may need to be limited to avoid unshimmable inhomogeneities. Stainless steel or fiberglass reinforcing can be substituted in place of ferrous reinforcing within concrete structures.

- Introduction of metal objects into the procedure room must be restricted. Metal detectors are installed at some sites but are not recommended by the ACR MR Safety Guidelines.

- The magnet's computer room should be beyond the 10-gauss line to avoid damage to magnetic media, such as computer disks, tapes, and so on.[31]

- Incandescent lamps with reinforced tungsten filaments are advised; the reinforced filament mitigates the magnet's effect of shortening the lamp's life span. Direct current is preferred to alternating current.

MRI Safety Considerations

- The American College of Radiology (ACR) has developed MR Safety Guidelines in an effort to eliminate or reduce preventable accidents in the MR suite (see Appendix B).[32] Portions of these guidelines include site planning considerations, such as the division of any MR suite into four distinct safety zones:
  - Zone I is unrestricted and is outside of the MR suite.
  - Zone II is semirestricted and includes reception, waiting, dressing, and other patient support areas. People in zone II are under the supervision of MR personnel.
  - Zone III is restricted and includes the areas immediately surrounding the scan room (such as the control room) or other areas where access by unscreened individuals or ferromagnetic objects can result in serious injury or death as a result of interactions with the magnet.
  - Zone IV is highly restricted and is the scanner room itself. Zone IV, by definition, is located within Zone III. No one is permitted within Zone IV without direct supervision by specially trained MR personnel.

- The entrance to the MR scanning room should be observed at all times by specially trained MR personnel. The design of the suite—including the location, configuration, and sight lines from the control room—should accommodate this requirement. If multiple magnet rooms are provided, shared MR control rooms may facilitate the ability of staff to observe the entrance to each magnet room.

- The term "MR environment" describes the volume within the 5–gauss line surrounding the magnet (the area within which the static magnetic field is higher than or equal to 5 gauss).[33]
- There is a distinction between an object or device that is considered MR–safe and one that is MR–compatible.[34]
  - "MR–safe" means that it will not cause harm–as a projectile object, due to excessive heating, or due to excessive torque–from magnetic or radio–frequency forces emitted from the magnet. An example of an MR–safe device is a nonferromagnetic oxygen tank.
  - "MR–compatible" means that an object or device is MR–safe and that it will not distort the MR image or be distorted or damaged by the MR equipment (without necessarily causing harm). An example of a MR–compatible device is a specially designed physiologic monitor, made for use within an MR environment.
  - An MR–safe device, however, can be non–MR–compatible. Therefore, it is essential that there be some way of testing (and in some instances physically restraining) any object to see if it is both MR–safe and MR–compatible before it has a chance to enter the scan room.
  - Because some devices that may not be MR–safe or MR–compatible are likely to be used in a surgical environment, the safety screening of such devices in an intraoperative MR suite (a hybrid space consisting of both an operating room and an MR scanner, as described in chapter 15, "Imaging Beyond the Radiology Department") can be more difficult than in a purely diagnostic MR suite.
  - An instrument that is MR–safe or –compatible within a 1.5 T environment may not be safe or compatible within a 3.0 T environment, or it may be compatible outside the 5–gauss line but not within it.[35] Similarly, a device may be compatible within an MR suite before the magnet is upgraded but not after, if the performance and specifications of the magnet change.[36] According to researchers at Brigham and Women's Hospital, "Even minute quantities of magnetic material in an instrument may completely degrade an image, although the materials may not be sufficiently magnetic to cause translational or rotational forces."[37]
- The following MR safety issues were presented at the Association of periOperative Registered Nurses 2005 World Congress by Angela Kanan, RN, and Elizabeth Gasson, RN, and should be considered when planning an intraoperative MR suite:

- Magnet properties that can affect patient safety, instruments, and equipment include:
  - The magnet's magnetic field (always present for most magnets)
  - Rapid changes in the magnetic field (present only during MR imaging)
  - Radio–frequency energy (present only during MR imaging)
- Potential hazards include:
  - Ferrous objects can become projectiles.
  - Ferrous implants can be caused to move within the body.
  - Non–MR-safe items (such as certain implants, EKG leads, medication patches, and tattoos) can cause burns due to RF–induced heating.
- Any instrument or device that may be used within the MR environment should be tested (with a strong handheld magnet) to ensure it is not magnetic, then color–coded to identify whether it is both safe and compatible.[38]

Design and Planning Considerations for Nuclear Medicine
(figure 12-25)
Single–photon emission computed tomography (SPECT) is a common nuclear medicine imaging technique. Sometimes the terms "SPECT" and "gamma camera" are used interchangeably, although not all gamma cameras are SPECT cameras.

Functional Requirements

- When locating a nuclear medicine room, it should be remembered that the patient may be given a radioactive dose either hours or minutes before the exam. He or she may be asked to remain in the vicinity or return later for a scan that could last from 20 minutes to 3 hours. Ideally, these patients should not be required to traverse the entire radiology department, both for reasons of convenience and because a patient who has been administered a radioactive substance may cause disturbances to nearby gamma cameras that are in use.
- Consideration should be given to locating the scanning room near cardio–neuro diagnostics if nuclear stress testing will be performed for cardiac studies. Emergency resuscitation equipment and personnel should be readily available. Nuclear medicine (especially PET/CT) has many oncology applications. When nuclear medicine rooms are used for oncology, they should be located near that service when possible.

Figure 12-25 Nuclear medicine room. Courtesy of Anshen + Allen, Architects.

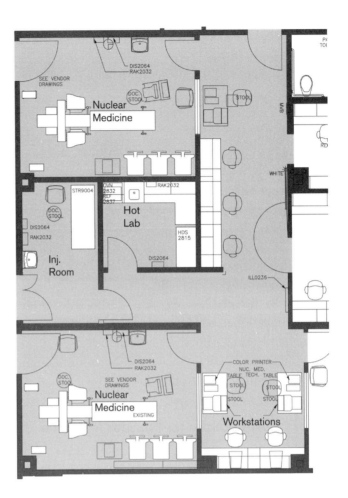

- The patient should be in a darkened room without visual or auditory stimuli prior to the exam.
- A hand-washing fixture and casework should be provided in the scanning room.
- A dedicated shielded patient toilet should be provided within the suite.
- Suite circulation should be divided into controlled and noncontrolled zones. Controlled zones—where radioactive materials are used—will be restricted (for example, no food is permitted within controlled zones).
- Adequate storage for equipment and supplies in the scanning room and adjacent support areas helps minimize staff travel time.
- Ample storage space should be provided for multiple collimators, treadmill, EKG, and other ancillary equipment.
- If more than one gamma camera is located in the scanning room, each unit must be spaced a certain distance from the others and at a specified angle to them.

- Gamma cameras should not be placed near MRI rooms or other sources of electromagnetic interference (EMI) such as large motors and major electrical panels because the cameras are very sensitive to EMI.

Human Factors

- Patient privacy should be allowed for, especially if more than one gamma camera is located in each scanning room.

Technical Issues: Hot Lab

A radiation–protected hot lab should be provided, including:

- Base cabinets, often with a stainless steel countertop, sink, sliding drawers, and structural reinforcement.
- A lead–lined under–counter refrigerator.
- Lead–lined containers or a safe for storing and working with radioactive substances. The work area may include long "extended hands" for holding radioactive vials, radiation shields, and an enclosure of interlocking bricks that provide radiation shielding. The entire work area can sit on the reinforced countertop.
- A 100 percent exhaust radioisotope hood, specially designed for this purpose (optional in some instances).
- An approved system of radioactive waste collection and disposal, including a shielded area for radioactive waste decay. A radiation decay room where radiation–contaminated linens and supplies can be held until their radioactive half-life declines to a safe level should be provided near or adjacent to the hot lab.

Technical Issues: Dose Room/Uptake Room/Injection Room

A dose room should be provided for the administration of radiopharmaceuticals. This space should include:

- A patient chair
- An exam light
- A hand-washing fixture
- An approved system of radioactive waste collection and disposal
- A small work surface for dose calibration
- A xenon gas delivery system, where required

Technical Issues: General

- Although the floor, walls, and ceilings of the gamma camera nuclear medicine procedure room may not require radiation shielding, radioactivity from the hot lab, radiopharmacy, and even "hot" patients may disturb sensitive imaging equipment in the immediate vicinity. For this reason, lead–lined partitions are common, especially for separating gamma cameras from incidental radiation coming from the hot lab or dose administration area. Freestanding or mobile radiation shields are useful for shielding the technologist from radiation emitted from the patient. Radiation protection requirements should be provided per the direction of a certified medical or health physicist.

- Special structural support for floor–mounted equipment in the exam room and work spaces in the hot lab may be required.

- Adequate access space and structural capacity should be provided for installation and/or replacement of large equipment.

- An air exhaust system, a gas scavenger system, and negative air pressure relative to adjoining spaces may be required.

- Special exhaust devices, such as a gas trap or low wall returns, may be required if gaseous radiopharmaceuticals will be used for ventilation scans.

- Easily cleanable, nonporous materials and surfaces that can be readily decontaminated should be used throughout the nuclear medicine suite. Seamless floor covering and work surfaces are preferred.

- Special provisions for receiving, holding, and disposing of radioactive substances must be considered. For example, if radioactive materials are delivered during off hours, special secure holding containers may be required at the point of delivery.

- After a certain predetermined time has elapsed, radioactive substances may be disposed of as nonradioactive waste. In all instances, the appropriate regulatory agencies should be contacted to verify current storage and disposal requirements.

Design and Planning Considerations for Positron Emission Tomography/Computed Tomography (PET/CT) (figure 12-26)

PET and PET/CT are a form of nuclear medicine. Therefore, many of the considerations for nuclear medicine listed above will apply.

PET scanners have traditionally been mostly limited to academic medical centers and other specialty centers, due to their high capital cost, high maintenance and staffing costs, requirement for a nearby cyclotron, and limited reimbursement. However, in recent years favorable changes in reimbursement policies set by the Centers for Medicare and Medicaid Services (CMS), availability of regional radioisotope distribution centers (reducing

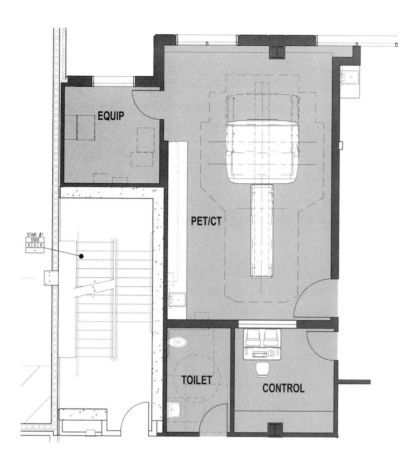

Figure 12-26 PET/CT room. Courtesy of Anshen + Allen, Architects.

the need for an on-site cyclotron), and the growing use of PET beyond on-cology applications–such as cardiac and stroke functional imaging–have led to more frequent PET installations. In addition, the emergence of hybrid PET/CT scanners has resulted in many PET scanner purchases being PET/CT scanners. PET/CT scanner installations must respond to siting requirements for both PET and CT scanners, as well as unique PET/CT requirements. This section describes general considerations for both PET and PET/CT site planning. As with other advanced imaging technology, specific requirements will vary among different vendors and among different equipment models. Therefore, it is suggested that vendor-specific and site-specific information be obtained for each project.

Functional Requirements

- The following spaces should be considered for a PET or PET/CT installation:
    - Scanning room
    - Control room
    - Injection room
    - Hot lab

- Radioactive decay room (if volumes are low, a decay safe in the hot lab may be adequate)
- Separate utility rooms for clean and soiled material
- Reading room
- Technologist work area
- Patient prep/holding area
- Shielded patient toilet
- Shielded consult room for post-exam consultation
- Staff toilet and other staff support spaces, such as a lounge and lockers

- PET/CT scan rooms are larger than typical PET or CT scan rooms.
- PET/CT rooms will require shielding–often significantly more shielding than would be required for either PET or CT alone. Consider heavier-gauge wall studs and increased floor and ceiling structural capacities to support the required shielding. Rooms likely to require the most shielding include:
  - Scanning room
  - Injection room
  - Hot lab[39]
- In many cases, patient prep/holding rooms will require shielding to prevent radiation from "hot" patients from affecting scan readings.
- If the PET or PET/CT scanner can be located within a nuclear medicine department, economies can be realized if radioactive material handing spaces and staffing do not need to be duplicated.
- The PET/CT scanner should be installed in a location that is convenient for patients from oncology as well as from other services (such as cardiology, psychiatry, and neurology). Some cancer centers have their own dedicated PET/CT scanners.

Human Factors

- Patients in prep/holding areas and in the injection room should be kept as calm and quiet as possible. Holding rooms should be able to be made dark, as the uptake duration for PET radioisotopes is typically longer than for other nuclear medicine radioisotopes.
- Patient privacy should be accommodated, especially if there are multiple positions in the holding area.

Technical Issues

- Although many newer CT scanners do not require dedicated equipment rooms for systems electronics, PET/CT scanners will likely require a dedicated equipment room and supplemental air-conditioning/chiller equipment. This may vary by manufacturer.

- Shielding requirements throughout the suite should be determined by a certified medical or health physicist familiar with shielding requirements for this type of equipment. Not all physicists qualified to determine shielding requirements for diagnostic radiology are qualified to determine PET or PET/CT shielding requirements.

- Some manufacturers recommend air-conditioning systems with two compressors. A backup unit permits the PET/CT system to remain operational during extended periods of repair of the primary air-conditioning system.

- PET/CT scanners should be kept some distance from sources of high electromagnetic interference, such as:
  - MRIs or other large magnets
  - Transformers
  - Large electric motors
  - High-powered radio signals

Notes

1. H. W. Fischer, *Radiology Departments: Planning, Operation, and Management* (Ann Arbor, MI: Edward Brothers, 1982), 5–6.

2. A. Kanan and E. Gasson, "Safety in an Intraoperative MRI Suite," poster presented at the Association of periOperative Registered Nurses World Congress 2005, Barcelona, Spain, September 2005.

3. E. Kanal, J. Borgstede, A. J. Barkovich, C. Bell, J. Felmlee, J. Froelich, E. Kaminski, E. Keeler, J. Lester, E. Scoumis, L. Zaremba, and M. Zinninger, "American College of Radiology White Paper on MR Safety," *American Journal of Roentgenology* 178 (2002).

4. E. Siegel and B. Reiner, "Radiology reading room design: The next generation," *Applied Radiology* 31, 4 (2002): 11–16.

5. D. Dakins, "How we work will revolve around the human element," 2001, www.diagnosticimaging.com/specialedition/digital.jhtml.

6. B. Rostenberg, "Success by design: Maximizing your digital environment," *Advance for Imaging and Oncology Administrators* 8, 12 (1998): 13–19; B. Rostenberg, "Desperately seeking solutions to digital reading room design," *Advance for Imaging and Oncology Administrators* 14, 5 (2004): 31–33. Portions of this section are excerpted from articles previously written by the author.

7. P. Nagy, E. Siegel, T. Hanson, L. Kreiner, K. Johnson, and B. Reiner, "PACS reading room design," *Seminars in Roentgenology* 38, 3 (2003): 244–55.

8. Siegel and Reiner.

9. Siegel and Reiner.

10. B. Rostenberg, "Ergonomics straightens its posture at SCAR 2004," *Diagnostic Imaging*, September 2004, 25–31.

11. Siegel and Reiner.

12. Siegel and Reiner.

13. A. Xthona, "Designing the perfect reading room for digital mammography," internal white paper of Barco n.v. Kortrijk, Belgium, 2003, www.barco.com.
14. Mammography Quality Standards Act, 42 USC 201:262b Pub L no. 102–539 (1992).
15. S. C. Horii, *Electronic Imaging Workstations: Ergonomic Issues and User Interface—Syllabus: A Special Course in Computers for Clinical Practice and Education in Radiology* (Chicago: Radiological Society of North America, 1992), 131.
16. Siegel and Reiner.
17. Herman Miller, Inc., *A Few Simple Facts on the Risky Business of Office Ergonomics* (Zeeland, MI: Herman Miller, 1992), 13.
18. Rostenberg, "Ergonomics straightens its posture at SCAR 2004."
19. Siegel and Reiner.
20. W. N. Rosch, "Does your computer—or how you use it—cause health problems?" *PC Magazine*, November 1991, 491.
21. Rosch, 494.
22. L. Rumreich and J. Johnson, "From traditional reading rooms to a soft copy environment: Radiologist satisfaction survey," *Journal of Digital Imaging* 16, 3 (2003): 262–69.
23. M. Harisinghani, A. Blake, M. Saksena, P. Hahn, D. Gervais, M. Zalis, L. Fernande, and P. Mueller, "Importance and effects of altered workplace ergonomics in modern radiology suites," *RadioGraphics 24* (2004): 615–27.
24. Rostenberg, "Ergonomics straightens its posture at SCAR 2004."
25. Rostenberg, "Ergonomics straightens its posture at SCAR 2004."
26. Rostenberg, "Ergonomics straightens its posture at SCAR 2004."
27. H. Laufman, ed., *Hospital Special Care Facilities: Planning for User Needs* (New York: Academic Press, 1981), 478.
28. S. Jenkins, *The Medical Imaging Planner* (Gallatin, TN: EDI Design Service, 1998), 41; www.edidesignservice.com.
29. ECRI, "Healthcare Product Comparison System: Scanning systems, magnetic resonance imaging," Plymouth Meeting, PA, May 2004, 9.
30. ECRI, 9.
31. Jenkins, 47.
32. Kanal et al.
33. ECRI, 7.
34. Kanan and Gasson.
35. T. Gilk, "The new 'MR safe': Language changes for the FDA," *MRI Newsletter*, August 2005; www.mri-planning.com.
36. S. Silverman, F. Jolesz, R. Newman, P. Morrison, A. Kanan, R. Kikinis, R. Schwartz, L. Hsu, S. Koran, and G. Topulos, "Design and implementation of an interventional MR imaging suite," *American Journal of Roentgenology* 168 (1997): 1465–71.
37. Silverman et al., 1468.
38. Kanan and Gasson.
39. G. Sayed, "PET, PET-CT scanner siting issues." *Imaging Economics*, July 2004.

CHAPTER 13

Physical Properties Influencing Design

Physical properties associated with both imaging procedures and imaging equipment must be considered when planning and designing a new facility. Some phenomena, such as the effects of ionizing radiation, are present only after the equipment has been installed and the facility is operational. However, other considerations–such as the size and weight of equipment–come into play during design and construction as well as after the facility becomes operational. These physical properties must be taken into account throughout design, construction, and occupancy.

Construction specialties (such as radiation barriers that compensate for unique physical forces) protect occupants in adjacent areas from the harmful effects of forces originating from within the procedure room. Other barriers, such as magnetic and RF shielding, prevent external forces from disturbing image acquisition within the procedure room, in addition to preventing those forces that originate in the procedure room from disturbing equipment outside the room.

This chapter examines the key physical properties of imaging procedures and related issues that must be considered when designing an imaging facility. These include the size and weight of the imaging equipment to be used, the type of protection needed from ionizing radiation, and special considerations for magnetic resonance imaging (MRI) installations.

Imaging Equipment Size and Weight

Most imaging equipment is large and heavy. Although it often is delivered as separate components and later assembled in the procedure room, even the smaller components can still be difficult to maneuver between the truck on which they are delivered and the room in which they are ultimately installed. Procedure room design must take into account equipment size and weight. Unfortunately, size and weight are not always thoroughly

considered when it comes to the route along which equipment is delivered. Some of the ways in which a magnet can enter the procedure room are through ceiling hatches, removable wall panels, or large exterior windows (figures 13–1 and 13–2). In some cases, a delivery route that cannot accommodate equipment transport can result in the unplanned partial demolition of a new facility in order to install or replace the equipment. A series of meetings (first during the early stages of design and then during the preparation of contract documents) involving the architect, the equipment vendor, the equipment installation coordinator, and the owner can do much to eliminate unnecessary installation surprises.

Often, special structural systems are required to support assemblies of imaging equipment or ancillary devices such as ceiling–mounted monitors or secondary radiation barriers. Heavy–gauge metal studs are required to support the weight of lead–lined partitions and accessory equipment. Partitions in procedure rooms should also be constructed of studs that are thicker than standard studs (typically a minimum of 6 inches) to accommodate the array of conduit and mounting assemblies that are placed in the wall. Special backing plates often are installed as part of the wall framing and are hidden behind the drywall. For ceiling–mounted equipment, secondary structural assemblies often are fastened to the building's structural beams and purlins. Typically, these assemblies are hidden behind a finished ceiling, such as a lay–in ceiling panel system.

Careful coordination is necessary for both wall and ceiling structural supports. In both cases, the support system usually is furnished and installed by the contractor but must meet the precise requirements specified by the equipment manufacturer. All parties must agree on which compo-

nents are to be a part of the contractor–furnished support system for the equipment and which ones are to be provided by the manufacturer as part of the equipment itself. If equipment selections are changed, often the capacity and location of the structural support also must be modified. However, a universal support system will minimize the need for modification for some modalities.

In addition, most states require a detailed, and often lengthy, review by structural regulatory officials prior to granting a building permit, and additional field inspections prior to granting a certificate of occupancy. If equipment is changed after the building permit is granted, the structural review may have to be repeated, causing significant delays. Often, both the structural components and the equipment itself require a long lead time to be manufactured and delivered. Excess capacity designed into the building systems may minimize the potential disruption caused by last–minute equipment changes.

In geographic locations that experience seismic activity, lateral bracing of equipment is required in addition to vertical structural support. Lateral bracing prevents equipment from falling over as a result of vibration or other movement caused by an earthquake. Lateral bracing, when required, usually applies to mechanical ducts, light fixtures, and essential utility lines, in addition to the individual components of imaging equipment and ancillary equipment.

Design of the building's structural system must also minimize excessive vibration, which can be transferred from other components of the building system. Interventional procedures and associated imaging modalities often have more stringent vibration criteria than do other imaging modalities.

Radiation Protection

Patients, staff, and the general public need to be protected wherever ioniz-ing radiation is present. Radiation barriers (such as lead–lined drywall, lead sheets, concrete, or lead–lined glass or acrylic sheets) must be strategically sized and located. Although a basic understanding of the physical princi-ples of ionizing radiation and the equipment planned for each room will assist the designer in planning the imaging facility, the exact requirements for radiation protection need to be calculated by a certified medical or health physicist. Often, the physicist is either employed by the owner or contracted as the owner's consultant (rather than as the architect's consult-ant). The information he or she will need may include:

- The make and model number, intended location, and move-ment characteristics of each piece of radiation–emitting equipment
- The location of wall-mounted cassette holders or flat–panel detectors
- The types of procedures to be performed in the room
- The average duration of a typical exposure and the room's hours of operation
- The type of occupancy of all adjacent rooms (including those above and below the procedure room)
- A floor plan showing equipment, control stations, doors, and room dimensions
- The average number of procedures and exposures each week

Based on this information, the physicist will calculate and prescribe the requirements for radiation shielding. For example, the physicist might pre-scribe that the north wall requires 2.5 pounds of lead per square foot up to a height of 7 feet above floor level between point A and point B, and 4 pounds of lead per square foot between point B and point C as indicated on the floor plans. After construction, a qualified testing agency should test and certify that the room has been built in accordance with the medical health physicist's requirements.

Radiation Protection Regulations

As previously mentioned, radiation protection calculations (based on mathematical formulas that determine the type and amount of protection required) must be made by a certified medical health physicist. The follow-ing is provided for information only and is in no way intended to suggest that anyone other than a certified medical health physicist should perform radiation protection calculations.

Radiation protection requirements are specified on both the local (state and municipality) and federal levels. Often, local requirements are more stringent than federal requirements, although this varies by location. In

1976, the National Council on Radiation Protection and Measurement (NCRP) published its Report No. 49, *Structural Shielding Design and Evaluation for Medical Use of X-Rays and Gamma Rays of Energies up to 10 MeV.*[1] Although many new techniques and devices for imaging have been developed since NCRP 49 was first written, the 1976 edition remained as the primary regulatory reference for determining radiation protection requirements for several decades. In 2004, the NCRP published Report No. 147, which now supersedes NCRP 49.[2] NCRP 147 provides more stringent shielding design guidelines and also includes shielding requirements for several diagnostic imaging modalities that were not covered in NCRP 49, such as computed tomography (CT), mammography, and bone mineral densitometry (DEXA).

Anyone involved in the design or planning of an imaging facility should become familiar with NCRP 147 and any additional regulations that will eventually supersede it. While the NCRP reports are written primarily for physicists, "sections of the reports should be of interest also to architects, hospital administrators, and others who are concerned with the planning of radiation facilities."[3]

The medical or health physicist's chief charge, as it relates to determining radiation protection barrier requirements, is to protect patients, staff, and public from excessive levels of radiation generated from radiographic equipment. The level of protection for radiation staff is described as a maximum permissible dose (MPD) or MPD equivalent. The MPD is a measure of accumulated radiation exposure and is stated in terms of millirems per week (mrem/wk). Radiology staff (occupational workers) wear personal monitoring devices that keep track of accumulated radiation exposure.

Modern X-ray equipment generally provides a lower level of radiation than does older equipment. At the same time, it is interesting to note that the acceptable level of mrem/wk has been reduced significantly over the years as more knowledge about the biological effects of ionizing radiation has become available. Therefore, even as most equipment is becoming safer, radiation protection barrier requirements in general have become more stringent. For example, if an existing room is reequipped with a similar but newer radiation emitting device, additional shielding may be required even if the previous room was compliant with the safety requirements applicable at the time of its initial design. Radiation itself has not changed, but our understanding of it and our philosophy about safety have.

Radiation protection can be achieved using a number of methods, each of which provides a means of protecting individuals against excessive radiation exposure. Methods of radiation protection include collimation, filtration, protective apparel, protective barriers, and other techniques. It is the inclusion of protective barriers that the architect will be most closely involved with.

The NCRP shielding reports provide formulas and criteria necessary to design safe protective barriers in both new construction and renovated facilities. Protective barrier design calculations should anticipate future needs of new equipment and processes–including increased workloads–where possible.[4]

Shielding design should be performed by a "qualified expert" as defined by the NCRP. The shielding designer should be engaged early in the design process, as the location of some radiation–emitting equipment, partitions, and doors may be affected by shielding design. In addition, all design drawings and calculations must be reviewed and approved by the relevant authorities prior to construction.[5]

Alternative materials and methods may be employed to achieve proper shielding protection where appropriate. After construction but prior to oc-cupancy, a radiation survey should be performed. If the survey demon-strates deficiencies or variations from the approved design intent, either the installed shielding will need to be modified or the installed equipment or operational procedures will need to be changed.[6]

The American Board of Radiology, the American Board of Health Physics, and the American Board of Medical Physics have certification cri-teria for people to be considered qualified in radiation protection and ra-diation shielding design. In most cases, the architect (and owner) should be prepared to furnish the following (and other) types of documentation and data to the physicist performing shielding design calculations:

A. Architectural
   1. Drawings of radiation rooms and adjacent areas (preferred scale: ¼ inch = 1 foot or larger), including position of radia-tion source, doors, and windows
   2. Information about occupancy below, above, and adjacent to radiation–emitting rooms
   3. Type of proposed or existing construction of floors, ceilings, and walls
B. Equipment
   1. Below 150 kV
      a. Purpose, such as therapy, radiography, fluoroscopy, special procedures, cystoscopy
      b. kV and expected weekly workload, if known
   2. 150 kV and above, including gamma beam apparatus
      a. kV or type of gamma source
      b. Rate of radiation emission
      c. Weekly workload, if known
   3. Possible future increases in workload or estimated volume of patients seen per room, per week[7]

In addition to the NCRP requirements, most states–and some local municipalities–have special codes describing radiation protection require-ments. These requirements vary considerably from one jurisdiction to another. For example, some states require that protective barriers be in-

stalled in the walls of all mammography suites. Other states do not require this because of the low level of radiation employed in mammography examinations.

Determination of Radiation Protection Requirements

A number of variables are used to determine requirements for radiation
protection that separates a source of radiation from occupants and adjacent
spaces. These variables include:

- *Weekly design exposure rate.* Weekly design exposure rate identifies the target level of radiation exposure to which an adjacent occupied area must be reduced. Each adjacent area
  should be identified as either controlled or noncontrolled. A
  controlled area is limited to radiation staff; a noncontrolled
  area is open to the public.
- *Distance.* Distance identifies how much space (usually expressed in meters) is between the radiation source and the
  area being protected. The greater the distance, the lower the
  requirements for radiation protection. Therefore, theoretically, a larger room will require less lead per square foot of
  wall area. However, the larger room will not necessarily cost
  less to protect. For one thing, a larger room has more surface area and thus may require greater quantities of lead
  (although not necessarily thinner lead sheets). In addition,
  the cost of lead is not always proportional to its thickness.
  Certain thicknesses of lead may cost more because of either
  their availability or complications in fabricating thin sheets
  of lead.
- *Workload.* Workload is expressed as milliampere–minutes
  per week (mA–min/wk) or the number of patients seen per
  room, per week.
- *Use factor or beam direction factor.* Use factor represents the
  amount of time (expressed as a percentage) that the X–ray
  beam is on, in which the radiation source directly strikes the
  protective barrier. The use factor for each wall may vary depending on the type of equipment installed and the types of
  procedures performed.
- *Occupancy factor.* Occupancy factor represents the amount of
  time (expressed as a percentage) in which each adjacent
  room or space is occupied. This factor suggests that if the
  occupancy of an adjacent room changes over time, radiation protection requirements also will change. Therefore, if a
  room's occupancy classification is likely to be upgraded in
  the future, additional protection might need to be added at
  that time or a higher–than–actual occupancy factor should
  be used in the initial calculations.

- *Maximum operating potential of the imaging equipment.* Maximum operating potential signifies the potential power of the equipment. It usually is expressed in terms of kilovolt peak (kVp). The X–ray tube's operating potential determines the intensity of the radiation and its ability to penetrate matter.[8]

Two types of protective barriers–primary and secondary–are considered, based on the characteristics of three types of radiation (primary radiation, scatter radiation, and radiation leakage). A primary or useful beam is defined as "radiation which passes through the window, aperture, cone, or other collimating device of the source housing." Of the three types, primary radiation is most intense. As a result, it usually requires a greater level of protection. Scatter radiation is defined as "radiation that, during passage through matter, has been deviated in direction." Scatter radiation is caused by a primary beam reflecting off an object, such as a piece of equipment or the patient. In theory, primary radiation, which usually is collimated or focused, rarely strikes a protective barrier without first passing through the patient and therefore becoming scatter radiation. However, protective barrier design calculations are conservative and often take into consideration the unlikely situation in which the primary beam might be energized without a patient in the room. Leakage radiation is defined as "all radiation coming from within the source or tube housing except the useful beam. Leakage radiation includes the portion of the direct radiation not absorbed by the protective source or tube housing as well as the scattered radiation produced within the housing." Scatter radiation and leakage radiation are both considered to be secondary radiation.[9]

Protective barriers that are irradiated directly by the imaging equipment's primary or useful beam are considered to be primary barriers. Barriers that are irradiated only by leakage or scatter radiation are considered to be secondary barriers. Primary barriers usually require a higher degree of protection than do secondary barriers. This is one reason that a description of the equipment, its movement characteristics, and the frequency of each type of examination should be given to the medical health physicist.

After the medical health physicist determines the appropriate level of radiation protection required for each barrier, he or she should provide a written report to the owner and the architect. The report should describe the required amount of lead, usually in terms of pounds per square foot. Where appropriate, alternative materials can be used in lieu of lead to achieve the required radiation protection. For example, approximately 4 inches of concrete provides the same degree of protection as 1/16 inch of lead.[10] However, concrete is typically used for radiation therapy barriers; it is rarely used as a protective barrier in low–energy–level diagnostic imaging facilities. Lead used for radiation barriers in these facilities is most commonly available in the form of sheet lead or lead–lined drywall. Where transparency is required, plate glass, leaded glass, and leaded acrylic sheets are available. Doors also are available with lead lining.

The recommendations of the medical or health physicist should be incorporated into the architect's contract documents so that the contractor will be able to include them as part of the facility construction. The physicist's written report should be kept in the architect's file for future reference. If the physicist is acting as the owner's agent, the architect might want to indicate on the contract documents that the criteria for protective barrier design are owner-furnished. The architect might want to include a clause in the specifications, for example: "The Owner shall engage a qualified radiological physicist certified by the American Board of Radiology or the American Board of Health Physicists to test shielded spaces for conformance with the Contract Documents. In the event that radiation protection fails to meet specification requirements, the Contractor shall remove substandard radiation protection and apply new at no cost to the Contract."

Design and Planning Issues

Radiation protection is just one of many issues that influence design and planning decisions. Such issues affect both the cost and safety of the facility, and often cost and safety are directly interrelated. Increased levels of radiation protection tend to increase construction costs. The goal of both the medical health physicist and the architect is to provide an appropriate level of protection without requiring unnecessarily excessive cost. The architect's ability to understand radiation-related implications of design decisions is essential to providing a safe, cost-effective, functional, and aesthetic environment. For example, openings in radiation barriers–such as doors, windows, and duct penetrations–should be located within secondary barriers where possible. The required shielding thickness will be less in a secondary barrier than in a primary barrier. The design of barrier penetrations will depend on a number of factors, including:

- The radiation energy level
- The radiation beam's orientation and field size
- The location of the opening and its orientation relative to the radiation source
- The geometrical relationship between the opening and the radiation source
- The geometrical relationship between the opening and the people, instruments, and other objects being protected[11]

Adjacencies

Because radiation protection is influenced as much by the occupancy of spaces adjacent to the imaging room as by the activities within the imaging room, the degree of radiation protection required can be reduced by modifying or controlling the adjacent occupancies. For example, a radiographic room located in the basement will have no occupants below it. Similarly, a radiographic room located on the top floor or at the exterior perimeter of the building also will have limited adjacent occupants.

Sometimes imaging departments are planned solely with the objective of reducing the cost of radiation protection. This is inappropriate. Although lead–lined partitions are somewhat heavier and costlier than standard dry-wall partitions, the premium paid for this type of construction is minor compared to the cost of other issues, such as adjacencies to interrelated departments, functionally efficient circulation routes, and the optimal size of procedure rooms. Radiation protection is one of many important issues that must be considered during design, planning, and construction. It cannot be ignored, but it also cannot be considered in the absence of other crucial issues.

Control Areas

The architect or planner may encounter various conceptually different arrangements for the technologist's control area with respect to the procedure room. One concept locates the control alcove within the room; another locates it in an adjacent but separate control corridor. A third concept provides a separate control room. (See the section "General Considerations for Control Corridors, Control Alcoves, and Control Rooms" in chapter 12, "Room Design.") The control alcove that is part of the procedure room provides for better personal communication between patient and technologist than the control corridor concept does, but it might make it more difficult for the technologist to access the staff work core. Each of these control area concepts may have different radiation shielding requirements.

Pregnancy and Radiation

Planners should be aware of special considerations involved in protecting the developing fetus from ionizing radiation. If ultrasound rooms or other spaces likely to be occupied by pregnant women are located adjacent to rooms that emit radiation protective barrier requirements must be carefully calculated. In the case of radiology staff members who become pregnant, either protective garments can be worn or the staff members' daily activities can be temporarily modified without jeopardizing their employment. Because this is such a sensitive issue with respect to health, safety, and equal opportunity employment laws, legal advice on this subject is suggested.

Construction of Radiation Barriers

In addition to lead–lined gypsum board, a number of other materials and products may be used as part of the protective barrier. These include leaded glass, acrylic lead glazing, lead–lined viewing windows, and lead–lined doors. Care must be taken when installing the protective barrier over fittings and accessories such as wall-mounted devices and even electrical receptacle boxes. Drywall screws set into the lead may require installation of lead disks to maintain a continuous protective barrier; however, some researchers believe that the disks themselves can cause discontinuity of the barrier. According to the NCRP reports, radiation shielding should be constructed in such a way that it is not impaired by penetrations in the barrier or by conduits or cables passing through it.[12]

Special attention also must be given to wall surfaces that contain multiple sections with different radiation protection requirements because each section may be a different thickness. For example, assume that one-third of a wall's area requires lead-lined gypsum board and the remaining area is adequately protected with standard drywall, the difference in thickness of the two materials will be noticeable unless the standard sheetrock is furred out to match the lead-lined material or unless both surfaces are covered with a plaster-like coating to float out the difference.

Although lead usually is placed on the inside surface of room partitions, it also can be placed on the "outboard" side of the wall studs. Sometimes this can simplify installation of room accessories and make future changes easier to achieve, because the radiation barrier is less likely to be disturbed when wall-mounted equipment and accessories are removed, replaced, or added.

Special Considerations for MRI Installations

Siting requirements for some MRI units have become simpler in recent years, in part because of the introduction of actively shielded magnets (which can preclude the need for heavy room magnetic shielding in some installations) and lighter magnets, while for others siting is more complex. On one hand, the space required for some magnets has been reduced, primarily due to active shield technology and the advent of smaller but more powerful computer systems. On the other hand, stronger magnets–such as the popular 3.0 T superconducting magnet–have more complex siting issues that must be considered. (See also the relevant sections in chapter 12, "Room Design.")

Many forces influence the optimal location of MRI units. For instance, the weight of most magnets requires that structural reinforcing be employed not only where the magnet will eventually be positioned but also along the route used to deliver and install it. However, physical characteristics of the magnet–such as size and weight–are not the only considerations for siting. The magnet's magnetic field can detrimentally interact with other devices if adequate shielding is not provided. Steel beams and other dense ferrous objects (primarily in the floor) can distort the homogeneity or uniformity of the magnetic field and thus detract from the image quality of the MR system. In addition, moving ferrous objects (such as automobiles and even light rail vehicles) can adversely affect the homogeneity of the magnetic field. Finally, the magnetic and RF forces emitted from the magnet can disturb, and in turn be disturbed by, other sensitive equipment in the area.

Because MRI does not employ ionizing radiation, X-ray shielding is not necessary. However, RF shielding is required to prevent external radio signals from masking the faint resonating radio-frequency emissions originating from the patient. In facilities with two or more magnets in close proximity and operating at the same frequency, the RF shield prevents cross-interference.

If the magnet is not self-shielded and is located near occupied or mechanical space, external magnetic shielding may be necessary to prevent the magnet's electromagnetic field from disturbing, and being disturbed by, objects and signals outside the procedure room. RF shielding enclosures are typically designed and installed by an MRI enclosure manufacturer, not by the architect or contractor. Magnetic shields are typically designed by the magnet manufacturer, and the MR shielding contractor engineers this design into a structural shield. In addition to shielding design considerations, architectural design should be sensitive to patient safety issues such as magnetic field, quench, acoustic and vibration issues, special construction requirements associated with the RF and magnetic shield, and unique utility requirements.

RF Interactions

Magnetic imaging uses signals of the same frequency as those used for various types of radio and television communications. The MRI unit is a very powerful radio transmitter and is itself a very sensitive radio receiver. To prevent interference from external RF signals, special shielding is required. Radio-frequency shields must completely envelop the imaging volume, which means that the entire area in which the MRI system is installed must be RF-shielded. Even access panels that are removed during magnet installation must include RF shielding to enclose the entire space when the panels are replaced (figure 13-3). RF shielding may be prefabricated, modular, or custom applied. It may be a freestanding structure or an integrally shielded room. Freestanding RF structures are common in animal research

Figure 13-3 The RF shielding enclosure surrounds the entire procedure room. © 2005 Lindgren R.F. Enclosures, Inc. All Rights Reserved.

facilities where appearance is of limited importance. In facilities for patients, however, integral shielding is more common. In either case, the RF shielding must be electrically isolated from all metal structural elements, electrical grounds, and finishes and must maintain its integrity around doors, walls, and mechanical and plumbing penetrations. The RF enclosure and all interior systems are grounded to earth at a single point called a ground stud.

Radio-frequency shielding materials need very high conductivity ratings. Although many materials work for this purpose, there are only a few that will provide high conductivity at a reasonable cost. The most effective and common material is pure copper. Copper is easily shaped and easily joined to provide good RF seams. It also forms a conductive oxide that protects it from corrosion, thus preserving its RF integrity. Galvanized steel is also commonly used in the form of thin-gauge sheets. Compared to copper, galvanized steel is somewhat less expensive. However, the zinc surface used in the galvanizing process forms a compound called white rust when it corrodes. This nonconductive rust is the main disadvantage of using steel shielding.

Aluminum is used less frequently for RF shielding. Although aluminum is less expensive than copper (though more expensive than galvanized steel), it corrodes easily and so can become nonconductive. Heavy-gauge aluminum (2–3 mm) has found a use in MRI shielding for something known as eddy current shielding. This is used for some of the new high-field-strength open-type magnets.

In order for the RF shielding to maintain its continuity, special details are required around penetrations in the room enclosure, as penetrations are the most vulnerable points in the RF shield. For example, through-the-wall plumbing lines can degrade the RF enclosure because water running through the pipes may disturb the magnet's RF signal and can cause grounding problems. If a sink is to be installed within the procedure room (although a sink just outside the procedure room is usually preferred), several precautions need to be taken. A specially tuned brass pipe waveguide should be used for each water line as well as the drain line and vent line. For water lines and drain lines, a minimum of 2 linear feet of PVC pipe should be installed on the exterior end of the waveguide. Local code restrictions and manufacturers' recommendations should be followed.

A large opening in the wall or ceiling will be required for installation and replacement of the magnet. However, once the magnet is installed, this opening will need to be completely sealed with RF shielding. This should be performed by the same company or individual that installs the rest of the RF enclosure to preserve the RF warranty. If the magnet needs to be replaced, the RF shielding surrounding the access opening will need to be removed and replaced in such a way that it continues to provide proper shielding.

Flooring

A number of types of floor construction that provide RF protection are available. Usually, the RF floor assembly is furnished and installed by the RF shielding vendor. However, the finish floor surface may be installed by the contractor. The RF floor of any enclosure is subject to considerable damage. The magnet's dead load bears directly on it. In addition, it may be damaged by water. (Floors in MRI rooms should be kept dry because water can affect the integrity of the RF enclosure.) Settling of the parent room can also damage the floor. Uneven subflooring can also create problems in RF floor installation.

Two types of RF floor construction are common. They include:

- An epoxy-layered floor that uses an epoxy substrate to both seal the parent floor from moisture and provide dielectric isolation for the enclosure. The resultant assembly is mono-lithic in nature, thereby providing a strong surface with high compressive strength. Most commercial floor coverings can be used with this type of floor.
- A wood core modular system that is constructed of wood panels faced with either galvanized steel or copper. This system, however, is not completely waterproof, and it is difficult to install over an uneven parent floor. It is somewhat easier to install this kind of floor system than it is to install an epoxy-layered floor, and it is slightly less expensive. However, a wood core modular system often requires a greater floor thickness than an epoxy-layered floor. In many cases, the underlying floor surface will need to be depressed in order for the door threshold to meet accessibility requirements.

RF Screens and Glazing at Control Windows

RF shielded control windows are composed of conductive mesh fabric, usually made of type 304 stainless-steel wire cloth, copper, or brass (figure 13-4). Often, two layers of mesh are provided. Each layer is separated by 1 to 2 inches, and the layers are electrically connected to the primary shield through the window frame assembly. Although glazing is not required for RF shielding purposes, it usually is beneficial to glaze the window opening to provide acoustic, temperature, and ventilation control. Glazing also serves to protect the RF mesh fabric from damage. The optical quality of RF windows from different manufacturers may vary significantly. An RF window that has poor optical quality will have a negative impact on staff.

The RF screen in the control room window should be blackened. In addition, the two pieces of screen can be rotated slightly to eliminate or minimize the moiré pattern that can result from superimposing multiple layers of screen.

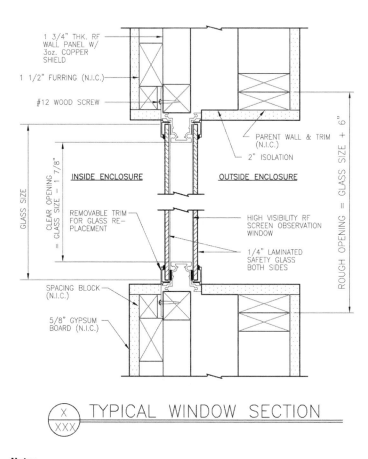

1 3/4" THK. RF
WALL PANEL w/
3oz. COPPER
SHIELD

1 1/2" FURRING (N.I.C.)

#12 WOOD SCREW

PARENT WALL & TRIM
(N.I.C.)

2" ISOLATION

INSIDE ENCLOSURE   OUTSIDE ENCLOSURE

GLASS SIZE

CLEAR OPENING =
GLASS SIZE - 1 7/8"

ROUGH OPENING = GLASS SIZE + 6"

REMOVABLE TRIM
FOR GLASS RE-
PLACEMENT

HIGH VISIBILITY RF
SCREEN OBSERVATION
WINDOW

1/4" LAMINATED
SAFETY GLASS
BOTH SIDES

SPACING BLOCK
(N.I.C.)

5/8" GYPSUM
BOARD (N.I.C.)

TYPICAL WINDOW SECTION

X / XXX

Figure 13-4 Section through typical RF control room window. © 2005 Lindgren R.F. Enclosures, Inc. All Rights Reserved.

Notes
Windows come with 1/4" safety glass on both sides.
Rough openings should be 6" larger than the nominal glass size (ie: 4'-0" x 3'-6" glass size = 4'-6" x 4'-0" rough opening).
Bottom elevation of rough opening is typically 2'-9" A.F.F. Check for exact location with the architect.

RF Doors

According to ETS–Lindgren, a company that produces shielding enclosures, "The door is the most critical component of the [RF] shielded enclosure. It is the only component subject to mechanical forces and daily wear and tear."[13] RF doors generally are available in two styles. One has an industrial appearance and is used in research applications where people are not treated. A second, architectural style is available for use in areas where human patients are treated. The RF door leaf has a conductive interior skin, usually made of copper, that provides the RF seal over the door aperture. "Fingerless" RF doors are also available. This type of door may provide a more durable RF seal than earlier designs. In addition to maintaining a complete RF seal, the architectural–style door must meet the accessibility requirements of the Americans with Disabilities Act and other local requirements. This requires a special handle and a low door threshold (figures 13–5 and 13–6).

Figure 13-5 Typical RF door detail.
© 2005 Lindgren R.F. Enclosures, Inc.
All Rights Reserved.

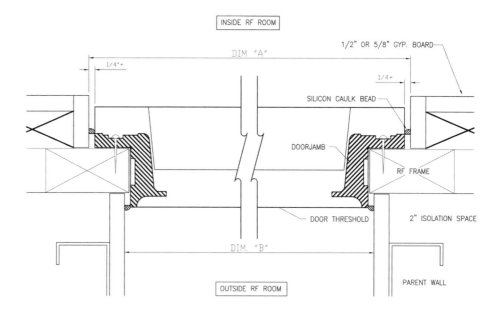

Figure 13-6 Section through typical RF
door. © 2005 Lindgren R.F. Enclosures, Inc.
All Rights Reserved.

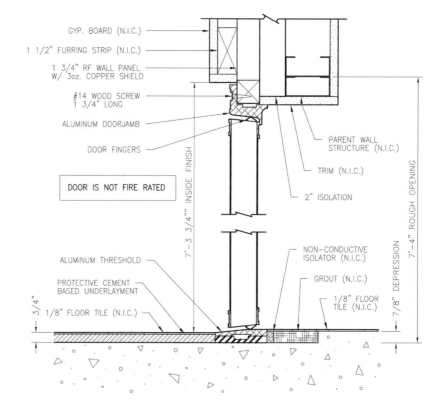

Notes:
RF doors are not fire rated. If a door requires a rating, an independent pocket door will be
required, (see page 13 of this section). Vision panels are available. If the slab is not depressed then
the customer is responsible for the installation of an approved ramp up to the RF door threshold.
Typical rough opening for a 4' x 7' RF door is 4'-6" x 7'-4"

Mechanical Waveguides and RF Electrical Filters

Although the RF enclosure must maintain its uniformity, certain objects will need to penetrate the procedure room envelope. These include HVAC ducts, electrical cables, medical gas lines, and other utility lines. All room utilities with the exception of HVAC ducts must enter the shield at the MRI penetration panel (figures 13–7 and 13–8). HVAC vents can be located anywhere within the enclosure, but ideally not more than one supply and return duct should penetrate the shield. Where ducts penetrate the enclosure, a waveguide–a honeycomb cluster of hexagonal tubing that provides maximum open-air space without disrupting RF integrity–is installed by the RF shielding vendor and coordinated with the work of the utility system subcontractors (figure 13–9). Usually, the length of a waveguide is four times its diameter.

Utilities that come to the shield in pipes are attached to a pipe penetration waveguide. Power lines are fed into the shielded area via power line filters. A quench pipe is a large waveguide connected to the outside in order to provide safe venting of helium gas in the event of a quench, a rapid boil-off of liquid helium in which cold helium gas is discharged. Special care must be used in the design and construction of the entire quench pipe due to mechanical stresses, pressure drops, moisture control, and acoustics.

Figure 13-7 All room utilities (except HVAC) must enter the procedure room through the penetration panel. © 2005 Lindgren R.F. Enclosures, Inc. All Rights Reserved.

Figure 13-8 Penetration panel. © 2005 Lindgren R.F. Enclosures, Inc. All Rights Reserved.

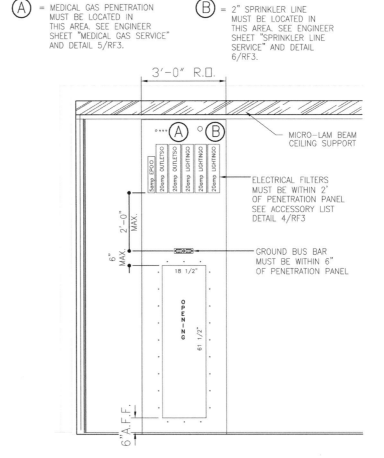

(A) = MEDICAL GAS PENETRATION MUST BE LOCATED IN THIS AREA. SEE ENGINEER SHEET "MEDICAL GAS SERVICE" AND DETAIL 5/RF3.

(B) = 2" SPRINKLER LINE MUST BE LOCATED IN THIS AREA. SEE ENGINEER SHEET "SPRINKLER LINE SERVICE" AND DETAIL 6/RF3.

PENETRATION PANEL ELEVATION DETAIL

Notes:
Panel is located within the RF shield at the direction of the architect. All system grounds must terminate at the ground bus bar. All mechanical and electrical systems, with the exception of HVAC ducts and sink vent/drain line, must enter the RF shield at this location. Size of the penetration panel is determined by the type of MRI system selected. All floor cable trenches, wall or ceiling mounte4d wire ways used for the MRI system will terminate at this location.

Magnetic Interactions

The magnetic force field has a great deal of influence on facility design because magnetic force can be damaging to both people and objects. The magnetic field extends in three dimensions from the magnet's center. The fringe field is the magnetic field extending beyond the magnet. Self-shielding magnets or external magnetic shielding of low-carbon steel or iron can be employed to redistribute or reduce the fringe field. The field is measured in gauss, an international unit equal to 0.00001 tesla.

Because magnetic force can be damaging to people and objects (it can disrupt operation of pacemakers and video monitors, and erase magnetic data from credit cards), gauss lines of an MRI instrument often are plotted

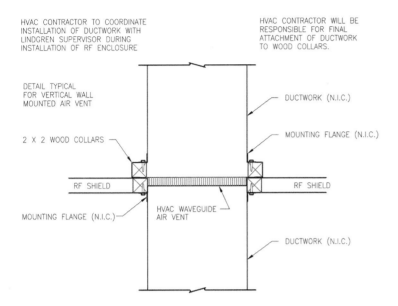

DUCT SUPPORTED INDEPENDANT OF
RF ROOM PANELS

HVAC CONTRACTOR TO COORDINATE
INSTALLATION OF DUCTWORK WITH
LINDGREN SUPERVISOR DURING
INSTALLATION OF RF ENCLOSURE

HVAC CONTRACTOR WILL BE
RESPONSIBLE FOR FINAL
ATTACHMENT OF DUCTWORK
TO WOOD COLLARS.

DETAIL TYPICAL
FOR VERTICAL WALL
MOUNTED AIR VENT

DUCTWORK (N.I.C.)

MOUNTING FLANGE (N.I.C.)

2 X 2 WOOD COLLARS

RF SHIELD   RF SHIELD

MOUNTING FLANGE (N.I.C.)

HVAC WAVEGUIDE
AIR VENT

DUCTWORK (N.I.C.)

Figure 13-9 A waveguide enables HVAC ducts to penetrate the shielding enclosure without disrupting the room's RF integrity. © 2005 Lindgren R.F. Enclosures, Inc. All Rights Reserved.

WAVEGUIDE AIRVENT

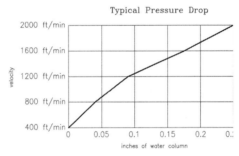

Typical Pressure Drop

Notes:
Waveguide air vent RF filters will collect dust over time reducing airflow. It is recommend that
a serviceable air filter be located on the inlet side of both supply and return air vents waveguides
Duct work materials externat to the RF shield can be of any selected type.
Duct work materials used within the RF shield must be non magnetic.
Ceiling air vent diffuser must be non magnetic.

on architectural and equipment drawings to locate three-dimensional area boundaries where public traffic should be excluded (figures 13–10A–D). A gauss plot is available from the equipment manufacturer and should be obtained during the early phases of design. Any area where the magnetic field is greater than 5 gauss is known as the exclusion zone. People with pacemakers or biostimulator devices must stay out of this area. The 5-gauss line should be contained within the examination room whenever possible. (One exception to this is the use of an unshielded magnet with no external shielding added to the room. Sometimes this is used in research applications to obtain the clearest image possible or when the

continues on page 318

Figure 13-10A-C The magnetic field extends in three dimensions around the magnet, and varies along each axis. © 2005 Lindgren R.F. Enclosures, Inc. All Rights Reserved.

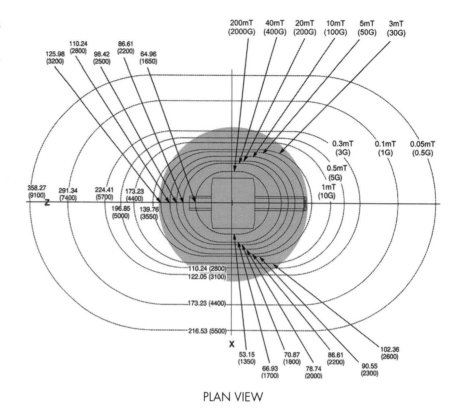

PLAN VIEW

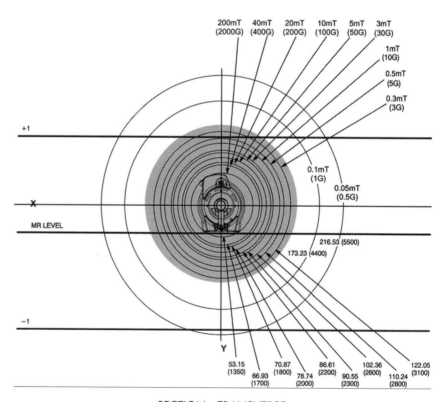

SECTION—TRANSVERSE

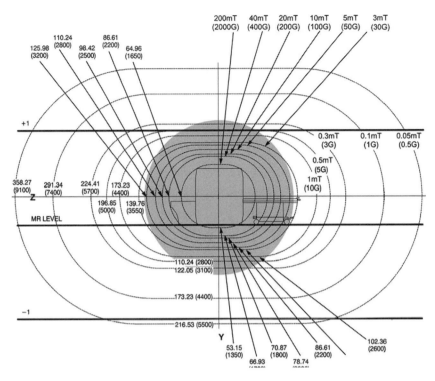

SECTION—LONGITUDINAL

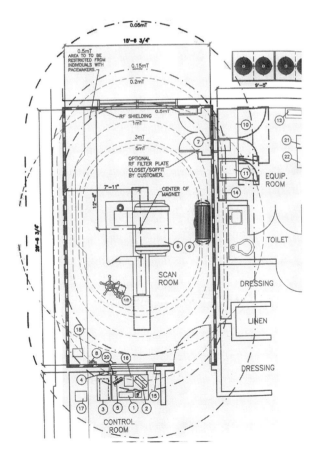

Figure 13-10D It is important to verify the strength of the magnetic field that extends into adjacent spaces and restrict its extent where necessary (see figure 12.24, page 286). © 2005 Lindgren R.F. Enclosures, Inc. All Rights Reserved.

continued from page 315

research program includes chemical shift spectroscopy. An unshielded magnet uses distance instead of magnetic shielding to control the force field. External magnetic shielding, which may degrade the image somewhat, is eliminated and so is the diminished image quality. Conventional wisdom suggests that the generated 1–gauss field be kept out of any areas not under the direct control of the magnet operator/owner. This is especially true for adjacent tenant lease areas.

Permanent and resistive magnets tend to be in the ultra–low– or low–field–strength group (less than 0.5 T) and have tighter, more compressed gauss plots than superconductive magnets. In most cases, the force field of permanent and resistive magnets is nearly contained within the confines of the equipment itself. In contrast, the force field of a superconductive magnet that is not actively shielded usually is much larger, often extending beyond the limits of the exam room. Actively shielded superconductive magnets typically contain their 5–gauss field within the exam room. Due to the larger force field, superconductive magnets that are not actively shielded are more challenging to site and require more space than do the other magnet types.

Magnetic shielding, which limits the magnet's fringe field, can either be integrated into the walls of the exam room or be designed as part of the magnet itself. A magnet that provides integral magnetic shielding is said to be self–shielded, either actively or passively. In either case, magnetic shielding can cost hundreds of thousands of dollars. A magnet that provides integral shielding adds this cost to the equipment budget; one that is passively shielded adds the cost to the construction budget.

There are four ways that an MR exam room can be magnetically shielded:

1. Use passive room shielding made of steel.
2. Use passive clamp–on ferrous shielding (which is integrated into the magnet's construction).
3. Use active electronic magnet shielding.
4. Use distance to eliminate the need for shielding.

Passive room shielding takes on a variety of shapes. When new magnets are shielded, the steel may only need to be installed at the top or along one side of the room. However, older, reconditioned high–field magnets usually need full-room magnetic shielding or a six-sided steel box enclosure. Full-room shields can weigh more than 100 tons. They tend to extend 2 to 4 feet below the finish floor level of the room and up to 12 feet above the floor level. The maximum thickness of the steel box is located normal to the axis of the magnet's bore. From there, it tapers to a thinner construction. When magnetic shielding is placed below the floor level of the exam room, the structural system of the room may need to be modified separately from the rest of the building's structural system.

Passive clamp-on ferrous shielding is available from the equipment vendor. Unlike the ferrous box integrated into the procedure room walls, clamp-on shielding attaches to the magnet directly. Clamp-on shielding must be precisely constructed so that no electronic shimming problems or gauss distortions are created within the magnetic field. This type of shielding is also heavy, often adding 30 tons to the weight of the magnet. Clamp-on shielding originally was more popular when few alternatives existed. Today, it is used less frequently than either passive room shielding or active shielding.

Active types of shielding available with superconductive magnets incorporate two magnets in one. The imaging magnet is wound around the core in one direction. Then another magnet is wound around the core in the opposite direction in order to compensate for and cancel out the fringe field of the first. This active shielding can reduce the extent of the 5-gauss line considerably, as compared to a nonshielded magnet. It compresses the magnetic field better than the passive system does, and it does not add as much weight to the installation. Actively shielded magnets were first introduced to the market in the late 1980s and early 1990s. They are available for most superconducting magnets and are often considered the system of choice when new MRI units are being planned and installed. For some site conditions, an actively shielded magnet and partial passive room shielding might be employed. Actively shielded magnets, however, are much more sensitive to environmental distortions than are the old-style free-field magnets. Installation sites for actively shielded magnets must be carefully selected.

Magnetic shielding works by entrapping magnetic flux near its source, keeping it away from what it is designed to protect. The property by which the shielding attracts the magnetic field lines to itself is called "permeability." Magnetic shielding materials, therefore, require high permeability ratings. Silicon steel is the most common material for most actively shielded systems. However, it cannot be used as an integrated RF/magnetic shielding material. Annealed low-carbon steel is another material employed in the manufacture of magnetic shields. It is used mainly for high-field-strength (7 T) investigational research magnets. Annealed low-carbon steel can be used for integrated RF/magnetic shielding. Nickel alloy is a material that has a very high permeability rating. However, it is rarely used in magnetic shields because of its prohibitive cost and high magnetic saturation levels.

As mentioned earlier, an unshielded magnet sometimes is used in research and clinical applications where the best possible image is required. Distance is used in place of steel to control the magnetic force field. Special caution (as determined by the magnet vendor) must be used to prevent people and certain objects from entering critical force fields.

In the early days of MRI, distance was thought to be the only way to shield a system. As a result, many of the early units were located in parking lots or remote locations within the facility. This approach led to countless operational inefficiencies and substantial challenges to architectural planners.

Regardless of how the magnet is shielded, both static and moving ferromagnetic objects can influence the homogeneity of the magnetic field. Shimming, a process in which the vendor compensates for magnetic inhomogeneity (formerly done by inserting pieces of iron around the magnet enclosure, but today primarily done electronically), can compensate for some imperfections in the magnet and static ferrous objects, such as steel beams. Active shimming does not compensate effectively for moving objects such as elevators, automobiles, and movable medical equipment. These must be kept a distance away unless additional magnetic shielding is installed. Shimming, or for that matter any external magnetic shielding, tends to somewhat compromise the clarity of the MR image.

Certain conditions relating to the facility's construction and its effect on the magnet's performance must be considered. However, as MRI technology improves, siting requirements also change. For each installation, current siting requirements should be verified with manufacturers.

For many magnets no ferrous material can be installed in close proximity to their isocenter, yet normal construction methods and practices can be followed outside the shielded space. The magnetic isocenter is:

- The point in the center of the magnet where the coordinates x, y, z = 0, 0, 0
- The point from which all critical measurements are taken for functions directly related to the placement of the magnet
- The point from which the cryogenic exhaust waveguide is typically located
- The point from which magnetic shielding is measured and placed
- The point from which the limit of the resulting magnetic field is measured

Vendors may specify the maximum amount of iron reinforcement that can be placed in the floor directly beneath or above the MRI unit. Fiberglass or stainless steel structural reinforcement is available as an alternative. If ferrous reinforcement is used in the floor, it should be distributed equally throughout the floor area. Exceeding vendor-specified limits can result in unshimmable conditions.

Often, a detailed analysis identifying the limitations imposed by the magnet's field is performed at the beginning of the design process. This analysis is important for proper magnet placement. It can be performed by either the magnet vendor or a special consultant. However, the service can be expensive. Additionally, the results of the analysis can affect the scope of the equipment purchase. For example, the analysis may lead the owner and architect to compare the cost of an actively shielded magnet with that of a passively shielded installation. If either the magnet or other critical objects in its vicinity are relocated during the design or construction phase, the analysis may need to be repeated.

For systems that require only the installation of an RF shield, the construction of the parent room can be relatively simple. However, some caution should be taken in selecting construction materials that will be used inside the parent room enclosure. Certain items must be made of nonferrous materials. These include lay-in ceiling grids and hangers, ceiling-mounted lighting fixtures, sprinkler lines and hangers, all cover plates and associated mounting screws, and HVAC ducts and hangers. Aluminum support grids should be used in place of standard metal supports for lay-in ceiling systems. However, items such as steel wall–furring channels and plasterboard screws are generally acceptable. Many ferrous fasteners that once were eliminated from the MR environment are now commonly used.

When MRI was first introduced, designers and builders went to great lengths to ensure that no ferrous materials were used in any aspect of MRI room design. Metal fabrications were often replaced by wood, fiberglass, or other nonferrous items. "Now, however, manufacturers generally agree that shimming of the magnet is able to compensate for [many] static ferrous building materials. The use of conventional construction techniques and materials [outside of the shielded room] greatly reduces the expense of constructing an MRI facility."[14]

Electromagnetic fields from power lines, motors, and transformers also can influence magnetic homogeneity. Electromagnetic sources may include nearby medical equipment, including other MR units. Minimum distances must be observed.

Space Required for RF and Magnetic Shielding

The MR procedure room is actually a room within a room, and thus the overall wall thickness of both rooms combined is greater than that of standard room construction. As mentioned previously, the parent room is constructed by the general contractor, whereas the shielding enclosure is fabricated and installed by the shielding contractor based on the dimensions of the parent room and the shielding requirements of the magnet. Depending on the type of enclosure used, the inside dimensions of the parent room may be as much as 4 to 10 inches greater in each direction than the inside dimensions of the shielding enclosure. This difference must be accounted for when the space is being planned. If not, the usable area inside the exam room may be smaller than desired.

When determining space requirements for imaging rooms, area dimensions usually are given in terms of usable net area or the actual space available inside the room excluding wall, floor, and ceiling finishes. The usable area within the MR procedure room is actually determined by the inside dimensions of the shielding enclosure, not the parent room. Thus the room's available usable area may be 40 to 60 net square feet less than the net area provide by the parent room. During programming, this space should be accommodated either in the area allocated to the room or as a separate line item.

At a minimum, the parent room walls should be covered with drywall. Prior to installing the shield, the space should be free and clear of utilities and other services. All roughed-in openings should be provided for doors, windows, the installation access panel, and the penetration panel. For systems requiring magnetic as well as RF shielding, the parent room may provide some structural support for heavy magnetic shielding. In such cases it must be engineered accordingly.

Magnetic Contamination

MR site planning analysis typically evaluates a potential site to verify if it is appropriate structurally, spatially, and in terms of EMI and RF interactions to accommodate a new MR imaging system. However, planners and administrators should also evaluate sites where an MRI has been or will be removed to provide space for other clinical uses. While the 5-gauss exclusion zone is typically considered to be safe for most occupants, the long-term accumulation of the magnetic field (even beyond the exclusion zone) can magnetically contaminate stationary ferrous materials, such as steel structural supports (such as beams, reinforcing bars, and structural supports) or shielding. After the magnet is removed, many of these magnetized objects will remain, especially if they are part of the building's construction.

Magnetic contamination can be problematic for the new occupants of the space. For example, image quality of advanced imaging equipment–especially PET/CT, CT and rotational angiography units–can be detrimentally affected by environmental magnetic contamination.[15] CRT monitors and other devices can also be affected. The potential for magnetic contamination is greater–and the area of impact can be larger–with very-high-field-strength magnets. In extreme cases, the entire space can become magnetized to a strength similar to that of a refrigerator magnet.[16]

According to Joe Weber, director of new product development at ETS/Lindgren, Inc., the biggest problem with residual magnetism is with new equipment–such as CT and PET scanners–that is installed in old MR suites, due to many of these new systems' ultrasensitive and precise technology.[17]

Safety

Stories of metal objects transformed into dangerous projectiles probably are more common than the occurrences themselves. Nonetheless, the MRI environment can be a hazardous area if safety precautions are misunderstood or not carefully followed. Because magnetic fields are invisible until their effects are made noticeable, these powerful forces of physics often are forgotten. Magnetic safety criteria relating to facility design–including recommendations of the American College of Radiology–are described in chapter 12, "Room Design," and Appendix B, "American College of Radiology White Paper on MR Safety."

A superconductive magnet consists of an electromagnet with windings composed of a special alloy. The alloy, immersed in liquid helium, is kept extremely cold to eliminate its electrical resistance. The magnet must remain at an extremely cold (cryogenic) temperature in order to efficiently produce the high magnetic field required. In the event that a superconductive magnet must be immediately shut down (perhaps to allow access to a critical patient), a substantial amount of helium may boil off. As mentioned earlier, this situation is known as a quench. It is a serious problem and may destroy the magnet, as well as create a safety hazard. Although helium is nonflammable and nonpoisonous, it is potentially harmful to health because it can dilute the oxygen content of the surrounding air. Ventilation requirements are specified by both the manufacturer and regulatory agencies. Usually, a minimum number of air changes per hour with outside air is specified. In addition, the magnet should be connected to an automatic ventilation system to prevent evaporation of helium into the procedure room. The magnet should never be energized without proper installation of quench venting and exhaust systems.

In many locations, code requires that an oxygen–monitoring system be installed to verify the oxygen content of the air. Special care must be taken when handling liquid helium or nitrogen. They are extremely cold and can cause severe burns when they come in direct contact with the skin.

Special venting in the form of a quench pipe must be installed, per the manufacturer's specifications, to keep helium from discharging into the procedure room. If a quench occurred, it would place very high stress on the ventilation system. Cryogenic vents should have the least number of bends or turns possible. Bends and turns may create back pressure within the ventilation system. In addition, the vent should be supported structurally to withstand increased gas pressure and velocity during a quench. A cryogen exhaust system has three components:

- The first component connects the magnet to the vent, and is supplied by the magnet supplier.
- The second component is the connection from the vent to the cryogen, and is supplied by the RF shielding contractor.
- The third component connects the cryogen to a vent pipe that extends to the building's exterior, and is supplied and installed by the contractor.[18]

The vent pipe must extend to the building's exterior, and its discharge point should be away from areas accessible to people (figures 13–11 and 13–12). In addition, a warning sign must be posted near the point of discharge cautioning people such as maintenance workers not to approach. The warning should be posted at the edge of nearby accessible roofs if the discharge point is below and hidden from view.

Figure 13-11 Cryogen vent inside an MRI procedure room. © 2005 Lindgren R.F. Enclosures, Inc. All Rights Reserved.

Acoustics

An MRI examination is an inherently noisy procedure. In particular, sounds originating from the gradient coils, which are activated during imaging, create a loud banging sound. This adds to the fear and anxiety that most patients already have about their encounter with this mysterious machinery. A significant number of MRI patients either fail to show up for their appointments or are unwilling to return for follow-up exams because of their fear of the noise and claustrophobia induced by the equipment.

Equipment manufacturers have not been entirely successful in reducing the noise generated by gradient coils. Architects and interior designers can mitigate the noise impact within the procedure room somewhat, although the greatest acoustic problems occur within the magnet's bore. Acoustic damping of the walls, floor, and ceiling of the procedure room softens the environment and provides an extra measure of comfort.

High sound pressure levels can result in structure–borne vibration. HVAC ducts and cryogen vents can become conduits for sound transmission. However, proper acoustic material selections and detailing can reduce the transmission of both airborne noises and those traveling through walls and partitions. For example, acoustically rated RF doors and windows can be specified, and consideration might be given to placing fabric-wrapped acoustic panels on the walls and acoustic panels with a high noise reduction coefficient on the ceiling, where permitted by code. While carpeting acts to control noise levels, many manufacturers discourage the use of carpeting at the patient couch location because it impedes the movement of patients as well as the dewars needed to periodically replenish the cryogen.

Figure 13-12 Cryogen vent at an external discharge point. © 2005 Lindgren R.F. Enclosures, Inc. All Rights Reserved.

In addition, carpeting is typically inappropriate to use within procedural areas for reasons of infection control. The finish surface of the procedure room floor should not be higher than adjacent floor surfaces or create high thresholds in doorways for reasons of disability access and movement of heavy equipment from room to room. In addition, such floor height differences may make it difficult to create an integral RF enclosure.

A variety of audio and video systems are available to mask noise and distract patients from thinking about the machinery or the medical procedure. Some systems include specially designed headphones and goggles that can be used near the magnet. Others consist of special television monitors on which patients can watch local television stations or their favorite videos. Still others include a mirror either in the form of glasses or mounted on a bracket placed near the patient's chest or feet. The patient then looks down the bore of the magnet to see a pleasant view of either a fixed or video image reflected in the mirror.

Most magnet manufacturers are attempting to design less-noisy machinery. However, sometimes artwork, views to the outdoors, or other visually interesting objects can effectively compensate for the acoustic disturbances inherent to most magnets by transferring the patient's awareness away from the noise. Some manufacturers offer equipment packages that include room design with features intended to comfort anxious patients, especially children and their families.[19] In addition, many magnets (especially those with ultra–low or low field strength) are now being designed to have an open bore. Such designs reduce the feeling of claustrophobia for many patients.

Lighting

Proper lighting in the MR exam room is important for both functional and aesthetic reasons. A minimum of two lighting levels should be provided. A lower level, for patient comfort, is desirable in the area around the magnet's bore and the patient couch. Direct lighting should be avoided in these areas. However, fluorescent lamps and certain types of electronic dimmers cannot be used because they create RF disruption and degrade the MR image quality. At the same time, standard incandescent lamps should be avoided because the magnetic field will quickly destroy their filament. Incandescent lamps with a special reinforced tungsten filament usually are recommended. The reinforced filament extends their life considerably. Direct–current lighting will serve better in the MR environment than will alternating–current lighting. Most MR manufacturers specify the use of direct–current lighting. High–power (3 watt) light–emitting diodes have entered the market and will likely become increasingly popular for MRI installations as their cost becomes lower. Daylighting in the MR exam room can be beneficial to both patients and staff.

A lighting level higher than that of the patient areas should be provided around the magnet's perimeter. This is necessary for servicing and routine maintenance and is typically provided by fluorescent lamps in nonferrous fixtures. Controls for these lights should be separate from those used during the patient exam. In some instances, a third type of lighting–additional task lighting–is needed for special procedures or examinations.

The control room adjacent to the exam room also should have two lighting levels that are of equal value to the levels in the exam room. Balancing the level of lighting in the two rooms will minimize glare along the control room window. For the same reason, direct daylight or artificial light should be controlled to minimize glare on the operator's console.

The technical equipment room can have a single lighting level. Preferably, its level should be equal to the service light level in the control and exam rooms.

Notes

1. National Council on Radiation Protection and Measurement, Report No. 49, *Structural Shielding Design for Medical Use of X-rays and Gamma Rays of Energies up to 10 MeV* (Bethesda, MD: NCRP, 1976), 1–3.
2. National Council on Radiation Protection and Measurement, NCRP Report No. 147, *Structural Shielding Design for Medical X-ray Imaging Facilities* (Bethesda, MD: NCRP, 2004).
3. NCRP 49.
4. NCRP 49.

5. NCRP 49.
6. NCRP 49.
7. NCRP 49 and NCRP 147.
8. B. R. Archer, "Radiation design criteria for diagnostic X-ray facilities: Part 1," paper presented at the annual meeting of the Radiological Society of North America, Chicago, 1991, 2.
9. NCRP 49, 46.
10. S. C. Bushong, *Radiologic Science for Technologists*, 3rd ed. (St. Louis: Mosby Year Book, 1984), 515.
11. NCRP 49, 14–15.
12. NCRP 49, 13.
13. ETS/Lindgren RF Enclosures, Inc., *MRI Shielded Architectural Site Planning Guidelines*, CD, 2005.
14. J. Malkin, *The Design of Medical and Dental Facilities* (New York: Van Nostrand Reinhold, 1980), 235.
15. M. Robb, "Magnetic contamination: The ghost of MRI past," *Radiology Today* 5, 21 (2004), http:www.radiologytoday.net/archive/rt_101104p22.shtml.
16. Robb.
17. Robb.
18. ETS/Lindgren.
19. Philips Medical Systems, Shelton, CT, Philips North America.

CHAPTER 14

Renovation Versus New Construction

O ne of the first steps in planning a new imaging service is to decide whether the project will involve new construction, renovation, or both. In some cases, however, one or the other option may not be feasible because of site constraints, schedule pressures, or other mitigating factors. For example, if adequate site area is unavailable, new construction would be impossible unless a portion of an existing structure is demolished. On the other hand, if existing facilities are fully utilized, there might be no suitable location for renovation without displacing existing services. In either case, a site and facility master plan should guide the process of deciding between renovation and new construction.

Other issues to consider when deciding on a construction strategy include:

- Comparative costs and project durations for each type of construction
- The extent that the existing facility conforms to current code requirements (renovation can lead to additional work that needs to be done in order for the renovation project to conform to all applicable codes and regulations)
- The evaluation of the remaining useful life of a renovated facility versus that of new construction
- The ability of each type of project to meet functional requirements (for example, providing functional adjacencies between related services such as imaging, surgery, and emergency services)
- The degree to which either renovation or new construction adheres to previously established long- and short-range planning objectives

- The amount of disruption that renovation may cause for existing ongoing services that are near the area of renovation
- The potential for renovation to cause infection- or health-related hazards (such as dust, contamination of air-handling systems, or excessive vibration) for existing ongoing nearby services

The impact of both new construction and renovation must therefore be considered in terms of future growth and flexibility, operational efficiency, longevity, safety, and code compliance.

This chapter examines key issues that must be considered when deciding whether to renovate an existing imaging facility or to build a new one. It also explores some of the unique considerations involved in planning renovation projects.

Key Questions in the Decision of Construction Approach

Renovation often is viewed as a less-expensive alternative to new construction because floors, foundations, and exterior walls already exist. Although renovation sometimes is the most cost-effective approach to construction, by no means is this always the case. If significant existing building and infrastructure components require extensive modification, renovation may end up requiring more work than new construction. Furthermore, if the area being renovated is supported by aging building systems (such as air handling, power, and structural), renovation could trigger upgrades to those systems in locations beyond the area of remodeling, thus significantly extending the project's scope and cost. In some cases, renovation might require the central plant to be expanded or possibly even replaced.[1] Additionally, some factors such as existing floor-to-floor heights cannot be easily changed. Therefore, the resulting renovation project may be less flexible and adaptable to change than new construction because the existing construction may act as a physical constraint limiting size, configuration, circulation patterns, and coordination of infrastructure systems.

Technically demanding programs such as imaging services have rigorous physical requirements. In particular, imaging facilities place significant demands on structural, plumbing, air-handling, and power capacities. Additionally, imaging equipment requires a higher floor-to-floor height than do many other types of equipment. Finally, the rapid development of imaging technology demands a facility that will accommodate change easily. Most of these criteria are more difficult to satisfy with renovation than with new construction.

On the other hand, new construction may be inappropriate for small projects or upgrades that can be accommodated by minor modifications to existing facilities. For example, a newly constructed two-room radiology expansion would be expensive relative to its size because the cost of new foundations, roofing, and so on must be amortized over the small area. Furthermore, numerous small additions to an existing campus tend to compromise the effectiveness of campus-wide master plans that provide a strategic direction for growth over time. Finally, renovation may be preferred over new construction if it will enable new services to be made available sooner than will new construction.

Many imaging projects involve expansion or upgrading rather than replacement of relatively new existing building systems. For this type of project, there may be significant value remaining in portions of the facility that require little or no work. Renovation may be the preferred alternative in such cases. However, numerous hidden costs may emerge even when newer facilities are remodeled.

Several important questions should be asked when deciding between renovation and new construction:[2]

1. What is the nature of the project? Is it mostly cosmetic, or is it functional? Projects primarily seeking to improve ambience, image, and aesthetics–without changing significant functional components–are often well suited to renovation. Projects that require major functional elements to be changed, however, are likely to trigger modification or even replacement of mechanical and electrical systems, as well as relocation of partitions, installation of new smoke and fire protection assemblies, and augmentation of structural capacities. If these amount to a significant scope of work, such projects may be more effective as new construction if that is an option.

    With the exception of minor administrative remodeling projects or replacement of equipment in a few rooms, renovation of an imaging facility almost always involves major functional changes. For most renovation projects, the potential cost savings come from not having to construct a new building core and shell. For these projects the foundation, exterior skin, and structural system can usually be reused with little or no alteration for the renovated design. Compared to new construction, the core and shell cost can be reduced by an average of 80 percent, but savings in other areas (such as internal partitions, electrical, plumbing, and air-handling devices) are often minimal.[3]

2. When was the existing facility built? If it was built after significant code changes were adopted by regulatory authorities having jurisdiction, it is more likely either to be code-compliant or to require less modification to become compliant. Older facilities are likely to have inadequate floor-to-floor heights, shorter structural spans, less resistance to vibration,

and hazardous materials such as asbestos. While the presence of any of these conditions should not automatically exclude renovation as an option, each is likely to add both cost and time to the project.[4]

3. For what purpose was the facility initially built? Facilities initially built for healthcare use are likely to have greater building systems capacities than, say, a commercial office building, which is likely to require structural, mechanical, electrical, and other systems upgrades in order to accommodate advanced imaging equipment, even if it to be used exclusively for ambulatory patients.

4. For what purpose will the new space be used? The extent of technical complexity required for the new use will affect how extensive renovation efforts need to be. If the renovated space will be used primarily to house radiology administrative staff and consists mostly of offices and conference space, the extent of renovation may be simple. If the space is to be used for imaging exam rooms, thus requiring more extensive infrastructure upgrades, renovation will be more complex and the potential uses of the space may be compromised.

5. Do applicable regulatory codes suggest that a comprehensive facility upgrade may be required? Some jurisdictions specify that if a certain percentage of a facility is being renovated, the entire building must be made code-compliant. These requirements can extend beyond the building's boundaries. For example, the Americans with Disabilities Act clearly describes the circumstances under which accessible routes of travel must be provided. These can–and often do–require replacement of elevators, doors, parking spaces, and sidewalks.

6. What will the impact of renovation be on daily operations? Providing ongoing services on a site where a new building is being constructed can be challenging; doing the same within, or directly adjacent to an area undergoing renovation is usually more disruptive. For example, noise, vibration, and airborne dust and dirt can compromise nearby imaging services, discourage staff (who may already be a challenge to recruit and retain), and cause potential health hazards. The AIA Guidelines for Construction and Equipment of Hospitals and Medical Facilities provide specific infection control risk assessments (ICRAs) to minimize the negative impact that construction may have on infection control.[5] In addition, service outages and temporary disconnection of services can be disruptive. Multiple construction

phases also required of most renovation projects may mean that imaging functions need to be temporarily relocated several times until the project is complete.

Special Considerations for Renovation Projects

Renovation projects involve a number of special considerations. The following subsections discuss these considerations in terms of planning, phasing, and cost.

Planning Considerations

An imaging department planned within the shell of an existing facility may be restricted by some of the physical features inherent in the present structure. For example, if the available area is smaller than desired, some spaces may wind up undersized. If the available area is adequate but its configuration is irregular, ideal room-to-room adjacencies may not be practical and the amount of space devoted to circulation may be excessive. If both the available area and the configuration of space are adequate but the location is remote from other related services, operational efficiencies may suffer.

A thorough analysis of the unique conditions inherent in renovation projects can help reduce the likelihood and impact of unexpected factors. Such an analysis involves consideration of questions in a variety of categories.

Available options for new construction versus renovation

- Do several options exist? If the proposed plan is to renovate existing space, is there adequate area on the site that provides an option for new construction? Similarly, if the proposed plan is for new construction, is renovation a possible alternative? If feasible alternatives exist, have comparative planning studies and cost estimates been prepared and compared for both renovation and new construction alternatives?
- Has a strategic plan been developed for the organization? Has a site and facility master plan been developed for the existing site or campus? If so, which renovation or new construction options (if any) most successfully achieve the goals set forth in both the strategic plan and the site and facility master plan?

Available area and configuration

- How much space is available in the proposed location, and is it of a regular configuration? If the space is oddly shaped, a greater amount of area may be needed to accommodate the desired program. For example, if the space is too narrow,

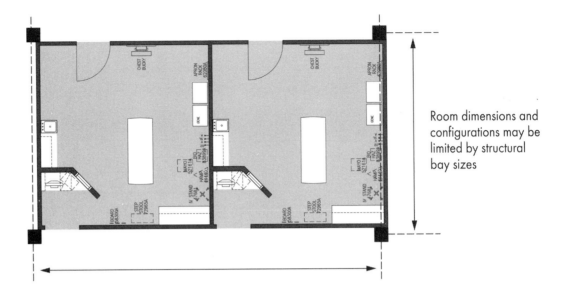

Room dimensions and configurations may be limited by structural bay sizes

Figure 14-1 Structural bay spacing relative to room configuration—two procedure rooms within a bay.

it may not accommodate a core layout with multiple procedure rooms off a central technologist work core. If the overall space is too long and narrow, resulting travel distances may become inappropriately long.

- Is the area subdivided by fixed elements such as stairs or shafts? If so, functional adjacencies may be difficult to achieve, resulting in operational inefficiencies such as long travel distances for staff and/or patients.

- What is the spacing of the existing structural columns? If they are closely spaced, it may be difficult to arrange multiple rooms adjacent to each other without having columns projecting into some of the rooms (figure 14–1). Shallow structural bays also may limit the depth or width of rooms that have corridors running alongside them (figure 14–2).

- What is the floor–to–floor height of the existing structure? Shallow floor–to–floor heights may not allow for an efficient arrangement of mechanical systems above functional areas (such as procedure rooms) and below beams and girders of the structural system. Inefficient mechanical (and other) system arrangements can lead to cost premiums for both initial construction costs and life–cycle operational costs.

Functional adjacencies

- If the renovation project involves relocating imaging services, is the proposed location near other related services? Does it allow for a separation of inpatient and outpatient traffic (if this is applicable to the project)? Does it allow for

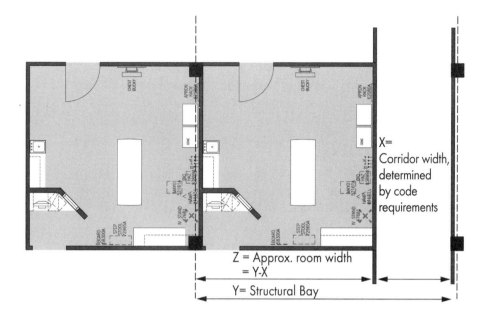

$X=$ Corridor width, determined by code requirements

Z = Approx. room width = Y-X

Y= Structural Bay

easy access to and from the emergency and surgery departments, as well as other required adjacencies?

- Will the renovated area disrupt the existing horizontal and/or vertical circulation routes serving other parts of the building? Can required exiting for the renovated area be easily accommodated without modifying corridors and/or exit paths beyond the boundary of the renovated area?

Future flexibility and adaptability

- What is the useful remaining life of all physical elements that are not being replaced? Will they limit the future use of the renovated area? Are any building systems that are not being replaced approaching their maximum capacities?
- Does the existing facility have a building system that is easy to modify? For example, a steel structural moment frame accommodates internal modifications more easily than a building with structural concrete shear walls.
- Was the existing facility specifically designed to easily accommodate future change? For example, are utility systems located in interstitial spaces that are separate from functional areas? Do structural and utility systems have reserve capacity to handle additional loads?
- Is there available "soft" space that could be used for future expansion within the facility? Is external expansion possible in the future? Would it be easy to integrate a technology dock into the plan for relocatable imaging services (such as those housed in trucks or other movable structures)?

Figure 14-2 Structural bay spacing relative to room configuration—a procedure room and a corridor within a bay.

Structure and infrastructure

- What is the loading capacity of the existing floors, walls, and roof area? How much supplemental structural modification will be needed to support the heavily concentrated loads of imaging equipment? Will required structural modifications affect operations in other areas of the building?

- Is the project located in a seismically active area? Does the existing structure conform to current structural requirements (structural code requirements often increase with each new major seismic event)? Is seismic stability provided by a braced frame or by shear walls, either of which may limit initial or future planning flexibility?

- Does the depth of beams limit vertical clearances and, thus, compromise the efficient layout of air-handling and other systems? Beam depth should be considered in conjunction with floor-to-floor height.

- Is there a convenient location for air-handling units to supply and exhaust air to and from the area of renovation? Will new vertical risers need to be added, thus disrupting functions above the area of renovation? Can the ductwork currently servicing the area of renovation be easily replaced without requiring major modifications to adjacent areas of the building that will remain operational? Is the area being renovated adequately supplied by IT/data closets?

- Is asbestos or another hazardous material present in the existing facility?

- Does the existing facility have a source of clean, uniform, uninterrupted power? Does the existing facility have adequate power capacity? Can power be efficiently distributed between the main power supply location and its points of use?

- Is an information network or communications system in place that will allow for electronic image management and picture archiving? If not, is it appropriate to install one, either throughout the entire facility or in portions of the facility?

- Can the existing fire protection system be easily modified to serve the area of renovation?

- Will the existing structure cause excessive vibration that would be disruptive to vibration-sensitive procedures (interventional imaging and MRI, for example)?

Code compliance

- To which codes and regulations must the facility conform? Will the renovation project require additional areas of the existing facility to be upgraded so that they conform to current codes? Will this project trigger the need for a more extensive upgrade elsewhere in the facility? (This may vary by jurisdiction and by the proposed scope of renovation.)

- How easy will it be to conform to current accessibility requirements? Has the existing facility been assessed for Americans with Disabilities Act compliance? If so, to what extent does it conform?
- Will structural codes require the primary structure to be upgraded?
- Is the intended occupancy different from the occupancy type that the facility was initially designed for? For example, if an existing office building (usually designed for business occupancy) is renovated to be used as a freestanding outpatient imaging center (the occupancy classification for this use may vary by location and by the particular nature of the proposed imaging procedures), the life-safety and exiting code requirements for the new occupancy type might exceed those attained by the building's construction. Furthermore, if patients become temporarily nonambulatory (often defined as "not capable of self-preservation") during some portion of the procedure, more stringent criteria for life safety and exiting might have to be met.

Phasing Considerations

There are many kinds of renovation projects. Some involve only a cosmetic upgrade; others require replacement of everything except the building's exterior skin and structural system. However, almost all renovation projects involve some degree of interim phasing regardless of the scope of renovation.

Renovation often involves adapting a space that is to be used for a new or different purpose. Unless the area to be renovated (and immediately adjoining areas) is already vacated or unless the scope of construction is so minor that it can be accomplished entirely during off-hours, it is likely that some functions will need to be temporarily relocated to enable construction to take place without disrupting existing services. With complex projects, numerous interrelated phases of temporary construction may need to be choreographed in order for these services to be provided throughout the course of construction.

Two types of renovation projects are common. These are:

1. In-place renovation, where imaging services are physically upgraded without being moved to a new location
2. Relocation projects, where an entire imaging service or department is relocated to an unoccupied portion of an existing building

Each type of renovation has advantages and disadvantages. Some may require a series of additional projects in order to free up unoccupied space for temporary or long-term relocation of services.

In-place renovation projects may be the sole alternative if adequate vacant space is unavailable elsewhere in the facility. However, even in-place renovation may require temporary relocation of some services. For example, if an existing imaging department is to be remodeled in place, it may be necessary to temporarily relocate some functions during construction (perhaps into a temporary modular structure or a semitrailer unit) and move them back once the work is complete.

Most renovation projects are more appropriately designed as relocation projects. One advantage of relocation is that the old service can usually operate in place until the new area is completed, thus significantly simplifying phasing and potentially eliminating the need for temporary interim relocation. In addition, construction disruption may be minimized if the area being renovated is not directly adjacent to occupied space. However, this approach requires that vacant space be available in the new location. If adequate vacant space is unavailable, multiple interrelated relocation projects may evolve in an effort to both create a vacant area and then utilize each area that consequently becomes vacant.

Cost Considerations

Often renovation is selected over new construction for one or all of the following reasons:

1. Adequate space is not available for new construction.
2. Adequate time is not available for new construction.
3. The existing area has a significant remaining useful life, making renovation construction relatively more appealing and easier to justify.
4. It is assumed that renovation is less expensive than new construction.

Although renovation sometimes is (but not always) more affordable than new construction, it is important to consider both the obvious and the less obvious cost components of renovation before selecting an approach. The obvious cost benefit of renovation is that some elements of a facility already exist and thus do not have to be built again. Some of the less obvious aspects of cost are discussed in the following subsections.

First Cost Versus Life-Cycle Costs

Any cost determination should include both initial construction costs and the life-cycle costs of maintaining, modifying, and operating the facility during the next decades. Most important, these costs should be amortized over the facility's expected life in order to compare the value of new construction dollars to renovation dollars.

Hidden Construction Costs

Most renovation projects involve myriad hidden conditions. As a result, the likelihood often exists that some previously unknown physical conditions will be discovered during the renovation process. Some hidden conditions can become very expensive to rectify. To reduce the potential impact of such surprises, the following steps should be taken:

- Existing conditions should be examined and documented as carefully as possible. This may require some degree of disruptive investigation, ranging from removing ceiling panels in order to visualize above-ceiling conditions to demolishing small areas in order to observe conditions that are not otherwise visible.
- If available, a set of drawings for the building's initial construction and subsequent modifications should be obtained and verified.
- An ample construction contingency (usually a higher percentage of construction than would be provided for new construction projects) should be provided.

Required Related Work Costs

Renovation work may require interim construction, phasing of work, and demolition. As a result, funds should be allocated for required interim construction, phasing, and demolition, as well as for final construction. If existing medical equipment–such imaging equipment–is to be reused, funds should be allocated for its removal, transport, and reinstallation. This applies to both renovation and new construction.

Plan Efficiency and Operational Costs

Several plan layouts that can be accommodated within the space available for renovation should be analyzed. Do physical constraints (such as size and configuration of the area, floor-to-floor height, and column spacing) limit the type of layout that can be accommodated? If optimal adjacencies and circulation routes cannot be achieved, operational inefficiencies may result. All plans should be examined closely to ensure that patient circulation and staff work flow are ideal and that imaging rooms and their associated support spaces are arrayed appropriately. The recurrent cost of operational inefficiency over time can easily exceed the one-time cost of construction.

Notes

1. M. Jackson, "Renovate or replace?" *Health Facilities Management* 18, 9 (2005): 23–26.
2. L. C. Bacher, "Deciding between renovation and new construction," *Health Facilities Management* 4, 7 (1991): 20–24.
3. Bacher.
4. Bacher.
5. *Guidelines for Construction and Equipment of Hospital and Medical Facilities* (Washington, DC: American Institute of Architects Press, 2001).

PART FIVE

TRENDS INFLUENCING TOMORROW'S IMAGING FACILITIES

CHAPTER 15

Imaging Beyond the
Radiology Department

The practice of medicine–and interventional procedures in particular–
has widely adopted imaging into many aspects of patient care. While
many imaging examinations take place within radiology departments
or dedicated imaging facilities, much of the impact of medical imaging extends well beyond these boundaries. This chapter examines innovative applications of imaging beyond the radiology department and explores how
these concepts are becoming central to healthcare delivery today, and will
become more so in the future. Specific design guidelines for many of these
techniques are also described in chapter 12, "Room Design."

The influence of medical imaging services across the continuum of
healthcare continues to grow as myriad medical specialties increase their
reliance on imaging data. All this while there is a growing focus on assessing and improving the quality and safety of patient care. Rapid development of advanced communication systems continues to enable the efficient
decentralization of imaging functions. Furthermore, new hybrid combinations of imaging and other medical services, such as image–guided surgery
(IGS), require novel facility designs with imaging equipment embedded
into what have historically not been imaging environments.

Radiologic images and their interpretations provide essential data to a
variety of healthcare providers. Timely dissemination of these data directly
affects patient care throughout the healthcare enterprise. In addition, many
procedures take place outside the radiology department, such as in the
emergency department (ED), the intensive care unit (ICU), the surgical suite,
and remote facilities such as ambulatory care clinics, urgent care centers,
and physicians' offices. Images are produced at these sites to facilitate rapid
care or, in the case of interventional services, to guide the procedure or assess the success of the intervention immediately. Images and reports are
used within these diverse areas to deliver patient care even when the image

acquisition occurs remotely. With modern PACS, multiple departments and individual physicians can obtain images and reports in real time.

While image acquisition and interpretation have historically been the responsibility of radiologists, many specialists now desire to have primary access to medical imaging equipment, control its use, interpret the images, and be financially remunerated for these services. Equipment vendors market specialized devices customized for specific nonradiology specialists. For example, some MRI and multi–detector computed tomography systems cater to cardiology, and some extremity magnets are designed primarily for orthopedic applications. Intensivists in the ICU and emergency physicians in the ED frequently need to review diagnostic images before the radiologist has prepared an interpretive report. Some obstetricians own their own ultrasound devices and interpret the images they acquire. The role of imaging in interventional care has expanded to include image guidance and real–time registration of patient anatomy during interventional procedures.

Imaging is an important component of many areas beyond the radiology department, with each area requiring unique architectural needs. Not only does facility design influence how well imaging equipment functions beyond the radiology department, but the location, layout, and configuration of the imaging suite can also affect whether practitioners collaborate or compete for access to it. This, in turn, affects patient care. The design of new facilities must account for emerging new collaborative relationships among various specialists. This planning must consider how patient safety and ergonomics influence how care is delivered. Such visionary planning may avert the costly duplication of space and equipment that might otherwise result from interdepartmental turf battles. Imaginative approaches must be implemented so that the same imaging equipment can be used for both inpatients and outpatients without the two types of patients encountering each other.

This chapter describes trends in imaging beyond the radiology department that are influencing the design of tomorrow's healthcare facilities in general, and imaging environments in particular. Each of these trends requires a working atmosphere that will be more collaborative and multidisciplinary than is typical today.

Imaging and Emergency Medicine

Rapid medical imaging and the equally rapid interpretation of those images are essential to emergency medicine. Numerous imaging techniques are routinely employed in the emergency department, and both the volume and the diversity of emergency imaging exams are continually growing. At the same time, a study reported at the 2004 annual meeting of the Radiological Society of North America (RSNA) claims that emergency departments throughout the nation could save millions of dollars a year and reduce unnecessary radiation exposure to patients if they followed American College of Radiology appropriateness criteria before ordering unnecessary imaging exams, especially CT studies.[1] There is ongoing debate regarding both the benefits and the cost of medical imaging in the ED, representing diverse opinions, such as those of emergency physicians, trauma surgeons, radiologists, and financial gatekeepers. Regardless of these debates, emergency medical imaging continues to grow due to the importance of rapidly obtaining essential anatomic and metabolic data that can influence the patient's course of treatment and outcome.

Most emergency and trauma departments are equipped to perform a variety of imaging examinations. The extent and sophistication of imaging equipment physically located within the ED depends, in part, on both the patient caseload and its proximity to the radiology department and other imaging services. In some hospitals where the imaging and emergency departments are adjacent, rooms used for urgent or emergency imaging examinations may be located within the imaging department and prioritized or even dedicated to emergency patients. An advantage of providing emergency imaging functions within the imaging department is that imaging staff do not need to leave the department and can perform other imaging functions when dedicated imaging rooms are not used for emergency patients.

Conversely, as either workload or the distance between the imaging and emergency departments increases, it may be more appropriate to locate imaging functions within the ED (Figure 15–1). There are advantages

Figure 15-1 Dedicated imaging in the emergency department. Courtesy of Anshen + Allen, Architects.

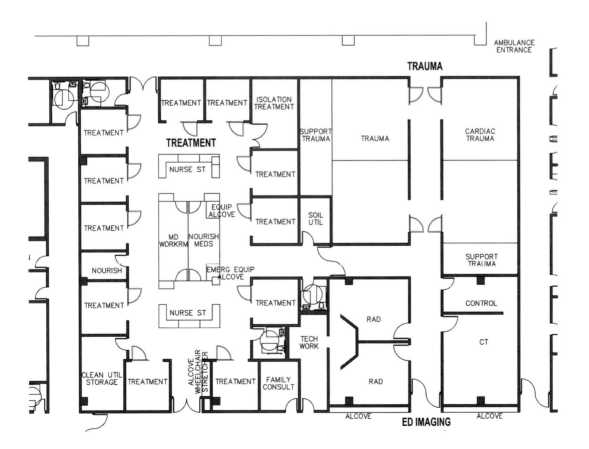

to providing imaging capabilities within the ED: emergency patients do not need to be transported away from the emergency department, emergency nurses and/or physicians do not need to leave the department to accompany and observe these patients, and scheduled nonemergency imaging exams in the radiology department are less likely to be canceled due to equipment in the radiology department being usurped for emergency needs. Patient transfers are associated with a several fold increase in medical errors and adverse outcomes, especially with sick patients.

A disadvantage to providing dedicated imaging equipment in the ED is that imaging staff may need to be either stationed in the ED or at least be on call and immediately available. This can be inefficient for radiology staff if the demand for emergency imaging is infrequent.

Imaging modalities commonly used for urgent and emergency patients include radiography, CT, ultrasound, angiography, and sometimes MRI. Many imaging needs can be accommodated in a general radiography room. This room can be used for emergency orthopedic patients and others requiring a variety of radiographic examinations who can either walk to or be wheeled from their exam room into the X-ray room. One rule of thumb suggests allocating one conventional X-ray room for every 20,000 to 25,000 annual visits, or one digital (cassetteless direct radiographic (DR)) X-ray room for every 30,000 annual visits.[2] This rule assumes that DR systems accommodate more patients than do conventional film-screen systems (see chapter 6, "Imaging Techniques").

For some trauma patients transport is inappropriate, even for a short distance. Therefore, EDs with a heavy trauma load often utilize a combina-

Figure 15-2 Imaging in multiple trauma bays—plan view.

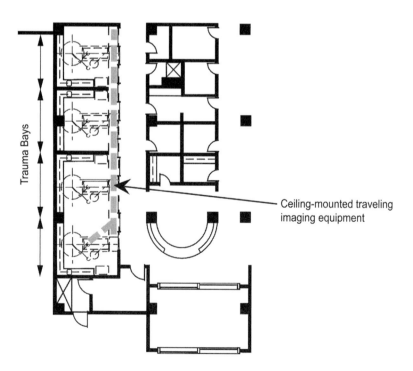

Ceiling-mounted traveling imaging equipment

tion of portable devices and fixed radiographic equipment specially de-signed for trauma rooms. This equipment can be used in single or multiple trauma bays. Some equipment vendors enable a series of trauma bays to be arranged in a row, with a single overhead, ceiling–mounted radiographic imaging tube that can be used within each bay (figures 15–2 and 15–3). Generally, special radiation protection is required above, below, and at the sides, including the corridor opening. OB/GYN exam rooms should not be located adjacent to X–ray equipment because of the potentially damaging effect of radiation on the fetus. Other types of trauma and emergency im-aging equipment are available for individual trauma bays. Radiation pro-tection requirements (which vary from state to state and by country) should be determined by a certified medical or health physicist for both fixed and portable X–ray equipment.

Many busy EDs have their own CT scanners, while other EDs utilize a CT unit located in the imaging department that is immediately accessible from the ED. Emergency departments benefit from a location that is adja-cent to diagnostic radiology so that patients have immediate access to CT scan facilities with only minimal movement. This enables patients requir-ing resuscitation timely CT access while the scanner remains functionally a part of diagnostic radiology for routine studies. Multidetector CT scanners provide remarkable images very quickly and are therefore extremely valu-able for evaluating both urgent and emergency patients, especially cardiac, stroke, and trauma patients. For example, if a patient presents in the ED with an acute stroke, a baseline CT can help determine if the stroke is due to a clot or a ruptured aneurysm. This, in turn, affects the treatment course.

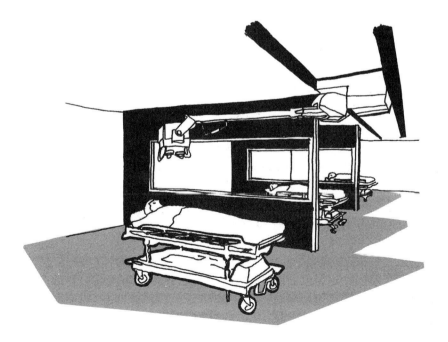

Figure 15-3 Imaging in multiple trauma bays—perspective view.

A clot would be treated medically, while an aneurysm might require endovascular placement of a stent and coils.[5]

Although an average annual volume of 30,000 emergency visits has historically been considered by many to be the minimum to justify a dedicated emergency CT scanner, the value of CT in the ED has grown in recent years. CT has become the workhorse for intra–abdominal and intracranial evaluation and is more commonly found in many of today's emergency departments than it was only a few years ago. The use of CT in the ED is expected to grow, eliminating many outdated types of examinations.

Advantages of CT include imaging speed, contrast resolution, and sensitivity, especially when imaging solid organs and certain intra–abdominal injuries. Disadvantages include the high cost of CT (and the associated desire to have expensive imaging equipment fully utilized), the lengthiness of involved studies (different from imaging speed), and the reality that unstable trauma patients should not be transported.[4]

Some EDs (and ICUs) have attempted to use portable CT scanners. However, the difficulty of transporting such equipment combined with its inferior imaging capabilities (as compared to fixed CT scanners) has led to only limited success. (Portable CT is also discussed later in this chapter, under the heading "Imaging in the Intensive Care Unit.")

Aggressive treatment within the first hour of trauma often makes the difference between survival and death. These procedures are often performed by multidisciplinary teams of emergency physicians, trauma surgeons, radiologists, and anesthesiologists.[5] Emergency access to an adjacent or nearby cardiac catheterization lab, angiography suite, and/or a computed tomography suite is key for the evaluation (and potential treatment) of critical patients, such as those with unstable coronary artery disease. Of these three modalities, computed tomography angiography is the least invasive. Often patients present to the ED with chest pain of unknown origin. Rapid evaluation of these patients is instrumental in accurately diagnosing and treating the cause of their chest pain. For example, at some hospitals, patients presenting with atypical chest pain (that is not an obvious and immediate clinical danger) are evaluated by CTA, which allows better evaluation of the patient's condition and provides for better-informed treatment decisions, such as immediate transfer to the cath lab versus further noninvasive testing.[6]

Some hospitals are closely aligning their EDs with their cath labs so as to be able to quickly perform primary angioplasty, or the invasive opening of cardiac blood vessels via catheters in lieu of anticlotting drug administration. For example, at Centra Health in Virginia, "if patients presenting with chest pain are evaluated by an ED doctor, and if a heart attack is diagnosed, the patient is whisked to the cath lab for angioplasty."[7]

Ultrasound is a valuable tool in emergency medicine. It is used both alone and in conjunction with other imaging techniques. Advantages of ultrasound include speed, lack of exposure to ionizing radiation, ability to identify freely floating fluid (such as blood in the abdominal cavity due to blunt or penetrating trauma), relative low cost, portability, ease of operation, and ability to be utilized at the patient's bedside, thereby reducing the need to transport the patient. Ultrasound machines come in a variety of types and sizes, and new uses of ultrasound for emergency patients emerge continuously.

Once the patient's airway, breathing, and circulatory systems have been assessed, the next priority is often to determine if surgery (or another form of invasive therapy) is required. The detection of fluid (such as blood) in the pericardial sac or peritoneal cavity is often an indicator that immediate surgical intervention is necessary. An ultrasound technique known as focused assessment with sonography for trauma (FAST) has become an initial screening process of choice in many emergency departments.[8]

While CT remains the gold standard for rapidly evaluating damage to solid organs and some intra-abdominal injuries, transport to a CT scanner requires that a patient be hemodynamically stable.[9] In comparison, FAST screening can be done at the bedside. In addition, a FAST scan is less expensive than CT. Finally, CT often requires the administration of oral or intravenous contrast material, which may result in aspiration, renal failure, or an allergic reaction.[10] Repeated serial FAST scans can be useful in detecting changes in the amount of fluid that may be accumulating. Disadvantages of FAST include potential inability to distinguish between blood and other fluids, loss of image quality in patients who are obese and those with subcutaneous emphysema, varying image quality based on equipment age, and inferior image quality with small handheld ultrasound devices compared to larger mobile units.[11]

MRI scans of emergency patients are sometimes used for the evaluation of musculoskeletal injuries, to assess stroke, and patients with other neurological complications. Because of potential dangers of placing MRI units in an ED (flying objects, patients with metallic implants, pacemakers, etc.), MRI equipment is not often found within the ED. However, MRI use for emergency patients will likely increase in the future. In general, MRI is better than CT for imaging soft tissue, the central nervous system, and the male and female pelvis. Often MRI is the preferred first line of study for new-onset seizures and for evaluation of stroke. MRI is also preferred for imaging ligamentous injuries of the knee in orthopedic workups when plain films are negative for fractures. Alternatively, CT is preferred for the evaluation of occult, minor, and complex fractures that are not easily seen on radiographs.

Although the cost of MRI as an emergency evaluation tool has been debated, at least one Scandinavian study identifies potential cost savings associated with MRI evaluation of suspected wrist fractures.[12] The study claims MRI's improved visualization compared to X-ray has enabled caregivers to accurately rule out fractures, thus avoiding the cost of treating uncertain diagnosis where no fracture actually exists.

Figure 15-4 Specialized CT equipment and patient gurney for imaging of emergency patients.

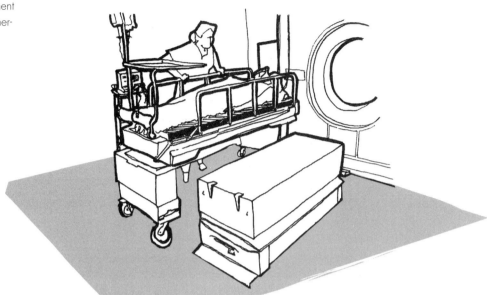

Specially designed gurneys and patient beds are desirable in the ED to minimize the need for patients to be transferred onto the patient table. Radiolucent tables are available for X-ray and CT exams, as are special nonferrous tables that can be used for MRI exams. Some equipment designed for trauma use enables the patient table, which usually is designed as part of the equipment, to be removed and replaced by the ED's own gurney (figure 15–4).

Radiographic rooms in the ED are typically supplemented by portable X-ray units and portable C-arms brought to patients' bedsides when transporting patients to the X-ray unit is inappropriate. Portable X-ray equipment, however, usually does not provide the same image quality as fixed equipment. Most portable X-ray equipment utilizes a removable, reusable phosphor plate that is placed in a plate reader, where the image is scanned; the plate is then erased to be ready for reuse. Facility planning must accommodate both the reader and an alcove or enclosed room where the portable equipment is stored and charged when not in use. Some vendors are developing direct capture portable X-ray units that do not require a plate reader.

Digital radiographic systems are a valuable asset in the ED because images are readily available for viewing by radiologists and emergency physicians simultaneously. One RSNA survey supports the notion that the transition to filmless imaging improves technologist productivity, but also points out that realized benefits of this enhanced productivity can be diminished in an unpredictable ED environment, compared to a more predictable radiography department.[13]

Among the various types of digital radiographic systems available, direct radiography is often preferable over computed radiography for stationary X-ray rooms within the emergency department because DR eliminates the need for the radiology technologist to physically carry a cassette to a plate reader (see chapter 6, "Imaging Techniques"). DR, however, is more expensive than CR. Conversely, CR is more common for portable imaging equipment, as DR detectors are fragile and subject to damage (and replacement expense) if dropped. Many believe that DR systems are more appropriate for areas such as the ED, where patient volumes are high, while CR systems are better suited for areas such as the ICU, where portable imaging is frequently performed.[14] Both CR and DR technologies continue to evolve as the two techniques appear to be converging. Some DR vendors are introducing portable units, and some CR manufacturers are offering cassetteless systems with automated plate handling.[15]

According to Dr. Henrik Thomsen, head of radiology at Copenhagen University Hospital in Herlev, Denmark (where the emergency department transitioned directly from film to DR), DR enables technologist staff to spend more time interacting with patients. Since digital DR images are available for review almost instantaneously, they can be checked by the radiographer in the room. Some radiographers working in EDs with DR imaging technology report a reduced incidence of shoulder and elbow pain compared to when they worked in an analog environment. This is attributed to no longer having to carry heavy film cassettes.[16]

A PACS workstation where soft-copy images can be read should be provided in the ED for use by emergency physicians. A dedicated PACS workstation is not required; one can configure a standard PC into a PACS workstation with the addition of a medical-grade video card and a bright monitor. The advantage of this is that clinicians can use one PC to access all information systems. Although radiologists should be able to read and interpret emergency images rapidly from the imaging department (or elsewhere), emergency physicians will also want immediate access to these images prior to or during consultations with the radiologist. PACS workstations in the ED must be located, configured, and designed to be visually and audibly secure, in keeping with HIPAA regulations.

Teleradiology, which transmits medical images to remote sites, typically over wide area networks (WANs), can be useful in the ED. It enables a sole radiologist to interpret diagnostic images from multiple emergency facilities or to interpret images remotely from his or her home or office. Teleradiology is particularly useful in rural emergency departments where around-the-clock access to a radiologist may not be possible or in any facility where radiologists are in short supply. Using teleradiology, an emergency physician can consult with a remote radiologist to interpret an ED-acquired image or to help determine whether a patient should be transported to a more acute setting. Radiologists in other time zones (such as Australia and India) frequently contract with U.S. hospitals and radiology practices to interpret images when it is nighttime in the United States. This is referred to as a "nighthawk."

In summary, the following should be considered when designing an emergency department with dedicated imaging services either within the department, or located for immediate access within an adjacent imaging department:

- Because various imaging modalities (CT, ultrasound, MR, etc.) are used for evaluating multiple types of patients (urgent, emergent, trauma, etc.) in the ED, imaging equipment should be placed so that it is accessible from all parts of the ED without requiring patients or staff to travel through other high-activity areas.
- Provide direct access between cast rooms and X-ray, and between trauma/resuscitation and CT.
- Some EDs routinely screen many patients with some form of imaging exam as part of the triage process. Locating imaging equipment near triage (perhaps with direct access from triage) can be advantageous. Many EDs have increased their use of CT scans for initial patient evaluation.
- Consider a CT scanner constructed to function as a "doorway" for high-volume EDs so that every severe trauma patient could be scanned on the way into the ED. Information acquired during the scan could be made available to the medical team when the patient arrives in the trauma bay, operating room, or elsewhere.
- If walk-in and ambulance entrances are remote from each other, locate imaging services so that they are easily accessible from each entrance.
- Locate ED imaging services so that both emergency and imaging staff and technologists have convenient access, and in such a way that patients do not require lengthy transport.
- Provide storage alcoves for portable imaging equipment, CR plate readers, and other necessary items. Consider allocating 5–6 percent of total layout space for storage. Remember that some equipment (such as a portable C-arm) is often composed of several components, all of which require storage that does not block the corridor. Be sure alcoves are sized to accommodate all equipment components. Provide electrical receptacles for charging parked portable equipment.
- Emergency imaging rooms should be sized larger than general imaging rooms used for similar procedures, in order to facilitate the rapid, safe transport of patients into the imaging room. Emergency patients are often accompanied by ancillary equipment (i.e., ventilators, infusion pumps, IV poles, etc) and multiple personnel and may need to be transferred to either radiolucent gurneys in the X-ray

examination space or nonferrous gurneys or beds before entering the MR examination space.

- Minimize built-in storage within the imaging room. Movable storage provides greater flexibility for maneuvering patients or accommodating unforeseen circumstances.

- Out-swinging doors should not swing into corridors, to avoid creating a potentially hazardous obstacle for others traveling in the corridor. While dual-leaf doors providing a 6- or 8-foot clear opening improve access into the room, they require special hardware to adequately shield against X-ray transmission. In the future, new materials–which will be lighter and less expensive–will likely provide greater X-ray protection for room shielding.

- Design PACS reading areas for visual and acoustic privacy, thus accommodating HIPAA and other privacy requirements.

- Design PACS reading areas with adjustable ambient light, in order to improve diagnostic capability.

- Identify "soft" or expansion space where additional imaging equipment can be added in the future if volume projections indicate such a need.

- Consider a dedicated trauma elevator in the ED, especially if critical imaging services must be located on another floor.

- When imaging equipment is located in the ED, provide adequate support space, such as chairs in a separate waiting area, gurney holding space, nurse work area, patient toilet, technologist work area, and imaging equipment storage.

- A technology dock (discussed in a later section of this chapter) containing specialized imaging equipment, such as CT or MRI, can be used for some emergency patients if (1) it is located nearby, (2) it is easily accessible, and (3) some provision is made for separating emergency from nonemergency traffic.

Imaging in the Intensive Care Unit

Routine and nonroutine imaging exams in the intensive care unit have a direct impact on the course of patients' care. Similar to the emergency department, rapid and accurate interpretations of these exams made available to caregivers are essential to clinical decision making that often modifies patient management. Prompt radiographic examinations are necessary after certain invasive procedures and for monitoring periodic changes in patients' physiologic status.

In the ICU, imaging is complicated by the fact that most patients cannot be easily moved; their physiologic functions (such as respiration) are compromised; physiologic monitoring devices and associated lines, wires, and catheters obstruct image acquisition; and most patient rooms do not easily accommodate the necessary cadre of people and imaging equipment.

Imaging modalities most useful in the ICU include radiography, fluoroscopy, angiography, CT, ultrasound, and sometimes MRI. X-ray equipment is useful for thoracic and abdominal imaging, especially chest X-rays, which are routinely acquired in the ICU. While portable C-arms are used frequently to verify the placement and position of catheters, tubes, and artificial valves, a catheterization lab or angiography room often provides better visualization for those patients who can be moved. Rapid access to a cath lab is also beneficial when invasive procedures must be performed, such as inserting catheters or pacemakers and verifying their placement; however, direct access to such a room is not always possible.

Some MRI vendors are developing MR-compatible isolettes to enable premature infants in the neonatal intensive care unit (NICU) to undergo MRI examinations. Such devices enable a fragile newborn to be transferred to the MR suite and be imaged while being carefully monitored throughout the examination. Ample storage space is required in the NICU to park the MR-compatible isolettes when they are not in use.

CT is useful for a variety of exams in the ICU, including pulmonary angiography for the evaluation of pulmonary emboli. Multidetector computed tomography is particularly helpful in imaging patients with compromised respiratory function, because acquisition times can be very quick (for example, 30 seconds for the entire thorax).

Various forms of ultrasound, including echocardiography, are valuable imaging tools for assessing both anatomy and physiology such as blood flow. Miniature, portable, and handheld ultrasound devices are both affordable and easily available in the ICU. In particular, compact, battery-operated laptop handheld echocardiography (HHE) machines may facilitate bedside assessment whenever a patient's condition abruptly deteriorates.[17] In addition to the diagnostic value of ultrasound, an emerging therapeutic technique known as focused ultrasound can be performed even with portable devices.[18] (Focused ultrasound is described later in this chapter, in the section "Imaging and Cardiology.")

While HHE is more commonly used in outpatient clinics and coronary care units, one study examined the effectiveness of HHE for mechanically ventilated patients in the general ICU, where bedside echocardiography can be more challenging.[19] Compared to conventional transthoracic echocardiography (TTE), HHE can be performed more rapidly. While HHE cannot provide the comprehensive assessment that TTE does, "the versatility and ease of use of this small portable device constitutes a definite advantage in the settings of crowded ICUs and emergency rooms. . . . [At] its present stage of development HHE may be considered a screening modality that extends the clinical evaluation of ventilated patients at beside, but should not be considered an alternative to conventional echocardiography, especially in hemodynamically unstable patients."[20]

Handheld ultrasound is also an asset in the NICU, where it is used to rapidly perform hour-by-hour assessments, essential to evaluating the quickly changing status of neonates. Prior to the availability of easy-to-use handheld ultrasound, conventional ultrasound equipment–or experienced technologists to operate it–was frequently unavailable, especially at night or on the weekend.[21]

Decisions regarding portable versus stationary imaging equipment in the ICU must weigh the need to frequently image patients who cannot be transported safely against the quality and cost of various types of bedside imaging. While the quality of most portably acquired images has significantly improved in recent years, it is still inferior to the quality of images acquired from fixed equipment. Yet it is often difficult to justify providing a fixed image acquisition room in or near the ICU unless several ICUs are co-located in close proximity, thus increasing image volumes and justifying the investment.

As with emergency medicine, some patients can be transported to stationary imaging rooms, but for many critically ill patients imaging equipment must be brought to them. A combination of portable imaging devices and larger patient rooms has enabled new types of bedside imaging to take place.

Portable X-ray equipment used in the ICU is similar to that used in surgery, except that the imaging tube used in the ICU tends to be smaller. As in the ED, space should be provided on the unit for portable C-arm storage (and associated equipment components, such as the control console and charger), and patient rooms should be sized and configured to accommodate portable imaging devices. Space is also needed for plate readers where computed radiography is utilized.

A few hospitals have experimented with portable CT scanners brought to the ICU (and the ED) in lieu of transporting critically ill patients to the radiology department. As with portable CT in the ED, it has not proven extremely effective, due primarily to the difficulty of transporting the equipment and its less than ideal image quality. In some cases, the portable scanner is transported to a special procedure room within the intensive care unit where the exam is performed. In other scenarios, CT scans are actually performed at the bedside within the patient room. While the cost of a portable CT examination is higher than a stationary CT scanner, some patients simply cannot be moved safely to a fixed unit. One study concluded, "If a medically stable patient . . . that does not require nurse monitoring is imaged, the transportable scanner probably would not be cost-effective. Conversely, if the patient . . . is very ill such that leaving the ICU would place them at great medical risk, the transportable scanner will be medically and economically more valuable."[22] Another study found that portable CT (PCT) "performed within an ICU assures optimal treatment of patients during a CT examination. Portable CT had more time exposure and required more personnel resources than examination in the IS [interventional suite]. All

PCT examinations performed directly in the patient's room demonstrated the diagnostic value and had direct therapeutic consequences."[23] Inpatient CT scanners that are located close to ICUs and other inpatient units are another way to minimize patient transport.

The ICU (like the ED) is an area that benefits from an enterprise-wide digital image and information management system. Compared to other parts of the hospital, the ICU typically experiences the greatest number of images that must be reacquired due to poor image exposure or patient positioning. It is where film images are likely to become lost and where lost films have an enormous detrimental impact on patient outcomes. It is also where intensivists cannot wait long for radiologist image interpretations without compromising patient care. Digital image management enables ICU physicians to view images both immediately and concurrently with radiologists, while simultaneously discussing their findings with allied caregivers.

While modalities such as CT and ultrasound are inherently digitally based, plain film radiography (general X-ray) is often the last modality to go to digital acquisition at many facilities. Yet general radiography is one of the most commonly used imaging modalities in the ICU, and digitally acquired X-rays (especially chest X-rays) rarely need to be retaken (due to their wide exposure latitude), are not easily lost, and typically result in lower radiation exposure to the patient compared to analog systems.

Digital radiography is typically in the form of either computed radiography, which utilizes a reusable phosphor imaging plate that must be uploaded in a plate reader, or direct radiography, which bypasses the plate reader and directly loads the acquired image into the PACS (see chapter 6, "Imaging Techniques"). While DR systems enable more efficient work flow and are often preferable for fixed imaging equipment, their availability is limited for portable imaging systems. DR equipment is also more expensive than CR equipment.

CR and DR imaging systems in the ICU can lead to improved staff efficiency and patient management, as well as better communications among diverse caregivers. According to Lt. Cmdr. Tim Duncan, MD, staff radiologist and PACS director at the Naval Medical Center in San Diego:

> The radiologists are much more efficient in reading as a result of CR. The ICU clinicians have the ability to pick up the phone and talk to the radiologist while everyone has the same set of images in front of them.[24]

The system allows for correction of marginal-quality images, resulting in fewer retakes and faster treatment decisions. The Naval Medical Center also found that CR eliminated many problems associated with lost films and improved staff efficiency, as technologists no longer had to constantly carry their plain film X-ray back and forth between the ICU and the radiology department for processing.[25]

Figure 15-5 Remote patient monitoring in the eICU®. Photo courtesy of INOVA Health System © 2005.

In addition, with CR or DR systems, support staff are no longer needed to hang films or physically archive films. This is accomplished through standard PACS/RIS protocol. Although some support personnel may be able to be eliminated or reassigned to more productive assignments, new specialized staff with information technology (IT) skills are needed. In addition to the quantifiable benefits of digital radiography in the ICU are the less tangible benefits of improved patient care.[26]

PACS workstations (or PACS-capable PCs) should be provided within the ICU. Configurations with two monitors are usually preferable—one for viewing the most recent image and the other for viewing the image immediately preceding the most recent image, so that the two can be compared. The workstation area should be large enough to enable a small group of physicians to discuss the images and should be located away from patient rooms and public traffic to keep conversations from being overheard. Controlled lighting should be provided to avoid glare on the monitors, and the monitors should be located in such a way that the operator does not need to frequently move his or her head to view the images.

Similar to the way PACS enables remote interpretation of digitally acquired medical images, some ICUs are beginning to be designed for remote patient observation, monitoring, and medical consultation as part of a trademarked concept known as the Electronic Intensive Care Unit (eICU®) (figure 15-5), sometimes generically referred to as remote ICU monitoring. The eICU® model is an effort to compensate for the shortage of available intensivists (physicians who specialize in critical care medicine). Intended to supplement, not replace, on-site critical care nurses and doctors, the eICU® electronically links several ICUs to a remote data/observation center where specialists can make "virtual house calls," conferring with both patients and their providers while having full visual access to each as well as digital access to medical images, tests, and physiologic monitoring devices.

According to Molly Joel Coye, MD, MPH, CEO of the Health Technology Center, "The electronic ICU . . . is the cutting edge of technologies that will increasingly distribute just-in-time medical consultation to almost any care setting. . . . It can speed throughput and reduce errors, complications and deaths. . . . [The] technology is already being carried beyond the ICU onto medical-surgical floors and into emergency departments by a mobile unit that includes monitor inputs and two-way visual and verbal communication. In some respects, this follows the pattern that some early adopters of PACS have developed, with regional and even more distant redistribution of imaging acquisition and reading."[27]

In addition, some mobile robots—such as those developed by InTouch Health—enable physicians to make virtual rounds on medical/surgical as well as intensive care nursing units. Such devices combined with enterprise-wide advanced information systems provide myriad types of medical information at the bedside as well as at the procedure table.

While new forms of advanced bedside imaging bring extended capabilities to the critical care team, many caregivers cannot take advantage of these extraordinary tools because ICU patient rooms are often too small, poorly configured, or both. It is not unusual for an older ICU room to be 200 net square feet in size or smaller. However, many new—and newly renovated—ICU patient rooms are designed at 260 to 320 NSF in size; in rare cases, they are as large as 400 NSF.[28] New ICU rooms are often zoned with distinct caregiver, patient, and family zones to facilitate both the delivery of critical care medicine and patient and family convenience (figure 15-6). Enlarged ICU room size reflects sensitivity to accommodating bedside testing and bedside imaging, as well as an emphasis on patient and family amenities.[29] It also represents a significant construction cost increase. New ICU rooms are often zoned with distinct caregiver, patient, and family zones to facilitate both the delivery of critical care medicine and patient and family convenience.

Typically, the caregiver zone is closest to the corridor, is accessed through sliding glass breakaway doors, and is sized and configured to enable myriad portable imaging devices—and their associated personnel—to acquire medical images of the bedridden patient. Supplies, data entry devices, and hand-washing fixtures may occupy the caregiver zone of the room, in addition to portable imaging equipment.

The type and variety of patients treated in any given patient room affect the type of imaging equipment that may be brought in. In some hospitals, intensive care units are organized by disease type—such as cardiac, oncology, or pediatric ICUs—where both medical and surgical patients may be treated. In other facilities, individual ICUs may treat multiple types of patients, and suites are typically segregated into medical and surgical ICUs.

A concept known as the universal bed model minimizes the need for patients to be transferred from an ICU bed to an acute care bed by designing patient rooms (and the entire nursing unit in which they are located) in such a way that the unit can accommodate acute care, transitional care, and

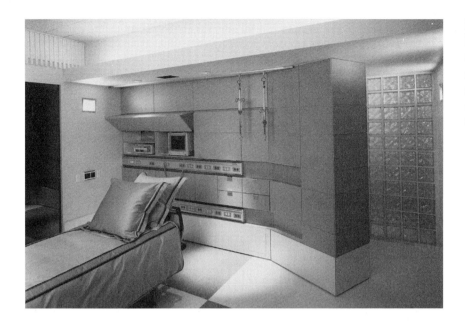

Figure 15-6 As hospitalized patients have become increasingly more acutely ill, patient rooms need be larger and designed for multiple types of bedside care, including advanced imaging studies. © 2005 Farshid Assassi. Designed by Anshen + Allen, Architects with Orlando Diaz Acuny.

intensive care patients. A variation of the universal bed model–sometimes referred to as the acuity–adaptable bed model–attempts to accommodate a smaller range of patient types (such as acute and transitional, or transitional and intensive) to reduce the design and staffing challenges of the one–size-fits-all concept. Similarly, an acuity–convertible room (or suite) could become an acuity–adaptable room (or suite)–and thus cover a broader range of patient acuity–with a minor physical renovation of the space.[30]

While most acute care nursing units are designed with fire–rated corridors and doors, most ICUs are designed in a configuration and with materials and assemblies in such a way that the fire marshal (or other authorities having jurisdiction) consider the unit to be a "suite" in terms of life safety and emergency exiting. Most regulatory agencies are more restrictive regarding the placement of portable imaging equipment, plate readers, and other ancillary devices within rated corridors of acute care nursing units than they are with regard to placing those devices in alcoves off the general circulation routes of special–use suites such as ICUs. In either instance, however, such equipment must not encroach upon the required clear exit path.

Acute care patients are generally able to be transported to image acquisition rooms and so require less bedside imaging than do room–bound intensive care patients. Patient rooms designed with power columns or overhead booms tend to accommodate multiple patient positions (and multiple positions of imaging equipment) more easily than do rooms designed with headwalls. Patient rooms with decentralized nurse/charting stations adjacent to the patient room enable staff to better observe patients, regardless of bed orientation.

On average, almost half of all ICU patients come from the emergency department, and slightly more than one quarter of all ICU patients come from surgery or interventional procedure areas of the hospital. As surgical and interventional procedures continue to become less invasive—and therefore require less postsurgical ICU observation and monitoring—there may be a rebalancing of the surgical and medical ICU patient mix in the future, with the number of surgical patients declining and the number of medical patients increasing. This, in turn, will influence the type and frequency of imaging needs for ICU patients.

In summary, when designing an intensive care unit to accommodate a variety of medical imaging needs, consider the following:

- Provide immediate access to and from the emergency department, surgery, cath lab, and other imaging rooms.
- Size and configure patient rooms to accommodate various portable imaging devices and associated personnel.
- Anticipate a broader array of types of imaging equipment being used at the bedside.
- Plan patient rooms to accommodate more bedside procedures, such as endoscopy and bronchoscopy.
- Design ICU suites and rooms for robust enterprise-wide information technology, including remote monitoring systems.
- Locate PACS workstations on the unit, and provide visual and acoustic screening to help keep patient data and clinical conversations confidential.

Imaging and Surgery

Design of surgical suites capable of incorporating tomorrow's state-of-the art medical imaging systems is one of the most complex design challenges to be found within the healthcare environment. This is due in part to the diversity and intricacy of surgical procedures and the complexity of imaging systems used to support them. In addition to the typical design requirements of general imaging facilities, surgical imaging facility design must also meet the needs of infection control, restricted work flow, and advanced human factors engineering that support increasingly multifaceted interactions among the surgical team, image acquisition equipment, and the images themselves.

Imaging procedures associated with surgery can be divided into two categories: (1) those performed on surgical patients presurgically or postsurgically outside the surgical suite and (2) those performed during surgery within the surgical suite. The primary focus of this section is imaging performed within the sterile field of the surgical suite and, in particular, the implication of these techniques on facility design.

The mutual roles of surgeons and radiologists are rapidly evolving. The relationship between surgery and radiology can at times be described as both cooperative and competitive. As new procedures—such as the placement of stents—further dissolve some of the apparent boundaries between surgery and interventional radiology (as well as interventional cardiology),

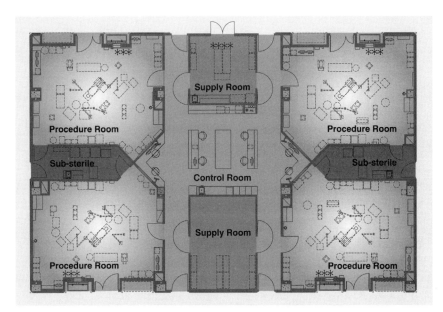

Figure 15-7 Some operating rooms are designed with adjacent control rooms to accommodate the increased use of image guidance in the future. Courtesy of Anshen + Allen, Architects.

OPERATING ROOM WITH ADJACENT CONTROL ROOMS

opportunities for mutual support and understanding among these medical specialties are on the rise. As each subspecialty becomes increasingly complex, the need for multispecialty collaboration and interdepartmental alliances also becomes more urgent.

In addition, new types of personnel are becoming common in the collaborative surgical imaging environment. For example, as advanced imaging continues to become increasingly dependent on advanced computing power, surgical information technologists are spending more time in the surgical suite. Similarly, as many surgical procedures become more reliant on image guidance, surgical imaging technologists (similar to MR or CT techs in the diagnostic imaging department) are needed to run advanced image acquisition and transmission systems. Some new operating room designs provide imaging control rooms to facilitate surgical image guidance and to better accommodate surgical imaging technologists and surgical information technologists (figure 15-7). Guidance devices may use previously acquired data to localize the disease process, but in the future they will increasingly provide reregistration of patient anatomy and confirmation of the success of the procedure. This means that the advanced surgical suite will contain not only the image guidance systems but also the ability to acquire new CT or MR data as the procedure progresses.

While many surgical procedures are performed with the assistance of robotic devices, instrument handling in the OR can also benefit from robotic assistance, also known as computer–assisted surgery (CAS). In the distant future it is likely that some surgical personnel such as scrub nurses may be assisted, or even replaced by robotic or automated material handling systems, such as the surgical scrub robot–a pick–and–place robotic system based on automated systems found in nonmedical professions, such as automotive assembly lines.[31] For example, a voice-controlled Surgical Instrument Server (known as Penelope) assisted in its first surgical case in 2005 at New York's Columbia–Presbyterian Hospital. "The one-armed Penelope can automatically grab surgical instruments when called for ('scalpel please!') and then pick it up and put it back when it's no longer in use, while at the same time keeping track of everything that's used in order to make sure that nothing is accidentally left behind."[32]

The impact of robotics in surgery affects the architectural design of operating rooms and other procedure rooms where robotic devices may be used. The size of robots requires that additional floor space be allocated to the OR, and their utility requirements introduce yet another set of cables and cords that must be accounted for. Conversely, the potential replacement of some scrub personnel by robotic devices could reduce the amount of space required in the OR. Coordination of the location and movements of both surgical assist devices and surgical imaging devices will become more complex as the technology continues to advance.

The popularity and efficacy of many medical imaging techniques used in surgery are in constant flux, due in part to the continuous development of new medical imaging technologies. As a result, the facility requirements for surgical imaging change rapidly and frequently. The pace of change for surgical procedures seems instantaneous compared to the long duration between facility design and occupancy. Therefore, specific design solutions for surgical imaging must accommodate near-term imaging technology, while more general long-range design strategies anticipate the eventual impact of future imaging developments. The imaging needs of today and the near future can be accommodated in the specific details of operating room configuration and layout, coordination of fixed and movable equipment, coordination of ceiling-mounted devices, and the provision of electrical power, data, air-handling, and cooling services. The longer-range design drivers of surgical imaging–such as the convergence of minimally invasive surgery and interventional radiology–can be accommodated by robust infrastructure capacities and by anticipating how work flow will change in the future. Various forms of medical imaging in the operating room–radiography, fluoroscopy, ultrasound, and more recently CT, MRI, and even PET–may be installed with fixed and portable units alike. These imaging modalities are integral to many surgical procedures and in some instances help reduce the invasiveness of surgery by providing better visualization, real-time image guidance, and more accurate localization. Furthermore, the coordination of presurgical and postsurgical images with surgical procedures links surgery to other forms of medical imaging–such as those used in cardiology, oncology, and orthopedics–that take place outside the operating room.

Minimally Invasive Surgery and Image-Guided Surgery
Numerous surgical procedures are performed as minimally invasive surgery (MIS), an approach that has revolutionized surgery in recent decades.

Image-guided surgery (IGS) systems—a common companion to MIS during neurosurgery, and becoming more common in other types of surgery—integrate preoperative and intraoperative images with tracking technology that correlates surgeons' movements, thus enabling them to observe their real-time location and orientation. This ultimately shortens procedure times and improves surgical outcomes.[33]

MIS uses video-based imaging technology and small incision port access for instruments, instead of larger open incisions. During MIS, one or several small incisions are made. A cavity for better visualization is created by insufflating the abdomen, performing single lung ventilation in chest surgery, or infusing saline for joint arthroscopy. Ports are used to introduce specialized instruments that carry out complex procedures including suture, ablation, tumor resection, and almost any other procedure that can be accomplished with traditional open surgery. MIS procedures are considerably less invasive than conventional surgery and require less patient recovery time.

One significant difference between conventional surgery and MIS is that in conventional surgery anatomy is viewed directly, while in minimally invasive procedures the surgeon typically views anatomy indirectly through a video system by observing images displayed on a monitor or other display device. Thus the design of MIS procedure rooms is driven by unique ergonomic and lighting constraints. Various imaging modalities, such as ultrasound, may be used in conjunction with MIS, further increasing the use of monitors to visualize anatomy.

Since the early introduction of MIS, surgical procedures have evolved to rely more heavily on the use of indirect observation of the procedure via optical visualization combined with other forms of medical imaging. In addition, four-dimensional (3-D with motion) and even five-dimensional (4-D with metabolic data) images require that surgeons, interventionalists, and radiologists interact more rigorously with medical images than they did with static films affixed to light boxes. As a result, design requirements for bringing images into the OR are more complex than they were in a film environment. Yet while many surgical imaging procedures benefit from their integration into enterprise-wide picture archiving and communication systems, the surgical suite is sometimes the last area to become connected to the PACS network.

Operating room design needs to accommodate various forms of image reconstruction to help orient the surgeon.[34] The placement of monitors displaying medical images in the OR is influenced by the type of surgical procedure being performed, who is using the images, and the types of images being displayed. The most up-to-date suites are now being designed with video routing equipment that can be controlled from within the sterile field by the surgeon. The surgeon has access to any medical data being created in the room during the procedure as well as the ability to access data from electronic medical records, from the PACS, or even remotely from outside the facility. During some surgeries,

[s]urgeons view various types of information, such as electronic medical records, laparoscopic images, radiology data and pathology data. There is also an increasing trend toward image-guided surgery (IGS). As a result, ORs must implement a system for viewing images that allows surgeons to be able to switch from multiple sources of images. . . . For example, a surgeon may ask that an image from the PACS workstation be displayed on a screen to the left of the OR table and the images from the endoscope be displayed to the right.[35]

Some surgeons may prefer images to be displayed during every case, and may have specially trained circulating nurses or operating room technicians manipulate the images.[36] Other surgeons prefer to access the images themselves while in the sterile field, and thus require wireless or voice-controlled access to the images.

The primary user, the surgeon, is typically scrubbed and not in a position to use a keyboard or mouse. Therefore, either more people need to be involved in the process of selection or manipulation of images, such as a circulating nurse, or hands-free tools, such as foot pedals or speech recognition, need to be employed.[37]

Access to PACS images and other data within the sterile field is provided in a number of ways, and some approaches appear to be more successful than others. For example, some surgical suites utilize cart-mounted monitors—sometimes referred to as COWs (computers on wheels)—while others incorporate wall-mounted displays. Computer carts, however, can result in a plethora of interconnecting wires and cables, posing a safety hazard, and can be a source of bacteria and other contaminants brought into the sterile field. While wireless computer systems reduce the number of cables needed, they do not eliminate them entirely. Alternatively, wall-mounted displays (either surface-mounted or on articulating arms), while eliminating many of the cables, are inflexible and cannot be as easily moved. In addition, they must also be large enough to be viewed from a distance. A third and preferable alternative—displays on ceiling-mounted booms with articulating arms—are easily movable and do not require distance viewing. However, they may conflict with the movement of other ceiling-mounted devices, such as surgical lights, anesthesia equipment, and radiation shields, unless the path of travel of each device in the room is carefully coordinated. In addition, fixed boom locations that are ideal for one type of procedure may not work well for other procedure types. Thus the placement of ceiling booms is challenging for universal ORs intended to accommodate any type of surgical procedure. Proper location of boom mounts is essential for this reason. While no solution is ideal, the preferred approach for most ORs is ceiling-mounted towers on flexible booms. The type and size of the OR will determine the number of booms (typically two or three) and their location.

Often, a pair of ceiling-mounted flat-panel monitors provides surgeons with a view of what is visualized through the laparoscope. Some surgeons

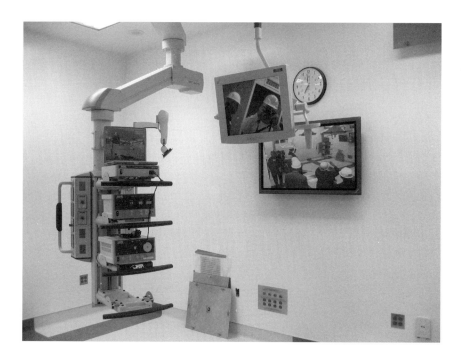

Figure 15-8 Minimally-invasive OR with ceiling-mounted and wall-mounted flat-panel displays.

wear special headsets or goggles that project a view into their visual field, and some institutions are experimenting with virtual–reality, and augmented–reality (where images are projected onto the patient) to provide image guidance. One manufacturer's approach to augmented reality, which is still in the research and development stage, uses a headset that superimposes prerecorded ultrasound, MR, or CT images on real-time video images that approximate the surgeon's field of view. These combined images are then virtually registered with tracking markers placed on the patient. The resulting augmented–reality image is projected onto miniature screens placed directly in from of the surgeon's eyes. This device gives surgeons two simultaneous views of the patient. One is the actual view of the patient's surface; the other is a virtual view of what exists below the visible surface.[38]

> [This] should mean less–invasive procedures that are faster, more ac-
> curate, and require less medication. Such claims have already at-
> tracted the attention of neurosurgeons, interventional radiologists
> and orthopedic surgeons, many of whom have already signed up to
> test the device in clinical trials.[39]

In addition to various image display devices, a wide–screen, flat-panel monitor affixed to one wall of the OR (mounted at eye level for standing individuals) can help orient the entire surgical team through various forms of image guidance (figure 15–8). While it is architecturally desirable to design one universal operating room that accommodates multiple types of surgical procedures, various types of surgical procedures–neurosurgery, trauma, cardiac surgery, and so on–may each suggest a different array and quantity of monitors in the OR.

With respect to flat-panel displays, LCD displays tend to provide a sharper image than do plasma screens, can be viewed more easily from an angle, and are less susceptible to glare. In addition, images on LCD displays are less likely to become burned in (compared to those on plasma screens) in the OR, where one image may be displayed for a long duration.[40]

Since the surgical team is performing arduous, slow, and delicate manipulative procedures while indirectly viewing their actions via an array of monitors, proper ergonomic and human factors design is essential for comfort and safety. In addition, lighting design requirements for the OR are complex and often contradictory. For example, lighting must be dimmable where images are projected on monitors, yet other surfaces in the OR–such as the surgical site–must be highly illuminated. Ambient lighting in the operating room cannot be too dim because ample lighting is needed for the various activities taking place, such as the circulation of nurses and the movement of equipment and supplies.

Some facilities, such as the UCLA Center for Health Sciences–Westwood Hospital and McGill University Health Centre–Montreal General Hospital, incorporate green theatrical gels over individually switched ceiling lights.[41] The green illumination–similar to the lighting in submarines and air-traffic-control rooms–apparently enables images on flat-panel monitors to be seen better and with less glare and eye fatigue than would be the case with whiter light, while maintaining a relatively high ambient light level throughout the OR. This design feature may be particularly beneficial in reducing fatigue induced medical errors.

Ultrasound-Guided Surgery

Ultrasound guidance is commonly incorporated into a variety of surgical procedures. Real-time ultrasound guidance is common for localizing tumors during cranial and spinal neurosurgery, for evaluating anatomy and metabolic activity of the heart, and for visualizing obstructions (such as stones) during surgical procedures of the kidneys, liver, and pancreas.

Ultrasound was once restricted to neonatal intracranial surgery because the incompletely closed skull of the infant easily accommodates the insertion of ultrasound probes, which formerly were larger than those now available. But today, miniature ultrasound probes are commonly used in adult brain surgery as well to assist the surgeon in localizing intracranial tumors and providing safe, nonradioactive guidance beneath the brain's surface.

In addition to its diagnostic value, ultrasound can be used as a form of therapy. High-intensity focused ultrasound (HIFUS, or sometimes FUS) concentrates ultrasonic frequencies to create heat. An ultrasound transducer produces focused acoustic energy that passes through the skin and heats targeted tumors, causing cell death. The focused sound wave is relatively harmless everywhere except at its focal point, though it is important that the focal point avoid any nerves.[42] Among other applications, focused

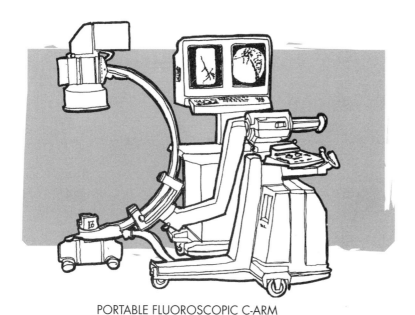

PORTABLE FLUOROSCOPIC C-ARM

ultrasound is used to treat uterine fibroids, brain tumors, and breast tumors, with MR guidance to determine a safe trajectory and to monitor heat deposition. Pioneering radiologist Dr. Ferenc Jolesz and his colleagues at Brigham and Women's Hospital in Boston have developed innovative applications of MRI–guided cryoablative therapies and MRI–guided focused ultrasound technology built into the MRI scanner table. Under MR guidance, focused ultrasound is used to target lesions and thermally ablate them percutaneously (through the skin). In some instances, FUS is used to ablate brain tumors. Gene therapy medications can be systematically applied prior to FUS treatment in order to improve its impact.[45]

New uses for ultrasound in the OR are continuously emerging. However, the facility requirements associated with intraoperative ultrasound are relatively few and simple compared to other imaging modalities. Lighting levels in the OR should be designed to facilitate easy viewing of ultrasound monitors without causing glare on the screen and without compromising the light quality required for surgery. Additionally, space should be allocated for storage of portable ultrasound equipment.

Intraoperative Radiography and Fluoroscopy

Radiography/fluoroscopy is useful in a variety of surgical procedures. Portable equipment such as a mobile C–arm (figure 15-9) is frequently employed, and provides greater flexibility than does fixed equipment. Built–in ceiling–mounted imaging equipment was more popular when the image quality of portable equipment was less satisfactory than it is today.

Some facilities selectively equip operating rooms with built–in X–ray equipment, including angiographic patient tables. These rooms can be used by surgeons, cardiologists, and interventional radiologists for a variety of procedures, including vascular, cardiothoracic, open surgical, percutaneous,

Figure 15-10 Ceiling-mounted radiation protection in the OR.

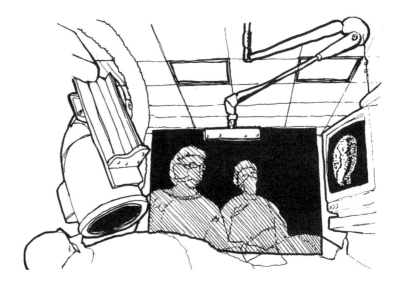

and combined procedures.[44] The integration of high-end angiographic imaging equipment within the OR provides real-time tabletop image guidance for surgical assessment. However, typical angiographic systems have user interface designs that are not ideal for use within the operating room, due to various physical limitations. As one study notes:

> Limited patient accessibility was observed, sometimes leading to uncomfortable positions for the operating physicians. Patient transfer [onto the angiographic table] was considered inadequate. Cleaning of the system was rated as poor.[45]

Where fixed radiographic equipment is provided, it should be installed in such a way that it does not interfere with ceiling-mounted surgical equipment and enables the imaging tube to be moved away from the center of the room when not in use. Additionally, it must be able to be easily cleaned and serviced. However, advances in portable X-ray equipment design have resulted in portable X-ray images that now approach the quality of those produced by fixed equipment. Because of the complex nature of the operating room environment and the need for an OR to accommodate changing daily functional requirements, portable equipment is more desirable than fixed equipment if adequate image quality can be achieved.

Surgical staff must be protected from both direct radiation exposure and scatter radiation. While adequate protection can be provided by wheeled or ceiling-mounted radiation shielding, these devices are cumbersome and frequently impair access to the sterile field. In addition, both ceiling-mounted shields (figure 15-10) and those that roll on wheels require space and have the potential to interfere with the movement of other essential equipment. In addition to fixed and mobile radiation protection barriers, most surgeons wear personal protective gear, including lead aprons, thyroid shields, and glasses, during procedures that generate radiation exposure.

Regardless of whether imaging equipment is fixed or portable–and even though some portable equipment may emit only low levels of radiation and contain integral radiation protective construction–radiation protection requirements should be determined by a certified medical or health physicist. (See the section "Radiation Protection" in chapter 13, "Physical Properties Influencing Design.") In some states, lead–lined (or equally protected) wall, floor, and ceiling surfaces and glazing are required by code in ORs that are likely to incorporate radiographic imaging. Radiation protection is especially important when pregnant women occupy adjacent areas.

Space should be provided for storage of portable X–ray equipment and ancillary devices, such as plate readers (when removable cassette systems are used). In addition, space should be provided for movable carts that may be used for transporting ancillary imaging devices and monitors. Circulation of radiography–related equipment, supplies, and people must be planned in conformance with the special clean and soiled circulation restrictions of the surgical suite.

Accessories such as overhead monitors, apron racks, and other devices must be incorporated into the OR layout without interfering with the many surgical devices that also are necessary. Often, the specific location of these items is determined by personal preference and is related to the specialized traffic in the OR and the ability to thoroughly clean the surgical suite.

Cystoscopy and Endoscopy Procedures

Cystoscopy and endoscopy procedure rooms, while physically part of the surgical suite, are often located off their own corridor and configured as a discrete area within surgery. In addition to various surgical procedures, a number of diagnostic procedures may take place in these rooms. Many are performed on an outpatient basis. For example, cystography is an X–ray technique used to detect abnormalities in the bladder by injecting contrast material via a catheter into the urinary tract.

In addition to the use of cystoscopes (small tubelike optical instruments used to visualize the interior of the bladder), X–ray images also may be obtained. The cysto room usually contains special imaging equipment that may be built into the construction of the urology table. The urology table and the cysto room itself require special cleaning capabilities because many procedures involve irrigating the examination site. A work room and X–ray control area should be adjacent to and directly accessible from the cysto room.

MRI-Guided Surgery

Many surgeons and radiologists are focusing attention on performing surgical procedures under MRI guidance. This concept is sometimes referred to as magnetic resonance therapy (MRT) or intraoperative magnetic resonance therapy (IMRT–not to be confused with intensity–modulated radiation therapy, which uses the same acronym but is a distinctive form of radiation therapy and is discussed under "Imaging and Oncology" later in this chapter).

MRI has a unique ability to distinguish between healthy and abnormal tissue due to its sensitivity to changes in tissue temperature.[46] This attribute is of great value to surgeons removing tumors and conducting procedures such as cryosurgery and other thermal ablations where changing tissue characteristics can be detected with MRI. Studies indicate that up to 80 percent of brain tumors and 30 percent of breast tumors removed by lumpectomies are not completely removed during surgery, and healthy tissue is sometimes cut or damaged because tumor margins are difficult to visualize accurately.[47] Under MRI guidance, however, surgeons can operate more precisely because the tumor's margins are more clearly defined. With intraoperative MR image–guided surgery, "a back and forth rhythm quickly establishes itself between surgery and radiology, between imaging and re-moving and re-imaging the tumor."[48]

The first IMRT suite in the United States was opened in 1994 at Brigham and Women's Hospital in Boston, where other MRI–guided surgical suites have since been installed. The 1994 IMRT suite was initially designed to overcome a number of physical challenges, including:

- Development of a magnet that provided the surgical team with sufficient access to the patient
- Development of a magnet from which either the patient could be quickly removed or the magnetic field could be quickly terminated if the patient required emergency stabilization
- A magnet that could be kept surgically clean
- Development of nonferrous surgical instruments and life support equipment that could be used in an MRI environment (some of these already existed)
- Surgical lights and other accessories that could be used in an MRI environment
- An RF–shielded enclosure that would enable emergency access to the patient if necessary
- Development of a quiet magnet, or apparatus worn by the surgical team to block noise generated by the gradient coils
- Development of video and computer monitors that neither disturb nor are disturbed by the magnetic field

Numerous types of magnets and various facility configurations have been developed for Intraoperative MRT. Each requires unique human factor and team design considerations, and each has its own set of advantages and disadvantages. For example, the second intraoperative MRT installation at Brigham and Women's Hospital aligns three rooms: one containing a 3 T MRI, another containing a PET/CT scanner, and a third–between the other two rooms–containing a surgical theater with fluoroscopy, ultrasound, and optical imaging. This suite, known as the Advanced Multimodality Image-Guided Operating Room (AMIGO), is designed to integrate various imaging modalities within one surgical environment (see Appendix A).[49]

According to Dr. Michael Vannier, professor of radiology at the University of Chicago:

> This type of imaging for surgery [such as AMIGO] touches virtually all the surgical subspecialties, and is an important test ground for the development of other new technologies as well. [Integrating] several imaging modalities enables new procedures that would not otherwise be possible, offering real outcome benefits for the patient. Many other technologies in development have breakthrough potential, and could very easily eclipse the practice as it exists today. The forefront of change is really in image–guided intervention. Those who understand and accommodate these changes will do very well, and those that do not, face a perilous future.[50]

Blurring the Boundaries Between Surgery and Interventional Radiology

In many ways surgical and interventional radiology procedures are becoming similar, as are the spaces in which they take place. Several discrete factors are creating conditions to align surgery and interventional radiology, thus forecasting the need to consider a more collaborative procedural environment.

These forces include technical, social, economic, and political pressures mandating that facilities be shared among specialists and used flexibly, productively, efficiently, and safely. Associated operational and physical design changes require assessing the team and individual competencies required to operate these modalities efficiently and safely. The result is a more adaptable physical environment in which surgeons, radiologists, anesthesiologists, and cardiologists as well as other physicians and technologists can work cooperatively; the various types of equipment they use can be shared, rather than duplicated; and the infrastructure is designed in anticipation of accommodating the rapid medical technology advances associated with procedural medicine.

On one hand, much of surgery is becoming less invasive. On the other hand, much of medical imaging is becoming more interventional. For example, a growing number of radiology procedures are therapeutic activities that treat as well as seek clinical information. Similarly, many surgical procedures now benefit from advanced forms of image guidance that enable surgeons to better visualize relevant anatomic and physiologic data.

Most traditionally designed operating theaters cannot accommodate the plethora of advanced imaging equipment or the multitude of specialists necessary for many cases. Similarly, many traditionally designed imaging procedure rooms do not provide the surgical environment needed to control the flow of materials, supplies, and people or the air quality required for invasive procedures. Yet interventional radiology procedure rooms–where both diagnostic and therapeutic procedures have historically taken place–are now being used more for surgery-like therapeutic procedures because new advances such as high-speed computed tomography angiography and magnetic resonance angiography are quickly assuming the diagnostic workload and taking those cases out of the interventional procedure room. As a result, many surgical procedures traditionally performed exclusively within an operating room are now routinely performed within a variety of advanced procedure rooms, and many of the diagnostic procedures traditionally performed within interventional procedure rooms are now being performed in the diagnostic imaging environment. This change in location and levels of expertise requires rethinking anesthesia support and access to ensure safe outcomes in areas which in the past created little physiological perturbations, such as within the MRI suite.

In addition, novel hybrid concepts that integrate advanced image guidance modalities into the surgical environment have recently begun to be developed in selective medical centers throughout the nation. These include the seamless integration of various forms of MRI, PET, CT, ultrasound, and radiographic imaging devices as part of the image-guided surgery room. Each involves a reexamination of work flow, infection control, various forms of shielding, and safety issues. In addition, a host of endoscopic, endovascular, and transluminal procedures also integrate therapeutic interventions with various forms of image guidance and are thus also candidates for inclusion within the integrated interventional platform.

The nature of procedure rooms themselves is becoming more flexible. For example, interventional radiology and interventional cardiology (cath lab) procedure rooms tend to be similar in how they are designed but formerly were somewhat dissimilar in how they were equipped. When imaging equipment was analog-based, each room had a different size of image intensifier–for example, one sized for detailed cardiac procedures, and the other sized for broader peripheral procedures. However, today's digitally equipped rooms benefit from new flat-panel detectors that can accommodate both cardiac and peripheral procedures.[51] Thus one room can be used for a variety of procedure types, with its workload changed either on a daily basis or adjusted over a period of months or years. This approach to universal room design is a first step toward increasing flexibility and minimizing turf battles. With innovative planning and skilled diplomatic leadership, a universal approach can be used to design a common footprint accommodating a wide range of surgical, interventional radiological, and cardiac procedures.

The convergence of surgery and imaging requires more than just a rethinking of how procedure rooms are designed. It warrants a more aggressive redesign of an entire interventional platform or multifunctional procedure zone without the discrete departmental boundaries that typically foster internal competition among specialists, isolate specialists from one another, and lead to the inefficient duplication of rooms, equipment, and personnel in separate medical service lines. The integrated interventional platform suggests a new approach to both room design and departmental design that anticipates new types of equipment, new roles of personnel, and changes in work flow.

Decades ago, Harold Laufman, MD, observed that well-intentioned architects have historically attempted to "design away infection" with the creation of the clean-core surgical suite, which endeavored to separate the flow of clean and soiled traffic.[52] At the time the clean-core concept first emerged, few interventional imaging rooms were part of the surgical platform. Most were placed in the back of the diagnostic imaging department, where little if any separation of clean and soiled traffic was considered.

While the clean-core concept remains a useful planning model for the efficient flow of materials into and out of operating rooms, the physical convergence of surgery and interventional radiology suggests an environment where diverse types of supplies need to be managed in unison. While many surgical procedures utilize a significant amount of reusable supplies and instruments, many interventional radiology procedures use disposable supplies and catheters. Reevaluating how surgical supply cores are actually used might better accommodate various types of material simultaneously.

In many ways interventional imaging is becoming more like minimally invasive surgery. Thus, the need to restrict traffic around the interventional suite and cardiac catheterization laboratory is more important than when procedures were less complex and more diagnostic in nature. At the same time, some of the early architectural concepts of surgical infection control are now being reassessed, leading to more relaxed protocols for controlled flow within the surgical suite and divergent opinions about the impact that clean-core layouts actually have on improving infection control and patient care. In contrast, greater emphasis is being placed on design that encourages better hand-washing technique and compliance with infection control guidelines.

More stringent flow control for interventional imaging environments and more lenient rules for configuring surgical suites are resulting in newly emerging layouts that are applicable to both service lines. This new planning model includes clusters of procedure rooms surrounding a staff core and control room (similar to that used to support the cath lab or angiography suite) instead of surrounding a clean supply core (see figure 15-7, page 361).

As image guidance becomes more crucial for many surgical procedures, two new types of staff positions are emerging: surgical technologists (to operate imaging equipment used during surgery), and surgical information technologists (to manage the data used during surgery). Both personnel need immediate access to the procedural environment without necessarily entering the procedure room/sterile area. A central staff core provides such access without disrupting flow through the procedure room (see figure 10-4 on page 213).

Similarly, as both imaging and surgery become more computer-driven and as advanced image and information systems become more integral to both imaging and surgery, the need for computer server cabinets within the vicinity of the procedure room has become crucial. Often these are better located directly adjacent to the procedure room rather than within it. Ideally, the server cabinets can be placed near the central staff core/control area.

Another advantage of the integrated interventional platform—where operating rooms, interventional rooms, cath labs, and even endoscopic suites are co-located—is that scarce patient preparation and recovery space, personnel, and equipment can be consolidated in a flexible configuration that supports multiple service lines, rather than duplicating these areas in separate locations. The overall prep/recovery area still needs to be sized appropriately for the comprehensive number of surgical, interventional, cath, and endoscopic prep/recovery positions, and it needs to be subdivided into intimate elements rather than remain on a massive scale. Compared to separate decentralized surgical, interventional, cath and endoscopic recovery suites, individual prep/recovery zones within the comprehensive centralized suite can swing more easily to accommodate varying census volumes. In addition, recovery staff may become cross-trained to support myriad patients' needs, including both cardiac and surgical patients and ranging from patients undergoing conscious sedation for minimally invasive procedures to those requiring fast-acting general anesthesia for more traditional surgical interventions.

While architectural planning and design for uncertain future conditions is challenging, it is usually less complex than the political and territorial issues that must be addressed in order to develop a successful design. Turf issues surrounding the integrated interventional platform, however, are growing in their complexity as revenue streams, reimbursement policies, and equipment ownership trends become more varied.

For example, in many cases vascular surgeons, interventional radiologists, and interventional cardiologists all compete for patients requiring certain interventional procedures, such as the placement of a drug-eluting stent. Historically, surgeons and cardiologists controlled patient referrals, while radiologists controlled equipment. However, as vendors continue to develop specialty equipment (such as cardiac MRIs and cardiac CT scanners) and market these devices for specialists to purchase, and as some interventional radiologists are now seeking their own patient referrals, competition for patients, space, and equipment has become more intense.

In order to avoid expensive and unnecessary duplication of space and equipment used for similar procedures but fed by different revenue streams, intrepid executive decision makers are striving to establish a more shared and less duplicative integrated interventional platform. The most successful endeavors involve a close collaboration between informed and diplomatic design professionals and visionary yet steadfast executive management.

The integrated interventional platform is a planning framework designed to support a diverse array of procedures in universally designed procedure rooms. Each procedure room can be equipped for a variety of needs without having to modify the overall flow of people and materials throughout the suite.

In particular, the integrated interventional platform assumes the operating room of the future is likely to look and feel more like today's catheterization lab (with electronics equipment and a control area adjacent to but separate from the procedure room itself) than like yesterday's operating room (with only minimal provisions to integrate image guidance and data management into the surgical procedure). In addition, the integrated interventional platform anticipates that advanced forms of image guidance—not yet available today—will need to be assimilated into the suite with minimal disruption to ongoing services. Thus, procedure rooms are clustered together for the future conversion of adjacent rooms into hybrid configurations, such as intraoperative MRI/ORs or MRI/PET/ORs.

Imaging and Surgery in the Future

Tomorrow's surgical suites—designed to incorporate advanced imaging systems into the surgical process—will continue to evolve into new configurations, perhaps similar to today's cardiac cath lab with dedicated control rooms and closets for electronics and a telecommunications server. Additionally, the further development of electronic medical records, surgical simulation, and full-body scanning will affect how surgical procedures are performed and who performs them. Not only will advanced information and imaging systems integrated into the surgical theater improve productivity, but they will significantly reduce medical errors and improve patient safety.

According to Richard Satava, MD—a visionary surgeon at the University of Washington, and a pioneer in the U.S. Department of Defense's development of advanced robotic surgery and virtual telepresence surgery (where patient and surgeon can be in two separate locations)—developments in surgical training using simulation to practice surgical technique will radically affect both surgical procedures and surgical facility design. They will also affect the competencies of the surgical team members to perform in emergency conditions.

Accordingly, patients will undergo a comprehensive total body scan prior to their surgical procedure, which after postprocessing will become a dynamic patient medical record (figure 15-11). Using this data set to rehearse the surgical procedure, surgeons will hone their skills on surgical simulators, editing out their mistakes, in much the same way we currently edit text in word-processing software to perfect a written manuscript.[53]

Figure 15-11 In the future, the electronic medical record may be created post-operatively from a functional and anatomic total body scan. Image courtesy of Richard Satava, MD.

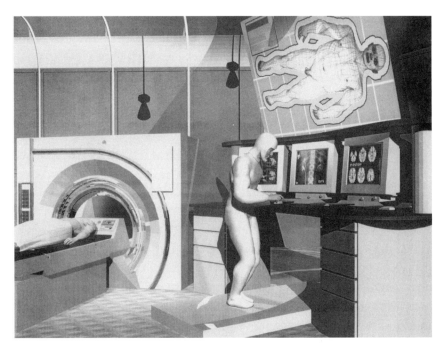

FUTURISTIC TOTAL BODY SCAN

The scenario will be one in which the surgeon performs the virtual operation on the patient's image, "edits" the procedure until it is perfect, then pushes the "operate" button and a "perfect" operation is performed, with all the errors edited out. This will take surgery from the Industrial Age, or "typewriter mentality" of today and into the "word processor" stage of the Information Age.[54]

In this scenario, advanced anatomic and physiologic image acquisition and monitoring systems become a virtual electronic patient record, upon which the surgical procedure is choreographed:

With total–body scanning or organ–specific scanning, it is possible to get an information representation of the patient. Thus preoperative planning, surgical rehearsal, intraoperative navigation and postsurgical outcomes can all be automatically integrated through the use of the robotic system. . . . The robotic system is not a machine; rather it is an information system with "arms." And a computed tomography scanner is not an imaging system; it is an information system with "eyes." Thus the entire spectrum of surgical care, from pre–operation to post–operation, can be integrated in "information space" to enhance surgical care in "real space."[55]

Circulating nurses might be replaced by robotic instrument handlers. The surgeon may conduct the procedure remotely, either from an adjacent control room or from a remote data center similar to the control center of the eICU® (see "Imaging in the Intensive Care Unit" earlier in this chapter). Ultimately, the patient may be the only person in the operating room, and

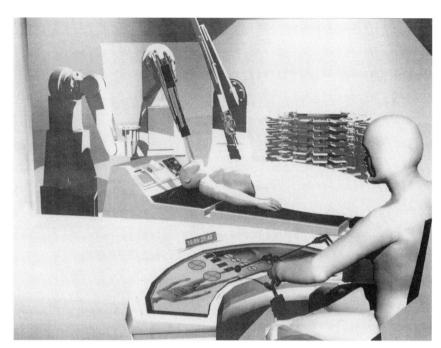

PROCEDURE ROOM OF THE FUTURE

the room itself can be made infection–free through the use of microwave or infrared radiation (figure 15-12).

Dr. Satava describes the preoperation, surgery, and postoperation processes as follows:

> The patient is brought to the preoperative holding area and is anesthetized on a "smart stretcher" that continuously monitors all the vital signs, biochemical parameters, etc. The patient is properly positioned for surgery and taken through a total body scan. The anatomic structures from the scan are fused with the biochemical and physiologic parameters from the smart stretcher in a single database that results in a representation of the patient in information space.

> Once the patient has been prepared [irradiated], the entire sterile system, including the stretcher, is moved to a clean room. . . . The smart stretcher "docks" with the robotic system inside the OR, and instantly shares information about the patient with the robotic system, including automatic registration.[56]

Design Considerations for Surgical Imaging Facilities
The following should be considered when designing a surgical suite that accommodates various forms of advanced medical imaging:

- If specialized intraoperative imaging equipment–such as MRI–is likely to be used both for surgical image guidance and overflow diagnostic imaging (not related to surgery), provide two routes of access to the imaging suite. One route should pass through the controlled surgical corridor, and the other should bypass the surgical corridor.

- Even if dual routes are provided to the imaging suite, only one door (which can be constantly monitored) should enter the MRI exam room to restrict unauthorized access. Preventing ferrous objects from entering the magnet room is essential and may be more challenging in an intraoperative environment than in a purely diagnostic MRI suite.
- The specific design of an intraoperative MRI suite will be based on a number of variables, including:
  - The type of magnet being used (open versus closed; stationary versus movable; high field strength versus low field strength, etc.)
  - The location of the I-MRI suite (within the surgical suite, adjacent to the surgical suite, or remote from the surgical suite)
  - The number of procedure rooms accommodating both imaging and surgical procedures (one room for both MRI imaging and surgical procedures; one room for MRI imaging and another room for surgical procedures; one room for MRI imaging, another room for surgical procedures, and a third room for other forms of imaging such as PET/CT)
  - For multiple room configurations, whether RF shielding extends beyond the MRI room or surrounds only the MRI room (which then must be separated from the other rooms by a movable RF-shielded door) (figure 15-13)
- Anticipate the evolution of some operating rooms becoming more like cardiac catheterization labs, with dedicated control rooms and electronics equipment storage rooms.
- Identify a zone within the surgical suite where future advanced imaging modalities–perhaps unknown at the time of initial suite design–may be added. Locate this zone to minimize disruption when it is renovated. Provide excess structural, power, air-handling, and data capacities in anticipation of future technology integration (yet understand that the excess capacities may or may not be adequate once the future technology emerges).
- Provide multiple lighting systems in the operating room, to accommodate both the needs of surgery and the needs of image display.
- Where electronic charting stations are provided within the operating room, orient them so that the person doing the charting can observe the surgical procedure without having to physically turn around.

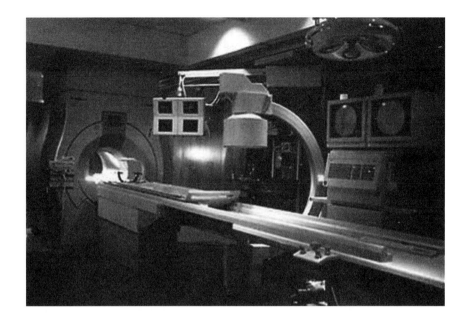

Figure 15-13 Hybrid procedure room with MRI and interventional radiology/cardiology. Image Courtesy of Philips Medical Systems.

Imaging and Cardiology

Many of the imaging techniques described under the headings of "Imaging and Emergency Medicine," "Imaging in the Intensive Care Unit," and "Imaging and Surgery" have specific cardiac applications. Cardiac imaging includes noninvasive cardiac diagnostics and screening, invasive cardiac diagnostic and therapeutic imaging, and image guidance to support cardiovascular surgical procedures. These forms of cardiac imaging are performed in a variety of locations, such as hospitals, outpatient facilities, designated heart centers, or private physicians' offices. Some of the most significant technological advances regarding cardiac imaging surround developments in molecular imaging (such as PET and PET/CT), multidetector CT (MDCT), dedicated cardiac MRI, MR angiography (MRA), and ultrasound–especially ultrasound–activated microbubbles used for targeted drug and gene delivery.

Noninvasive Cardiac Imaging

CT, MR, ultrasound, and cardiac nuclear imaging are used to perform noninvasive cardiac imaging studies for various types of cardiac illnesses and injuries. For example, coronary artery disease (CAD) typically involves both anatomic abnormalities (such as thinning of the muscular walls between the heart's chambers) and atypical cardiac processes (such as irregular blood flow and chemistry). Therefore, functional imaging techniques–such as PET, CT, and MRI scans–that measure cardiac behavior and chemical composition in addition to physical structure are important components of cardiac imaging.

Perfusion imaging examines blood flow and is used in conjunction with cross–sectional imaging that depicts the structure of the heart and related vessels. Because blood flow abnormalities often precede dysfunctional muscular activity in patients with CAD, perfusion imaging offers the potential to detect early stages of cardiac disease. "At present, nuclear cardiology is the most widely used noninvasive approach for assessing myocardial perfusion. Other imaging techniques, such as contrast echocardiography and magnetic resonance imaging have been recently proposed as alternative methods for the evaluation of myocardial perfusion."[57]

Multidetector CT has increased the utility of CT cardiac imaging primarily due to its improved acquisition speed as well as its high-quality spatial resolution. Diagnostic cardiac angiography studies using computed tomography instead of invasive catheter angiography are revolutionizing cardiac imaging. Compared to traditional catheter angiography, computed tomography angiography (CTA) is noninvasive, is less expensive, and requires little or no patient recovery. Multidetector CT has made CTA possible by recording multiple slices of data simultaneously, thus shortening scan durations. Faster scans provide clearer images within shorter durations; many can be performed within a breath hold. While CTA can be performed on 16-slice CT scanners, many believe 64-slice CT is becoming the gold standard for CTA. However, 256-slice CT scanners are being clinically tested. Currently, in order to procure good images, a patient's heart rate must be slowed to about 60 beats per minute or less; CT scanners with a higher number of slices produce good image quality with faster heart rates.

There is ongoing debate as to whether CTA should be used for routine asymptomatic cardiac screening or only for noninvasive diagnosis of patients predisposed for cardiac abnormalities. Some view CTA "as a screening device to actually bring more people to the interventional table," where cardiac disease can be properly treated.[58] Yet others are concerned that CTA could be overused, and claim, "There's no evidence at the present time that it's effective or cost-effective in clarifying risk for asymptomatic patients. This is not something that's ready to be a screening test; there's too much radiation and contrast given to justify the approach.[59]

In addition to diagnostic CT angiography studies, MDCT is frequently used in rapid assessment of cardiac patients presenting to the ED. Because a CT chest exam takes only minutes (in contrast, angiography takes hours), it is used to rapidly rule out or confirm a variety of heart- and great-vessel-related problems. "Medical centers save costs by taking less staff to support a patient until the diagnosis is made, and they improve emergency care by cutting the time patients spend being imaged before being stabilized and acutely managed."[60]

Ultrasound is used to view both cardiac anatomy and blood perfusion. Echocardiography (a specialized type of cardiac ultrasound, and a traditional cardiac imaging workhorse) with color Doppler capabilities provides real-time information about blood flow within the heart. Advanced uses of ultrasound include the delivery of oxygen (or pharmacological agents) to the myocardium via tiny microbubbles less than 6 microns in size. Ultrasound contrast agents containing encapsulated microbubbles are injected intravenously and directed to specific organs, such as the heart. Ultrasound waves are then used to burst the microbubbles, releasing their contents to the targeted site. The microbubbles also provide quantitative analysis of spatial and temporal characteristics of blood flow, thus enhancing ultrasound images and improving their diagnostic accuracy.[61]

Nuclear cardiac imaging–especially PET and PET/CT–records metabolic cardiac activity. PET and SPECT studies examine blood perfusion and oxygen uptake of patients either at rest or under the stress of a mechanical treadmill (or pharmacologically induced stress). Hybrid PET/CT and SPECT/CT automatically correlate precise cardiac CT data with metabolic PET (or SPECT) images by co-registering the two types of images, thus providing exquisite anatomic and metabolic information within one comprehensive data set.

Interventional Cardiac Imaging

Interventional cardiac imaging procedures examine both blood perfusion and electrical conductivity within the heart. In addition to acquiring diagnostic data via a catheterization procedure, the catheter and associated devices are used to perform therapeutic procedures, such as opening compromised vessels, altering the heart's electrical conductivity, or surgically repairing structures (such as valve repairs).

Procedures involving vascular blood flow are often referred to generically as catheterization procedures and are typically performed in a cardiac catheterization laboratory. Procedures involving the heart's electrical conductivity are known as electrophysiology (EP) procedures (or studies) and may be performed in an EP lab. Sometimes the EP lab is generically called a cath lab.

Both rooms can be similar in layout but are often equipped slightly differently. Historically, EP labs have not required the same complex imaging equipment common to most cath labs, but recent advances in EP procedures now require equally sophisticated imaging tools.[62] Catheterization and EP procedures are typically performed under fluoroscopic guidance; often in conjunction with ultrasound guidance as well. Some fluoroscopic cath and EP systems enable an ultrasound transducer to directly plug into the angiography system, thus eliminating the need for the entire ultrasound unit to be wheeled in. It is also becoming common for MR and CT data to be ported into cath and EP labs.

Rapid changes in interventional cardiac imaging are currently under way, and these changes affect the volume, type, and location of imaging procedures performed in the cath lab. Historically, both diagnostic and therapeutic cardiac exams have been routinely performed in cardiac cath and EP labs. However, advances in MDCT, CTA, MRA, and cardiac nuclear imaging are shifting much of the diagnostic imaging load out of the cath lab and into less invasive or noninvasive CT, MR, and nuclear medicine environments. While many cath labs still perform both diagnostic and invasive procedures, the majority of cases are clearly shifting toward mostly invasive procedures and will continue to do so in the years to come.

Cath and EP studies can be performed in an operating room if it is equipped with the proper imaging systems. Conversely, many cardiovascular surgical procedures that were once restricted to operating rooms are now routinely performed in cath and EP labs. Most cath and EP labs are designed to meet surgical standards of air changes, infection control, and so on. It is not uncommon to locate cath and EP labs within–or adjacent to–the surgical suite, thus creating an opportunity to consolidate certain equipment, real estate, and staff (especially those related to patient prep and recovery activities), although this approach is not supported universally. Some practitioners prefer to separate interventional cardiology from surgery and interventional radiology due to both territorial issues and concerns about the skill sets of cross-trained support staff.

A primary difference between a cath lab and an interventional radiology suite–the latter being where peripheral vascular studies, rather than coronary studies, are performed–lies in specific attributes of the imaging equipment; in particular, the image intensifier. Coronary studies utilize a smaller image intensifier, whereas peripheral vascular studies use a larger one. New equipment, utilizing flat-panel detectors, can more easily flex between coronary and peripheral imaging, thus enabling one room to swing across both specialties. This is important, as interventional radiologists and cardiologists are more aggressively reaching into each other's markets than in the past. A multipurpose room that accommodates both coronary and peripheral vascular studies can provide clinical flexibility, especially at sites where both volumes are growing.[63]

A cath lab with two fluoroscopic C-arms–for two simultaneous views of the heart–is called a biplane lab. A biplane lab should be sized slightly larger than a single-plane lab. Biplane labs are less common than they were years ago, with the exception of pediatric cath labs, some EP labs, and neuroangiography suites, which still use biplane equipment.

EP and cath labs are sometimes equipped with stereotactic magnetic catheter guidance systems (not to be confused with MRI image guidance). Magnetic catheter guidance is used to delicately manipulate the complex movement of ferrous-tipped catheters, rather than to produce MR images. Rooms with these systems installed typically require magnetic shielding and upgraded structural capacities. Also, the equipment is space-intensive, and unless the room is oversized, it may restrict use of the space when non-catheter guidance procedures are performed.

The proliferation of advanced imaging systems used for cardiac exams, combined with strategic marketing of cardiac-specific imaging devices and imbalances in supply and demand for both interventional radiologists and cardiologists, has led to intense competition between the specialties. Competition for equipment ownership and patient referral patterns is compounded by varying opinions regarding who should read and interpret cardiac images. While most cardiologists claim they are more familiar with the nuances of cardiac anatomy and pathology, most radiologists believe they are more familiar with the subtleties of CT, MR, and nuclear medicine images and data. As a result, both the American College of Radiology and the American College of Cardiology have established minimum training and reading volume standards in an effort to set minimum competency levels in each respective area.[64]

Imaging and Oncology

Cancer care encompasses a wide range of activities, including research, patient education, screening, diagnostic procedures, therapeutic procedures, post-treatment consultation, and palliative care. Cancer treatment may include surgical oncology, medical oncology (chemotherapy), radiation oncology, or some combination of those. While cancer is still the first or second (depending on the survey source) leading cause of death in the United States, patient outcomes are steadily improving, and many cases of cancer are detected earlier as a result of technological advances in imaging, treatment planning, and improved treatment protocols. Another factor contributing to improved outcomes is the continued collaboration among imaging and oncology specialists.

While medical imaging is instrumental to all aspects of oncology, it is often most closely aligned with cancer screening, diagnosis, and various forms of therapy. Specifically, oncology-related imaging includes various screening examinations (such as mammography and colonoscopy), diagnostic and staging examinations (such as chest radiography, PET/CT, and various types of image-guided biopsies), computer-aided detection (CAD, also sometimes referred to as computer-aided diagnosis) tools (such as pattern recognition systems used in conjunction with mammography), interventional oncology procedures (such as radio-frequency ablations and cryotherapy), radiation therapy (RT) simulation (including fluoroscopic, CT and MR simulation), radiation therapy treatment components (including onboard imaging, tomotherapy, intensity-modulated radiation therapy [IMRT], and image-guided radiation therapy [IGRT]). Other specialty devices and procedures—such as gamma knives, cyber knives, and stereotactic radiosurgery (using linear accelerators to perform percutaneous noninvasive interventions)—are also used in conjunction with oncology-related imaging. In addition, molecular imaging is instrumental in analyzing genetic and cellular structure, both to detect factors that may cause cancer and to treat cancer at a cellular level. The various forms of imaging used in conjunction with oncology treatment each have unique design requirements.

Mammography

Mammography is used for both screening and diagnosis of cancer. In addition, some mammography devices are used to perform biopsies and other invasive procedures. Many mammography examinations are radiographic, but ultrasound and magnetic resonance mammography are also common. While mammography is predominantly performed on women, men occasionally require mammography exams, and facilities should be designed to accommodate this requirement by providing the opportunity for separate–albeit infrequent–flow of male patients.

Because screening patients (who consider themselves healthy and undiagnosed) may be less inclined to seek voluntary screening exams in a facility that they identify as a "cancer center," screening mammography is often separated from diagnostic mammography by locating it in a women's health center or other ambulatory care setting. However, some sites combine screening mammography and diagnostic mammography in one location in an effort to minimize the duplication of equipment, space, and staff. In such cases, it may be beneficial to separate screening and diagnostic patients by time, such as offering screening exams on certain days and diagnostic exams on others. If, however, screening and diagnostic patients are seen concurrently, facility layout should physically separate the two populations as much as possible. At sites where stereotactic mammography is used to perform needle location procedures, a discrete and direct path of travel from the stereotactic mammography room to a surgical procedure room should be provided, because a gowned patient is likely to be wheeled in a chair to the procedure room with a needle placed in her breast to identify the procedural site location.

The economics of screening versus diagnostic mammography differ greatly due to disproportions between the cost of performing each exam and typical reimbursement rate structures. In essence, it is difficult for screening mammography to be profitable; thus its cost is often offset by financial gains from diagnostic mammography and other resultant procedures. Yet screening mammography environments have a high consumer choice component and so require sensitive and supportive ambience and visible patient amenities, sometimes similar to spalike settings. Therefore, facility design for mammography services must be considered as a continuum of care from both a design perspective and an economic perspective.

Radiographic mammography has been one of the last imaging modalities to go digital because of the need for very high spatial and contrast resolution images. Yet digital mammography systems have become common. Challenges of digital mammography include both the cost of the equipment and large digital file sizes. Advantages of digital mammography include the ability to incorporate computer–aided detection (CAD) tools to assist radiologists in reviewing mammograms and rendering a diagnostic interpretation.

PET/CT

Since it first became commercially available in 2001, hybrid PET/CT has proven invaluable in cancer detection, staging, monitoring, and treatment planning. PET scanning is the modality of choice for oncology functional imaging to determine biological characteristics of cells, thus potentially detecting cancer in its early stages. PET, however, has poor spatial resolution and thus does not provide a clear picture of anatomic structure. In contrast, multidetector CT provides excellent spatial resolution but usually identifies little, if any, metabolic data. Combined simultaneously acquired and co-registered PET and CT images, however, exhibit a new level of diagnostic power greater than the sum of the parts.[65] At many institutions, such as Memorial Sloan–Kettering Cancer Center, in New York City, PET/CT images have been used effectively to reduce the number of required postprocedural invasive procedures, such as biopsies.

> The quality of images has given clinicians more confidence in their ability to monitor patients' outcomes and has obviated many unnecessary tests. In fact, the new scanners produce images so detailed that physicians have found cancers they probably would not have detected through other non–invasive imaging exams.[66]

Due to the tremendous value of hybrid PET/CT and gradually improving reimbursement for PET/CT procedures, the majority of PET scanners sold in the United States in recent years have been hybrid PET/CT scanners, rather than standalone PET scanners. Considerations in planning for PET/CT include significant shielding requirements in the scan room, larger room size than general CT scan rooms, dedicated equipment chillers for some models, the likely need for multiple shielded uptake rooms to maintain high patient throughput (in part due to longer uptake durations and higher radioactivity levels of injected radioisotopes), provisions to accommodate radioactive isotopes in a department other than nuclear medicine (where they are commonly handled), and concerns about full–time utilization of expensive PET/CT equipment.[67] While most diagnostic CT scanners found in imaging departments are heavily used, an oncology–based PET/CT scanner is likely to have lower utilization unless it is part of a high-volume specialty cancer center. However, attempting to use the scanner as a backup unit for diagnostic imaging is likely to inappropriately introduce nononcology patient traffic into the oncology setting. In addition, oncology CT simulators and PET/CT scanners differ from equipment typically used for diagnostic CT. The bore of the oncology CT simulator is often larger to accommodate simulation of radiation therapy (although large–bore diagnostic scanners also have been introduced to accommodate bariatric, interventional, and trauma patients). In addition, PET/CT scanners are increasingly being installed within nontraditional settings such as medical office buildings and freestanding imaging centers, thus presenting unique facility design and regulatory challenges.

Radiation Therapy, IMRT, IGRT, and Simulation

The integration of medical imaging with radiation therapy and RT treatment planning creates opportunities for unprecedented collaboration among medical specialists. Compared to cardiac imaging, where advanced technology appears to accelerate competition and turf battles between cardiologists and radiologists, advances in oncology-related imaging seem to foster collaborative relationships between oncologists and radiologists. Oncology imaging appears to make both specialties aware of the myriad opportunities each has to support one another.

For example, radiologists and radiation oncologists typically have different perspectives on how they participate in cancer treatment. Radiologists are usually most concerned about defining the shape and nature of a malignancy, while radiation oncologists, radiation physicists, and dosimetrists may focus more on how to calculate treatment trajectories to irradiate the tumor site by using sophisticated 3-D treatment-planning workstations. Advanced imaging techniques now help these various perspectives come together due to the quality of information they can provide for each other.[68]

The sheer volume of images encourages both specialties to collaborate, and the precision of the data acquired means that collaborative efforts can result in more precise targeted therapy with less collateral damage to healthy tissue. Nowhere is this truer than with intensity-modulated radiation therapy (an advanced technique that has revolutionized the way radiation treatment is delivered to more precisely target malignancies and avoid surrounding healthy tissue) and image-guided radiation therapy (which integrates various forms of medical imaging tools with radiation therapy equipment in order to more accurately monitor and guide treatment delivery).

Compared to 3-D conformal radiation, in which the intensity of the treatment beams is constant, IMRT delivers radiation through multiple pencil-thin rays whose intensity is dynamically varied, or modulated, in order to safely navigate through complex structures composed of both healthy and malignant tissue. "The technology combines computer-generated images and inverse treatment planning software to deliver the tightly focused radiation beam that matches the 3D shape of the tumor."[69]

IGRT is beneficial in correlating radiation treatment with previously performed simulation and to continuously monitor changes in anatomic structure through the course of treatment, which may be ongoing for several weeks or months. Patients may not be placed in the exact position they were in during the simulation. Even when patients are placed in the same position for each treatment, the targets themselves do not necessarily remain static for tumors can shift over the course of treatment. As a result of these shifts, it is possible that radiation may not reach the desired targets and instead damage healthy tissues.[70]

Tumor localization during treatment setup through image-guided beam delivery has become a standard of care. While standalone ultrasound devices are commonly used to help localize tumors just prior to treatment, IGRT offers linear accelerator gantry-based alternatives for tumor localization. IGRT compensates for potential misregistration by integrating image guidance into the linear accelerator. Various approaches to IGRT–such as on-board imaging (OBI)–vary by manufacturer. Some devices utilize ultrasound probes and 3-D tracking systems. Others use general X-rays with robotically controlled arms, while still others integrate CT scanning technology in the radiation treatment device. In most cases, discrepancies between preplanned treatment parameters and real-time image guidance devices are calculated by the treatment software, so the patient's position and/or the dose trajectory can be adjusted accordingly.

The first critical step for advanced radiation treatment techniques such as IMRT and IGRT is advanced pretreatment imaging, used for treatment planning–both to identify malignancies more accurately and to uncover them earlier in their developmental process. In addition, state-of-the-art radiation therapy image management systems are necessary to effectively analyze and manipulate complex images and data sets throughout the process from detection and planning, through simulation, therapy, and follow-up. Many cancer centers have transitioned from darkrooms and film-based portal images (used to manually correlate treatment with changes in anatomy over the course of treatment) to integrated digital image management systems that allow for seamless movement of data between image acquisition modalities, simulation and linear accelerators. Therefore, a robust and flexible data infrastructure backbone is essential in today's oncology facility to move images and treatment plans through the enterprise.

Many cancer centers own and manage their own advanced image acquisition devices (PET/CT, CT, MR, and ultrasound) or are closely aligned with associated facilities that acquire and share this data. This growing trend underscores the importance of close functional relationships and physical adjacencies between cancer-related medical imaging facilities and cancer treatment centers. Many of these advanced pretreatment imaging techniques affect throughput volumes and durations. "Industry analysts suggest that large volumes of cancer cases and the mounting use of advanced techniques such as IMRT increases the time needed to plan the delivery of patient treatments; thus impacting the desire to implement dedicated CT scanners.[71]

In addition, fluoroscopic simulation–which was once standard in most cancer centers–has been widely replaced by CT simulation, and in some instances by MR simulation. Treatment planning utilizes many types of images–PET, CT, MR, and ultrasound–to more accurately define target volumes. Some imaging modalities are better suited to specific cancers. For example, MR is useful in brain, head, neck, pelvic, and central nervous system tumors, while PET imaging can highlight hypermetabolic cellular activity in various tumor types.[72] Many of these data sets are fused together, either at the time of acquisition or through postprocessing. Several companies are working on PET/MR scanners; however, they are not commercially available at the time of this writing.

Figure 15-14A Linear accelerator that integrates sensitive design with appropriate radiation protection. © Peter Sellar Klik Photography. Architect: Farrow Partnership Architects.

Some IMRT and IGRT applications require larger rooms to accommodate the size of linear accelerator equipment with integrated ancillary devices. Some IGRT applications place both a CT scanner and a linear accelerator within one vault. The amount of radiation shielding (which, depending on the materials used, can exceed 5-foot thicknesses at the primary barrier) may be influenced by IMRT. Room size may also be affected by the types of radiation procedures being performed. For example, stereotactic radiosurgery may increase the total radiation dose per treatment, and total body irradiation may require a wider room (at least to one side of the accelerator) in order to accommodate radiation over the entire body surface.

Many alternatives to basic poured-in-place concrete exist for constructing linear accelerator vaults and other types of high-energy radiation procedure rooms. For example, combinations of steel and concrete, high-density concrete, and concrete with a magnetite admixture can all be used to reduce the overall wall thickness while still maintaining adequate radiation shielding properties. As another alternative, synthetic radiation shielding materials–such as Ledite block–can be used to significantly reduce both the horizontal and vertical overall dimensions of the vault while maintaining internal room clearances. Other room design variations include vaults with a maze but no door, vaults with a door but no maze, vaults with a maze and two doors, and vaults with sliding doors instead of swinging doors. Each approach has advantages and disadvantages with respect to shielding efficiency, requirements for additional structural support systems, appearance, overall dimensions, and dependability of the door(s)

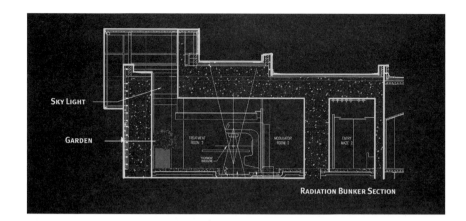

Figure 15-14B Linear accelerator—sectional view. © Farrow Partnership Architects Inc.

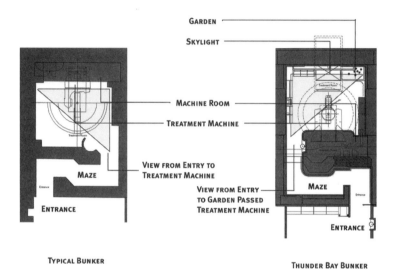

Figure 15-14C Linear accelerator—plan view. © Farrow Partnership Architects Inc.

to function properly. Some companies construct prefabricated radiation therapy facilities, complete with the linear accelerator and associated shielding installed, in an effort to reduce the construction duration.

Regardless of how the room is designed, radiation shielding calculations need to be determined by a certified radiation physicist. Not all radiation physicists who are qualified to determine shielding requirements for lower-energy diagnostic imaging environments are qualified to determine shielding requirements for high-energy radiation therapy enclosures. The medical planner and interior architect should work collaboratively with a qualified radiation physicist to design the radiation therapy room. A basic knowledge of radiation shielding design principles and a collaborative working relationship with a qualified radiation health physicist can result in innovative design that is both safe and aesthetically desirable (figures 15–14A–C).

Several therapeutic modalities are used in conjunction with radiation oncology, medical oncology, and surgical oncology to combat cancer. Generically referred to as interventional oncology, these techniques include cryoablation, microwave ablation, radiofrequency ablation, and brachytherapy (implantation of radioactive seeds, sometimes referred to as high dose radiation, or HDR). They are relatively noninvasive treatments used to destroy tumors without the trauma of open or minimally invasive surgery. They usually have short patient recovery durations and typically enable patients to resume normal lifestyle activities postprocedure, thus reducing the overall economic burden of cancer care. For this reason, continued growth of interventional oncology is projected. Many of these procedures may likely replace some of the more invasive procedures that are currently being performed. Cryoablation, in which low-temperature freezing is used to destroy tissue in situ, is a thermal ablation technique. Other thermal ablation techniques heat tissue, typically using radio-frequency or microwave energy. For example, radio-frequency ablation is often used for palliative treatment of patients whose cancer is not well suited for surgical removal. Many interventional oncology ablative procedures are conducted in concert with radiation therapy, chemotherapy, and surgical treatment.

While ultrasound and CT are commonly used to guide the placement of probes used in interventional oncology, MR has unique capabilities to identify thermal properties of tissue, and so it is also used to guide interventional procedures. Special MR scanners with high-intensity focused ultrasound (HIFUS) devices integrated into the MR couch enable MR guidance of HIFUS treatment of fibroids and other anomalies "by concentrating the focal point of ultrasound waves to transfer the energy to cells, heating and destroying them. This technique could eventually be used to open the blood-brain barrier or to perform targeted therapy delivery by bursting drug-laden microbubbles."[73] (See "MRI-Guided Surgery" under the section "Imaging and Surgery" earlier in this chapter.)

In an ideal radiation oncology department layout, it is desirable to have a dedicated minor procedures room or ambulatory surgery suite to perform brachytherapy procedures, where radioactive seeds are placed internally within the patient as a form of radiation therapy. Other special procedure rooms—such as a HIFUS room—are also desirable.

Technology Docks

A technology dock is a structure where mobile trailers or other types of portable imaging enclosures can be parked in order to become an extension to a medical imaging facility. Most imaging modalities—including MRI, CT, and PET—are capable of being installed inside relocatable or mobile trailers. This enables the temporary use of these modalities or enables multiple users to share expensive equipment. Mobile units that remain at one site can reduce equipment and facility installation time and provide coverage when other equipment is not operational. When modular construction or relocatable trailers are used, it is especially important that human factors and aesthetics be given adequate consideration within these confining spaces. If not, the imaging facility's image and market appeal can be significantly diminished.

The technology dock has three distinct benefits:

1. It enables the temporary use of imaging equipment during construction or renovation of more permanent facilities. The dock can also be used for temporary placement of expensive equipment that may become outdated, without having to commit to permanent construction to house it. This is beneficial if there is a plan to upgrade specific imaging equipment in the future but also a desire not to wait until the improved technology is available. For example, if there is a need for a high–field–strength magnet today but it is likely that a higher–field–strength magnet will be permanently installed within a year, a technology dock can provide immediate access to the interim magnet. The dock also allows for imaging equipment to be upgraded with minimal changes to the physical plant.

2. A technology dock allows some types of equipment to be available at a lower cost because movable equipment can be shared among multiple providers using it at separate sites. This is most beneficial in sparsely populated locations where volumes at any one facility are low but several locations together may be able to more fully utilize a specific advanced imaging technology. Because equipment can be shared (perhaps one mobile trailer travels to two or three hospitals each week), equipment costs also can be shared. However, for some equipment (such as MR), the unit may require recalibration, shimming, and other types of adjustment each time it is relocated.

3. Compared to a permanent facility, which may take years to design and build, mobile equipment often is more quickly and readily available. In some states, mobile imaging installations are reviewed by the Department of Transportation (DOT) and not state planning agencies or building departments, although many state agencies are becoming more involved in regulating mobile healthcare structures. In either case, requirements of the Americans with Disabilities Act (ADA) will apply.

Technology docks provide an additional advantage in seismically active locations or sites prone to other natural disasters. If provided with adequate emergency power, water supply, structural, sewage capabilities, and communications systems, mobile facilities may be able to be activated if the adjacent permanent structure becomes temporarily nonoperational, or can be brought back online quickly once essential services are restored.

Although mobile imaging facilities might be appropriate in some instances where quick installation is the single most important factor or where sharing equipment among sites is necessary, mobile installations are more likely to be a temporary or partial solution than a long-term remedy. However, whenever a technology dock is incorporated into facility design, special attention should be given to issues of convenience and image (see chapter 8, "Design Concepts"). For example, access to the dock from the imaging department should be direct, convenient, and protected from adverse weather conditions. Adequate vehicular and pedestrian access should also be provided. This may be difficult at some dense urban sites. Too often, support spaces in technology docks–such as waiting, dressing, and clerical areas–are designed with minimal amenities and to lesser design standards than the permanent structures.

The following should be considered when planning a technology dock:

- Is the dock easily accessible? Do users have to walk through the parking lot to reach it? Is it close enough to other imaging procedure areas so that staffing efficiency and patient safety can be maintained? Will the dock be accessible only from the main facility or will it also have its own entrance? If it has its own entrance, how will this affect patient and staff work flow and circulation? How will having a separate entrance affect patient registration and related work flow?

- Are the mobile unit's patient and staff support spaces of a similar quality to those in other parts of the facility?

- Site access must allow a large semitrailer to deliver the mobile unit to the dock. Specific slope and clearance criteria should be available from the manufacturer of the unit.

- The pedestrian connection between the dock and the main facility should be short, level, and protected from adverse weather conditions, if possible.

- Will services provided at the dock be needed by inpatients? Will regulatory agencies permit inpatients to be treated in the dock? If so, will special construction modifications be required for this?

- Some imaging modalities may be adversely affected by excess vibration. Certain MRI units may be affected by large, moving ferrous objects such as trucks, automobiles, and nearby elevators. MRIs in mobile trailers may be adversely affected by the ferrous environment of the site, especially if the trailer is moved among various sites and not always parked at the exact same location when it returns to a given site. In some instances, if the trailer is not adequately magnetically shielded, or if large moving or stationary ferrous objects are present near the magnet (even large concentrations of reinforcing steel), the magnet may need to be shimmed each time it is moved, in order to provide accurate images.[74]

- When an MRI is installed, people will need to be kept out of a 5-gauss exclusion zone that may extend beyond the boundary of the physical enclosure. Physical barriers may be required. Signage identifying the 5-gauss boundaries should be coordinated with facility-wide signage systems.

- Some imaging modalities will need special service access. For example, superconducting magnets will require periodic cryogen replenishment. People–including staff and maintenance personnel–must be protected from cryogen discharge points. If a magnet quenches, extremely cold and thus dangerous cryogen gas will be expelled though the discharge outlet. This point must be clearly identified by signage, and access to this point must be prevented by fencing, landscaping, or other barriers.

- Utility requirements (such as power, water, cooling, sewage, and communication) should be coordinated with the mobile equipment vendor. Some imaging equipment requires an uninterruptible power supply system to ensure uniform power. Required clearances should be verified for adequate airflow. Consideration should be given to providing additional utility hookups and excess capacity that might accommodate additional equipment in the future.

- In cold climates, modifications to the trailer or the trailer site may be necessary to prevent freezing and/or to maintain comfort. Windbreaks may be necessary in windy areas.

Notes

1. J. Brice, "Application of ACR appropriateness criteria in ER could save billions," November 30, 2004, from http://www.diagnosticimaging.com/webcast04/showArticle.jhtml?articleID=54201252.

2. J. Huddy, *Emergency Department Design: A Practical Guide to Planning for the Future* (Dallas, TX: American College of Emergency Medicine, 2002), 164.

3. C. H. Harris, "CT and therapy," *Medical Imaging* 18, 3 (2003): 38–43.

4. S. Hughes, "Evaluating thoracoabdominal trauma with ED ultrasonography," *Official Journal of the American Academy of Physician Assistants* 16 (2003): 57–62.

5. M. O. Philipp, K. Kubin, M. Hormann, and V. M. Metz, "TK," Radiological emergency room management with emphasis on multidetector-row CT. *European Journal of Radiology* 48, 1 (2003): 2–4.

6. C. P. Kaiser, "Cardiac imaging: Cardiologists move to protect MR and CT turf," *Diagnostic Imaging* 26, 11 (2004): 61.

7. R. Haugh, "The rise and uncertain future of cath labs," *Hospitals and Health Networks* 78, 9 (2004): 52–54, 56.

8. Hughes.

9. Hughes.

10. Hughes.

11. Hughes.

12. K. Sandrick and J. Bonner, "MR workup for wrist fracture saves time and money," *Diagnostic Imaging Europe*, April 2004, available at http://dimag.com/db_area/archives/europe/2004/0404.news1.die.shtml.

13. D. Page, "PACS productivity boost proves elusive for ED technologists," *Diagnostic Imaging*, December 2002, available at http://www.diagnosticimaging.com/showArticle.jhtml?articleID=47901511.

14. D. Page, "CR and DR come to the rescue in emergency departments," *Diagnostic Imaging*, November 2005, 29.

15. R. Smith, "DR and CR, today and tomorrow," *Imaging Economics* 17, 12 (2004): 43–45.

16. Sandrick and Bonner; Smith, "DR and CR."

17. P. Vignon, C. Chastagner, B. François, J. M. Martaille, S. Normand, M. Bonnivard, and H. Gastinne, "Diagnostic ability of hand-held echocardiography in ventilated critically ill patients," *Critical Care* 7, 5 (2003): 84–91.

18. Vignon et al.

19. Vignon et al.

20. Vignon et al.

21. V. Burgjalov, P. Srinivasan, S. Baumgart, and A. R. Spitzer, "Handheld, portable ultrasound in the neonatal intensive care nursery: A new, inexpensive tool for the rapid diagnosis of common neonatal problems," 22, 6 (2002): 478–83.

22. W. Mayo–Smith, J. Rhea, W. Smith, C. Cobb, I. Gareen, and G. Dorfman, "Transportable versus fixed platform CT scanners: Comparison of costs," *Radiology* 226, 1 (2003): 63–68.

23. Mayo–Smith, "Transportable versus fixed platform CT scanners: Comparison of costs."

24. Quoted in R. Smith, "Naval Medical Center in San Diego: CR in the ICU," *Imaging Economics*, August 2002, available at http://www.imagingeconomics.com/library/200208–20.asp.

25. Smith, "Naval Medical Center."

26. Smith, "Naval Medical Center."

27. M. J. Coye, "The e–ICU and new business models in health care," *Hospitals and Health Networks* 79, 5 (2005).

28. D. K. Hamilton, ed., *ICU 2010: ICU Design for the Future* (Concord, CA: Center for Innovation in Health Facilities, 2000), 61–75.

29. Hamilton, ed., 307–17.

30. Hamilton, ed., 71.

31. P. Rojas, "The Penelope surgical instrument server makes its debut," posted June 29, 2005, www.endgadget.com/entry/1234000010048684.

32. Rojas, "The Penelope surgical instrument server makes its debut."

33. E. Chesson, "Viewing images in the OR," *Health Imaging and IT*, July 2004, 40–44.

34. F. Jolesz, and R. Kinkinis. The role of imaging in the operating room of the future. Administrative Radiology. 1992 Nov;11(11):43–6.

35. Chesson, "Viewing images in the OR."

36. Chesson, "Viewing images in the OR."

37. Chesson, "Viewing images in the OR."

38. L. Conley, "And no, it's not for seeing through clothes," *Fast Company*, July 2005, 32.

39. Conley.

40. Chesson, "Viewing images in the OR."

41. K. Johnson, "New high-tech surgery units help MUHC forge ahead," May 2005, www.much.ca/media/ensemble/2005may/technology.

42. H. F. Hodder, "Bloodless revolution: Twenty-first-century surgery," *Harvard Magazine*, November–December 2000.

43. E. Barnes, "CARS suite of the future sees key role for image-guided intervention," www.AuntMinnie.com, June 23, 2005.

44. E. Fosse et al., "Integrating surgery and radiology in one suite: Multicenter study," *Journal of Vascular Surgery* 40, 3 (2004): 494–99.

45. Fosse et al.

46. Hodder.

47. Hodder.

48. Hodder.

49. Hodder.

50. Barnes.

51. L. Fratt, "Inside the state of the art cardiac cath lab," *Health Imaging and IT* 3, 3 (2005): 22–26.

52. H. Laufman, *Hospital Special-Care Facilities* (New York: Academic Press, 1981).

53. R. M. Satava, "The operating room of the future: Observations and commentary," *Seminars in Laparoscopic Surgery* 10, 3 (2003): 99–105.

54. Satava.

55. Satava.

56. Satava.

57. "The Many Ways to Myocardial Perfusion Imaging," RedNova News, 2005, available at http://www.rednova.com/news/health/155452/the_many_ways_to_myocardial_perfusion_imaging.

58. C. H. Harris, "Multifunction multislice: Slicing it by function," *Health Imaging and IT* 3, 2 (2005): 48–52.

59. S. Jersild, "CT angiographers predict widespread reimbursement," *Diagnostic Imaging Supplement*, February 2005, 2–4.

60. K. Sandrick, "MSCT tackles acute chest pain in emergency room," *Diagnostic Imaging Supplement*, February 2005, 12.

61. S. B. Feinstein, "The powerful micro-bubble: From bench to bedside, from intravascular indicator to therapeutic delivery system and beyond," *American Journal of Physiology* 287, 2 (2004): H450–57.

62. Fratt.

63. Fratt.

64. L. Thompson, "ACR sets standards for noninvasive cardiac imaging," June 5, 2005, available at www.auntminnie.com.

65. C. P. Kaiser, "PET/CT fusion proves its value," *Diagnostic Imaging* 24, 6 (2002): 36–43.

66. Kaiser.

67. D. Townsend, N. Hall, and D. Barker, "State of the art in PET/CT," *Imaging Economics* 17, 9 (2004): 57–62.

68. K. Sandrick, "PET/CT drives changes in art and geometry of oncology," *Diagnostic Imaging*, February 2005, 6–14.

69. E. Chesson, "Advances in radiation oncology," *Health Imaging and IT* 3, 5 (2004): 52–56.

70. Chesson, "Advances in radiation oncology."

71. Chesson, "Advances in radiation oncology."

72. Chesson, "Advances in radiation oncology."

73. J. Lowers, "New techniques expand arsenal of tumor therapies," *Diagnostic Imaging*, February 2005, 11–12.

74. T. Gilk, "Imaging trailer docks: Making mobile MRIs work for you," *MRI Newsletter*, Junk Architects, PC, February 2005.

CHAPTER 16

Future
Vision

In the hundred-plus years since Wilhelm Conrad Roentgen first discovered X-rays, medical imaging has been transformed from what was once a questionable curiosity into the backbone of medical treatment, an admired and respected profession, and a multibillion-dollar international industry. Medical imaging is at once one of the most expensive aspects of today's healthcare delivery and potentially one of the most cost-saving.

As the second century of medical imaging unfolds, imaging facility design will surely undergo as much—and likely more—transformation as it has since its inception. While it may be challenging to predict the precise details of how imaging and imaging facilities will change, it is possible to envision with some confidence the general aspects of each that will transpire. Similarly, while it is difficult to design a new medical imaging facility today that will accommodate all the specific details of tomorrow's imaging needs, it is possible to design flexibility strategies into current designs that will likely help any building and its infrastructure adapt to tomorrow's needs. These techniques and strategies have been described throughout this book.

This concluding chapter identifies several aspects of medical imaging—and their associated facility design ramifications—that will characterize the imaging facility of the future. While many of these attributes have already begun to emerge, they are all likely to attract expanded interest and scrutiny in the coming years.

The Ever-Expanding Digital Enterprise

Since the time of the first radiographic installations, one of the most significant rules of imaging facility planning had been the need to reduce travel distances by placing darkrooms in close proximity to where images were initially acquired. For decades, as film processing techniques evolved and improved, so did the design rules for planning film-based imaging departments. Now that enterprise-wide digital image and information management solutions are being implemented universally, the very foundation of imaging facility design is being reinvented. This affects not only detailed imaging department planning but also the very way radiologists and other radiologic personnel communicate and interact with other healthcare providers and their patients.

The physical boundaries of the radiology department have eroded, and imaging now permeates multiple hospital departments, such as the ED, the ICU, surgery, oncology, and cardiology. Similarly, the operational boundaries of each facility have expanded to encompass multiple inpatient, outpatient, and even non–healthcare facilities (such as educational, retail, and community service facilities) within their network. Many facilities are aligned with collaborating institutions in different time zones.

Medical imaging facility design in the future will focus less on individual departments or buildings in isolation and more on how the users of each facility interact with others within their region and around the globe. Information technology will become an increasingly important element of facility design and will continue to represent an increasingly large percentage of overall construction dollars. While wireless communication techniques continue to evolve, facility infrastructure and cable distribution networks will not diminish in importance; rather, they will continue to be more robust and ubiquitous.

Tomorrow's electronic medical record may originate from the data collected as a patient first seeks medical treatment, either physically presenting to a place of treatment or virtually communicating with medical caregivers. According to Dr. Richard Satava, a visionary surgeon at the University of Washington, "With total–body scanning, or organ-specific scanning, it is possible to get an information representation of the patient."[1] Using simulation tools and multimedia software, that information representation can be converted into a medical record providing the basis for myriad activities ranging from physicians virtually rehearsing invasive treatment protocols to identifying potential adverse medication contraindications. Tomorrow's imaging facility will be replete with intelligent communications technology fully integrated into each room and throughout the enterprise.

The Transition to Ambulatory Healthcare Delivery

As more patients (many of whom will require more complex medical treatment) continue to be cared for in nonhospital settings, the capabilities of outpatient imaging centers will approach those of today's hospitals, but the distinction between inpatients and outpatients will become more apparent, due to their varying degrees of acuity. For many, the hospital will be the treatment site of last resort, and only the most critically ill patients will be admitted. As a result, hospital-based imaging will become more specialized, and the ability of image acquisition devices to travel to bedridden patients will likely replace the present requirement for most patients to be transported to stationary imaging suites.

Alternative types of ambulatory healthcare facilities have already emerged, including retail-oriented diagnostic imaging centers, centers for advanced medicine, and bedless hospitals. Many of these outpatient imaging centers are physician-owned and cater to well-insured customers. Therefore, many facility owners and managers place a priority on design, image, and branding (see "Patient-Focused and Sustainable Design Strategies," below). Similarly, facility operators will strive to develop models of improved staffing efficiency and patient throughput. Many will learn from non–healthcare best-practice models, such as those establishing new standards of customer service in the retail, hospitality, and entertainment industries. Hospital providers will be forced to improve their facilities' efficiency and ambience in order to remain competitive.

Additional new models for outpatient imaging will evolve, and scrutiny of conflict-of-interest self-referrals will also continue. Legislation restricting specialty care facilities that disproportionately skim off the well-insured—and thus redistribute the burden of indigent care upon other providers—will continue to be passed. Tomorrow's ambulatory imaging facilities will have more rigorous structures and infrastructures and will be capable of offering many of the sophisticated imaging services currently offered primarily in hospitals today. Structural, power, data, and air-handling systems will become more robust than those found in today's typical outpatient buildings. Floor-to-floor heights will grow in order to accommodate more complex imaging equipment and their associated building systems.

Ambulatory patients will undergo increasingly complex interventional image guided procedures without needing to be admitted to the hospital. Building and licensure codes and regulations that govern outpatient imaging facility design and operations will need to be overhauled in order to better reflect the needs of "extreme" ambulatory patients, many of whom will become temporarily incapable of self-preservation while being treated in tomorrow's imaging facilities.

The Impact of Molecular and Functional Imaging

Much of medical imaging possesses the capability of revealing physiologic and metabolic function in addition to anatomic structural data. This suggests not only that many physicians may require substantial retraining in order to make the most of these new capabilities but also that many medical maladies can be detected earlier and thus treated more effectively.[2]

The facility design implications of future developments in molecular imaging are numerous. For example, screening exams will likely grow in importance as data demonstrate that early detection improves patient outcomes and saves lives. If screening volumes increase and more disease is detected early, therapeutic volumes will also increase, resulting in greater overall utilization of both diagnostic and therapeutic imaging services.

Molecular imaging has already had a beneficial accelerating impact on oncology and cardiac treatment, and it will likely have a similar impact on other medical subspecialties. Finally, molecular imaging will likely contribute to the increased growth of those imaging modalities well suited to revealing metabolic data and similarly the decreased utilization–and perhaps eventual demise–of anatomic–only modalities. In particular, in the future there will be considerable growth in advanced imaging tools such as CT, MR, and PET and a corresponding decline in general radiographic and fluoroscopic devices, which currently contribute to the majority of imaging exams.

Mandates to Reduce Medical Errors and Improve Patient and Staff Safety

Our current healthcare system is rampant with preventable medical errors. The Institutes of Medicine of the National Academies have highlighted the need to reduce medical error rates, as identified in the landmark publications *To Err Is Human: Building a Safer Health System, Crossing the Quality Chasm: A New Health System for the 21st Century,* and *Keeping Patients Safe: Transforming the Work Environment of Nurses.*[3]

Facility design plays a significant role in enabling caregivers to reduce errors and improve safety by providing a safer physical environment and by helping to improve work process which can lead to reduced errors and increased safety. Several improvement strategies incorporate "lean" operations (as developed as part of the Toyota production system) that eliminate activities that are undesirable but often not apparent.[4] Opportunities identified in the Institutes of Medicine publications where facility design can help improve error and safety outcomes include:

- Visual controls–where work processes and their indicators are in plain view so staff can readily see the status of activities at a glance
- Streamlining physical plant layouts–to optimize the flow and sequence of work processes
- Point–of–use storage–where frequently used supplies, equipment, information, and procedural protocol documentation are readily accessible at the location where they will be used in order to reduce time spent hunting for them[5]

The Institutes of Medicine study identifies seven root causes of waste in the hospital environment:

- Poor utilization of resources (resources deployed or stored at the wrong place, the wrong time, and wrong quantities)
- Excess motion (poorly designed workplaces and work processes that contribute to excess caregiver motion)

- Unnecessary waiting (poorly designed work processes–such as process complexity and inaccessible information–that require caregivers to unnecessarily wait to provide necessary care)
- Transportation (inefficient transport of resources and inventory due to poor facility layout, policy, or processes)
- Process inefficiency (unnecessary steps in patient care, inefficient execution of processes, or unplanned interruptions)
- Excess inventory (wasteful practice of storing more inventory or employing more personnel than is necessary)
- Defects/quality control (mistakes caused by distractions or lack of standardization)[6]

Tomorrow's imaging facility designer will be asked to justify critical design decisions with evidence substantiating their beneficial outcomes, rather than simply relying on intuition or anecdotal inference. One technique used to help improve error and safety outcomes is the design of "same-handed" procedure rooms, as described in chapter 12, "Room Design." Same-handed rooms are rooms of a similar functional type (such as a group of general radiography rooms) that are configured and equipped identically or at least very similarly so that staff will know where in the room to find supplies and how to travel through the space (see figure 12-5 on page 244). For example, rather than mirroring two X-ray rooms around one shared control alcove, same-handed X-ray rooms would each have its own control alcove, entrance door, and supply cabinets in the same configuration and orientation as the other room. Where same-handed rooms are provided, it is sometimes beneficial to have some distinct identifying characteristic–such as a unique color or piece of artwork–to aid staff in remembering which room they are in.

Radiation safety and MRI safety are two areas unique to medical imaging that present architects and engineers with opportunities to design safer environments. Both of these issues are described in chapter 12, "Room Design," and chapter 13, "Physical Properties Influencing Design." The National Council on Radiation Protection and Measurements (NCRP) published its Report No. 147, on radiation shielding design methodologies, in 2004. It is a long-overdue update to its previous Report No. 49, from 1976. While most imaging equipment has become safer, with each new model improving upon its predecessors, the maximum permissible radiation dose that is considered to be safe has decreased over time. Thus, requirements for shielding of radiation-emitting equipment and associated procedure rooms have continually become more stringent. This trend is expected to continue in the future, as radiation safety in general will receive increasingly careful scrutiny. New materials will emerge, thereby enabling rooms to be safely shielded with less weight and lower cost, and with greater flexibility.

The American College of Radiology (ACR) has developed a white paper describing recommended safety guidelines they believe should be incorporated into any MRI facility.[7] As magnet field strength continues to grow and as magnets are being placed in a variety of nontraditional environments (such as retail centers, physicians' offices, and image–guided surgical suites), magnet safety will continue to be an important challenge. The future development of hybrid technology–such as MRI devices in surgical suites–will complicate the criteria according to which designers must create safe environments.

Patient-Focused and Sustainable Design Strategies

The imaging facility of tomorrow will maximize its impact on patients while minimizing its impact on the environment. Patients, their families, and their advocates will be afforded dignity, privacy, and choices ranging from how their care is provided to where it is provided and even their ability to control the physical environment in which their care is delivered. Patients will be increasingly informed, alert and aware of the procedures they undergo, and similarly the procedural environment will be designed with much greater attention to patients' needs and desires, such as acoustic privacy, natural and controlled lighting, and convenient access. Scheduling, consultations, and follow–up care will be streamlined and convenient as a result of lessons learned from successful consumer industries.

The environment will similarly cater to highly qualified–but increasingly scarce–caregivers. Recognizing that staff and faculty spend longer hours in the imaging facility than do patients, owners and managers will require architects to leverage opportunities for a facility design that supports their recruiting and retention objectives, as well as those that provide opportunities for philanthropic donations from grateful patients.

Design and construction will cause minimal damage to the natural environment. Materials will be selected based not only for their environment–friendly characteristics once installed but also on the basis of the impact they have on the environment during the processes of production, packaging, and transport. Imaging facilities will be constructed to easily adapt to continuous new developments in medical technology without requiring substantial renovation, and they will be built to endure longer. Tomorrow's imaging facility will produce greatly reduced quantities of waste, while being able to convert its medical waste into energy used to heat and power its own operations.[8]

Notes

1. R. M. Satava, "The operating room of the future: Observations and commentary," *Seminars in Laparoscopic Surgery* 10, 3 (2003): 102.
2. D. Ellis, "The future of imaging," *Hospitals and Health Networks Online*, October 11, 2005, http://www.hhnmag.com/hhnmag/jsp/articledisplay/jsp?dcrpath=HHNMAG/PubsNews.

3. Institutes of Medicine, *To Err Is Human: Building a Safer Health System* (Washington, DC; National Academy Press, 2000); Institutes of Medicine, *Crossing the Quality Chasm: A New Health System for the 21st Century* (Washington, DC: National Academy Press, 2001); Institutes of Medicine, *Keeping Patients Safe: Transforming the Work Environment of Nurses* (Washington, DC: National Academy Press, 2004).

4. Institutes of Medicine, *Keeping Patients Safe*, 257.

5. Institutes of Medicine, *Keeping Patients Safe*, 256–76.

6. Institutes of Medicine, *Keeping Patients Safe*, 258, Table 6-1.

7. E. Kanal, J. P. Borgstede, et al., "American College of Radiology white paper on MR Safety," *American Journal of Roentgenology* 178 (2002): 1335–47.

8. Anshen + Allen Website. Medergy–Waste to Renewable Energy. http://www.anshen.com/US/portfolio/portfolio.php?project=medergy&category=science_centers.

PART SIX

APPENDICES
& INDEX

Case Studies

The following descriptions of imaging facilities illustrate a variety of architectural solutions to numerous operational and physical design challenges. The material in this appendix is based on project descriptions prepared by the architects who designed these projects.

Appendix A-1

UCLA Westwood Replacement Hospital
Non-Invasive Radiology Department

Owner: UCLA Medical Center
Executive Architects: Perkins + Will
Design Architects: I. M. Pei, Architect, and Pei Partnership Architects
Consulting Architect: RBB Architects Inc.

The Non-Invasive Radiology Department is part of the new $900 million, 525-bed UCLA hospital, scheduled to open in 2006 as the Ronald Reagan UCLA Medical Center. The building gross area is approximately 1,040,000 square feet and consists of eight floors above grade and two basement levels. Non-invasive imaging is located on the first level, directly adjacent to the Emergency and Observation Unit, and encompasses approximately 31,000 DGSF.

Scope of services include adult and pediatric inpatient diagnostic radiology and fluoroscopy, IVP/tomography, ultrasound, CT, and MRI. Most outpatient services are provided separately in the Medical Plaza (other than Emergency, invasive procedures, and specialized high-tech imaging such as open MRI). The department was designed around a filmless model, with capability to continue using a dual system during the move-in transition period.

UCLA, Non-invasive Imaging Department.
Courtesy RBB Architects Inc.

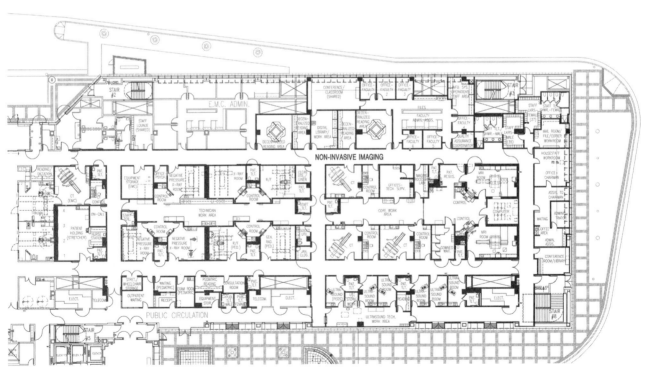

Peak staffing: 161 people, including 26 physicians and 4 managers.

All procedure rooms were designed and planned to provide maximum flexibility for various (multifunctional) procedures. Room sizes and shapes were standardized. Similar rooms were co-located to allow for flexibility to change as needs evolve (with minimal construction costs and down time). Soft spaces were strategically located so as to be easily converted to procedure rooms if needed.

Features

- Dedicated Emergency Department CT scan room, directly adjacent to Trauma Room. Built-in overhead X-ray units in both trauma bays.
- Procedure rooms were located around a central tech work core to separate staff work areas from inpatient traffic. Configuration allows for rapid response by locating tech work areas central to patient areas.
- Centralized and decentralized reading rooms, including trademark UCLA-designed central reading room stations for four workstations each.

Appendix A-2

UCLA Westwood Replacement Hospital Radiology Reading Room

Owner: UCLA Medical Center
Architect: RBB Architects Inc.

For the new hospital, UCLA is redesigning the radiologist workplace using modeling and computer simulation. The new design focuses on flexibility, lighting conditions, and noise reduction in rooms shared by multiple users performing diagnostic tasks or holding conferences with referring physicians. To reengineer the workspace ergonomics, new technologies were integrated, including custom cabinets, indirect dimmable lights, sound-absorbent partitioning, and a geometric arrangement of workstations to allow for better privacy while optimizing space occupation. Innovations in design included adjustable flat-panel monitors, integration of videoconferencing and voice recognition devices, and retractable keyboards for optimal space utilization. An overhead compartment protecting the monitors from ambient light was also used as an accessory light box and rear-projection screen for conferences. These illustrations present the design and computer simulation of virtual reading rooms with different room setups and different lighting combinations.

The Next Generation

With the rapid evolution of flat-panel display technology, we foresee that multiple monitors will soon be replaced by a single high-resolution display panel. This panel will accommodate single or multiple images displayed in various arrangements. New technology will also allow display panels to be curved for more convenient viewing of a large-surface display.

While most workstation functions will be voice-activated, some features will also be activated through a convenient electronic command panel. Touch-sensitive panels with customized icons will be used in place of keys on conventional keyboards. Innovative software design will allow for specific "keys" to be tailored to specific tasks. This creates a more flexible and customized user interface and design.

Discussion and Conclusions

The 3-D modeling techniques allow for better planning and innovation of ergonomics in the workspace. 3-D computer models are a much more cost-effective means of obtaining realistic representations in place of full-scale or subscale mock-ups.

This process allowed us to correct and improve some weaknesses and conceptual errors in our initial design and to add specific features that enhanced the design and ergonomics of the radiologists' working environment.

UCLA, reading room prototype.
Courtesy RBB Architects Inc.

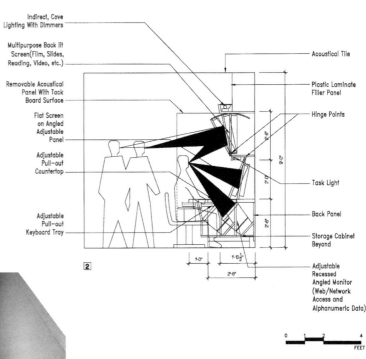

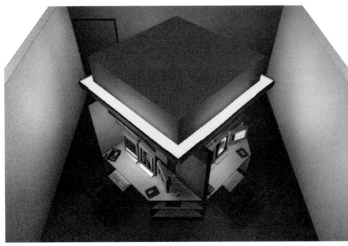

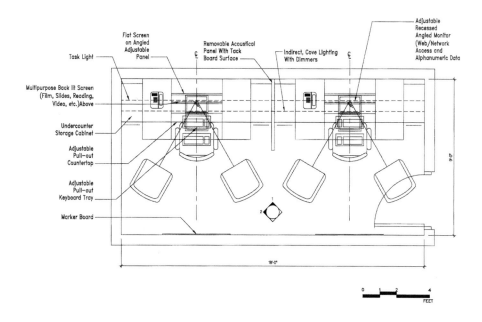

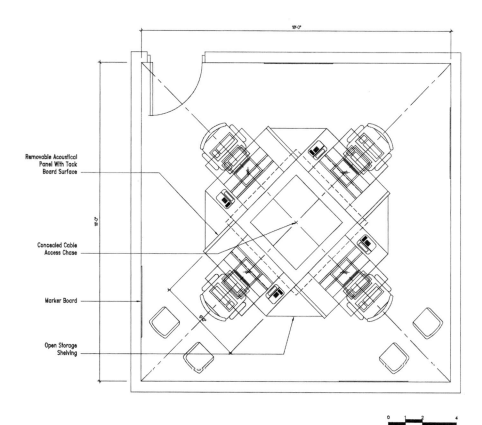

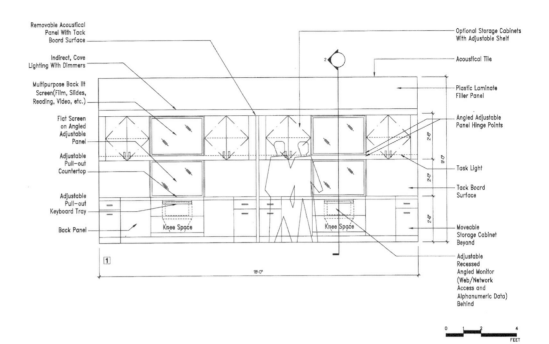

Removable Acoustical
Panel With Tack
Board Surface

Indirect, Cove
Lighting With Dimmers

Multipurpose Back lit
Screen(Film, Slides,
Reading, Video, etc.)

Flat Screen
on Angled
Adjustable
Panel

Adjustable
Pull-out
Countertop

Adjustable
Pull-out
Keyboard Tray

Back Panel

Knee Space

Knee Space

Optional Storage Cabinets
With Adjustable Shelf

Acoustical Tile

Plastic Laminate
Filler Panel

Angled Adjustable
Panel Hinge Points

Task Light

Tack Board
Surface

Moveable
Storage Cabinet
Beyond

Adjustable
Recessed
Angled
Monitor
(Web/Network
Access and
Alphanumeric Data)
Behind

1

18'-0"

2'-8"

9'-0"

2'-0"

2'-8"

0   1   2   4
FEET

UCLA, reading room prototype.
Courtesy RBB Architects Inc.

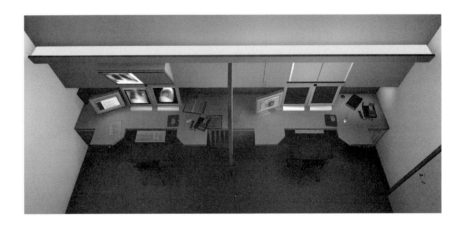

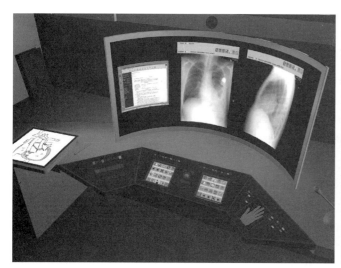

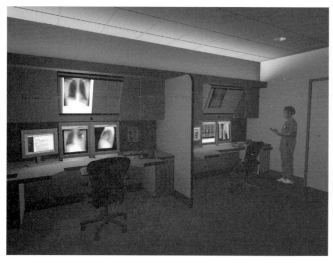
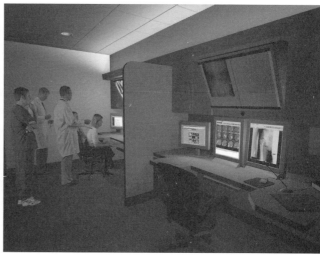

Appendix A-3

UCLA Westwood Replacement Hospital—Interventional Floor

Owner: UCLA Medical Center
Executive Architects: Perkins + Will
Design Architects: I. M. Pei, Architect, and Pei Partnership Architects
Consulting Architect: RBB Architects Inc.

The new 525-bed UCLA Westwood Replacement Hospital comprises three hospitals: the Ronald Reagan Medical Center, the Mattel Children's Hospital at UCLA, and the NeuroPsychiatric Hospital. The facility is a tertiary/quaternary hospital with high acuity levels and complex medical cases. A key component of the hospital is the second-floor Interventional Platform, which consolidates all interventional and procedural functions, including patient intake and recovery, on a single floor under a single administrative leadership.

The Interventional Platform aggregates nursing care for prep and recovery, image-guided procedural spaces, and management for all interventional services and staff/support functions. The combination of like services and spaces allows for more effective staffing, higher staffing skill levels, elevated consistency of quality and process, and better utilization of program space. Consolidating these like functions both spatially and administratively further enhances and supports a more multidisciplinary and interactive environment for enhanced patient care and clinical research.

The Interventional Platform includes:

- 23 operating rooms
- 2 intraoperative MRI operating rooms
- 6 cardiac cath/EP labs
- 8 interventional radiology labs
- 5 endoscopy/bronchoscopy rooms
- 59 prep/recovery spaces

Each of the procedural areas is designed with a peripheral corridor for patient, staff, and equipment access in groups of four to six rooms. Scrub sinks and holding spaces for beds and stretchers, as well as mobile equipment, are provided off this corridor. Windows on these corridors provide natural light and views for staff members, who often do not have time to leave the floor during long shifts.

A central supply/work core is included in each room grouping to allow for convenient access to supplies, instruments, case carts, and material. In the interventional labs, space for control areas and staff work areas is included within this core. By utilizing a similar modular procedure room configuration, future flexibility for room equipping and usage is ensured. This design feature also facilitates the realignment of procedure rooms from clean to sterile environments and vice versa as protocols and codes change (see diagram).

Given the number of procedure rooms and patient care spaces on the second floor, all nonessential functions are located on the third and ground floors. The third floor houses all staff support spaces such as locker rooms, lounges, resident/fellow workspaces, conference rooms, and on-call rooms. Staff locker rooms are connected directly to the operating room suite via a dedicated "clean" stair. In addition, the satellite pathology lab is located on the third floor, connected via pneumatic tube and video system.

While the third floor is dedicated for staff use, the ground floor is reserved for patients and their families. On the day of a procedure, the patient will arrive on the ground floor and check in at the Family Waiting Room. Located immediately adjacent to the dining commons, the check-in is convenient to both the Children's Hospital and Medical Center entrances. Patients will be escorted to the Interventional Platform suite on the second floor while family members remain on the ground level.

UCLA, interventional platform.
Perkins + Will, Executive Architect.

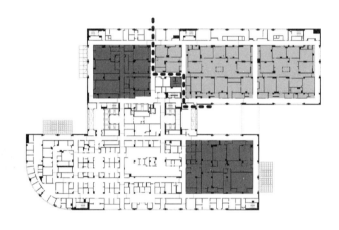
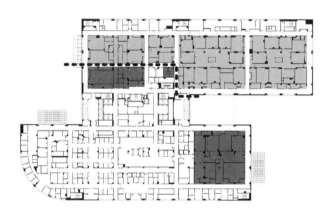
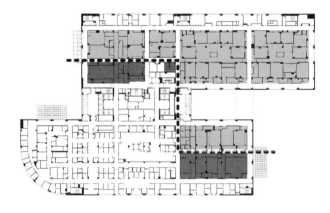
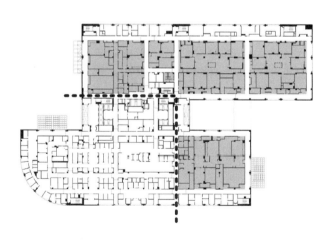

Flexible Interventional Platform

Sterile Environment

Non-Sterile Environment

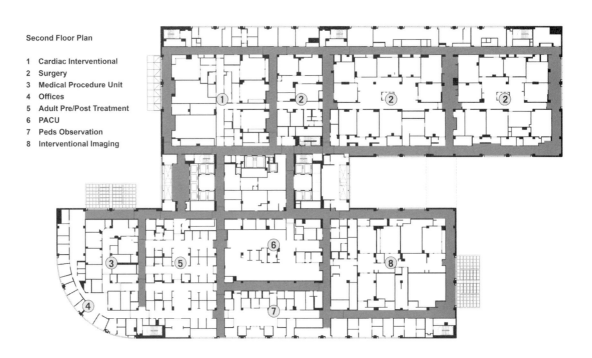

Second Floor Plan

1   Cardiac Interventional
2   Surgery
3   Medical Procedure Unit
4   Offices
5   Adult Pre/Post Treatment
6   PACU
7   Peds Observation
8   Interventional Imaging

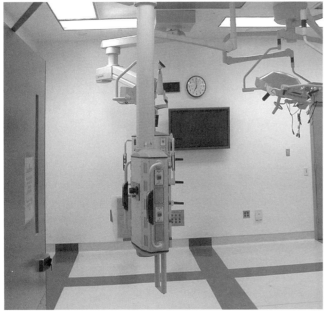
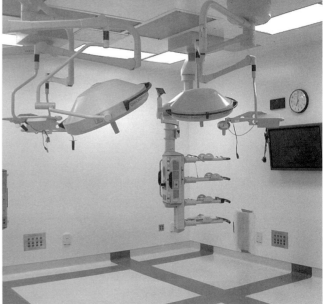

UCLA, interventional platform.
Perkins + Will, Executive Architect.

Appendix A-4

Foothills Medical Centre—Intraoperative Magnetic Resonance Imaging

Owner: Calgary Regional Health Authority
Architect: Stantec
Size: 2600 m^2
Date: 1998

The Intraoperative MRI at the Foothills Medical Centre in Calgary, Alberta, is the first facility of its kind in the world. By placing MRI equipment within the operating room, images may be obtained during successive stages of a surgical procedure. This enables entirely new procedures for neurosurgery, and new means of saving lives.

The requirements of an intraoperative system required the development of entirely new technologies and an entirely new facility to house them. Issues of grounding and isolation, structural deflection, service access, and nonferrous equipment, including the design of a titanium operating table, have been successfully addressed.

Foothills Medical Centre, Intraoperative Magnetic Resonance Imaging facility. Courtesy of Stantec Architecture Ltd.

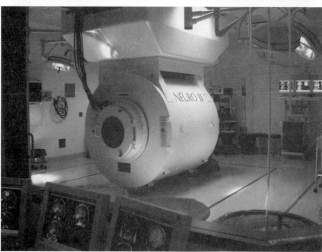

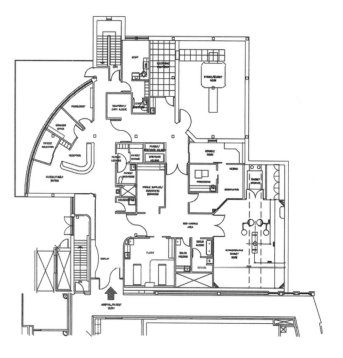

Appendix A-5

Brigham and Women's Hospital Advanced Multimodal Image Guided Operating Room Suite (AMIGO)

Owner: Brigham and Women's Hospital
Architect: Payette
Total square footage: 13,000 NSF
Phase I: 6,500 NSF
Phase II: 6,500 NSF
Estimated Completion: 2006
Program Components: MRI, operating rooms, PET

The Advanced Multimodal Image Guided Operating Room Suite (AMIGO) is a cooperative endeavor between Brigham and Women's Hospital and General Electric to develop facilities for image guided interventional procedures that will change the paradigm for therapeutic care of patients.

Using advanced technology in magnetic resonance (MR), positron emission tomography (PET), and computed tomography (CT)–all commonly used in current hospital procedures–the AMIGO Suite will be capable of providing image-guided surgery, which will allow extensive visualization and ablation of soft tissue. Innovative features of the AMIGO Suite will include motorized operating tables that will move a patient during a procedure from the OR to the MR or PET room through automatic doors.

AMIGO is an integrated environment to support percutaneous, endovascular, open surgical, and focused ultrasound procedures. A procedure room, MRI room, and PET/CT room can be modularly utilized, based on the scheduled procedure. The procedure room will be equipped with a surgical microscope, fluoro X-ray, sophisticated patient table, navigation system, and 3-D ultrasound, and will also serve as a test bed for endoscopy and optical imaging. The devices integrated here do not need to be MRI-compatible. The

Brigham and Women's Hospital, Advanced Multimodal Image Guided Operating Room (AMIGO). Courtesy of Payette, Computer Generated Image.

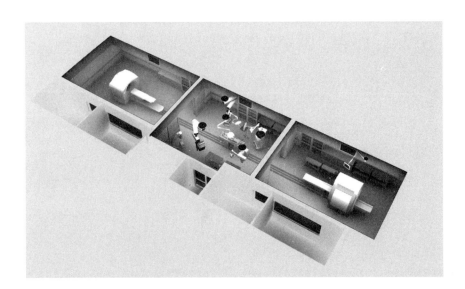

three-room solution demands a means to safely move the patient between stations while maintaining sterility. The surgical table enables motorized movement along tracks in the floor. The tabletop manually transitions from the surgical table to the MRI and PET/CT tables.

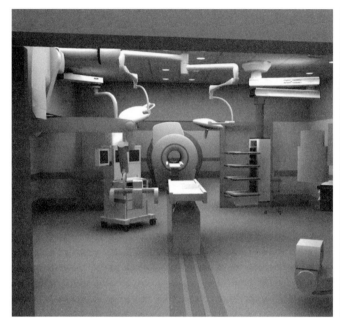 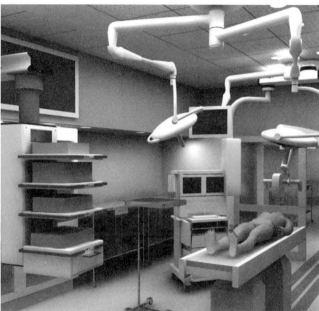

1   CONTROL ROOM
2   SCRUB STATION
3   SUB STERILE
4   PET SCANNER
5   OPERATING ROOM
6   3T MRI
7   COMPUTER ROOM
8   PATIENT TOILET

0 2' 4' 8'   16'   32'   64'

American College of Radiology White Paper on MR Safety

Emanuel Kanal,[1] James P. Borgstede,[2] A. James Barkovich,[3] Charlotte Bell,[4]
William G. Bradley,[5] Joel P. Felmlee,[6] Jerry W. Froelich,[7] Ellisa M. Kaminski,[1]
Elaine K. Keeler,[8] James W. Lester,[9] Elizabeth A. Scoumis,[1] Loren A. Zaremba,[10]
Marie D. Zinninger[11]

Received January 8, 2002; accepted after revision March 5, 2002.

[1] Department of Radiology, Magnetic Resonance Services, University of Pittsburgh Medical Center, 200 Lothrop St., Pittsburgh, PA 15213–2582.

[2] Penrose St. Francis Health System, Colorado Springs, CO 80907.

[3] Department of Neuroradiology, Rm. L 371, University of California at San Francisco, 505 Parnassus Ave., San Francisco, CA 94143–0628.

[4] Department of Anesthesiology, Yale University School of Medicine, 333 Cedar St., P. O. Box 208051, New Haven, CT 06520–8051.

[5] Department of Radiology, Long Beach Memorial Medical Center, University of California, Irvine, 403 E. Columbia St., Long Beach, CA 90806.

[6] Department of Radiology, Mayo Clinic, 200 1st St. S.W., Rochester, MN 55902–3008.

[7] Department of Radiology, Hennepin County Medical Center and The University of Minnesota, 701 Park Ave., Minneapolis, MN 55415.

[8] National Electrical Manufacturers Association, Philips Medical Systems, 595 Miner Rd., Cleveland, OH 44143.

[9] Durham Radiology Associates, Ste. 500, 4323 Ben Franklin Blvd., Durham, NC 27704.

[10] Office of Device Evaluation, Center for Devices and Radiological Health, U.S. Food and Drug Administration, 9200 Corporate Blvd., HFZ–470, Rockville, MD 20850.

[11] American College of Radiology, 1891 Preston White Dr., Reston, VA 20191.

Address correspondence to: M. D. Zinninger.

AJR 2002; 178:1335–1347

0361–803X/02/1786–1335

The following is a report of the American College of Radiology Blue Ribbon Panel on MR Safety, chaired by Emanuel Kanal, MD, FACR, to the Task Force on Patient Safety, chaired by James P. Borgstede, MD, FACR. Under the auspices of the Task Force, the panel met in November 2001 consisting of the following members: A. James Barkovich, MD; Charlotte Bell, MD (Anesthesia Patient Safety Foundation); James P. Borgstede, MD, FACR; William G. Bradley, MD, PhD, FACR; Joel Felmlee, PhD; Jerry W. Froelich, MD; Ellisa M. Kaminski, RTR, MR; Emanuel Kanal, MD, FACR; Elaine K. Keeler, PhD, (NEMA); James W. Lester, MD; Elizabeth Scoumis, RN, BSN; Loren A. Zaremba, PhD (FDA); and Marie D. Zinninger (American College of Radiology Staff). The following document is intended to be used as a template for MR facilities to follow in the development of an MR safety program.

Recent articles in the medical literature and electronic/print media [1, 2] detailing Magnetic Resonance Imaging (MRI) adverse incidents involving patients, equipment, and personnel spotlighted the need for review. The Panel was charged with reviewing MR safety practices and guidelines and issuing new ones as appropriate for MR examinations and practices today

[5–7]. The document restates existing practices and articulates new ones. This document will continue to evolve, as does the MRI field.

There are potential risks in the MR environment, not only for the patient but also for the accompanying family members, attending healthcare professionals, and others who find themselves only occasionally or rarely in the magnetic fields of MR scanners, such as security or housekeeping personnel, firefighters, police, etc. These MR Safe Practices Guidelines have been developed to help guide MR practitioners regarding these issues and provide a basis for them to develop and implement their own MR policies and practices. It is intended that these MR Safe Practice Guidelines (and the policies and procedures to which they give rise) be reviewed and updated on a regular basis.

It is the intent of the American College of Radiology (ACR) that these MR Safe Practice Guidelines will be helpful as the field of MR evolves and matures, providing patient MR services that are among the most powerful, yet safest, of all diagnostic procedures to be developed in the history of modern medicine.

ACR Magnetic Resonance Safe Practice Guidelines

A. ESTABLISH, IMPLEMENT, AND MAINTAIN CURRENT MR SAFETY POLICIES AND PROCEDURES

1. All clinical and research magnetic resonance imaging sites should maintain MR Safety Policies and Procedures, which are to be established, implemented, maintained, and routinely reviewed and updated, as appropriate. The level of compliance by staff will be assessed and documented annually. The policies and procedures manual should be readily available to the MR professionals on site at all times of operation.

2. These policies and procedures should also be reviewed concomitant with the introduction of any significant changes in safety parameters in the MR imaging environment of the site's MR service (e.g., adding faster/stronger gradient capabilities, higher RF duty cycle studies, etc.) and updated as needed. In this review process, national and international standards and recommendations should be taken into consideration prior to establishing local guidelines, policies, and procedures.

3. Each site will name an MR Medical Director whose responsibilities will include ensuring that these MR Safe Practice Guidelines are established and maintained as current and appropriate for the site. It is the responsibility of the site's administration to ensure that the policies and procedures that result from these MR Safe Practice Guidelines are implemented and adhered to at all times by all of the site's personnel.

4. Procedures should be in place to ensure that any and all adverse events, MR safety incidents, or "near incidents" that occur in the MR site are to be reported to the Medical Director of the MR site in a timely fashion (e.g., within 24 hours/one business day of their occurrence) and used in continuous quality improvement efforts.

B. STATIC MAGNETIC FIELD ISSUES: SITE ACCESS RESTRICTION

1. Zoning

The MR site is conceptually divided into four Zones (Fig. 1 [in complete version of the ACR guidelines]) as follows.

a. Zone I: This includes all areas that are freely accessible to the general public. This area is typically outside of the MR environment itself and is the area through which patients, healthcare personnel, and other employees of the MR site access the MR environment.

b. Zone II: This area is the interface between the publicly accessible uncontrolled Zone I and the strictly controlled Zone III and IV (see below). Typically patients are greeted in Zone II and are not free to move throughout Zone II at will, but are rather under the supervision of MR Personnel (see Section 2b, below). It is in Zone II that the answers to MR screening questions, patient histories, medical insurance questions, etc., are typically obtained.

c. Zone III: This area is the region in which free access by unscreened non–MR Personnel and/or ferromagnetic objects and equipment can result in serious injury or death as a result of interactions between the individuals/equipment and the MR scanner's particular environment. These interactions include but are not limited to those involving the MR scanner's static and time varying magnetic fields. All access to Zone III is to be strictly restricted, with access to regions within it (including Zone IV, see below) controlled by, and entirely under the supervision of, MR Personnel (see Section 2b, below). Specifically identified MR Personnel (typically–but not necessarily only–the MR Technologists) are to be charged with ensuring that this MR Safe Practice Guideline is strictly adhered to for the safety of the patients and other non–MR personnel, the healthcare personnel, and the equipment itself. This function of the MR Personnel is directly under the authority and responsibility of the MR Medical Director or the Level Two–designated (see section 2b, below) physician of the day for the MR site.

Zone III regions should be physically restricted from general public access–for example, by key locks, pass-key locking systems, or any other reliable physically restricting method that can differentiate between MR Personnel and non–MR Personnel. The use of combination locks is to be discouraged as combinations often tend to become more widely distributed than initially intended, resulting in site restriction violations being more likely with these devices. Only MR Personnel shall be provided with free access, such as the access keys/pass keys, to Zone III regions.

There should be NO exceptions to this guideline. Specifically, this includes hospital/site administration, physician, security, and other non–MR Personnel (see Section 2b, below). Non–MR personnel are not to be provided with independent Zone III access until such time as they undergo the proper education and training and become MR Personnel themselves. Zone III regions or at the very least the area within them wherein the static magnetic field's strength exceeds 5–gauss should be clearly marked and demarcated as being potentially hazardous.

d. Zone IV: This area is synonymous with the MR scanner magnet room itself–i.e., the physical confines of the room within which by definition, will always be located within Zone III as it is the MR magnet and its associated magnetic field that generates the existence of Zone III itself. Zone IV regions should also be clearly marked and demarcated as being potentially hazardous due to the presence of very strong magnetic fields. As part of the Zone IV site restriction, all MR installations should be installed in such a way as to provide for direct visual observation by Level II MR Personnel to access pathways into Zone IV regions. By means of illustration only, the MR Technologists would be able to directly observe and control, via line of site or via video monitors, the entrances or access corridors to Zone IV regions from their normal positions when stationed at their desks in the scan control room.

Zone IV/MR magnet rooms should be clearly marked with a lighted sign and red light stating, "The Magnet Is On." Except for resistive systems, this sign/red light should be illuminated at all times and should be provided with a backup energy source to continue to remain illuminated for at least 24 hours in the event of a loss of power to the site.

In case of cardiac or respiratory arrest or other medical emergency within Zone IV for which emergent medical intervention and/or resuscitation is required, appropriately trained and certified MR Personnel should immediately initiate basic life support and/or CPR as required by the situation WHILE the patient is being emergently removed from the MR magnet room/Zone IV to a predetermined magnetically safe location. ALL PRIORITIES SHOULD BE FOCUSED ON STABILIZING (E.G., BASIC LIFE SUPPORT WITH CARDIAC COMPRESSIONS AND MANUAL VENTILATION) AND THEN EVACUATING THE PATIENT AS RAPIDLY AND SAFELY AS POSSIBLE FROM THE MAGNETIC ENVIRONMENT THAT MIGHT RESTRICT SAFE RESUSCITATIVE EFFORTS.

Further, for logistical safety reasons, the patient should always be removed from ZONE IV (the magnet room itself) to the prospectively identified location where full resuscitative efforts are to continue.

Quenching the magnet (for superconducting systems only) is not routinely advised for cardiac or respiratory arrest or other medical emergency, since quenching the magnet itself and having the magnetic field dissipate could easily take more than a minute. Furthermore, as quenching a magnet can theoretically be hazardous, ideally one should evacuate the magnet room, when possible, for an intentional quench. One should rather use that time wisely to initiate life support measures while removing the patient from Zone IV/the MR magnet room to a location where the strength of the magnetic field(s) is insufficient to be a medical concern. ZONE III AND ZONE IV SITE ACCESS RESTRICTION MUST BE MAINTAINED DURING RESUSCITATIONS AND/OR OTHER EMERGENT SITUATIONS FOR THE PROTECTION OF ALL INVOLVED.

2. MR Personnel/Non–MR Personnel

a. All individuals working within at least Zone III of the MR environment should be documented to have completed successfully at least one of the MR site's approved MR safety live lectures or prerecorded presentations as approved by the MR

Medical Director. Attendance should be repeated at least annually, and appropriate documentation should be provided. These individuals shall be referred to henceforth as MR Personnel.
b. There are two levels of MR Personnel.
1. Level One MR Personnel: Those who have passed minimal safety educational efforts to ensure their own safety as they work within Zone III regions will be referred to henceforth as Level One MR Personnel.
2. Level Two MR Personnel: Those who have been more extensively trained and intensively educated in the broader aspects of MR safety issues including, for example, issues related to the potential for thermal loading/burns, direct neuromuscular excitation from rapidly changing gradients, etc., shall be referred to henceforth as Level Two MR Personnel. It is the responsibility of the MR Medical Director of the site not only to identify the necessary training, but also to identify those individuals that qualify as Level Two MR Personnel. It is understood that the Medical Director of the MR site will be one whose education and experience in MR safety qualifies them for designation as Level Two MR Personnel.
c. All those not having successfully complied with these MR safety instruction guidelines shall be referred to henceforth as Non–MR Personnel.
3. Patient/Non–MR Personnel Screening
a. ALL Non–MR Personnel wishing to enter Zone III regions of the MR Site must have first successfully passed an MR safety screening process to be performed by authorized MR Personnel. Only MR Personnel are authorized to perform an MR safety screen prior to permitting Non–MR Personnel into Zone III areas.
b. Metal Detectors
   The usage of metal detectors in MR environments is NOT recommended. Reasons for this recommendation include, among others:
1. They have varied–and variable–sensitivity settings.
2. The skills of the operators can vary.
3. Today's metal detectors cannot detect, for example, a 2 × 3 mm, potentially dangerous ferromagnetic metal fragment in the orbit, near the spinal cord, or heart, etc.
4. Today's metal detectors do not differentiate between ferromagnetic and nonferromagnetic metallic objects/implants/foreign bodies.
5. Metal detectors should not be necessary for the detection of large metallic objects such as oxygen tanks on the gurney with the patients. These objects are fully expected to be detected–and physically excluded–during the routine patient screening process.
c. Non–MR Personnel should be accompanied by, or under the immediate supervision and visual/verbal contact with, one specifically identified Level Two MR Person for the entirety of the duration during which the Non–MR Personnel remain within Zone III or Zone IV restricted regions. However, it is acceptable to have them in a changing room or restroom not in visual contact in Zone III as long as personnel and the patient can verbally communicate with each other.

In the event of a shift change, lunch break, etc., no Level Two MR Personnel shall relinquish their responsibility to supervise the Non–MR Personnel still within Zone III or Zone IV under their charge until such supervision has been formally transferred to another of the Level Two MR Personnel of the MR Site.
d. Non-emergent patients should be MR safety screened on-site by a minimum of two separate individuals. At least one of these individuals should be one of the Level Two MR Personnel of the MR site. At least one of these two screens should be performed verbally/interactively.

Emergent patients and their accompanying Non–MR Personnel may be screened only once providing that the screening individual is one of the site's Level Two MR Personnel.

There should be no exceptions to this.
e. Any individual undergoing an MR procedure must remove all readily removable metallic personal belongings and devices on or in them (e.g., watches; jewelry; pagers; cell phones; body piercings, if removable; contraceptive diaphragms; metallic drug delivery patches; and clothing items that may contain metallic fasteners, hooks, zippers, loose metallic components, or metallic threads; cosmetics containing metallic particles, such as eye makeup). It is therefore advisable to require that the patients or research subjects wear a site–supplied gown with no metal fasteners during the MR procedure when feasible.
f. All patients/Non–MR Personnel with a history of a potential ferromagnetic foreign object penetration must undergo further investigation prior to being permitted entrance to Zone III of the MR site. Examples of acceptable methods of screening include patient history, plain x-ray films, prior CT or MR of the questioned anatomic area, or access to written documentation as to the type of implant or foreign object that might be present. Once positive identification has been made as to the type of implant/foreign object that is within a patient, best effort assessments should be made to attempt to identify the MR compatibility or MR safety of the implant/object. Efforts at identification might include written testing on the implant prior to implantation (preferred), product labeling regarding the implant/object, peer-reviewed publications regarding MR compatibility, and MR safety testing of the make/model/type of the object, etc. MR safety testing would only be of value assuming that the object/device has not been altered since such testing had been published.

All patients who have a history of orbit trauma by a potential ferromagnetic foreign body for which they sought medical attention are to have their orbits cleared by either plain x-ray orbit films (two views) [8, 9] or by a radiologist's review and assessment of contiguous cut prior CT or MR images (obtained since the suspected traumatic event) if available.
g. Conscious, non-emergent patients and research and volunteer subjects are to complete written MR safety screening questionnaires prior to their introduction into Zone III regions. Family/guardians of non-responsive patients or of patients who cannot reliably provide their own medical histories are to complete a written MR safety screening questionnaire prior to

their introduction into Zone III regions. These completed questionnaires are then to be reviewed orally with the patient/guardian/research subject in their entirety prior to permitting the patient/research subject to be cleared into Zone III regions.

The patient/guardian/research subject as well as the screening MR staff member must both sign the completed form. This should then become a part of the patient's medical record. No empty responses will be accepted–each question MUST be answered definitively with a "Yes" or "No" or provide specific further information as requested. A sample of a pre–MR screening form is provided (Appendixes 2–5). This is the minimum information to be obtained; more may be added if the site so desires.

h. Screening of the patient/Non–MR Personnel with, or suspected of having, an intracranial aneurysm clip should be performed as per the separate MR Safe Practice Guideline addressing this particular topic (see section K, below).

i. Screening of all unconscious/unresponsive patients and/or patients who cannot provide their own reliable histories, or when the history cannot be reliably obtained from others, regarding prior possible exposures to surgery, trauma, and/or metallic foreign object history/exposure, in whom an MR examination is deemed clinically indicated/necessary:

1. If no reliable patient metal exposure history can be otherwise obtained and if the requested MR examination cannot reasonably wait until such a time that a reliable such history might be obtained, it is recommended that such patients be physically examined by Level Two MR Personnel. All areas of scars or deformities that might be anatomically indicative of an implant such as on the chest or spine region, etc., and whose origins are unknown and which may have been caused by ferromagnetic foreign bodies, implants, etc., should be subject to plain film radiography (if such recently obtained plain films or computer tomographic or magnetic resonance studies of such areas are not already available). The investigation described above should be made to ensure that there are no potentially harmful embedded/implanted metallic foreign objects or devices. All such patients should also undergo plain film imaging of the skull/orbits and chest to exclude metallic foreign objects (if recently obtained such radiographic and/or MR information is not already available).

2. Monitoring of patients is sometimes necessary in the MR scanner. The potential for thermal injury from possibly excessive radio frequency power deposition exists. Sedated, anesthetized, and/or unconscious patients may not be able to express symptoms of such injury. This potential for injury is greater on especially higher field whole-body scanners (e.g., 1 Tesla and above). Much patient monitoring information can be satisfactorily acquired via pulse oximetry and/or other means without utilization of electrocardiographic tracing and its inherent thermal injury risks. Patients who require EKG monitoring and who are unconscious, sedated, and/or anesthetized should be examined with potential repositioning, after each imaging sequence, of the EKG leads and any other electrically conductive material with which the patient is in contact. Alter-

natively, cold compresses or ice packs could be placed upon all necessary electrically conductive material that touches the patient during scanning.

j. Final determination of whether or not to scan any given patient with any given implant, foreign body, etc., is to be made by the Level Two designated attending MR radiologist, or the MR Medical Director, or specifically designated Level Two MR Personnel following criteria for acceptability for MR scanning predetermined by the Medical Director.

k. All Non–MR Personnel (e.g., patients, volunteers, varied site employees and professionals, etc.) with implanted cardiac pacemakers, autodefibrillators, diaphragmatic pacemakers, and/or other electromechanically activated devices on whose function the Non–MR Personnel is dependent should be precluded from the MR magnet room/Zone IV and physically restrained from the 5–gauss line unless specifically cleared in writing by a Level Two MR Personnel–designated radiologist attending physician or the Medical Director of the MR site. In such circumstances, specific defending risk/benefit rationale should be provided in writing and signed by the authorizing radiologist.

Should it be determined that Non–MR Personnel wishing to accompany a patient into an MR scan room require their orbits to be cleared by plain film radiography, a radiologist must first discuss with the Non–MR Personnel that plain x-ray films of their orbits are required prior to permitting them access to the MR scan room. Should they still wish to proceed with access to Zone IV and/or within the 5–gauss line, and should the attending radiologist deem it medically advisable that they do so (e.g., for the care of their child about to undergo an MR study), written informed consent should be provided by these accompanying Non–MR Personnel prior to their undergoing x-ray examination of their orbits.

l. MR scanning of patients/prisoners/parolees with metallic prisoner restraining devices or radiofrequency ID/tracking bracelets could lead to theoretical potential adverse events including: 1) ferromagnetic attractive effects and resultant patient injury, 2) possible ferromagnetic attractive effects and potential damage to the device and/or its battery pack, 3) radio frequency (RF) interference with the MR imaging study and secondary image artifact, 4) RF interference with the functionality of the device, 5) RF power deposition and heating of the bracelet tagging device or its circuitry and secondary patient injury (if the bracelet would be in the anatomic volume of the RF transmitter coil being imaged). Therefore, in cases where requested to scan a patient/prisoner/parolee wearing radiofrequency tagging bracelets and/or metallic handcuffs or anklecuffs, request that the patient be accompanied by the appropriate authorities who can and will remove the restraining device prior to the MR study and be charged with its replacement following the examination.

m. Firefighter/Police/Security safety considerations: For the safety of firefighters and other emergent services responding to an emergent call at the MR site, it is recommended that all fire alarms, cardiac arrests, or other emergent service response calls originating/located in the MR site should be forwarded simultaneously to a specifically designated individual from amongst the site's MR Personnel. This individual should, if possible, be on-site prior to the arrival of the firefighters/emergent responders to ensure that they do not have free access to Zone III or Zone IV. The site might consider assigning appropriately trained security personnel, who have been trained and designated as MR Personnel, to respond to such calls.

In any case, all MR sites should arrange to prospectively educate their local fire marshals/firefighters associations and police/security personnel about the potential hazards of responding to emergencies in the MR suite.

It should be stressed that even in the presence of a true fire (or other emergency) in Zone III and/or Zone IV, the magnetic fields may be present and fully operational. Therefore, free access to Zone III or Zone IV by firefighters and/or other Non–MR Personnel with air tanks, axes, crowbars, other firefighting equipment, guns, etc., might prove catastrophic or even lethal to those responding or others in the vicinity.

As part of the Zone III/IV restrictions, all MR sites must have clearly marked MR-compatible fire extinguishing equipment physically stored within and readily accessible to Zone III/IV regions. All Non–MR compatible fire extinguishers and other firefighting equipment should be restricted from being brought into Zone III regions.

For superconducting magnets, the helium (and the nitrogen as well, in the older magnets) is not flammable and does not pose a fire hazard directly. However, the liquid oxygen that can result from the supercooled air in the vicinity of the released gases might well increase the fire hazard in this area. If there are appropriately trained and knowledgeable MR personnel available during the emergency to ensure that emergency response personnel responding to the fire call are kept out of the MR scanner/magnet room and 5-gauss line, then quenching the magnet during response to an emergency or fire should not be a requirement.

HOWEVER, if the fire is in such a location where Zone III/IV needs to be entered for whatever reason by the firefighting and/or emergency response personnel and their firefighting and emergent equipment such as air canisters, crowbars, axes, defibrillators, etc., a decision to quench a superconducting magnet at that point should be VERY seriously considered to protect the health and lives of the emergent responding personnel in such an emergency situation. Should a quench be performed, appropriately designated MR personnel still need to ensure that ALL non–MR personnel (including and especially emergently responding personnel) continue to be restricted from Zone III/IV regions until the designated MR Personnel have personally verified that the static field is either no longer detectable or at least sufficiently attenuated so as to no longer present a potential hazard to one moving by it with, for example, large ferromagnetic objects such as oxygen tanks, axes, etc.

For resistive systems, the magnetic field of the MR scanner should be shut down as completely as possible and verified as such prior to permitting the emergency response personnel access to the magnet/Zone IV. For permanent or resistive or hybrid systems whose magnetic fields cannot be completely shut down, MR personnel should be available to warn the emergency response personnel that a very powerful magnetic field is still operational in the magnet room/Zone IV.

4. MR Personnel Screening

All MR Personnel are to undergo an MR screening process as part of their employment interview process to ensure their own safety in the MR environment. For their own protection and for the protection of the Non–MR Personnel under their supervision, all MR Personnel must immediately report to the MR Medical Director any trauma, procedure, or surgery that they experience or undergo in which a ferromagnetic metallic object/device may have become introduced within or on them. This will permit an appropriate screening to be performed upon the employee to determine the safety of permitting that MR Personnel–designated employee into the Zone III environment of the MR site.

5. Device/Object Screening

As part of the Zone III site restriction and equipment testing/clearing responsibilities, all sites should have ready access to a strong handheld magnet ($\geq$1000–gauss). This will enable the site to test external and even some superficial internal devices or implants for the presence of grossly detectable ferromagnetic attractive forces.

a. All portable metallic or partially metallic devices that are on or external to the patient (e.g., oxygen cylinders) are to be positively identified in writing as nonferromagnetic and either MR safe or MR compatible prior to permitting them into Zone III regions. For all device/object screening, all verification and positive identification should be in writing. Examples of such devices that need to be positively identified include fire extinguishers, oxygen tanks, aneurysm clips, etc.

b. If external devices/objects are demonstrated to be ferromagnetic and Non–MR safe/MR compatible, they may still, under specific circumstances, be brought into Zone III regions if, for example, they are deemed by MR Personnel to be necessary and appropriate for the care of the patient. They should only be brought into Zone III regions if they are under the direct supervision of specifically designated either Level One or Level Two MR Personnel who are thoroughly familiar with the device, its function, and the reason supporting its introduction into the Zone III designated region. The safe utilization of these devices at all times while they are present in Zone III will be the responsibility of a specifically named Level One or Two MR Personnel. This device must be appropriately physically secured or restricted at all times during which it is in Zone III regions to ensure that it does not inadvertently become introduced too close to the MR scanner and accidentally become exposed to static magnetic fields/gradients that might result in its becoming either a hazardous projectile or no longer accurately functional.

c. Never assume MR compatibility or safety information about the device if it is not clearly documented in writing. All unknown external objects/devices being considered for introduction beyond Zone II regions should be tested with a strong handheld magnet (≥1000–gauss) for ferromagnetic properties prior to permitting them entry beyond Zone II regions. The results of such testing as well as the date, time, and name of tester, and methodology used for that particular device should be documented in writing. If a device has not been tested and/or its MR compatibility/safety status is unknown, it should NOT be permitted unrestricted access beyond Zone II regions.

d. All portable metallic or partially metallic objects that are to be brought into Zone IV regions (i.e., the MR magnet room itself) must be labeled with either a green "MR Safe" label or a red "Not MR Safe" label. As noted in section 5 introduction above, testing for the purpose of this labeling is to be accomplished by the site's MR personnel by exposing the metallic object to a handheld magnet (≥1000–gauss). If grossly detectable attractive forces are observed between the metallic object or any of its components and the handheld magnet, it is to be labeled with a red label. If no such forces are observed, a green label is to be affixed to the device/object prior to its introduction into Zone IV.

e. Decisions based on published MR compatibility or safety claims should recognize that all such claims apply to specifically tested static field and static gradient field strengths. For example, "MR compatible up to 3.0 Tesla at gradient strengths of 400–gauss/cm," or "MR safe tested up to 1.5 Tesla up to maximum static gradient fields experienced in an unshielded 1.5 Tesla [manufacturer name] whole body MR scanner tested 1.5 feet within the bore."

f. It should be noted that alterations performed by the site on MR safe/compatible equipment or devices may alter the MR safety and/or compatibility properties of the device. For example, tying a ferromagnetic metallic twisting binder onto a sign labeling the device as MR compatible might result in artifact induction–or worse–if introduced into the MR scanner in that altered manner.

C. MR SAFE PRACTICE GUIDELINES: MR TECHNOLOGIST

1. MR Technologists should be ARRT Registered Technologists (RT). Furthermore, all MR Technologists must be trained as Level Two MR Personnel during their orientation, prior to being permitted free access to Zone III.

2. All MR Technologists will maintain current certification in American Heart Association Basic Life Support at the Health Care Provider level.

3. Except for emergent coverage, there will be a minimum of two MR technologists or one MR Technologist and one other individual with the designation of MR Personnel in the immediate Zone II through Zone IV MR environment. For emergent coverage, the MR Technologist can scan with no other individuals in their Zone II through Zone IV MR environment as long as there is in-house ready emergent coverage by designated Department of Radiology MR Personnel (e.g., radiology house staff, radiology attendings, etc.).

D. PREGNANCY-RELATED ISSUES

1. Healthcare practitioner pregnancies

Pregnant healthcare practitioners are permitted to work in and around the MR environment throughout all stages of their pregnancy [10]. This includes but is not limited to positioning patients, scanning, archiving, injecting contrast, entering the MR scan room in response to an emergency, etc. Although permitted to work in and around the MR environment, pregnant healthcare practitioners are requested not to remain within the MR scanner bore or Zone IV during actual data acquisition/scanning itself.

2. Patient pregnancies

a. Pregnant patients can be accepted to undergo MR scans at any stage of pregnancy if, in the determination of a Level Two MR Personnel–designated attending radiologist, the risk-benefit ratio to the patient warrants that the study be performed. The radiologist should confer with the referring physician and document this in the radiology report or the patient's medical record that:

1. The information requested from the MR study cannot be acquired via non–ionizing means (e.g., ultrasonography), and

2. The data is needed to potentially affect the care of that patient and/or fetus DURING the pregnancy, and

3. The referring physician does not feel that it is prudent to wait to obtain this data until after the patient is no longer pregnant.

b. MR contrast agent(s) should NOT be routinely provided to pregnant patients. This, too, is a decision that must be made on a case-by-case basis by the covering Level Two MR Personnel–designated attending radiologist who will assess the risk-benefit ratio for that particular patient.

c. It is recommended that pregnant patients undergoing an MR examination provide written informed consent to document that they understand the risks/benefits of the MR procedure to be performed, the alternative diagnostic options available to them (if any), and that they wish to proceed.

E. TIME VARYING GRADIENT MAGNETIC FIELD–RELATED ISSUES: INDUCED VOLTAGES

Types of patients needing extra caution: Patients with implanted or retained wires in anatomically and/or functionally sensitive areas (e.g., myocardium or epicardium, implanted electrodes in the brain) should be considered at higher risk especially from faster MR imaging sequences, such as echoplanar imaging (which may be used in such sequences as diffusion weighted imaging, functional imaging, perfusion weighted imaging, MR angiographic imaging, etc.). The decision to limit the dB/dt (rate of magnetic field change) and maximum strength of the magnetic field of the gradient subsystems during imaging of such patients should be reviewed by the Level Two MR Personnel–designated attending radiologist supervising the case/patient.

F. TIME VARYING GRADIENT MAGNETIC FIELD–RELATED ISSUES: AUDITORY CONSIDERATIONS

1. All patients/volunteers should be offered and encouraged to use hearing protection prior to their undergoing any imaging in the MR scanners.

2. All patients/volunteers in whom research sequences are to be performed (i.e., MR scan sequences that have not yet been approved by the Food and Drug Administration [FDA]) are to have hearing protective devices IN PLACE prior to initiating any such research MR sequences on these patient/volunteers. Without hearing protection in place, MR imaging sequences that are not FDA approved should not be performed on patients/volunteers.

G. TIME VARYING RADIOFREQUENCY MAGNETIC FIELD–RELATED ISSUES: THERMAL

1. All unnecessary and/or unused electrically conductive materials should be removed from the MR system before the onset of imaging. It is not sufficient to merely "unplug" or disconnect unused unnecessary electrically conductive material and leave it within the MR scanner with the patient during imaging. All electrical connections such as on surface coil leads, monitoring devices, etc., must be visually checked by the scanning MR Technologist prior to each scan to ensure the integrity of the thermal and electrical insulation.

2. For electrically conductive material, wires, leads, implants, etc., that are required to remain within the bore of the MR scanner with the patient during imaging, care should be taken to ensure that no large caliber electrically conducting loops (including patient tissue; see Section g, 5, below) are permitted to be formed within the MR scanner.

3. For electrically conductive material, wires, leads, implants, etc., that are required to be within the bore of the MR scanner with the patient during imaging, care should be taken to place thermal insulation (including air, pads, etc.) between the patient and the electrically conductive material during imaging, while simultaneously attempting to (as much as feasible) keep the electrical conductor from directly contacting the patient during imaging. It is also appropriate to try to position the leads/wires as far as possible from the inner walls of the MR scanner if the body coil is being used for radio frequency transmission. When it is necessary that such electrically conductive leads directly contact the patient during imaging, consideration should be given to prophylactic application of cold compresses or ice packs to such areas.

4. Depending on specific magnet designs, care may be needed to ensure that the patient's tissue(s) do not directly come into contact with the inner bore of the MR imager during the MR imaging process. This care is especially important for several higher field MR scanners. The manufacturers of these devices provide pads and other such insulating devices for this purpose, and manufacturer guidelines should be strictly adhered to for these units.

5. It is also important to ensure that the patient's own tissues do not form large conductive loops. Therefore, care should be taken to ensure that the patient's arms/legs not be positioned in such a way as to form a large–caliber loop within the bore of the MR imager during the imaging process. For this reason, it is preferable that patients be instructed not to cross their arms or legs in the MR scanner.

6. Skin Staples/Superficial Metallic Sutures: Patients requested to undergo MR studies in whom there are skin staples or superficial metallic sutures (SMS) may be permitted to undergo the MR examination if the skin staples/SMS are not ferromagnetic and are not in the anatomic volume of RF power deposition for the study to be performed. If the nonferromagnetic skin staples/SMS are within the volume to be RF irradiated for the requested MR study several precautions are recommended, as follows:

a. Warn the patient and make sure that they are especially aware of the possibility that they may experience warmth or even burning along the skin staple/SMS distribution. The patient should be instructed to report immediately if they experience a warmth or burning sensations during the study (and not, for example, wait until the "end of the knocking noise").

b. It is recommended that a cold compress/ice pack be placed along the skin staples/SMS if this can be safely clinically accomplished during the MR imaging examination. This will help to serve as a heat sink for any focal power deposition that may occur, thus decreasing the likelihood of a clinically significant thermal injury/burn to adjacent tissue.

7. For patients with extensive and/or dark tattoos including tattooed eyeliner, in order to decrease the potential for radio frequency heating of the tattooed tissue it is recommended that cold compresses or ice packs be placed onto the tattooed area(s) and kept in place throughout the MR imaging process if these tattoos are within the volume in which the body coil is being used for RF transmission. This approach is especially appropriate if fast spin–echo (or other high RF duty cycle) MR imaging sequences are anticipated to be used in the study. If another coil is being used for RF transmission, a decision must be made if high RF transmitted power is to be anticipated by the study protocol design. If so then the above precautions should be followed in that case as well. Additionally, patients with tattoos that had been placed within 48 hours prior to the pending MR examination should be advised of the potential for smearing or smudging of the edges of the freshly placed tattoo.

8. The unconscious/unresponsive patient should have any/all attached leads covered with a cold compress/ice pack at the lead attachment site for the duration of the MR study prior to the initiation of scanning.

9. Patients in whom there are long electrically conductive leads such as Swan–Ganz thermodilution cardiac output capable catheters, Foley catheters with electrically conductive leads, etc., should be considered at risk for MR studies if the body coil is to be used for RF transmission over the region of the electrically conductive lead. This is especially true for higher field systems and for imaging protocols utilizing fast spin echo or other high RF duty cycle MR imaging sequences. Each such patient should be reviewed and cleared by an attending Level Two ra-

diologist and a risk benefit ratio assessment performed prior to permitting them access to the MR scanner.

H. CRYOGEN-RELATED ISSUES

1. For superconducting systems, in the event of a system quench it is imperative that all personnel/patients be evacuated from the MR scan room as quickly as safely feasible and the site access be immediately restricted to all individuals until the arrival of the MR equipment service personnel. This is especially so if cryogenic gases are observed to have vented partially or completely into the scan room itself, as evidenced in part by the sudden appearance of white "clouds" or "fog" around or above the MR scanner. As noted in Section B.2.m above, it is especially important to ensure that all police/fire response personnel are restricted from entering the MR scan room with their equipment (axes, air canisters, guns, etc.) until it can be confirmed that the magnetic field has been successfully dissipated, as there may still be considerable static magnetic field present despite a quench or partial quench of the magnetic field.

2. It should be pointed out that room oxygen monitoring was discussed by the MR Blue Ribbon Panel and rejected at this time because the present oxygen monitoring technology was considered by industry experts to not be sufficiently reliable to allow for continued operation during situations of power outages, etc.

I. CLAUSTROPHOBIA/ANXIETY/SEDATION—ANALGESIA/ ANESTHESIA MR SAFE PRACTICE GUIDELINES

Adult and pediatric patient anxiolysis, sedation, analgesia, and anesthesia for any reason should follow established American College of Radiology (ACR) [11, 12], American Society of Anesthesiologists (ASA) [13-16], and JCAHO standards [17].

J. CONTRAST AGENT SAFETY MR SAFE PRACTICES

1. Contrast agent administration issues

No patient is to be administered prescription MR contrast agents without orders from a duly licensed physician. Intravenous injection-qualified MR technologists may start and attend to peripheral intravenous access/lines if they have undergone the requisite site-specified training in peripheral IV access and have demonstrated and documented appropriate proficiency in this area. IV-qualified MR technologists may administer FDA-approved gadolinium-based MR contrast agents via peripheral intravenous routes as a bolus or slow or continuous injection, as directed by the orders of a duly licensed site physician.

a. Administration of these agents is to be performed as per the ACR policy (Res.1-H, 1987, 1997)

- The ACR approves of the injection of contrast material and diagnostic levels of radiopharmaceuticals by certified and/or licensed radiologic technologists and radiologic nurses under the direction of a radiologist or his or her physician designee who is personally and immediately available, if the practice is in compliance with institutional

and state regulations. There must also be prior written approval by the medical director of the radiology department/service of such individuals; such approval process having followed established policies and procedures, and the radiologic technologists and nurses who have been so approved maintain documentation of continuing medical education related to materials injected and to the procedures being performed.

2. Prior contrast agent reaction issues [18]:

a. Adverse events after intravenous injection of gadolinium seem to be more common in patients who had previous reactions to an MR contrast agent. In one study, 16 (21%) of 75 patients who had previous adverse reactions to MR contrast agents reacted to subsequent injections of gadolinium. Patients with asthma also seem to be more likely to have an adverse reaction to gadolinium. Patients with allergies also seemed to be at increased risk (~2.0-3.7 times, compared with patients without allergies). Patients who have had adverse reactions to iodinated contrast media are more than twice as likely to have an adverse reaction to gadolinium (6.3% of 857 patients).

b. At present there are no well-defined policies for patients who are considered to be at increased risk for having adverse reaction to MR contrast agents; however, the following recommendations are suggested: patients who have previously reacted to one MR agent can be injected with another agent, if they are restudied, and at-risk patients can be pre-medicated with corticosteroids and, occasionally, antihistamines [18].

c. All patients with asthma, allergic respiratory histories, prior iodinated and/or gadolinium-based contrast reactions, etc., be followed more closely as they are at a demonstrably higher risk of adverse reaction.

K. MR SAFE PRACTICE GUIDELINES REGARDING MR SCANNING OF PATIENTS IN WHOM THERE ARE/MAY BE INTRACRANIAL ANEURYSM CLIPS

1. In the event that it is unclear whether a patient does or does not have an aneurysm clip in place, plain films should be obtained. Alternatively, if available, any cranial plain films, CT or MR examination that may have already been taken in the recent past (i.e., subsequent to the suspected surgical date) should be reviewed to assess for a possible intracranial aneurysm clip.

2. In the event that a patient is identified to have an intracranial aneurysm clip in place, the magnetic resonance examination should not be performed until it can be documented that the type of aneurysm clip within that patient is MR safe/compatible. All documentation of types of implanted clips, dates, etc., MUST be in writing and signed by a licensed physician. Phone or verbal histories and histories provided by a non-physician are not acceptable. Fax copies of operative reports, physician statements, etc., are acceptable as long as a legible physician signature accompanies the requisite documentation. A written history of the clip itself having been appropriately tested for ferromagnetic properties (and description of the testing methodology used) prior to implantation by the operating surgeon is also considered acceptable if the testing follows the

ASTM (American Society of Testing and Materials) established Deflection Test methodology.

3. All implanted intracranial aneurysm clips that are documented in writing to be composed of titanium (either the commercially pure and/or the titanium alloy types) can be accepted for scanning without any other testing necessary.

4. All non-titanium intracranial aneurysm clips manufactured 1995 or later for which the manufacturer's product labeling continues to claim MR compatibility may be accepted for MR scanning without further testing.

5. Clips manufactured prior to 1995 require either pre-testing (as per the ASTM Deflection Test methodology) prior to implantation or individual review of previous MR imaging of the clip/brain in that particular case, if available. By assessing the size of the artifact associated with the clip relative to the static field strength on which it was studied, the sequence type, and the MR imaging parameters selected, an opinion may be issued by one of the site's Level Two MR attending radiologists as to whether the clip(s) demonstrate significant ferromagnetic properties or not. Access to the MR scanner would then be based on that opinion.

6. HAVING SAFELY UNDERGONE A PRIOR MR EXAMINATION (WITH AN ANEURYSM CLIP–OR OTHER IMPLANT–IN PLACE) AT ANY GIVEN STATIC MAGNETIC FIELD STRENGTH IS NOT IN AND OF ITSELF SUFFICIENT EVIDENCE OF ITS MR SAFETY OR COMPATIBILITY, AND SHOULD NOT BE SOLELY RELIED UPON TO DETERMINE THE MR SAFETY OR COMPATIBILITY STATUS OF THAT ANEURYSM CLIP (OR OTHER IMPLANT). Variations in static magnetic field strength, static magnetic field spatial gradient, orientation of the aneurysm clip (or other implant) to the static magnetic field and/or static field gradient, rate of motion through the spatial static field gradient, etc., are all variables that are virtually impossible to control/reproduce. These variables may well have not resulted in adverse event in one circumstance but may result in significant injury or death on a subsequent exposure. Case in point: A patient who went blind from interactions between the metallic foreign body in the retina and the spatial static fields of the MR scanner entered the magnet and underwent the entire MR examination without difficulty. He only went blind on the way out of the MR scanner at the completion of the examination.

7. Barring availability of either pre-testing or prior MR imaging data of the clip in question, a risk/benefit assessment and review must be performed in each case individually. Further, for patients with intracranial clips with no available ferromagnetic and/or imaging data, should the risk/benefit ratio favor the performance of the MR study, the patient/guardian should provide written informed consent that includes death as a potential risk of the MR imaging procedure prior to permitting that patient to undergo an MR examination.

Acknowledgments

We wish to acknowledge the assistance and support provided by Jeffrey Hayden, ACR MRI Accreditation Program, and Tamar Whipple, ACR.

References

1. Chaljub G, Kramer LA, Johnson RF III, Singh H, Crow WN. Projectile cylinder accidents resulting from the presence of ferromagnetic nitrous oxide or oxygen tanks in the MR suite. *AJR* 2001; 177:27–30

2. ECRI hazard report: patient death illustrates the importance of adhering to safety precautions in magnetic resonance environments. *Health Devices* 2001; 30:311–314

3. Shellock FG, Kanal E, SMRI Safety Committee. Policies, guidelines, and recommendations for MR imaging safety and patient management. *J Magn Reson Imaging* 1991; 1:97–101

4. Kanal E, Shellock FG, SMRI Safety Committee. Policies, guidelines, and recommendations for MR imaging safety and patient management. *J Magn Reson Imaging* 1992; 2:247–248

5. Shellock FG, Kanal E, SMRI Safety Committee. Guidelines and recommendations for MR imaging safety and patient management. III. Questionnaire for screening patients before MR procedures. *J Magn Reson Imaging* 1994; 4:749–751

6. American College of Radiology. MRI monograph: safety and sedation. Reston, VA: American College of Radiology, 1996

7. American College of Radiology. American College of Radiology standard for performing and interpreting magnetic resonance imaging (MRI). Reston, VA: American College of Radiology, 2000

8. Jarvik JG, Ramsey S. Radiographic screening for orbital foreign bodies prior to MR imaging: is it worth it? (editorial) *Am J Neuroradiol* 2000; 21:245–247

9. Seidenwurm DJ, McDonnell CH III, Raghaven N, Breslau J. Cost utility analysis of radiographic screening for an orbital foreign body before MR imaging. *Am J Neuroradiol* 2000; 21:426–433

10. Kanal E, Gillen J, Evans JA, Savitz DA, Shellock FG. Survey of reproductive health among female MR workers. *Radiology* 1993; 187:395–399

11. American College of Radiology. American College of Radiology standard for adult sedation/analgesia. Reston, VA: American College of Radiology, 2000: res. 17

12. American College of Radiology. American College of Radiology standard for pediatric sedation/analgesia. Reston, VA: American College of Radiology, 1998: res. 36

13. American Society of Anesthesiologists. Updated practice guidelines for sedation and analgesia by non-anesthesiologists. Park Ridge, IL: American Society of Anesthesiologists, August 2001

14. American Society of Anesthesiologists. Guidelines for non-operating room anesthetizing locations. Park Ridge, IL: American Society of Anesthesiologists, 1994

15. American Society of Anesthesiologists. Standards for basic anesthetic monitoring. Park Ridge, IL: American Society of Anesthesiologists, 1998

16. American Society of Anesthesiologists. Standards for post anesthesia care. Park Ridge, IL: American Society of Anesthesiologists, 1994

17. Joint Commission on Accreditation of Health Care Organizations. Standards and intents for sedation and anesthesia care: comprehensive accreditation manual for hospitals. Chicago: Joint Commission on Accreditation of Health Care Organizations, 2001: report no. TX. 2-2.4.1

18. American College of Radiology Committee on Drugs and Contrast Media. Manual on contrast media, 4.1 ed. Reston, VA: American College of Radiology, 1998

Appendix 1: Personnel and Zone Definitions

Personnel

Non–MR Personnel: Patients, visitors, or facility staff who do not meet the criteria of Level One or Level Two MR Personnel.

Level One MR Personnel: Individuals who have passed minimal safety educational efforts to ensure their own safety as they work within Zone III regions will be referred to as Level One MR Personnel (e.g., M.R.I. department office staff, patient aides).

Level Two MR Personnel: Individuals who have been more extensively trained and educated in the broader aspects of MR safety issues, including issues related to the potential for thermal loading/burns, direct neuromuscular excitation from rapidly changing gradients, etc., will be referred to as Level Two MR Personnel (e.g., M.R.I. Technologists, Radiologists, Radiology Department nursing staff).

Zones

Zone I: This includes all areas that are freely accessible to the general public. This area is typically outside of the MR environment itself, and is the area through which patients, healthcare personnel, and other employees of the MR site access the MR environment.

Zone II: This area is the interface between the publicly accessible uncontrolled Zone I and the strictly controlled Zone III (see below). Typically the patients are greeted in Zone II and are not free to move throughout Zone II at will, but are rather under the supervision of MR Personnel. It is in Zone II that the answers to MR screening questions, patient histories, medical insurance questions, etc., are typically obtained.

Zone III: This area is the region in which free access by unscreened Non–MR Personnel and/or ferromagnetic objects and equipment can result in serious injury or death as a result of interactions between the individuals/equipment and the MR scanner's particular environment. These interactions include but not limited to those with the MR scanner's static and time varying magnetic fields. All access to at least Zone III is to be strictly restricted, with access to regions within it (including Zone IV) controlled by, and entirely under the supervision of, MR Personnel.

Zone IV: This area is synonymous with the MR scanner magnet room itself; Zone IV, by definition, will always be located within Zone III as it is the MR magnet and its associated magnetic field, which generates the existence of Zone III itself.

Non–MR Personnel should be accompanied under the immediate supervision and visual contact with one specifically identified Level Two MR Person for the entirety of their duration within Zone III or Zone IV restricted regions.

Level One and Two MR Personnel may move freely about all zones.

Appendix 2: Safety Screening Form for MR Procedures

Date_____ Name (first middle last) _____

Female [ ] Male [ ] Age_____ Date of Birth_____ Height_____Weight_____

1. Why are you having this examination (medical problem)?_____

YES   NO

2. Have you ever had an MRI examination before and had a problem?_____

If YES, please describe:_____

3. Have you ever had a surgical operation or procedure of any kind?_____

If YES, list all prior surgeries and approximate dates:_____

_____

_____

4. Have you ever been injured by a metal object/foreign body (e.g., bullet, BB, shrapnel)?

_____ If YES, please describe:_____

_____

_____

5. Have you ever had an injury from a metal object in your eye (metal slivers, metal

shavings, other metal object)?_____

If YES, did you seek medical attention? — — — — — — — — — — — — — — — — —

Describe what was found: _____

_____

6. Do you have a history of kidney disease, asthma, or other allergic respiratory disease?

_____

7. Do you have any drug allergies?— — — — — — — — — — — — — — — — — — —

If YES, please list drugs: _____

_____

8. Have you ever received a contrast agent/x-ray dye used for MRI, CT, or other x-ray or

study?_____

9. Have you ever had an x-ray dye or MRI contrast agent allergic reaction? _____

If YES, please describe:_____

_____

_____

10. Are you pregnant or suspect you may be pregnant?_____

11. Are you breastfeeding?_____

12. Date of last menstrual period_____ Postmenopausal?_____

Appendix 3: MR Hazard Checklist

THE FOLLOWING ITEMS MAY BE HARMFUL TO YOU DURING YOUR
MR SCAN OR MAY INTERFERE WITH THE MR EXAMINATION.

Please mark on the drawings provided the location of any metal inside your body or site
of surgical operation.

You must provide a Yes or No for every item. Please indicate if you have or have had
any of the following:

YES NO

____ ____ Any type of electronic, mechanical, or magnetic implant. (Type_____)

____ ____ Cardiac pacemaker

____ ____ Aneurysm clip(s)

____ ____ Implanted cardiac defibrillator

____ ____ Neurostimulator

____ ____ Biostimulator (Type _____)

____ ____ Any type of internal electrode(s) or wire(s)

____ ____ Hearing aid

____ ____ Implanted drug pump (e.g., insulin, Baclofen, chemotherapy, pain medicine)

____ ____ Halo vest

____ ____ Spinal fixation device

____ ____ Spinal fusion procedure

____ ____ Any type of coil, filter, or stent (Type_____)

____ ____ Any type of metal object (e.g., shrapnel, bullet, BB)

____ ____ Artificial heart valve

____ ____ Any type of ear implant

____ ____ Penile implant

____ ____ Artificial eye

____ ____ Eyelid spring

____ ____ Any type of implant held in place by a magnet (Type_____)

____ ____ Any type of surgical clip or staple

____ ____ Any I.V. access port (e.g., Broviac, Port-a-Cath, Hickman, Picc line)

____ ____ Medication patch (e.g., nitroglycerin, nicotine)

____ ____ Shunt

____ ____ Artificial limb or joint (What and where_____)

____ ____ Tissue expander (e.g., breast)

____ ____ Removable dentures, false teeth or partial plate

____ ____ Diaphragm, IUD, Pessary (Type_____)

____ ____ Surgical mesh (Location_____)

____ ____ Body piercing (Location_____)

____ ____ Wig, hair implants

____ ____ Tattoos or tattooed eyeliner

____ ____ Radiation seeds (e.g., cancer treatment)

____ ____ Any implanted items (e.g., pins, rods, screws, nails, plates, wires)

____ ____ Any hair accessories (e.g., bobby pins, barrettes, clips)

____ ____ Jewelry

____ ____ Any other type of implanted item (Type_____)

I attest that the above information is correct to the best of my knowledge. I have read
and understand the entire contents of this form and I have had the opportunity to ask
questions regarding the information on this form.

Patient signature_____

MD/RN/RT signature_____

Date_____

Print name of MD, RN, RT_____

Appendix 4: Instructions for the Patients

1. You are urged to use the ear plugs or headphones that we supply for use during your MRI examination since some patients may find the noise levels unacceptable and the noise levels may affect your hearing.

2. Remove all jewelry (e.g., necklaces, pins, rings).

3. Remove all hair pins, bobby pins, barrettes, clips, etc.

4. Remove all dentures, false teeth, partial dental plates.

5. Remove hearing aids.

6. Remove eyeglasses.

7. Remove your watch, pager, cell phone, credit and bank cards, and all other cards with a magnetic strip.

8. Remove body piercing objects.

9. Use gown, if provided, or remove all clothing with metal fasteners, zippers.

Appendix 5: Hazard Checklist for MRI Personnel

For MRI Office Use Only

Patient Name_____

Patient ID Number_____

Referring Physician_____

Procedure_____

Diagnosis_____

Clinical History_____

Hazard Checklist for MRI Personnel

YES NO

____ ____ Endotracheal tube

____ ____ Swan-Ganz catheter

____ ____ Extraventricular device

____ ____ Arterial line transducer

____ ____ Foley catheter with temperature sensor and/or metal clamp

____ ____ Rectal probe

____ ____ Esophageal probe

____ ____ Tracheotomy tube

____ ____ Guidewire

Excerpt from the American Institute of Architects Academy of Architecture for Health Guidelines for Design and Construction of Hospital and Healthcare Facilities, 2001 edition, pages 46–52. Reproduced with permission.

7.10 Imaging Suite

7.10.A. General

*7.10.A1. Equipment and space shall be as necessary to accommodate the functional program. The imaging department provides diagnostic procedures. It includes fluoroscopy, radiography, mammography, tomography, computerized tomography scanning, ultrasound, magnetic resonance, angiography, and other similar techniques.

7.10.A2. Most imaging requires radiation protection. A certified physicist or other qualified expert representing the owner or appropriate state agency shall specify the type, location, and amount of radiation protection to be installed in accordance with the final approved department layout and equipment selections. Where protected alcoves with view windows are required, a minimum of 1'–6" (0.45 meter) between the view window and the outside partition edge shall be provided. Radiation protection requirements shall be incorporated into the specifications and the building plans.

*7.10.A3. Beds and stretchers shall have ready access to and from other departments of the institution.

7.10.A4. Flooring shall be adequate to meet load requirements for equipment, patients, and personnel. Provision for wiring raceways, ducts, or conduits shall be made in floors, walls, and ceilings. Ceiling heights shall be permitted to be higher than normal. Ceiling-mounted equipment shall have properly designed rigid support structures located above the finished ceiling. A lay-in type ceiling shall be permitted to be considered for ease of installation, service, and remodeling.

7.10.B. Angiography

*7.10.B1. Space shall be provided as necessary to accommodate the functional program.

7.10.B2. A control room shall be provided as necessary to meet the needs of the functional program. A view window shall be provided to permit full view of the patient.

*7.10.B3. A viewing area shall be provided.

7.10.B4. A scrub sink located outside the staff entry to the procedure room shall be provided for use by staff.

*7.10.B5. Patient holding area.

7.10.B6. Storage for portable equipment and catheters shall be provided.

AUTHOR'S NOTE: *Regulatory codes and guidelines take several years to develop, ratify and adopt. As a result, they can be out of date even at the time they are first published. For example, the AIA guidelines make several references to film darkrooms and only limited reference to PACS systems. In addition, the AIA guidelines are developed as minimum—not necessarily recommended—guidelines. The 2001 guidelines excerpted in this appendix have been superseded by the 2006 guidelines, which were not available at the time of this book's publication. The imaging chapter of the 2006 guidelines, however, includes few—if any—sustentative changes to the 2001 text.*

7.10.B7. Provision shall be made within the facility for extended post–procedure observation of outpatients.

7.10.C. Computerized Tomography (CT) Scanning

7.10.C1. CT scan rooms shall be as required to accommodate the equipment.

7.10.C2. A control room shall be provided that is designed to accommodate the computer and other controls for the equipment. A view window shall be provided to permit full view of the patient. The angle between the control and equipment centroid shall permit the control operator to see the patient's head.

7.10.C3. The control room shall be located to allow convenient film processing.

7.10.C4. A patient toilet shall be provided. It shall be convenient to the procedure room and, if directly accessible to the scan room, arranged so that a patient can leave the toilet without having to reenter the scan room.

7.10.D. Diagnostic X-Ray

*7.10.D1. Radiography rooms shall be of a size to accommodate the functional program.

*7.10.D2. Tomography, radiography/fluoroscopy rooms.

*7.10.D3. Mammography.

7.10.D4. Each x-ray room shall include a shielded control alcove. This area shall be provided with a view window designed to provide full view of the examination table and the patient at all times, including full view of the patient when the table is in the tilt position or the chest x-ray is being utilized. For mammography machines with built-in shielding for the operator, the alcove shall be permitted to be omitted when approved by the certified physicist or state radiation protection agency.

7.10.E. Magnetic Resonance Imaging (MRI)

7.10.E1. Space shall be provided as necessary to accommodate the functional program. The MRI room shall be permitted to range from 325 square feet (30.19 square meters) to 620 square feet (57.6 square meters) depending on the vendor and magnet strength.

*7.10.E2. A control room shall be provided with full view of the MRI.

*7.10.E3. A computer room shall be provided.

*7.10.E4. Cryogen storage.

*7.10.E5. Darkroom.

7.10.E6. When spectroscopy is provided, caution shall be exercised in locating it in relation to the magnetic fringe fields.

*7.10.E7. Power conditioning.

*7.10.E8. Magnetic shielding.

*7.10.E9. Patient hold area.

7.10.E10. Cryogen venting is required.

7.10.F. Ultrasound

7.10.F1. Space shall be provided as necessary to accommodate the functional program.

7.10.F2. A patient toilet, accessible from the procedure room, shall be provided.

7.10.G. Support Spaces

The following spaces are common to the imaging department and are minimum requirements unless stated otherwise:

7.10.G1. Patient waiting area. The area shall be out of traffic, under staff control, and shall have seating capacity in accordance with the functional program. If the suite is routinely used for outpatients and inpatients at the same time, separate waiting areas shall be provided with screening for visual privacy between the waiting areas.

If so determined by the hospital Infection Control Risk Assessment, the diagnostic imaging waiting area shall require special measures to reduce the risk of airborne infection transmission. These measures shall include enhanced general ventilation and air disinfection techniques similar to inpatient requirements for airborne infection isolation rooms (see Table 7.2 in the complete version of guidelines document). See the "CDC Guidelines for Preventing the Transmission of Mycobacterium Tuberculosis in Health Care Facilities."

7.10.G2. Control desk and reception area.

7.10.G3. Holding area. A convenient holding area under staff control shall be provided to accommodate inpatients on stretchers or beds.

7.10.G4. Patient toilet rooms. Toilet rooms with handwashing stations shall be provided convenient to the waiting rooms and shall be equipped with an emergency call system. Separate toilets with handwashing stations shall be provided with direct access from each radiographic/fluoroscopic room so that a patient can leave the toilet without having to reenter the R&F room. Rooms used only occasionally for fluoroscopic procedures shall be permitted to utilize nearby patient toilets if they are located for immediate access.

7.10.G5. Patient dressing rooms. Dressing rooms shall be provided convenient to the waiting areas and x-ray rooms. Each room shall include a seat or bench, mirror, and provisions for hanging patients' clothing and for securing valuables.

7.10.G6. Staff facilities. Toilets and staff lounge with lockers shall be permitted to be outside the suite but shall be convenient for staff use. In larger suites of three or more procedure rooms, toilets internal to the suite shall be provided.

7.10.G7. Film storage (active). A room with cabinet or shelves for filing patient film for immediate retrieval shall be provided.

7.10.G8. Film storage (inactive). A room or area for inactive film storage shall be provided. It shall be permitted to be outside the imaging suite, but must be under imaging's administrative control and properly secured to protect films against loss or damage.

7.10.G9. Storage for unexposed film. Storage facilities for unexposed film shall include protection of film against exposure or damage and shall not be warmer than the air of adjacent occupied spaces.

7.10.G10. Offices for radiologist(s) and assistant(s). Offices shall include provisions for viewing, individual consultation, and charting of film.

7.10.G11. Clerical offices/spaces. Office space shall be provided as necessary for the functional program.

7.10.G12. Consultation area. An appropriate area for individual consultation with referring clinicians shall be provided.

7.10.G13. Contrast media preparation. This area shall be provided with sink, counter, and storage to allow for mixing of contrast media. One preparation room, if conveniently located, shall be permitted to serve any number of rooms. Where pre-prepared media is used, this area shall be permitted to be omitted, but storage shall be provided for the media.

7.10.G14. Film processing room. A darkroom shall be provided for processing film unless the processing equipment normally used does not require a darkroom for loading and transfer. When daylight processing is used, the darkroom shall be permitted to be minimal for emergency and special uses. Film processing shall be located convenient to the procedure rooms and to the quality control area.

7.10.G15. Quality control area. An area or room shall be provided near the processor for viewing film immediately after it is processed. All view boxes shall be illuminated to provide light of the same color value and intensity for appropriate comparison of several adjacent films.

7.10.G16. Cleanup facilities. Provisions for cleanup shall be located within the suite for convenient access and use. It shall include service sink or floor receptacle as well as storage space for equipment and supplies. If automatic film processors are used, a receptacle of adequate size with hot and cold water for cleaning the processor racks shall be provided.

7.10.G17. Handwashing stations. Handwashing stations shall be provided within each procedure room unless the room is used only for routine screening such as chest x-rays where the patient is not physically handled by the staff. Handwashing stations shall be provided convenient to the MRI room, but need not be within the room.

7.10.G18. Clean storage. Provisions shall be made for the storage of clean supplies and linens. If conveniently located, storage shall be permitted to be shared with another department.

7.10.G19. Soiled holding. Provisions shall be made for soiled holding. Separate provisions for contaminated handling and holding shall be made. Handwashing stations shall be provided.

7.10.G20. Provision shall be made for locked storage of medications and drugs.

7.10.G21. Details and finishes; mechanical; electrical. See Section 7.28 for details and finishes; 7.31 for mechanical; and 7.32 for electrical.

7.10.H. Cardiac Catheterization Lab (Cardiology)

Note: The number of procedure rooms and the size of the prep, holding, and recovery areas shall be based on expected utilization.

7.10.H1. The cardiac catheterization lab is normally a separate suite, but shall be permitted to be within the imaging suite provided that the appropriate sterile environment is provided. It can be combined with angiography in low usage situations.

7.10.H2. The procedure room shall be a minimum of 400 square feet (37.16 square meters) exclusive of fixed cabinets and shelves.

7.10.H3. A control room or area shall be provided and shall be large enough to contain and provide for the efficient functioning of the x-ray and image recording equipment. A view window permitting full view of the patient from the control console shall be provided.

7.10.H4. An equipment room or enclosure large enough to contain x-ray transformers, power modules, and associated electronics and electrical gear shall be provided.

7.10.H5. Scrub facilities with hands-free operable controls shall be provided adjacent to the entrance of procedure rooms, and shall be arranged to minimize incidental splatter on nearby personnel, medical equipment, or supplies.

7.10.H6. Staff change area(s) shall be provided and arranged to ensure a traffic pattern so that personnel entering from outside the suite can enter, change their clothing, and move directly into the cardiac catheterization suite.

7.10.H7. A patient preparation, holding, and recovery area or room shall be provided and arranged to provide visual observation before and after the procedure.

7.10.H8. A clean workroom or clean supply room shall be provided. If the room is used for preparing patient care items, it shall contain a work counter and handwashing station. If the room is used only for storage and holding of clean and sterile supply materials, the work counter and handwashing stations shall be permitted to be omitted.

7.10.H9. A soiled workroom shall be provided which shall contain a handwashing station and a clinical sink (or equivalent flushing rim fixtures). When the room is used for temporary holding or soiled materials, the clinical sink shall be permitted to be omitted.

7.10.H10. Housekeeping closet containing a floor receptor or service sink and provisions for storage of supplies and housekeeping equipment shall be provided.

7.10.H11. The following shall be available for use by the cardiac catheterization suite:

a. A viewing room.

b. A film file room.

7.11 Nuclear Medicine

7.11.A. Equipment and space shall be provided as necessary to accommodate the functional program. Nuclear medicine may include positron emission tomography, which is not common to most facilities. It requires specialized planning for equipment.

7.11.B. A certified physicist or other qualified expert representing the owner or state agency shall specify the type, location, and amount of radiation protection to be installed in accordance with final approved department layout and equipment selection. These specifications shall be incorporated into the plans.

7.11.C. Flooring should meet load requirements for equipment, patients, and personnel. Floors and walls should be constructed of materials that are easily decontaminated in case of radioactive spills. Walls should contain necessary support systems for either built-in or mobile oxygen and vacuum, and vents for radioactive gases. Provision for wiring raceways, ducts or conduits should be made in floors, walls, and ceilings. Ceilings may be higher than 8'-0" (2.44 meters). Ceiling-mounted equipment should have properly designed rigid support structures located above the finished ceiling. A lay-in type ceiling should be considered for ease of service, installation, and remodeling.

7.11.D. Space shall be provided as necessary to accommodate the functional program. Where the functional program calls for it, the nuclear medicine room shall accommodate the equipment, a stretcher, exercise equipment (treadmill and/or bicycle), and staff.

7.11.E. If radiopharmaceutical preparation is performed on-site, an area adequate to house a radiopharmacy shall be provided with appropriate shielding. This area should include adequate space for storage of radionuclides, chemicals for preparation, dose calibrators, and record keeping. Floors and walls should be constructed of easily decontaminated materials. Vents and traps for radioactive gases should be provided if such are used. Hoods for pharmaceutical preparation shall meet applicable standards. If pre-prepared materials are used, storage and calculation area may be considerably smaller than that for on-site preparation. Space shall provide adequately for dose calibration, quality assurance, and record keeping. The area may still require shielding from other portions of the facilities.

*7.11.F. Positron Emission Tomography (PET)

7.11.G. Nuclear medicine area when operated separately from the imaging department shall include the following:

7.11.G1. Space shall be adequate to permit entry of stretchers, beds, and able to accommodate imaging equipment, electronic consoles, and if present, computer terminals.

7.11.G2. A darkroom on-site shall be available for film processing. The darkroom should contain protective storage facilities for unexposed film that guard the film against exposure or damage.

7.11.G3. When the functional program requires a centralized computer area, it should be a separate room with access terminals available within the imaging rooms.

7.11.G4. Provisions for cleanup shall be located within the suite for convenient access and use. It shall include service sink or floor receptacle as well as storage space for equipment and supplies.

7.11.G5. Film storage with cabinets or shelves for filing patient film for immediate retrieval shall be provided.

7.11.G6. Inactive film storage under the departmental administrative control and properly secured to protect film against loss or damage shall be provided.

7.11.G7. A consultation area with view boxes illuminated to provide light of the same color value and intensity for appro-priate comparison of several adjacent films shall be provided. Space should be provided for computer access and display terminals if such are included in the program.

7.11.G8. Offices for physicians and assistants shall be provided and equipped for individual consultation, viewing, and charting of film.

7.11.G9. Clerical offices and spaces shall be provided as necessary for the program to function.

7.11.G10. Waiting areas shall be provided out of traffic, under staff control, and shall have seating capacity in accordance with the functional program. If the department is routinely used for outpatients and inpatients at the same time, separate waiting areas shall be provided with screening or visual privacy between the waiting areas.

7.11.G11. A dose administration area as specified by the functional program, shall be provided and located near the preparation area. Since as much as several hours may elapse for the dose to take effect, the area shall provide for visual privacy from other areas. Thought should be given to entertainment and reading materials.

7.11.G12. A holding area for patients on stretchers or beds shall be provided out of traffic and under control of staff and may be combined with the dose administration area with visual privacy between the areas.

7.11.G13. Patient dressing rooms shall be provided convenient to the waiting area and procedure rooms. Each dressing room shall include a seat or bench, a mirror, and provisions for hanging patients' clothing and for securing valuables.

7.11.G14. Toilet rooms shall be provided convenient to waiting and procedure rooms.

7.11.G15. Staff toilet(s) shall be provided convenient to the nuclear medicine laboratory.

7.11.G16. Handwashing stations shall be provided within each procedure room.

7.11.G17. Control desk and reception area shall be provided.

7.11.G18. Storage area for clean linen with a handwashing station shall be provided.

7.11.G19. Provisions with handwashing stations shall be made for holding soiled material. Separate provisions shall be made for holding contaminated material.

7.11.G20. See Section 7.28 for details and finishes; 7.31 for mechanical; and 7.32 for electrical.

Index